THE PRESBYTERIAN HYMNAL COMPANION

THE PRESBYTERIAN HYMNAL COMPANION

LindaJo H. McKim

Westminster/John Knox Press
Louisville, Kentucky

Book design by Christine Schueler

First edition

This book is printed on acid-free paper that meets the American National Standards Institute Z39.48 standard. ♾

Published by Westminster/John Knox Press
Louisville, Kentucky

PRINTED IN THE UNITED STATES OF AMERICA
9 8 7 6 5 4 3

Library of Congress Cataloging-in-Publication Data

McKim, LindaJo.
The Presbyterian hymnal companion / LindaJo McKim. — 1st ed.
p. cm.
Includes bibliographical references and index.
ISBN 0-664-25180-3 (pbk. : alk. paper)

1. Presbyterian Church (U.S.A.)—Hymns—History and criticism. 2. Hymns, English—History and criticism. 3. Presbyterians—Hymns.
I. Presbyterian hymnal. II. Title.
ML3176.M4 1993
264′.0513702—dc20 92-17830

CONTENTS

PREFACE

The preparation of this work has been enhanced by a number of people. The members of the selection committee chose hymns with wonderful stories that deserve to be told. Robert H. Kempes and James G. Kirk encouraged my research and supported my editorial decisions during the formation of *The Presbyterian Hymnal*. I particularly want to thank Melva W. Costen, chair of the committee who was and continues to be one of my dearest friends. We look forward to learning from her as she continues to research African-American religious music.

I owe a great deal to the members of the support staff who worked with me day in and day out while the hymnal was in process, particularly Benita Lippman, Bonnie Karnes, and Ada Allen.

I am grateful for the love of my spouse, Don, and our children, Stephen and Karl, who sacrificed prime time with me from the beginning of the hymnal project to the close of these pages so that the work could be accomplished.

Finally, I would like to dedicate this companion to *The Presbyterian Hymnal* to the memory of Ford Lewis Battles, Calvin scholar, translator, musician, teacher, and friend. He instilled in me the desire to look deeply into the structure of hymns in order to learn of the faith of those who composed them.

Advent 1991

INTRODUCTION

Since its publication in 1990, *The Presbyterian Hymnal: Hymns, Psalms, and Spiritual Songs*, together with its ecumenical edition, *Hymns, Psalms, and Spiritual Songs*, has enjoyed wide and enthusiastic acceptance. Churches in the Presbyterian Church (U.S.A.) and other ecumenical bodies have found it to be a rich collection of texts and music that give glory to God. They have also found the hymnal presenting the best of historic traditions as well as contemporary compositions for today's churches. The hymnal continues to enrich a variety of congregations in the whole household of Christian faith.

It was a privilege to be editor of *The Presbyterian Hymnal.* The texts and tunes were selected by a committee of eighteen persons who reflected the breadth and diversity of the Presbyterian church. The committee was chaired by Melva W. Costen and worked from April 1985 until July 1989. Throughout its work, the committee sought to produce a hymnal to fulfill the directives of the General Assemblies of 1980 and 1983 that the book be developed "using inclusive language and sensitive to the diverse nature of the church." A massive number of texts and tunes were considered until the final 605 hymns were selected.

During my time as editor when I traveled throughout the country, frequently I was asked if a "companion" to the hymnal would be developed. What was in mind here often was the *Handbook to The Hymnal*, a volume edited by William Chalmers Covert and published in 1935 as a supplemental resource for the Presbyterian Church in the U.S.A.'s new book *The Hymnal*, published in 1933. This handbook offered backgrounds and comments on hymns, authors, tunes, and composers of each of the hymns and responses in *The Hymnal.* Calvin Weiss Laufer was associate editor of the volume. From the Introduction to the book, it appears that approximately forty others were engaged in writing various sections. Often pastors would tell me they consulted this enduring resource.

Since 1933 the Presbyterian Church (U.S.A.) and its antecedents have produced three other hymnals. *The Hymnbook* published in 1955 had representatives of five Presbyterian and Reformed denominations on its committee. *The Worshipbook—Services* (1970) and *The Worshipbook—Services and Hymns* (1972) provided worship and liturgical resources as well as a selection of hymns to supplement current Presbyterian hymnody. Neither of these two volumes had companion works.

The expanded nature of the third hymnal, *The Presbyterian Hymnal* (1990), in terms of greater diversity of types of music as well as inclusion of much newer music from the rich period of hymn writing in the past two decades means an accompanying "companion" is now necessary. My work as editor entailed research into the origins and evolution of texts and tunes for each of the hymns. This provided the basic groundwork as I sought to produce this volume to supplement the hymnal by indicating sources, backgrounds, and primary information about each of the pieces.

In most cases, information is presented about the hymn itself, its publication history and any special notes; the author, with biography given with the first of the author's hymns; and the tune, with mention of its origins, translators, arrangers, or harmonizers. In some instances stories about the hymn or someone involved with it are included to give a fuller picture.

My purpose throughout has been to provide a resource for the church's pastors, musicians, and laypersons who wish to know more about the splendid hymns that help them praise and glorify God. Scholars and others interested in Christian hymnody will find resources here for their further studies as well. The book is not a theological analysis of the hymns or solely a collection of interesting anecdotes about each of the pieces. It provides historical information so we will see and appreciate the hymns in their broader contexts as God's good gifts to the church conveyed through a number of talented and dedicated people.

Many printed works have been immensely helpful throughout this labor. In particular, mention should be made of that incomparable source of knowledge *The New Grove Dictionary of Music and Musicians*, edited by Stanley Sadie and published in twenty volumes. Along with the original Grove's it provided information at innumerable points. The splendid doctoral dissertation of Marilyn Kay Stulken, now published as the *Hymnal Companion to the Lutheran Book of Worship*, was of great help with information on persons and pieces common to both *The*

Presbyterian Hymnal and the *Lutheran Book of Worship.* Other standard works such as John Julian's *A Dictionary of Hymnology* (1892; 2nd rev. ed., 1907) and Charles W. Hughes' *American Hymns Old and New* (1980) have also been frequently consulted. No one studying the church's hymnody can fail to acknowledge the works of the late Erik Routley which have added so much to our understanding. A whole host of smaller, specialized studies have been invaluable as well. Many of these are indicated in the Selected Bibliography.

In addition to printed materials, I owe a debt of thanks to all who corresponded with me and talked with me on the telephone to provide data that could not be found in any books. Hymn authors, tune composers, translators, harmonizers, and family members and acquaintances have been generous with their time and efforts to help me fill in information not available anywhere else. Without their efforts, much material about more contemporary pieces would not be present. Future editions of this volume can take additional knowledge into account as it becomes available.

It has not been possible to document the sources of all information fully. This would have made the book much too technical in nature for its primary purposes, which are to provide fuller and more accessible use of *The Presbyterian Hymnal* and to supply background information that can be useful in a variety of ways, including for teaching and preaching ministries in the church. Where sources have disagreed, judgments have had to be made. I look forward to receiving further information to correct or supplement that given here so an even fuller companion might be presented someday.

It is hoped the appearance of this companion volume within a short period after the publication of *The Presbyterian Hymnal* will add to the excitement and interest in the hymnal throughout the church. It has been an intensive task to undertake this work on my own in a relatively short time. Similar types of companions to other recent denominational hymnals published prior to *The Presbyterian Hymnal* are not yet available. But I hope producing this volume in this time frame will provide a ready source of information and also add right now to an appreciation for the church's hymns as a means of praising God. My purpose accords with that of the writers for the *Handbook to The Hymnal* in 1935: "To place these facts before the hymn lovers of the Church, and to quicken their interest in hymns in general and especially in the hymns of the new Hymnal, is the purpose of this Handbook" (p. xi). As those writers saw it, the informative materials "may be used to intensify the spiritual meaning of the hymns and enhance the personal interest and singing cooperation of the people" (p. xii). That guiding purpose is still my own.

ANTECEDENTS OF *THE PRESBYTERIAN HYMNAL*

1539–1562 Evolution of the Genevan Psalter authorized by John Calvin

1719 Isaac Watts' *The Psalms of David Imitated in the Language of the New Testament* to which hymns were added

1802 *The Psalms of David Imitated in the Language of the New Testament, and Applied to the Christian State and Worship*, by Isaac Watts. Approved and allowed by the General Assembly

1813 *An Imitation of the Psalms of David, Carefully Suited to Christian Worship, Being an Improvement of the Presbyterian Church in the United States, to Be Used in Churches and Private Families.* Approved by the General Assembly

1831 *Psalms and Hymns Adapted to Public Worship, and Approved by the General Assembly of the Presbyterian Church in the United States of America*

1842 *Psalms and Hymns, Adapted to Social, Private, and Public Worship*

1843 Report of a Hymnal committee appointed in 1838, submitting a revision of *Psalms and Hymns*, published as the official Hymnal

1847 A New School Hymnal, *The Church Psalmist*

1852 An Old School Hymnal, *The Presbyterian Psalmodist*, edited by Thomas Hastings

1857 *The Church Psalmist* to which 155 hymns were added

1866 *The Hymnal of the Presbyterian Church* representing the final break with metrical psalmody

1874 *Book of Hymns and Tunes Comprising The Psalms and Hymns for the Worship of God, Approved by the*

General Assembly of 1866, arranged with appropriate tunes, and an Appendix, Prepared by the Presbyterian Committee of Publication, by Authority of the General Assembly of 1873. Richmond: Presbyterian Committee of Publication, 1874

1874 *The Presbyterian Hymnal,* recognized as official, following the Reunion of 1870

1887 *The Psalter* published by the United Presbyterian Board of Publication in Pittsburgh

1895 *The Hymnal,* Dr. Louis Benson's epoch-making work, setting a new standard for church hymns

1901 *The New Psalms and Hymns Published by Authority of The General Assembly of the Presbyterian Church in the United States A.D. 1901*

1911 *The Hymnal,* revised with many changes designed to render the book more adaptable to congregational use

1912 *The Psalter* published by the United Presbyterian Board of Publication in Pittsburgh

1927 *The Presbyterian Hymnal Published by Authority of the Presbyterian Church in the United States*

1927 *The Psalter Hymnal* published by the United Presbyterian Church of North America

1933 *The Hymnal,* edited by Clarence Dickinson and Calvin W. Laufer

1955 *The Hymnbook,* edited by David Hugh Jones

1972 *The Worshipbook—Services and Hymns,* prepared by The Joint Committee on Worship

1990 *The Presbyterian Hymnal: Hymns, Psalms, and Spiritual Songs,* edited by LindaJo McKim

—Adapted from *Handbook to The Hymnal,* ed. William Chalmers Covert and Calvin Weiss Laufer (Philadelphia: Presbyterian Board of Christian Education, 1935), pp. xx–xxi, and Morgan F. Simmons, "Hymnody: Its Place in Twentieth-Century Presbyterianism," in *The Confessional Mosaic: Presbyterians and Twentieth-Century Theology,* ed. Milton J Coalter, John M. Mulder, and Louis B. Weeks (Louisville, Ky.: Westminster/John Knox Press, 1990), pp. 162–186.

CHRISTIAN YEAR

1 Come, Thou Long-Expected Jesus

Tune: STUTTGART

This hymn is one of eleven penned by Rev. Charles Wesley (1707–1788) appearing in *The Presbyterian Hymnal* (1990).

Charles Wesley was the eighteenth child of Samuel and Susanna Wesley. In 1735 he came to colonial Georgia as secretary to General Oglethorpe, having previously received both deacon's and priest's orders. But it was a personal conversion experience on Whitsunday 1738 under the influence of the Moravians that gave him "rest in his soul" and released in him the gift of hymn writing. He is known to have written more than 6,000 hymns and by some counts as many as 6,500. Although he dedicated his life to the Methodist movement, he never relinquished his ordination in the Church of England.

The text appeared in *Hymns for the Nativity of Our Lord* (1744). Lampe published it in 1746 in the first of several tracts bearing the name "Festival Hymns." It was not in the *Wesley Hymn Book* until the revision of 1875. It appears here in an unaltered form.

The focus of the hymn is the celebration of the first Advent of Jesus as it looks forward to the second advent. Israel's messianic expectation is fulfilled in this child. Here is to be born the king who will break the bonds of "fear and sin," the "dear desire of every nation" (Hag. 2:7), and "the hope of all the earth."

STUTTGART is one of the hymn tunes found in Christian Friedrich Witt's *Psalmodia Sacra* (1715), where it is the setting for "Sollt' es gleich bisweilen scheinen." It is speculated that the tune was originally written as a psalm setting and became associated as a chorale tune because of its superior nature. The tune's name does not carry on the German custom of naming the tune for the text for which it serves as a setting. Witt was born in Altenburg 1660 and died in Gotha in 1716.

2 Come, Thou Long-Expected Jesus

Tune: HYFRYDOL

The text was written by Charles Wesley (1744). For comments on the hymn text and author see hymn 1.

HYFRYDOL, composed by Rowland Hugh Prichard (1831), is one of many fine Welsh tunes which have made their mark on hymnody. An interesting fact about this tune is that with one exception the melody lies within the first five notes of the scale.

Rowland Hugh Prichard (1811–1887) was a gifted song leader and tune writer who was born in Bala, Wales, where he spent most of his life. This tune was written before his twentieth birthday and was first published in his collection *Cyfaill y Cantorion (The Singer's Friend)* (1844). Prichard moved to Holywell Mill in 1880, where he served as an assistant to the loom tender in the Welsh Flannel Manufacturing Company's mill.

3 Comfort, Comfort You My People

Tune: PSALM 42

The German of this hymn was written by Johannes Olearius. It is based on Isaiah 40:1–8. Originally written for the feast of St. John the Baptist (June 24) it is now commonly sung during the Advent season. The hymn was first included in *Geistliche Singe-Kunst* (1671). This collection contained over twelve hundred hymns, three hundred two of them were by Olearius.

Johannes Olearius (1611–1684) was born in Saxony, Germany, where his father, also a hymn writer, was pastor of St. Mary's Church. The younger Olearius was educated at the University of Wittenberg (M.A. 1632; D.D. 1643). He was superintendent of Querfurt and then court preacher to August, Duke of Sachsen-Weissenfels. In 1657 he was made a member of the Consistory and in 1664 general superintendent. When the Duke died he was given similar posts by Duke Johann Adolf at Weissenfels, where he remained until his death. Besides his hymn collection, Olearius published a commentary of the entire Bible, and various devotional books.

The English translation is by Catherine Winkworth (1827–1878) and appears in her collection *The Chorale Book for En-*

gland (1863). Winkworth was perhaps the foremost translator of German hymns. She was born in London and spent most of her life in Manchester but moved with her family to Clifton, Bristol, in 1862. She promoted women's higher education through the Clifton Association and helped found Clifton College. Her book *Christian Singers of Germany*, a history of the rise and progress of the German Chorale, has long been of interest to musicologists. Winkworth died suddenly of heart disease while visiting Savoy, France. A tablet on the wall of Bristol Cathedral states that she "opened a new source of light, consolation, and strength in many thousand homes." Winkworth's translation has been altered for *The Presbyterian Hymnal* (1990).

PSALM 42 is from the Genevan Psalter (1551). It quickly found its way to Germany, where it became associated with several texts, including the funeral hymn "Freu dich sehr, o meine Seele" published in *Harmoniae Sacrae* (1613). Among Lutherans the tune is commonly titled FREU DICH SEHR. The present arrangement and harmonization are from the *Pilgrim Hymnal* (1958).

4 Creator of the Stars of Night

Tune: CONDITOR ALME SIDERUM

The text is a ninth-century Latin hymn sung during Advent at Vespers. Another form of the text, "Creator alme siderum," which is the product of revisions of Pope Urban VIII, also exists.

The translation is based on one by John Mason Neale that appeared in his *Hymnal Noted* (1851). The present form is a product of the committee on translations for *The Hymnal 1940.*

John Mason Neale (1818–1866) was born in London and educated at Trinity College, Cambridge, and Downing College. He was ordained a deacon in 1841 and a priest in 1842. Neale was closely associated with E. J. Boyce and Benjamin Webb (see hymn 83) of the Oxford Movement. He was one of the founders of Ecclesiological Society, commonly titled the Cambridge Camden Society. In 1846, Neale became warden of Sackville College, East Grinstead, where he remained until his death.

Neale's deep interest in Latin and Greek hymns led him to translating them. His ability to maintain the sense of the original text while creating a wonderful English poem is unsurpassed. His writings include *Mediaeval Hymns and Sequences* (1851), *The Hymnal Noted* (1851), *Hymns of the Eastern Church* (1862), *Original Sequences, Hymns, and Other Ecclesiastical Verses* (published posthumously), and *Essays on Liturgiology and Church History* (1863). In addition one eighth of the hymns in the original edition of *Hymns Ancient and Modern* (1861) were either written or translated by Neale.

CONDITOR ALME SIDERUM is a Sarum plainsong melody from the early Middle Ages (ninth century), always associated with the text. The harmonization is that of C. Winfred Douglas for *The Hymnal 1940.*

C. (Charles) Winfred Douglas (1867–1944) was born in Oswego, New York. He studied at Syracuse University (B.Mus. 1891) and St. Andrew's Divinity School. He was ordained deacon in 1893 and became curate of Church of the Redeemer, New York City. Because of a lung problem he moved to Evergreen, Colorado (1897–1907), where he began services that led to the founding of the Mission of the Transfiguration. He was ordained a priest in 1899 and became canon residentiary of St. Paul's Cathedral, Fond du Lac, Wisconsin. Douglas was an authority on Gregorian chant and applied his knowledge of plainsong to his ministry of music at St. Mary's, Peekskill, New York (1906–1944). His book *Church Music in History and Practice* (1937) is an extended study of his adaptation of plainsong for American usage. Douglas was music editor of the Protestant Episcopal hymnals of 1916 and 1940.

5 Let All Mortal Flesh Keep Silence

Tune: PICARDY

This hymn is the "Prayer of the Cherubic Hymn" from the Liturgy of St. James of Jerusalem. It is sung at the beginning of the Liturgy of the Faithful during the presentation of the bread and wine. Once thought to be written by James the Less, the Liturgy of St. James was devised for use in Jerusalem. The rite is the basis of all other Eastern Orthodox rites. A literal English translation was published in Neale and Littledale's *Translations of the Primitive Liturgies* (1868–1869). The metrical translation was rendered by Gerard Moultrie in the second edition of Shipley's *Lyra Eucharistica* (1864).

Gerard Moultrie (1829–1885) was born in Rugby Rectory, England, and educated at Rugby and Exeter College, Oxford (B.A. 1851; M.A. 1856). After several chaplaincies, he served as vicar of Southleigh (1869) and then warden of St. James College (1873). He held these positions until his death. In addition to his hymn translations from Greek, Latin, and German, Moultrie was the author of several hymn collections.

PICARDY is a French folk melody transcribed as sung by Mme. Pierre Dupont. It was published in *Chansons populaires des provinces de France,* IV (1860). The present adaptation is from *The English Hymnal* (1906).

6 Jesus Comes with Clouds Descending

Tune: HELMSLEY

The text was written by Charles Wesley and published in *Hymns of Intercession for All Mankind* (1758), where it was designated for the Second Sunday of Advent. For a biographical sketch of Wesley, see hymn 1.

There is evidence that Wesley adapted an earlier hymn, credited to John Cennick, which was performed in the Moravian Chapel at Dublin in 1750. Cennick's text appeared in a *Collection of Sacred Hymns* (1750). A longer form of the hymn was prepared by Martin Madan in 1760, who combined portions of Wesley's text with the original stanzas of Cennick.

HELMSLEY was composed by Thomas Olivers, who adapted a melody he heard being whistled. John Wesley called the tune OLIVERS and included it in *Sacred Melody* (1765). In Martin Madan's *Collection of Hymn and Psalm Tunes* (1769) it appeared in its present form and bore the name HELMSLEY.

Thomas Olivers (1725–1799) was born in Wales, orphaned at the age of four, and received little in the way of formal education. He became a shoemaker's apprentice and throughout his life followed that vocation. After hearing a sermon of George Whitefield he was led to join the Methodist Society at Bradford-on-Avon. In 1753 he became an evangelist traveling throughout

England and Ireland until his death in 1799. Olivers is buried in Wesley's tomb at City Road Chapel cemetery.

The harmonization is that of Ralph Vaughan Williams for *The English Hymnal* (1906).

Ralph Vaughan Williams (1872–1958), the youngest of three children, was born in Down Ampney, Gloucestershire, and raised in Surrey. He showed a gift for music and received his early training from his aunt. Later he studied at the Royal College of Music and Trinity College. Renowned as the most important English composer of his generation, Vaughan Williams' contributions to the world of music are too numerous to mention. (See Stanley Sadie, ed., *The New Grove Dictionary of Music and Musicians* 19:569f.). But his work as music editor of *The English Hymnal* (1906) was extremely important. In that collection are some tunes he wrote himself along with thirty-five to forty folk tunes he adapted. He also edited *Songs of Praise* (1925) and *The Oxford Book of Carols* (1928).

7 Lord Christ, When First You Came to Earth

Tune: MIT FREUDEN ZART

This text by Walter Russell Bowie was written for *Songs of Praise* (1931) at the request of one of the collection's editors who had asked for an Advent hymn in the Dies Irae mode. Bowie became one of few American hymnists included in an English hymnal.

Walter Russell Bowie (1882–1969) was born in Richmond and educated at Harvard University (B.A. 1904; M.A. 1905) and Virginia Theological Seminary (B.D. 1909; D.D. 1919). After his ordination to the Episcopal priesthood (1909), he was rector of Emmanuel Church, Greenwood, Virginia (1909–1911); St. Paul's Church, Richmond (1911–1923); and Grace Church, New York City (1923–1939). He was professor of practical theology and dean of students at Union Theological Seminary, New York City (1939–1950), and then (1950–1955) professor of homiletics at Virginia Theological Seminary (now the Protestant Episcopal Theological Seminary in Virginia). Bowie held lectureships at Philadelphia Divinity School, Yale Divinity School, and Seabury-Western Theological Seminary. He was editor of the *Southern Churchman* and wrote many books, including *The Story of the Bible, The Bible Story for Boys and Girls, Finding God Through St. Paul, The Master, a Life of Jesus,* and *The Living Story of the New Testament.* In addition, Bowie, was a member of the committee that produced the Revised Standard Version of the Bible (1946). He died at Alexandria, Virginia.

MIT FREUDEN ZART was the setting for Georg Vetter's "Mit Freuden zart zu dieser Fahrt" in his collection *Kirchengeseng darinnen die Heubtartickel des Christlichen Glaubens gefasset,* 1566 (also called the Bohemian Brethren's *Kirchengeseng,* 1566). An earlier version of the tune was the setting for Psalm 138, "Il faut que de tous mes esprits," in the Genevan Psalter of 1551.

8 Lift Up Your Heads, Ye Mighty Gates

Tune: TRURO

This hymn was written by Georg Weissel (1590–1635). The text is based on Psalm 24 and was published seven years after Weissel's death in *Preussische Fest-Lieder* (1642). The son of a judge and burgomaster, Weissel studied at the universities of Königsberg, Wittenberg, Leipzig, Jena, Strassburg, Basel, and Marburg. In 1623 he became pastor of the newly built Altrossfahrt Church at Königsberg, where he remained until his death. He wrote about twenty hymns.

The translation from German is by Catherine Winkworth (1855). For comments on Winkworth, see hymn 3.

TRURO is found in the two-volume *Psalmodia Evangelica,* edited by Thomas Williams (1789), where it served as the setting of an Isaac Watts text. In the collection it is written for three voices and bears no composer's name. Little is known of Thomas Williams.

Elsewhere the tune has been attributed to music historian Dr. Charles Burney (1726–1814). Burney was an English organist, composer, and author of *General History of Music*, a four-volume work.

The harmonization is by Lowell Mason (1792–1872), musician and composer. For comments on Mason, see hymn 40.

9 O Come, O Come, Emmanuel

Tune: VENI EMMANUEL

The origins of this Latin hymn are quite interesting. In the ninth century (or earlier) a series of seven Advent antiphons were sung at Vespers the week prior to Christmas both before and after the Magnificat. Each of these antiphons began with "O" followed by a biblical title for the Messiah. The seven antiphons began as follows: "O Sapientia"—O Wisdom; "O Adonai"—O Lord (Ex. 3:15); "O Radix Jesse"—O Root of Jesse (Isa. 11:10); "O Clavis David"—O Key of David (Isa. 22:22; Rev. 3:7); "O Oriens"—O Dayspring (Mal. 4:2; Luke 1:78); "O Rex"—O King; "O Emmanuel"—O God with us (Isa. 7:14; Matt. 1:23). In the twelfth century, according to John Mason Neale (see hymn 4), or the thirteenth century, according to Percy Dearmer (see hymn 459), an unknown poet chose five of the antiphons, rearranged them 7, 3, 5, 4, and 2, added a refrain reminiscent of Zechariah 9:9 and produced a hymn. (For more on the development of this hymn see John Julian, ed., *A Dictionary of Hymnology* 1:73.) The earliest source of the hymn today is *Psalteriolum Cantionum Catholicarum* (1710). In *Mediaeval Hymns and Sequences* (1851), Neale's translation began "Draw nigh, draw nigh, Emmanuel." He revised it for the first edition of *The Hymnal Noted* (1852). Later, the text was revised for *Hymns Ancient and Modern* (1861).

The text in *The Presbyterian Hymnal* (1990) a composite. Stanzas 1 and 2 are from Neale and stanza 3 is from a translation of Henry Sloane Coffin (1877–1954) in *Hymns of the Kingdom of God* (2nd ed., 1916).

VENI EMMANUEL was found in a French Missal in the National Library of Lisbon by Neale, who took it to his friend and collaborator Thomas Helmore. Helmore's adaptation of the tune was the setting for Neale's translation in *The Hymnal Noted,* Part II (1856). The subject of much speculation, the tune was thought to have been created by Helmore from fragments of Kyrie melodies. But John Stainer and George S. Barrett's *Dictionary of Musical Terms* (1881) quoted Helmore stating the tune "was copied by the late J. M. Neale from a French Missal." Further, *The Musical Times*, September 1966, reported the discovery of the melody in a fifteenth-century *Processional* belonging to a group of French Franciscan nuns. Originally VENI EMMANUEL was the tune for the funeral responsory "Libera me."

Thomas Helmore (1811–1890) was born in Kidderminster and educated at Oxford. The son of a Congregationalist minister, Helmore was ordained in the Church of England (1840) and became curate of St. Michael's Lichfield and priest-vicar in the cathedral. In 1842 he became vice-principal and precentor at St. Mark's College, Chelsea, where he coached the students to sing daily choral services in the chapel. Psalms and responses were chanted by the entire student body unaccompanied. Helmore's success led to his appointment as Master of the Children of the Chapel Royal (1846). During his lifetime he was the authority on the Anglican plainsong, but his lasting mark was establishing a choral tradition in English parish churches. With Neale he produced three hymn collections.

The harmonization is by John Weaver. For comments on Weaver, see hymn 565.

10 On Jordan's Bank the Baptist's Cry

Tune: WINCHESTER NEW

The text of this Advent hymn was written in Latin by Charles Coffin (1676–1749). It appeared in the *Paris Breviary* and *Hymni Sacri Auctore Carolo Coffin*, both published in 1736. It bore the title Jordanis oras praevia. In 1701, Coffin became a member of the faculty of Beauvois College and in 1712 its principal. He was named rector of the University of Paris (1718). Some of his Latin poems were published in 1727 and his complete works were published in two volumes in 1755.

The English translation by John Chandler (1806–1876) first appeared in *Hymns of the Primitive Church* (1837). As one of the first of the Oxford group to publish translations, he mistook the *Paris Breviary* as an ancient work rather than a collection from the eighteenth century with the majority of its hymns by Charles Coffin. Chandler, who was born in England and educated at Corpus Christi College, Oxford, was ordained in 1831 and succeeded his father as vicar of Witley. He died at Putney.

WINCHESTER NEW is from *Musikalisches Handbuch* (1690). For comments on the tune, see hymn 444. The harmonization is by William Henry Monk. For comments on Monk, see hymn 543.

11 O Lord, How Shall I Meet You?

Tune: VALET WILL ICH DIR GEBEN

This hymn "Wie soll ich dich empfangen?" was written by Paul Gerhardt. It was first published in Christoph Runge's *D.M. Luthers und anderer vornehmen geistreichen und gelehrten Männer geistliche Lieder und Psalmen* (1653). The English is by Catherine Winkworth and others. In the present collection, the second person pronouns have been updated.

Paul Gerhardt (1607–1676) was born in Gräfenhaynichen and educated at the University of Wittenberg (1628–1642). Gerhardt went to Berlin to tutor Anna Maria Barthold, who later became his wife (1655). He was pastor at Mittenwalde (1651–1657) and assistant at St. Nicholas' Church, Berlin (1657–1666), where he was removed from the pulpit by Elector Friedrich Wilhelm, a Calvinist. He became archdeacon at Lubben (1668), remaining there until his death. His wife and four of their five children preceded him in death. Gerhardt wrote over one hundred hymns. Johann Georg Ebeling (see hymn 21) edited and published the first collection of Gerhardt's hymns (1666–1667).

For comments on Winkworth, see hymn 3.

VALET WILL ICH DIR GEBEN was composed by Melchior Teschner for the text of the same name by Valerius Herberger, written after a five-month period in 1613 when bubonic plague had killed some two thousand people in the community of Fraustadt.

Melchior Teschner (1584–1635) was born in Fraustadt and studied philosophy, theology, and music at the University of Frankfort. He also studied in Wittenberg. In 1609 he was called to his hometown to teach school and serve as precentor to Herberger but became pastor of Oberpritschen church after the death of Adam Krause. Teschner died as a result of the Cossack invasion of 1635.

The harmonization is by William Henry Monk as the setting for "All Glory, Laud, and Honor" (see hymn 88) in *Hymns Ancient and Modern* (1861), where the tune was named ST. THEODULPH. For comments on Monk, see hymn 543.

12 People, Look East

Tune: BESANÇON

The text is by Eleanor Farjeon and first appeared in Part 3, "Modern Texts Written for or Adapted to Traditional Tunes," of *The Oxford Book of Carols* (1928; reset 1964). It is titled "Carol of Advent." For comments on Farjeon, see hymn 469.

BESANÇON is an old Besançon carol tune which originally appeared in Bramley and Stainer's collection of 1871. It was one of forty-two carols in the collection titled *Christmas Carols New and Old.* The tune was used as a setting for "Shepherds, Shake Off Your Drowsy Sleep" and was titled CHANTONS, BARGIÉS, NOUÉ, NOUÉ.

The harmonization is that of Martin Shaw for *The Oxford Book of Carols* (1928). Martin Edward Fallas Shaw (1875–1958) was born in London and studied at the Royal College of Music as a student of Charles Villiers Stanford (see hymn 264), and C. Hubert H. Parry (see hymn 224). He became organist and choirmaster at St. Mary's, Primrose Hill (1908–1920), St. Martin's in the Fields (1920–1924). Later he was master of music at Guild House (1924–1935) and then music director for the diocese of Chelmsford (1935–1945). With Percy Dearmer (see hymn 459), Ralph Vaughan Williams (see hymn 6), and George Wallace Briggs (see hymn 503), he edited *Children's Church* and *Songs of Praise* (1925), *The Oxford Book of Carols* (1928), and *Hymns for This Time of War* (1940). He encouraged the revival of English folk music and with his brother Geoffrey was honored with the Lambeth Doctor of Music degree (1932). Shaw's *Principles of English Church Music Composition* was published in 1921.

13 Prepare the Way

Tune: BEREDEN VÄG FÖR HERRAN

The text of this hymn, originally in Swedish, was written by Frans Mikael Franzén and published in *Prof-Psalmer* (1812). After the hymn received poor reviews, Franzén revised it for the *Svenska Psalm-Boken* (1819).

Frans Mikael Franzén (1772–1847) was born in Uleaborg, Finland, of Swedish parents. He entered Abo Academy in 1785. After his father's death, he returned home for a short time but returned to Abo and earned a master's degree. In 1790 he entered Uppsala University to study philosophy, then went back to Abo to write his dissertation. He was made librarian at Abo (1794) and later professor of the history of literature (1798). Franzén was ordained in 1803 and served several pastorates in both Finland and Sweden. It was Franzén's relationship with Archbishop Johan Olof Wallin that led to his excellent contribution to hymnody. Together they prepared both collections cited above. In 1834, Franzén was appointed bishop of Härnösand, where he remained until his death.

The translation, a composite, was adapted by Charles P. Price and was one of sixteen contributions he made to *The Hymnal 1982.* Price was born in Pittsburgh in 1920 and educated at Harvard University, Virginia Theological Seminary, and Union Theological Seminary in New York City. He studied piano with Elizabeth and Ferguson Webster (1935–1942) and was ordained as a deacon and priest in the Episcopal Church, Diocese of Pittsburgh. He served churches in Pennsylvania and New York City before becoming a professor at Virginia Theological Seminary (1956–1963). From 1963 to 1972 he was preacher to the university and Plummer Professor of Christian Morals at Harvard University before returning to Virginia Seminary as professor of systematic theology (1972–1989).

Price was a member of the Standing Liturgical Commission (1967–1985) and the Committee on Texts for *The Hymnal 1982* (1976–1982), as well as deputy to the General Convention (1976–1985) and chaplain to the House of Deputies (1979–1985) for the Episcopal Church. His books include *Introducing the Proposed Book of Common Prayer* (1976) and, with Louis Weil, *Liturgy for Living* (1979). A number of his hymns and translations appear in *The Hymnal 1982.*

BEREDEN VÄG FÖR HERRAN was included in *Then Swenska Psalmboken* (1697), which was the music edition of the 1695 revision of Jesper Swedberg's hymnal of 1694. The arrangement found in *The Presbyterian Hymnal* (1990) is from the *American Lutheran Hymnal* (1930).

14 Savior of the Nations, Come

Tune: NUN KOMM, DER HEIDEN HEILAND

This hymn is one of twelve definitely ascribed to Ambrose by the late John Julian. Both Augustine (372) and Pope Celestine (430) point to Ambrose as the author. Although schooled as a lawyer, at the age of thirty-five Ambrose was elected bishop of Milan. He was the father of Latin hymnody and was known for introducing antiphonal singing into the Western church. As a bishop he is best known for his fight against Arianism. In 1523 Martin Luther translated the text from Latin into German. For comments on Luther, see hymn 240.

The Presbyterian Hymnal (1990) uses an altered version of the 1850 translation by William Morton Reynolds (1812–1876). Reynolds' translation appeared in his edited work *Hymns, Original and Selected, for Public and Private Worship, in the Evangelical Lutheran Church* (1851). He was a Lutheran pastor and educator who in his last years became an Episcopal priest.

NUN KOMM, DER HEIDEN HEILAND is an adaptation of a medieval Latin plainsong. The tune was first found in the Einsiedeln *Hymnal* (twelfth-thirteenth century). The present form is from *Eyn Enchiridion* (Erfurt, 1524). The harmonization is from *Songs of Syon* (1910).

15 Rejoice! Rejoice, Believers

Tune: LLANGLOFFAN

The text was written by Laurentius Laurenti and appears in his *Evangelia Melodica* (1700). This hymn, considered his finest, had ten stanzas and was originally titled "For the 27th Sunday after Trinity." It is based on the parable of the ten maidens in Matthew 25 and images from Revelation 20 and 21.

Lorenz Lorenzen (1660–1722) was born in Schleswig, Germany, and educated at the University of Rostock (1681), then Kiel (1683), where he studied music. While there, Lorenzen Latinized his name to Laurentius Laurenti. In 1684 he became cantor and director of music in Bremen, where he died in 1722. A product of the Pietistic movement, he was one its best hymn writers.

The translation is by Sarah Borthwick Findlater (1823–1907), sister of Jane Laurie Borthwick (see hymn 415). They were born in Edinburgh, where their father managed the North British Insurance Office. Sarah married Eric John Findlater, a pastor in the Free Church of Scotland. Findlater and her sister Jane's English translations were collected in *German Hymns from the Land of Luther*, which appeared in four volumes (1854–1862).

LLANGLOFFAN is a Welsh folk melody from Daniel Evans' *Hymnau a Thonau* (1865). It is a tune of unknown authorship.

The name is probably that of a farm or homestead but it could be the "Church of St. Gloffan." The present harmonization is from *The English Hymnal* (1906).

16 The Angel Gabriel from Heaven Came

Tune: GABRIEL'S MESSAGE

The text of this hymn was written by Sabine Baring-Gould (1834–1924). He was born in Exeter and educated in Germany, France, and Cambridge (M.A. 1856). He was ordained in 1864 and served a curacy in Horbury, then in Dalton. Upon the death of his father he inherited the family's estate at Lew-Trenchard, where he became both squire and rector in 1881. He remained there until his death.

Sabine Baring-Gould was a prolific writer, publishing thirty novels as well as several folk song collections. He was a pioneer in collecting English folk songs, transcribing from performances over one hundred ten songs in the three years between 1888 and 1891. Only Lucy Broadwood's folk songs *Sussex Songs* (1843, 1888) preceded the collection he edited with Rev. H. Fleetwood Sheppard, *Songs and Ballads of the West* (1891). Baring-Gould is known especially for the hymns "Onward, Christian Soldiers" and "Now the Day Is Over" (see hymn 541).

GABRIEL'S MESSAGE is a *cantique* melody from the Basque provinces located between southern France and northeastern Spain. The tune was arranged for this text and named GABRIEL'S MESSAGE by Charles Edgar Pettman (1865–1943) and John Wickham.

17 "Sleepers, Wake!" A Voice Astounds Us

Tune: WACHET AUF

This hymn known as the "king of chorales" was written by Philipp Nicolai while in Unna in Westphalia (1596–1598). The text is based on the parable of the "wise and foolish bridesmaids" in Matthew 25:1–13. (Several other scriptural passages are also present in the text and are noted in the Index of Scriptural Allusions in *The Presbyterian Hymnal*, 1990.) It was published in his devotional *Frewden-Spiegel dess ewigen Lebens*

(1599), composed during a time of widespread disease when thousands were dying. Nicolai wrote in the preface:

> To leave behind me (if God should call me from this world) as a token of my peaceful, joyful, Christian departure, or (if God should spare me in health) to comfort other sufferers whom He should also visit with the pestilence.

Two of the three hymns included in his work—"Sleepers, Wake!" and "O Morning Star, How Fair and Bright" (see hymn 69)—appear in *The Presbyterian Hymnal* (1990).

Philipp Nicolai (1556–1608) was born in Mengeringhausen in Waldeck and educated at the universities of Erfurt and Wittenberg (degree 1579; D.D. 1594). He held pastorates in Herdecke, Unna, and Hamburg. He was a controversial preacher best remembered for his opposition to both Roman Catholic and Calvinist views of the Lord's Supper. Following his participation in the ordination of a friend on October 22, 1608, he developed a fever and died four days later.

The English translation is by Carl P. Daw, Jr., for *The Hymnal 1982*, of the Episcopal Church. For comments on Daw see hymn 314.

WACHET AUF was composed by Nicolai as the setting for his text in the *Frewden-Spiegel.* "Everyone agrees that the chorale makes its last and greatest gestures in the two immortal melodies of Philipp Nicolai, WIE SCHÖN LEUCHTET [see hymn 69] and WACHET AUF" (Erik Routley, *The Music of Christian Hymns*, p. 26).

The harmonization is by Johann Sebastian Bach (1685–1750), arranged for his Cantata 140. Bach was born in Eisenach and received his music education first from his father, then his eldest brother. By eighteen he was an accomplished violinist, organist, and composer. He held several positions as organist in Arnstadt (1704–1707), Mühlhausen (1707–1708), and Weimar (1708–1717) before becoming court musician for Prince Leopold at Cöthen (1717–1723). From there he moved to Leipzig, where he was cantor at St. Thomas School and music director of the other Lutheran churches. He remained in Leipzig until his death. Bach was the greatest organist of his day and his genius as a crafter of music has never been surpassed. (For a listing of J. S. Bach's works, see Albert Schweitzer, *J. S. Bach*, trans. Ernest Newman; New York: Dover Publications, 1966.)

18 The Desert Shall Rejoice

Tune: STERLING

This text was written by Gracia Grindal and published in *Singing the Story* (1983), where it was set to ADVENT ROSE by Rusty Edwards (see hymn 19).

Gracia Grindal was born (1943) in Powers Lake, North Dakota, where she spent her early years. When she was twelve her parents moved to Salem, Oregon. She graduated from Augsburg College (1965), the University of Arkansas (M.F.A. 1969), and Luther Northwestern Theological Seminary. Grindal taught English at Luther College, Decorah, Iowa, where she was poet-in-residence (1968–1984). She is now associate professor of pastoral theology and ministry at Luther Northwestern Theological Seminary, St. Paul. She served on the text committee of the Inter-Lutheran Commission on Worship for the *Lutheran Book of Worship* (1978). She is a regular contributor to *The Hymn* and leads workshops on worship and hymnody throughout the United States. A noted poet and hymn writer, her *Lessons in Hymnwriting* is perhaps her greatest contribution to the American church to date.

STERLING was composed for this text by Joy F. Patterson, a member of the Presbyterian Hymnal Committee. It was named for Sterling Anderson, both pastor and friend to Patterson for more than thirty-five years. It was his encouragement that led her to write hymns and tunes. For more on Patterson, see hymn 194.

19 To a Maid Engaged to Joseph

Tune: ANNUNCIATION

The text was written by Gracia Grindal to celebrate the foretelling of Jesus' birth (the Annunciation) to Mary. It is based on Luke 1:26–38, the Common Lectionary reading for the Fourth Sunday of Advent, year B. For a biographical sketch of Grindal, see hymn 18.

ANNUNCIATION was composed by Rusty Edwards (1984) for this text at the request of Gracia Grindal. It was the second of their collaborative efforts. Previously they had produced "In the Dark of Easter Morning." The hymn first appeared in *Singing the Story* (1983). It has also appeared in *Hymnal Supplement* (1984) and *The United Methodist Hymnal* (1989).

Rusty (Howard M. III) Edwards was born in 1955 in Dixon, Illinois, and received his musical training at Interlochen Arts Academy, Michigan (1973), and the University of Nebraska, Lincoln (B.M.E. 1976). After a brief teaching career he attended Luther Northwestern Seminary, St. Paul (M. Div. 1985), and was ordained in Rosemont, Illinois, that same year. He received a D.Min. from the Graduate Theological Foundation, Notre Dame, Indiana, in 1990. Edwards was associate pastor of Trinity Lutheran Church, Moline, Illinois, prior to becoming senior pastor of Gloria Dei Lutheran Church, Rockford, Illinois, October 1991. Edwards' hymns and tunes appear in over thirty publications.

20 Watchman, Tell Us of the Night

Tune: ABERYSTWYTH

The text by John Bowring (1792–1872) was first published in 1825. Bowring was born at Exeter and studied philology, poetry, and politics, and edited the *Westminster Review*. A student of languages, by the time of his death he knew two hundred and could converse in one hundred. He held several official appointments: commissioner to France, British consul at Hong Kong, and governor of Hong Kong. He was twice a member of Parliament and was knighted by Queen Victoria (1854).

Bowring's extensive writings were published in thirty-six volumes, including two volumes of sacred poetry: *Matins and Vespers with Hymns and Occasional Devotional Pieces* (1823) and *Hymns: as a Sequel to Matins* (1825). In 1859 an attempt was made to poison him and his family while in China. His wife died as a result. Bowring returned to England and maintained a full schedule of lecturing and writing until his death in Exeter.

ABERYSTWYTH was composed by Joseph Parry for the Welsh text "Beth sydd i mi yn y byd" and published in *Ail Lyfr Tonau ac Emynau* (1879). For comments on Parry, see hymn 303.

21 All My Heart Today Rejoices

Tune: WARUM SOLLT' ICH

This hymn "Fröhlich soll mein Herze springen" was written by Paul Gerhardt (1653) and included in Johann Crüger's *Praxis Pietatis Melica* (1656). The original poem contained fifteen stanzas, but Catherine Winkworth reduced the number to ten when she translated it for her *Lyra Germanica* (2nd series, 1858). It appears in most collections with either three (*The Hymnbook,* 1955) or four stanzas (*The Worshipbook—Services and Hymns,* 1972). Winkworth's original first phrase read "All my heart this night rejoices." In an effort to extend the usefulness of the text the phrase was changed to "Once again my heart rejoices" or "All my heart today rejoices." All three phrases appear in common usage. For a biographical sketch of Gerhardt, see hymn 11. For comments on Winkworth, see hymn 3.

WARUM SOLLT' ICH was composed by Johann Georg Ebeling as the setting for "Warum sollt' ich mich denn grämen" in *Pauli Gerhardi Geistliche Andachten, bestehend in 120 Liedern mit 4 Singstimmen, 2 Violinen und General-bass* (1666–1667). The collection featured poems by Gerhardt set to music by Ebeling. The tune has also been named BONN and EBELING.

Johann Georg Ebeling (1637–1676) was cantor and member of the faculty at the Greyfriars Gymnasium and music director of St. Nicholas Cathedral, Berlin (1662–1668). Here he became acquainted with Gerhardt. A second collection, *Evangelischer Lustgarten Herrn Pauli Gerhard's,* with Ebeling's settings was published in 1669. Ebeling became professor of Greek, poetry, and music and cantor at Caroline Gymnasium, Stettin, Pomerania, in 1668 and retained that position until his death.

22 Angels, from the Realms of Glory

Tune: REGENT SQUARE

The text of stanzas 1–3 of this Christmas hymn was written by James Montgomery (1816). It was first published in the newspaper *The Sheffield Iris*, December 24, 1816. It also appears in his collection of original hymns of 1853. The fourth stanza is a doxology from the *Salisbury Hymn Book* (1857).

The son of Moravian missionaries, James Montgomery (1771–1854) was educated at a seminary of the Brethren at Fulneck, Yorkshire. In 1787 he left the seminary and became the assistant to Joseph Gales, printer of the *Sheffield Register* (1792). Two years later Gales left England under the threat of imprisonment and Montgomery took over the publication of the paper, changing the name to *The Sheffield Iris.*

Among his poetical works are *Prison Amusements* (1797), *The West Indies, Greenland and other Poems, Songs of Zion* (1822), *The Christian Psalmist* (1825), and *Original Hymns for Public, Private, and Social Devotion* (1853).

REGENT SQUARE was composed by Henry Thomas Smart and published in the English Presbyterian hymnal *Psalms and Hymns for Divine Worship* (1867). There it was the setting for Horatius Bonar's "Glory Be to God the Father." For more on the tune, see hymn 417.

Henry Thomas Smart (1813–1879) was born in London and educated at Highgate. He received his early music training from his father and then continued on his own. He studied law but after four years chose a musical career over both law and a commission in the East Indian Army. He served as organist at Blackburn Parish Church, St. Giles, Cripplegate; St. Philip's, Regent Street; St. Luke's, Old Street; and St. Pancras. Smart designed the organs for St. Andrew's Hall and Leeds Town Hall and was one of five organists asked to perform at the Exhibition in 1851. For further comments on Smart, see hymn 417.

23 Angels We Have Heard on High

Tune: GLORIA

This French carol is thought by some to have originated during the eighteenth century, but its earliest appearance is in *Nouveau recueil de cantiques* (1855). It first appeared in English in Henri Frederick Hemy's *Crown of Jesus Music*, Part II (London, 1862). The hymn's original author is unknown but according to

The Hymnal 1982 the English translation is by James Chadwick (1813–1882).

GLORIA is a tune of unknown authorship usually associated with these words. The arrangement is by Edward Shippen Barnes (1887–1958) for *The New Church Hymnal* (1937). Barnes was born in Seabury, New Jersey, and educated at Yale University (B.A.) and in Paris. Upon his return to the United States, he served as organist and choir director at the Church of the Incarnation and Rutgers Presbyterian Church, New York City; St. Stephen's Church, Philadelphia; and First Presbyterian Church, Santa Monica, California. Barnes wrote anthems, organ and choral works, services for the Episcopal Church, and an organ method book.

24 Away in a Manger

Tune: CRADLE SONG

The first two stanzas of this hymn were published in the Evangelical Lutheran Church in North America's collection *Little Children's Book for Schools and Families* (Philadelphia, c. 1885). The third stanza appeared in Charles H. Gabriel's *Vineyard Songs* (1892).

This hymn is of unknown authorship but it has often been attributed to Martin Luther. Luther, however, did not write the text, and it appears nowhere in his writings. The only known German version is in a collection published in Missouri in 1934.

Most likely the text is an American one written for the two hundredth anniversary of Luther's birth.

CRADLE SONG was composed by William James Kirkpatrick, a native of Pennsylvania, in 1895. The tune was written for this text and appeared in *Around the World with Christmas* (1895). The gentle rhythm and quiet tone make it especially suited for unison singing.

Throughout his adult life William James Kirkpatrick (1838–1921) was a businessperson with strong ties to the music industry. From 1858 to the end of his life he edited and compiled camp-meeting songs and gospel hymns. Along with A. S. Jenks he collected materials for *Devotional Melodies* and with J. R.

Sweeney compiled forty-seven songbooks. In addition, Kirkpatrick published forty songbooks on his own.

25 Away in a Manger

Tune: MUELLER

Stanzas 1–2 are from the *Little Children's Book for Schools and Families* (c. 1885) and stanza 3 appeared in *Gabriel's Vineyard Songs* (1892). For comments on the text see hymn 24.

MUELLER was first associated with the text in James R. Murray's *Dainty Songs for Little Lads and Lassies* (Cincinnati, 1887). While Murray was obviously the composer, the tune bore the initials J. R. M., but the heading read: "Luther's Cradle Hymn. Composed by Martin Luther for his children, and still sung by German mothers to their little ones."

James R. Murray (1841–1905) was born in Andover, Massachusetts, of Scot parents. He studied under Lowell Mason, George Root, George Webb, and William Bradbury. During the Civil War, Murray was in the Union Army. From 1868 to 1871 he served as music editor for Root and Cady in Chicago. He taught music in the public schools of Andover from 1871 to 1881, when he went to Cincinnati's John Church Company as an editor until his death.

The harmonization is by John Weaver (1986) for *The Presbyterian Hymnal* (1990). For comments on Weaver, see hymn 565.

26 Break Forth, O Beauteous Heavenly Light

Tune: ERMUNTRE DICH

This hymn was written in German by Johann Rist. It is based on Isaiah 9:2–7 and was first published in *Himmlische Lieder* (1st ed., 1641). Rist titled it "a hymn of praise on the joyful birth and incarnation of our Lord and Savior Jesus Christ." It was included in Johann Crüger's *Praxis Pietatis Melica* (1656).

Johann Rist (1607–1667) was born in Ottensen and educated

at the University of Rinteln. He served as a tutor to the children of a Hamburg merchant accompanying them to the University of Rostock, where he studied Hebrew, mathematics, and medicine. Later he became a tutor in Hamburg. In 1635 he married and became pastor at Wedel on the Elbe, where he remained until his death.

The English translation is by John Troutbeck (1873). Troutbeck (1832–1889) was born in Dacre, Cumberland, England, and educated at Rugby and University College, Oxford (B.A. 1856; M.A. 1858; D.D. 1883 by appointment of the Archbishop of Canterbury). He was ordained in 1855 and served as chaplain and priest in ordinary to the Queen, minor canon of Westminster (1869) and secretary to the New Testament Revision Committee (1870–1881). Troutbeck is best known for his *Manchester Psalter and Chant Book* (1867) and the *Westminster Abbey Hymn Book* (1883).

ERMUNTRE DICH was composed by Johann Schop, a personal friend of Rist. He provided the musical settings for *Himmlische Lieder* and composed *Geistliche Koncerte* (1643). Schop (c. 1600–c. 1665) was born in Hamburg and was a member of the court band in Wolfenbüttel (1615) and violinist at the Danish court. He was appointed director of music at Hamburg and later organist to the town and St. James Church.

The harmonization is by Johann Sebastian Bach (1734). For comments on Bach, see hymn 17.

27 Gentle Mary Laid Her Child

Tune: TEMPUS ADEST FLORIDUM

This text was written by Joseph Simpson Cook. Its simplicity of language makes the hymn particularly appropriate for children.

Joseph Simpson Cook (1860–1933) was born in Durham County, England, and moved to Canada at an early age. He graduated from Wesley College of McGill University, Montreal, and was ordained a Methodist minister. He later became a member of the United Church of Canada when the Methodists joined with several other Protestant denominations to form that body in 1925. He died in Toronto.

TEMPUS ADEST FLORIDUM first appeared in *Piae Cantiones* (1582). The collection by Theodoricus Petri was intended to preserve in Sweden the medieval songs and carols. Originally the tune was the setting for the spring carol "Spring Has Now Unwrapped the Flowers," but it is better known as the melody for John Mason Neale's (see hymn 4) "Good King Wenceslas."

The arrangement is by Ernest (Alexander) Campbell MacMillan and appeared in *The Hymnal* (1933) of the Presbyterian Church U.S.A. MacMillan (1893–1973), a lifelong Presbyterian, was born in Mimico, Canada, and by age ten played organ recitals at Massey Hall. In 1906 he won an award in advanced harmony from the University of Edinburgh. From 1908 to 1910 he was organist at Knox Church, Toronto, and studied at the universities of Toronto and Oxford (B.Mus. 1911). MacMillan went to Paris for further study and was attending the Bayreuth Festival of 1914 to hear Wagner when World War I broke out. He and a friend were detained for four years in Ruhleben prison camp, during which time he composed music for Swinburne's *Ode to England* for which he received a degree of Doctor of Music *in absentia* from Oxford (1918). He was also granted a B.A. in modern history by the University of Toronto during his imprisonment. After the war he returned to Canada to become organist and choir director of Timothy Eaton Memorial Church (1919–1925) before becoming principal and music director of the Toronto Conservatory of Music (1926–1942). From 1927 to 1952 he was dean of the music faculty of the University of Toronto. MacMillan became the first person outside the British Isles to be knighted (1935). Other honors include Hon. RAM (1938), Canada Council Medal (1964), Canadian Music Council Medal (1973), and honorary doctorates from nine universities in Canada and the United States. He died in Toronto.

28 Good Christian Friends, Rejoice

Tune: IN DULCI JUBILO

This medieval carol dates from the fourteenth century. The writer is unknown but the text has been ascribed to Peter of Dresden, who died around 1440. However, most scholars believe the hymn to be older than that. The oldest form of the carol is found in the Leipzig University Library, Codex 1305 (c. 1400). The text employs both Latin and German throughout. A German-language version appeared in Hanover in 1646. The carol also was published in *Piae Cantiones* (1582) using Latin and Swedish.

The English translation and paraphrase is by John Mason Neale and was published in *Carols for Christmas-tide* (1853). Neale coedited that volume with Thomas Helmore (see hymn 9). The first line of each stanza was altered from "Good Christian men, rejoice" to "Good Christian friends, rejoice" when published in the *Lutheran Book of Worship* (1978). For a biographical sketch of Neale, see hymn 4.

IN DULCI JUBILO is a German folk tune from the fourteenth century which has served as the setting for the text. The melody appeared in Joseph Klug's *Gesangbuch* (1535).

The harmonization in *The Presbyterian Hymnal* (1990) is by David Hugh Jones (1900–1983), editor of *The Hymnbook* (1955). His was a slight adaptation of John Stainer's (see hymn 509) harmonization composed in 1867 and appearing in *Christmas Carols New and Old* (1871).

29 Go, Tell It on the Mountain

Tune: GO TELL IT

Having heard the refrain, John Wesley Work II (sometimes Jr.) wrote the present stanzas of this hymn shortly after the turn of the century. It was included in the collection *American Negro Songs and Spirituals* (1940).

John Wesley Work II (1872–1925) was born, educated, worked, and died in Nashville. He majored in history and Latin at Fisk University (B.A. 1895; M.A. 1898), after which he was instructor of Greek and Latin until 1906 when he was appointed chair of the department.

Work and his brother, Frederick Jerome (1879–1942), were leading figures in the preservation, performance, and study of African-American spirituals. They published several collections of slave songs and spirituals, including *New Jubilee Songs as Sung by Fisk Jubilee Singers* (1901) and *Folk Songs of the American Negro* (1907). John Work II's treatise *The Folk Song of the*

American Negro (1915) was one of the earliest studies of African-American music undertaken by the descendant of an ex-slave. In 1923, Work was named president of Roger Williams University, Nashville, a position he held at the time of his death.

GO TELL IT is an African-American tune usually associated with this text arranged by John Wesley Work III (1902–1967), who continued the work begun by his father and uncle. The younger Work was educated at Fisk University (B.A.), Columbia University (M.A.), and Yale University (B.Mus.), after which he directed the glee club at Fisk for four years until his appointment as professor of music theory in 1931. Known as a composer and arranger, Work published a comprehensive collection of African-American folk music *American Negro Songs and Spirituals* (1940).

The harmonization is by Melva Wilson Costen. Born in 1933 in Due West, South Carolina, she was educated at Johnson C. Smith University (B.A. 1953), University of North Carolina (M.A.; Mus.Ed. 1964), and Georgia State University (Ph.D. 1978). She has taught music at both the public school and seminary level and now she serves as the Helmar Nielson Professor of Worship and Music at the Interdenominational Theological Center, Atlanta. Costen was chair of the Presbyterian Hymnal Committee.

30 Born in the Night, Mary's Child

Tune: (MARY'S CHILD)

This hymn was originally composed in 1964 for guitar by Geoffrey Ainger (b. 1925). It was harmonized by Richard D. Wetzel for inclusion in *The Worshipbook—Services and Hymns* (1972).

Richard D. Wetzel (b. 1935) served on the selection committee for *The Worshipbook—Services and Hymns* (1972) and has written *Frontier Musicians on the Connoquenessing, Wabash and Ohio*, a history of George Papp's Harmony Society from 1805 to 1906. While a student, Wetzel cataloged the Warrington Music Collection at Pittsburgh Theological Seminary.

31 Hark! The Herald Angels Sing

Tune: MENDELSSOHN

The text was written by Charles Wesley during his early productive period and was first published in *Hymns and Sacred Poems* (1739). Originally the poem began, "Hark, how all the welkin rings, Glory to the King of kings." Wesley himself altered the text in 1743 and many more alterations have been made through the years. (See John Julian, ed., *A Dictionary of Hymnology* 1:487:1.) The present first line is from George Whitefield's *A Collection of Hymns for Social Worship* (1753). For a biographical sketch of Wesley, see hymn 1.

MENDELSSOHN is an adaptation from a composition by Felix Mendelssohn. The original composition was for male chorus and orchestra, *Festgesang an die Künstler*, Opus 68, 1840. It was composed to commemorate the four hundredth anniversary of the invention of printing.

Felix Mendelssohn-Bartholdy (1809–1847) was born in Hamburg, Germany. He was the grandson of the Jewish philosopher Moses Mendelssohn; however, Felix was raised Lutheran. His musical ability was noted early. He became accomplished on the piano and organ and at twelve he began to compose. At seventeen he composed his overture to *A Midsummer Night's Dream*. He revived an interest in the study and performance of Bach, conducting the *St. Matthew Passion* one hundred years after its first performance. Much of his life was spent in composing and performing his own compositions throughout Europe. The untimely death of his sister, Fanny, sent him into despair and ultimately led to the deterioration of his own health and death, six months after hers, in Leipzig.

The melody of the hymn was taken unaltered from the second movement of the composition. It was adapted and harmonized by William Hayman Cummings as the setting for the Wesley text and was first published in Richard R. Chope's *Congregational Hymn and Tune Book* (1857).

Born in Devon, England, William Hayman Cummings (1831–1915) served as a choirboy at St. Paul's Cathedral and sang the alto arias for the premiere performance of *Elijah* in 1846, directed by Mendelssohn himself. Cummings was principal of Guildhall School of Music (1896–1910). Today he is remembered primarily for his scholarship and his music library.

32 Hark! The Herald Angels Sing

Tune: MENDELSSOHN

The text was written by Charles Wesley. For comments on the text, see hymn 31. For a biographical sketch of Wesley, see hymn 1.

MENDELSSOHN was composed by Felix Mendelssohn. For comments on the tune and the composer, see hymn 31.

The descant and harmonization are by David Valentine Willcocks. Willcocks was born in 1919 in Newquay, England, and received his early music education at Westminster Abbey (1929–1933). He was a scholar at Clifton College and King's College, Cambridge (1939–1940). After a varied musical career he returned to King's College as organist and choir director. He was made a fellow of King's College (1958), commander of the Order of the British Empire (1971), and was knighted (1977).

His 1973 recording of Handel's *Messiah* is unique in that all the soprano arias were sung in unison by the boy sopranos of King's College choir. His musical setting of *The Festival of Nine Lessons and Carols* served as the basis for *Carols for Choirs* (1961; rev., 1985), the collection from which the present descant and harmonization are taken.

33 Sheng Ye Qing, Sheng Ye Jing Holy Night, Blessed Night

This hymn originated in the Mandarin area of China and was written by Weiyu Zhu and Jingren Wu in 1921. The English paraphrase is by Kathleen Moody for the Christian Conference of Asia's *New CCA Hymnal* (1990).

The tune was composed by Qigui Shy for *The New Hymns of Praise* (1983). It was harmonized by I-to Loh using the pseudonym Pen-li Chen (1987) for the *New CCA Hymnal* (1990).

I-to Loh (b. 1936) has been professor of church music at Taiwan Theological College and the Asian Institute for Liturgy and Music at St. Andrew's Theological Seminary, Manila, Philippines. He edited *The New Songs of Asian Cities* (1972), *Hymns from the Four Winds* (1983), and the *New CCA Hymnal* (1990). Loh is currently a Ph.D. candidate in music at the University of California, Los Angeles.

34 In Bethlehem a Babe Was Born

Tune: DISCOVERY

This hymn, text and tune, was written just before Christmas 1986. The author Barbara Mays says:

> There is no real story behind the writing. It was one of those middle of the night experiences. I just put myself in that place in Bethlehem. I imaged the events of the story surrounding the birth of Jesus and wrote the hymn in an evening.

Mays was born in Anderson, Indiana, in 1944 and graduated from Indiana University (B.S. in Communications 1965). Prior to her work as publisher of Friends United Press (1981–1988) she worked in the newspaper industry. At present she is director of the United Way for two counties in Indiana. She has several published pieces and currently serves on the committee preparing a new hymnal for the Society of Friends. She lives in Richmond, Indiana.

DISCOVERY was composed by Mays with the text. The harmonization is by John Weaver (1988) for *The Presbyterian Hymnal* (1990). For comments on Weaver, see hymn 565.

35 In Bethlehem a Newborn Boy

Tune: IN BETHLEHEM

The text of this hymn whose subject is the flight into Egypt (Matthew 2:13–16) was written by Rosamond E. Herklots. It first appeared in *Hymns and Songs*, a supplement published by the British Methodists in 1969.

Rosamond E. Herklots (1905–1987) was born in Masuri, North India, to British parents and educated at Leeds Girls' School and Leeds University, where she studied to be a teacher. But she found fulfillment as a secretary for a neurologist and later for the Association for Spina Bifida and Hydrocephalus of London.

Herklots began writing poetry in her childhood and turned to hymn writing in her adult years. She wrote over seventy hymns, many specifically with children in mind.

IN BETHLEHEM was composed by Wilbur Held for this text for *The Hymnal 1982*.

Wilbur Held (b. 1914) is a graduate of American Conservatory (B.M. and M.M.) and Union Theological Seminary School of Sacred Music, New York City (D.S.M. 1956). He also studied with Marcel Dupré and André Marchal when the two were in the United States. From 1946 until his retirement in 1978, Held was professor of organ and church music at Ohio State University College of the Arts and also organist and choirmaster at Trinity Episcopal Church, Columbus, Ohio (1949–1979). He now lives in Claremont, California. Held is the composer of numerous organ, choral, and solo works.

36 In the Bleak Midwinter

Tune: CRANHAM

This hymn text was written by Christina G. Rossetti as a poem. It was included in her *Poetical Works* (1904), where it is said the text was written before 1872. The text gained popularity through its publication in *The English Hymnal* (1906) with Holst's tune.

Christina G. Rossetti (1830–1894) was born in London to an Italian exile family. She received her education at home. Known for her beauty, she was a model for several artists of the day. She rejected two proposals of marriage on religious grounds.

Her poetry is collected in several published works, including *Goblin Market and Other Poems* (1862), *The Prince's Progress and Other Poems* (1866), *Poems* (1875), *A Pageant and Other Poems* (1881), and *Poetical Works* (1904).

CRANHAM was composed by Gustav Theodore Holst as a setting for this text in *The English Hymnal* (1906).

Gustav Theodore Holst (1874–1934) was born in Cheltenham and studied piano under his father's supervision. He attended the Royal College of Music (1893), studying first composition and then trombone. He was appointed teacher at James Allen Girls' School, Dulwich (1903), and he became director of music at St. Paul's Girls' School, Hammersmith (1905). He retained this position until his death in London. His compositions include works for stage, choir, orchestra, and songs for voice and piano.

37 Infant Holy, Infant Lowly

Tune: W ŻŁOBIE LEŻY

This Polish carol came to the attention of English-speaking audiences when Edith M. G. Reed's translation appeared in *Music and Youth* [also called *Piano Student*] (1925). The origin of the Polish text is unknown.

Edith Margaret Gellibrand Reed (1885–1933) was born in Middlesex, London, England, and educated at St. Leonard's School in St. Andrew's and Guildhall School of Music in London. She was an associate at the Royal College of Organists and was assistant editor of *The Music Student*, *Music and Youth*, and *Panpipe*. In addition, Reed wrote two Christmas plays and *Story Lives of the Great Composers*. She died in Herfordshire.

W ŻŁOBIE LEŻY (He lies in a cradle) found its way into England as a tune some fifty years before the text. It was harmonized by A. E. Rusbridge (1917–1969).

38 It Came Upon the Midnight Clear

Tune: CAROL

This text was written by Edmund Hamilton Sears while he was a pastor in Wayland, Massachusetts. It was first published in *The Christian Register* in December 1849. William Reynolds notes this is the first of the "carol-like hymns from the pens of American poets. Hymns stressing the social message of Christmas—'peace on earth, good will'—are distinctly American" (*Songs of Glory*, p. 142).

Edmund Hamilton Sears (1810–1876) was born in Sandisfield, Massachusetts, and educated at Union College, Schenectady, New York, and Harvard Divinity School (1837). In 1838 he became pastor at the First Unitarian Church, Wayland, Massachusetts, where he spent most of his pastoral career. For twelve years he edited the *Monthly Religious Magazine* in which many of his hymns appeared.

CAROL was composed by Richard Storrs Willis for "See Israel's Gentle Shepherd Stand" and published in *Church Chorals and*

Choir Studies (1850). In 1860 the tune was adapted to the present form.

Richard Storrs Willis (1819–1900) was born in Boston. He studied at Yale University (degree, 1841) and then with Felix Mendelssohn in Germany. When he returned to New York he became music critic for *The Albion*, the *New York Tribune*, and *The Musical Times*. He later edited *The Musical Times*, *A Musical World*, and *Once a Month*. Willis was vestryman in the Church of the Transfiguration in New York City. From 1861 to 1900 he lived in Detroit, where he died. His other compositions include anthems and secular songs.

39 Joyful Christmas Day Is Here

Tune: KURISUMASU

Both the text and the tune of this Japanese hymn are by Toshiaki Okamoto (b. 1907), a member of the Japanese Society for Rights of Authors, Composers and Publishers. The hymn first appeared in the book *Kodomo Sanbika 24*, published by the United Church of Christ in Japan (1966). There the hymn has enjoyed a wide circulation in the Sunday church school and is usually sung by children at Christmas.

The English translation of the text is by Sandra Fukunaga and Hidemi Itō (1981). Itō is a Methodist minister serving a parish in Los Angeles.

40 Joy to the World!

Tune: ANTIOCH

The text is by Isaac Watts (1674–1748), the father of English hymnody. Refusing an offer to be educated at Oxford, for which he would have had to become Anglican, Watts was educated for eight years at the nonconformist academy at Stoke Newington. He was called to be pastor of Mark Lane Independent Chapel in London (1701). Shortly after arriving, Watts became quite ill and remained a semi-invalid for the remainder of his life. Accepting the invitation of parishioner Sir Thomas Abney to spend a week at his country house, Watts stayed thirty-six years. He was noted as a writer of books on grammar, pedagogy, ethics, psychology, three volumes of sermons, twenty-nine treatises on theology—fifty-two works in all—plus over six hundred hymns.

Watts was fifteen when he wrote his first hymn. This began a musical revolution in Reformed worship. Hymns of human composition were thus introduced to the Anglican and Dissenting Churches of England. Watts was not the first to write hymns, but he was the first to have a method. Watts believed our songs are a human offering of praise to God. Therefore the words should be our own. The psalms if sung should be Christianized and modernized. Thus he wrote two types of hymns: those of human composition and those loosely based on psalms. Monuments to Watts stand in Abney Park, in Southampton Park, and in Westminster Abbey. There is also a memorial wall and a museum on the site of his birthplace.

ANTIOCH was adapted from two tunes of George Frederick Handel by Lowell Mason.

Born in Medfield, Massachusetts, Lowell Mason (1792–1872) directed a church choir at sixteen. In 1812 he moved to Savannah, worked as a bank clerk but remained active in church music as choirmaster of a Presbyterian church, and began to write hymn tunes. In 1827, Mason returned to Massachusetts and became the president of the Handel and Haydn Society of Boston. This organization made it possible for Mason's first collected works to be published. Mason founded the Boston Academy of Music in 1832. In 1855 he was awarded a Doctor of Music degree from New York University, the second such degree awarded in the United States.

Mason began an experimental music program in one public school in Boston the success of which led to the inclusion of music in the curriculum of all Boston public schools. He replaced the fuging-tunes and anthems of eighteenth-century America with "correct" harmonizations based on scientific principles from Europe, causing many to say his influence was a mixed blessing. He died in Orange, New Jersey, and his library was given to Yale University music library. For a complete listing of his works, see the article on Mason in Stanley Sadie, ed., *The New Grove Dictionary of Music and Musicians* 11:749. For comments on Handel, see hymn 59.

41 O Come, All Ye Faithful

Tune: ADESTE FIDELES

This hymn was written in Latin by John Francis Wade in the mid-eighteenth century. For many years the authorship of the hymn was questioned, but in 1946 an English vicar discovered a manuscript of the hymn signed by Wade. Since that time several other manuscripts of the hymn have been found, all signed by Wade.

John Francis Wade (1711–1786) was an Englishman living in Douay (Douai), France. He was a musician and calligrapher who made his living copying and selling music to the Roman Catholic community.

The English version is that of Frederick Oakeley. He translated the hymn for his congregation at Margaret Street Chapel (1841). The translation was first published in F. H. Murray's *A Hymnal for Use in the English Church* (1852).

Frederick Oakeley (1802–1880) was born in Shrewsbury, England, and educated at Christ Church, Oxford (B.A. 1824). He was ordained and served as prebendary of Lichfield Cathedral (1832) and preacher at Whitehall (1837) before going to Margaret Street (1839). A student of the Oxford movement, in 1845 he resigned all his appointments in the Church of England and joined John Henry Newman at Livermore. He was received into the Roman Church and became canon of Westminster (1852).

ADESTE FIDELES was composed by Wade for his text. In the earliest manuscript the rhythm was in 3/4. The tune is also known by the name PORTUGUESE HYMN because it was introduced as such into the Portuguese Chapel of London. The organist Vincent Novello (1781–1861) credited John Reading, the organist of Winchester Cathedral from 1675 to 1681, as the composer.

The present harmonization is from *The English Hymnal* (1906).

42 O Come, All Ye Faithful

Tune: ADESTE FIDELES

For comment on the text and tune, see hymn 41.

ADESTE FIDELES was composed by Wade for his text.

The harmonization is by Sir David Valentine Willcocks

(b. 1919) and is published in *Carols for Choirs* (1961; rev., 1985). For comments on Willcocks, see hymn 32.

43 O Little Town of Bethlehem

Tune: FOREST GREEN

This text by Phillips Brooks was written while he was pastor of Holy Trinity (Episcopal) Church, Philadelphia. On Christmas Eve 1865, Brooks traveled from Jerusalem to Bethlehem on horseback across the "Field of the Shepherds" and worshiped in the Church of the Nativity. No doubt his experience inspired him as he wrote the carol for the Christmas Sunday School service in 1868.

Phillips Brooks (1835–1893) was born in Boston and studied at the Boston Latin School, Harvard University (1859), and Episcopal Theological Seminary in Alexandria, Virginia. After his service at Holy Trinity (1859–1869) he became rector of Trinity Church, Boston (1869–1891), and then bishop of Massachusetts (1891). Known as the "Prince of the Pulpit," he was one of America's foremost preachers. His sermons are published and the first volume (1878) sold over two hundred thousand copies. They are considered classics of American literature.

FOREST GREEN was originally the melody for the English folk song "The Plowboy's Dream." It was arranged by Ralph Vaughan Williams and published in *The English Hymnal* (1906) as the setting for "O Little Town of Bethlehem." For a biographical sketch of Vaughan Williams, see hymn 6.

44 O Little Town of Bethlehem

Tune: ST. LOUIS

For comments on the text and the author, see hymn 43.

ST. LOUIS was composed by Lewis Henry Redner for this text. Redner was the organist, choir director, superintendent of the Sunday school, and teacher at Holy Trinity Church, Philadelphia, during the time Phillips Brooks was rector. Brooks asked Redner to compose a melody simple enough for children to sing easily. After he struggled to write a tune, the melody came to him during the night on the Saturday before the program. He composed the harmony the next morning prior to going to church. It was first published in *The Church Porch* (1874) and later in *The Hymnal* (1892).

Lewis Henry Redner (1831–1908) was born and educated in Philadelphia. At sixteen he entered the real estate business, and became successful and quite wealthy. He was church organist at several other churches before going to Holy Trinity in 1861. Through his efforts, an endowment fund was established which continues to support the work of the church in Philadelphia.

45 A La Ru
O Sleep, Dear Holy Baby

Tune: A LA RU

This is a Hispanic folk hymn from New Mexico. Both the English translation and the musical arrangement were made by John Donald Robb.

John Donald Robb (1892–1989) was born in Minneapolis and educated at Yale University and Harvard University. He practiced law until 1941, when he moved from New York to the University of New Mexico at Albuquerque, where he was professor and head of the music department. He retired in 1957.

Robb was a prolific composer. He wrote an opera, *Little Jo* (1947–1949); three symphonies, orchestral music, chamber music, and electronic pieces. He was also a collector of Hispanic folk music which was published in *Hispanic Folk Songs of New Mexico* (1954; rev., 1978) and *Hispanic Folk Music of New Mexico and the Southwest* (1980).

46 On This Day Earth Shall Ring

Tune: PERSONENT HODIE

This hymn is a product of the Protestant Reformation in Scandinavia. It is from *Piae Cantiones* (1582), a collection of seventy-four Latin hymns and school songs compiled and revised by Jacob Finno. The collection was published by Theodoric Petri in the Swedish-speaking province of Abo (now

Turku), Finland. The translation is by Jane Marion Joseph (1894–1929).

PERSONENT HODIE was one of the early Scandinavian Lutheran contributions to modern hymnody. It was written in 1360 but the present form of the tune is from *Piae Cantiones* (1582). The arrangement is by Gustav Theodore Holst (1924). It was published in *The Oxford Book of Carols*. For more on Holst, see hymn 36.

Also from *Piae Cantiones* are the tunes DIVINUM MYSTERIUM (see hymn 309), PUER NOBIS NASCITUR (see hymn 68), and TEMPUS ADEST FLORIDUM (see hymn 27).

47 Still, Still, Still

Tune: STILL, STILL, STILL

This Austrian carol was translated by George K. Evans for *The International Book of Christmas Carols* (1963), for which he served with Walter Ehret as coeditor and principal translator. The collection offers 164 carols, all with the original languages plus English translations.

George K. Evans (b. 1917) was educated at Rice University (B.A.), the University of Texas (M.A.), and George Peabody College for Teachers (Ph.D.). Throughout his career, he served as music supervisor and choral music director in high schools and colleges. He also was minister of music, choir director, and organist in various churches.

STILL, STILL, STILL is an Austrian melody associated with this text. It was arranged by Walter Ehret for inclusion in *The International Book of Christmas Carols* (1963).

Walter Ehret was born in 1918 in New York City, where he studied at the Juilliard School of Music (B.S.) and Columbia University (M.A.). He spent his career as a teacher in New Jersey and New York. His choirs have performed at Carnegie Hall and Madison Square Garden as well as on television and radio. Ehret was the author of the *Choral Conductor's Handbook* (1959), *Music for Everyone* (1960), *Time for Music* (1960), and the coauthor of *Functional Lessons in Singing* (1960), and *Growing with Music*. He has composed or arranged over one thousand choral arrangements.

48 Lo, How a Rose E'er Blooming

Tune: ES IST EIN' ROS'

This German carol probably dates from the fifteenth century, but the earliest source of the text is a manuscript from St. Alban's Carthusian Monastery preserved in the municipal library of Trier.

John Julian reports on two forms of the hymn. The first contains twenty-three stanzas and was published in *Alte Catholische Geistliche Kirchengesang* (1599), the second containing six stanzas was in *Andernach Gesangbuch* (1608).

The hymn is based on Isaiah 11:1 but originally referred to Mary as the rose. Sixteenth-century reformers sought to change the emphasis of the hymn to refer to Jesus.

Theodore Baker, American scholar and editor, translated the hymn around the turn of the century. The source of the present alteration is *Rejoice in the Lord* (1985). For comments on Baker, see hymn 559.

ES IST EIN' ROS' is a tune believed to be from the fourteenth or fifteenth century and was first published in *Alte Catholische Geistliche Kirchengesang* (Cologne, 1599). The present arrangement is that of Michael Praetorius, from his collection *Musae Sioniae*, VI (1609).

Michael Schulze (1571–1621) was born at Kreutzberg, Thuringia, Germany. After completing his education at the University of Frankfurt an der Oder, he Latinized his name from "Schulze" to "Praetorius." He was honorary prior of Ringelheim Monastery (1604). A serious student of music, he published three major works: *Musae Sioniae* (1605–1612), *Syntagma Musicum* (1615–1619), and *Musa Aonia* (1619).

49 Once in Royal David's City

Tune: IRBY

This hymn was written by Cecil Frances Alexander and included in her *Hymns for Little Children* (1848). She wrote it to illustrate the clause in the Apostles' Creed, "[I believe] in Jesus Christ . . . our Lord; who was conceived by the Holy Ghost, born of the Virgin Mary. . . . " Stanza 1 is a metrical version of Luke 2:4 and 7.

Cecil Frances Humphreys (1818–1895) was born in Dublin,

Ireland, and married (1850) Rev. William Alexander, later bishop of Derry. From childhood she wrote poetry. Some of her poems were published in *Verses from the Holy Scripture* (1846), *Narrative Hymns for Village Schools* (1853), *Poems on Subjects in the Old Testament* (1854, 1857), and *Hymns Descriptive and Devotional* (1858). She also contributed to a number of hymnals of the day. In addition to her writing, Alexander and her sister established a school for the deaf in Tyrone County, Ireland. She died in the bishop's palace in Londonderry.

IRBY was composed by Henry John Gauntlett for this text and included in *Christmas Carols* (1849). Later in *Hymns for Little Children* (1858) it was set as a solo with piano accompaniment.

Henry John Gauntlett (1805–1876) was born in Wellington, Shropshire, England, and at age ten (some say nine) was organist at Olney, Buckinghamshire, where his father was vicar. He studied law and was a successful lawyer for fifteen years (1831–1846) while holding various organist positions. In 1846 he was chosen by Felix Mendelssohn (see hymn 31) to play the organ part for *Elijah.*

Gauntlett was involved in the compilation of several hymnals, often supplying tunes, chants, and arrangements. It is said he composed over one thousand hymn tunes. In 1842, he became the first person in two hundred years to be granted the degree Doctor of Music by the Archbishop of Canterbury.

The harmonization is by Arthur Henry Mann composed while he was at King's College. For comments on Mann, see hymn 388.

50 Rise Up, Shepherd, and Follow

This African-American spiritual was included in Natalie Curtis Burlin's *The Hampton Series—Negro Folk-Sings* (1909). Aided by investigative work and phonograph records, Curtis produced this four-part work of African-American spirituals for the Hampton School, Virginia. James Weldon Johnson and J. Rosamond Johnson included it in their *Second Book of Negro Spirituals* (1926). It is based on the birth narrative in Luke 2:8–15.

In the preface to that volume James Weldon Johnson states his belief that this and other Christmas spirituals are probably from the period after the Emancipation and are therefore relatively late in their development.

The present form of the spiritual is from *Lead Me, Guide Me: The African-American Catholic Hymnal* (1987).

51 See Amid the Winter's Snow

Tune: HUMILITY

This text was written by Edward Caswall and was first published in *The Masque of Mary and Other Poems* (1858).

Edward Caswall (1814–1878) was born in Hampshire, educated at Brasenose College, Oxford (B.A. 1836; M.A. 1838), and became a priest in the Anglican Church. Deeply involved in the Oxford movement, he and his wife became Roman Catholics in 1847. After her death (1849), Caswall joined John Henry Newman and was reordained in 1852. The remainder of his life was devoted to service to the poor, the sick, and little children. Most of his writings and translations were during this period. They include *Lyra Catholica* (1849), *The Masque of Mary and Other Poems* (1858), *A May Pageant and Other Poems* (1865), and *Hymns and Other Poems* (1873).

HUMILITY was composed by John Goss in 1871. Goss (1800–1880) was born in Fareham, where his father served as organist. His early music training was at Chapel Royal and with Thomas Attwood at St. Paul's Cathedral. He then served as tenor in the chorus at Covenant Garden after which he became organist of Stockwell Chapel (1821). In 1824 he was appointed organist at St. Luke's, Chelsea, then he succeeded Attwood at St. Paul's (1838), a position he resigned in 1872. In 1827 he became professor of music harmony at the Royal Academy of Music, where he stayed for forty-seven years. He was knighted in 1872 and received a Doctor of Music degree from Cambridge in 1876. A noted teacher, his students included Sir Arthur Sullivan and Frederick Bridge.

His book *An Introduction to Harmony and Thoroughbass* (1833) went through thirteen editions. William Alexander Barrett, in *English Church Composers* (1877; rpt. London: S. Low, Marston and Co., Ltd., 1925, pp. 173–174), says of Goss, "His music is always melodious and beautifully written for the voices, and is remarkable for a union of solidity and grace, with a certain unaffected native charm."

52 Hitsuji Wa Sheep Fast Asleep

Tune: KŌRIN

This Christmas hymn is a favorite among the Japanese. It was written by Genzō Miwa in 1907. The text was revised, set to KŌRIN, and published in the Japanese hymnal *Kyodan Sambika* (1954).

The 1957 translation is by Rev. John A. Moss (b. 1925). It was first published in a slightly altered form with references to Luke 2:8–14 and Matthew 2:10–11 appearing on the hymn page, in *Hymns of the Church* (1963), the English language hymnbook of the United Church of Christ in Japan. This is the source of the hymn as it appears in *The Presbyterian Hymnal* (1990). May Murakami Nakagawa, a member of the Presbyterian Hymnal Committee, supplied the Japanese text. Moss is a United Church of Christ missionary living in Niigata, Japan.

KŌRIN was composed in 1941 by Chûgorȯ Torii (b. 1898). The melody and harmonization reflect Western influence throughout, but the final cadence retains a Japanese flavor. The tune was first published in *Kyodan Sambika* (1954).

53 What Child Is This

Tune: GREENSLEEVES

William Chatterton Dix wrote this text as a poem "The Manger Throne." It was published as a hymn in John Stainer's (see hymn 509) *Christmas Carols New and Old* (1871).

William Chatterton Dix (1837–1898) was born in Bristol,

England, and educated at Bristol Grammar School. He became manager of a Maritime Insurance Company in Glasgow. As a gifted writer he wrote two devotional books, translated hymns from Greek, and wrote several collections of poetry, including *Hymns of Love and Joy* (1861), *Altar Songs, Verses on the Holy Eucharist* (1867), *A Vision of All Saints* (1871), and *Seekers of a City* (1878).

GREENSLEEVES is a traditional English ballad which has been the setting for many different texts.

The tune was published twice in 1580, once by Richard Jones with the title "A new Northerne Dittye of the *Lady Greene Sleeves*" and once by Edward White using the title "A ballad, being the Ladie Greene Sleeves *Answere* to Donkyn his frende."

William Shakespeare (1564–1616) speaks of it through two of his characters in the *Merry Wives of Windsor* (1599). In act 2, scene 1, Mistresses Ford and Page are comparing love letters and as Mistress Ford shows hers she states, "I would have sworn his disposition would have gone to the truth of his words; but they do no more adhere and keep place together than the Hundredth Psalm to the tune of 'Green Sleeves.' " Again in act 5, scene 5, Falstaff says, "Let the sky rain potatoes; let it thunder to the tune of 'Green Sleeves.' "

One of its early appearances as a hymn tune was the Wait's carol found in *New Christmas Carols of 1642* where it is the setting for "The old year now is fled." By the seventeenth century "waits" were professional musicians employed as town minstrels.

John Gay's *The Beggar's Opera* (1795) used GREENSLEEVES as the tune for Macheath's aria after he has been condemned to death. The tune was first used as the setting for Dix's text in *Christmas Carols New and Old* (1871).

54 From Heaven Above

Tune: VOM HIMMEL HOCH

Martin Luther wrote this text for the Christmas Eve celebration of his family. The original text has fourteen stanzas in addition to one rearranged from the popular "Aus fremden Landen komm' ich her." It was published in Joseph Klug's *Geistliche Lieder* (1535). The translation is that of the Inter-Lutheran Commission on Worship for the *Lutheran Book of Worship* (1978). The group used Catherine Winkworth's English translation from *Lyra Germanica* (1st series, 1855) as the basis of its work. For comments on Luther, see hymn 240.

VOM HIMMEL HOCH was first published in Valentin Schumann's *Geistliche Lieder, auffs new gebessert und gemehrt* (1539) as the setting of the present text. Many attribute the tune as well as the text to Luther. The tune was used by Johann Sebastian Bach in his *Christmas Oratorio* with the text "Ah, Dearest Jesus, Holy Child."

The present harmonization is by Hans Leo Hassler (1564–1612), German organist and composer. He was born in Nuremberg and received his early music training from his father, the town musician. Hans became the first German of note to study in Venice, Italy (1584). He held several prominent positions, first as organist to Count Octavian II of Augsburg, then court organist to Emperor Rudolph II of Prague (1600), later organist to the Frauenkirche, and Kapellmeister and finally organist to Christian II, Elector of Saxony, Dresden (1604). Hassler suffered from tuberculosis and died while in the elector's employ. He is considered one of the founders of German music. His works included motets, psalms, litanies, and instrumental works as well as a large portion of sacred and secular choral compositions.

Another harmonization of this tune appears as the setting for "Lord Jesus Christ, Our Lord Most Dear" (see hymn 496).

55 That Boy-Child of Mary

Tune: BLANTYRE

This Christmas hymn was written by Tom Colvin in 1967.

Thomas Stevenson Colvin (b. 1925) is a minister in the Church of Scotland and a missionary to Africa. Most of his time on the field (twenty-years) has been in Malawi, where he now is involved with the Christian Council of Malawi's refugee work.

BLANTYRE is a Malawi melody adapted by Colvin for this text.

56 The First Nowell

Tune: THE FIRST NOWELL

This hymn is an old English carol and as such employs the Old English "Nowell" rather than the French *Noël.* Nowell is related to the Latin *Natalis*, meaning "birth or birthday."

The text is first found in *Some Ancient Christmas Carols* (1823).

THE FIRST NOWELL was first associated with this text in William Sandys' *Christmas Carols, Ancient and Modern* (1833). The arrangement is by Sir John Stainer (see hymn 509) from *Christmas Carols New and Old* (1871), which he edited with Henry Ramsden Bramley.

The alternate refrain was composed by Healey Willan in 1926. Willan (1880–1968) was born in Balham, Surrey, England, and educated at the resident choir school of St. Saviour's Church, Eastbourne. After advanced studies in organ and piano he immigrated to Toronto (1913) where he was head of the theory department of the university and also organist and choirmaster at St. Paul's Church. He held various positions at the university and was vice-principal, then principal, of the music faculty at Toronto Conservatory (1920–1950). He also was precentor of St. Mary Magdalene Church (1921–1968).

57 The Snow Lay on the Ground

Tune: VENITE ADOREMUS

According to John Julian's *Dictionary of Hymnology* this Anglo-Irish carol was published in two forms: In the *Crown of Jesus* (1862), it begins, "The snow lay on the ground" and is marked as sung to a "Christmas carol, sung in Rome by the Pifferari from the Abruzzi Mountains." In R. R. Chope's *Carols* (1875) the first line reads "The snow lay deep upon the ground."

The first two phrases of stanza 2 were altered from " 'Twas

Mary, daughter pure of holy Anne, That brought into this world the God made man."

VENITE ADOREMUS appears to have been a nineteenth-century melody contemporary with the text. It was adapted by C. Winfred Douglas for *The Hymnal 1940*; the harmonization was by Leo Sowerby also for that publication. For comments on Douglas, see hymn 4.

Leo Sowerby (1895–1968) was born in Grand Rapids and studied at the American Conservatory of Music, Chicago (M.A. 1918). He served as regimental bandmaster with the 332nd Field Artillery Band in both England and France (1917–1919). He became the first fellow of the American Academy in Rome, where he studied for three years. He participated in the Salzburg Festival for Contemporary Music in 1923. From 1924 to 1963 he was on the faculty of the American Conservatory. He also was organist and choirmaster of St. James Church (1927–1963). Sowerby had an interest in folk music which he turned into wonderful compositions. He won a Pulitzer Prize for his *Canticle of the Sun* (1946). He died at Port Clinton, Ohio.

58 While Shepherds Watched Their Flocks

Tune: WINCHESTER OLD

The text is by Nahum Tate. It is the one remaining hymn of the sixteen published in *The Supplement to the New Version* (1702). Its popularity is seen by its use in several languages. *Hymns Ancient and Modern* (1861) was the first collection to marry the text with the present tune.

Nahum Tate (1652–1715), the son of a minister, was born in Dublin, Ireland, and educated at Trinity College. He was made poet laureate of England (1690) to the Court of William and Mary (1689–1702) and royal historiographer in 1702. In 1696 Nicholas Brady and he produced *A New Version of the Psalms of David, fitted to the Tunes used in Churches* to replace *The Whole Booke of Psalmes, collected into Englishe Meter by Thomas Sternhold and John Hopkins* (1569) as the official psalter of the Church of England. Tate died in poverty in Southwark, London.

WINCHESTER OLD first appeared in Thomas Este's *Whole Booke of Psalmes* (1592). The harmonization is by George Kirbye (c. 1560–1634), who is credited with most of the arrangements and harmonizations in the collection. Este's *Psalmes* was the first work in which English tunes appeared with names assigned to them. The practice has continued ever since.

The descant is by Alan Gray (1923).

59 While Shepherds Watched Their Flocks

Tune: CHRISTMAS

The text is by Nahum Tate. For comments on the text and the author, see hymn 58.

CHRISTMAS is an arrangement of a melody from the opera *Siroe Re di Persia* (1728) by George Frederick Handel. The arrangement is by Lowell Mason. The tune was set to the aria "Non vi piacque" and also the English versification of Job 29:15, "I was eyes to the blind." For further comments on Mason, see hymn 40.

George Frederick (Frideric) Handel (1685–1759) was born at Halle, Saxony, and entered the University of Halle in 1702. However, a month later he became organist at the Calvinist Cathedral and after a year went to Hamburg. While in Hamburg, Handel befriended Johann Matheson, a popular musician of the day. It was here that Handel composed *Almira* (1705) and here he met Ferdinando de' Medici, who invited him to Italy. In Florence, he fell under the influence of Domenico Scarlatti and was able to assimilate the Italian opera style espoused by him. The opera *Agrippina* was composed during this period. Handel traveled to England first in 1710, finally settling there in 1712. He became a naturalized British subject in 1726. During Handel's long and prosperous career, he composed for most musical settings, including operas, theater music, odes, oratorios, sacred vocal music, cantatas, duets and trios with continuo, songs and hymns, English songs, orchestral works, concertos, solo sonatas, and keyboard pieces.

Handel was known to be a biblical scholar who chose the texts for which he wrote music. It has been reported that Handel was both quick to anger and equally quick to admit guilt when proven wrong. For a complete listing of Handel's works and a more complete biographical sketch, see the article by Winton Dean and Anthony Hicks in Stanley Sadie, ed., *The New Grove Dictionary of Music and Musicians* 8:83–140.

60 Silent Night, Holy Night
Stille Nacht, Heilige Nacht

Tune: STILLE NACHT

This Christmas hymn was written by Joseph Mohr for a Christmas festival at St. Nicholas Church, Oberndorf near Salzburg, Austria. The story is told that the organ was not functioning the day of the service and Mohr decided to write a new hymn that would not require organ accompaniment. He took it to his friend Franz Xaver Gruber and asked him to write a suitable tune. The two sang the new hymn as Gruber accompanied on the guitar. The village choir joined in repeating the last line of each stanza in four-part harmony.

Karl Mauracher came to repair the organ and Father Mohr sang the new hymn for him, giving him a copy of it. As Mauracher traveled from town to town repairing church organs he introduced the hymn to the people. In Zillerthal, a glovemaking family by the name of Strasser who were also singers heard the hymn and sang it at the Leipzig fair in 1831. It was published in the *Katholisches Gesang- und Gebetbuch für den öffentlichen und häuslichen Gottesdienst zunächst zum Gebrauche der katholischen Gemeinden im Königreiche Sachsen* (1838). In 1854, after some question as to authorship Gruber wrote a letter to Berlin detailing the events surrounding the creation of the hymn.

Joseph Mohr (1792–1848) was born in Salzburg and was a chorister at the cathedral there. He attended Salzburg University and was ordained a priest in 1815. He served several parishes, ending as vicar of Wagrein from 1837 until his death.

Franz Xaver Gruber (1787–1863) was born in Unterweizberg near Hochburg, Austria. His father did not want him to be a musician so Franz secretly took violin lessons and later studied organ. He was a teacher (1807–1829) and also organist at St. Nicholas Church (from 1816), where he met Mohr. Later he became teacher then headmaster at Berndorf. He is remembered for this tune.

German-speaking immigrants brought the hymn to America, where the first English version appeared in the 1849 Methodist hymnal. Nine years later the hymn was published in England. The most popular English translation is by John Freeman Young and was published in *The Sunday-School Service and Tune Book: Selected and arranged by John Clark Hollister* (1863).

John Freeman Young (1820–1885) was born in Pittston, Maine, and was educated at Wesleyan Seminary, Readfield, Maine, and Wesleyan University, Middletown, Connecticut. He graduated from Virginia Theological Seminary (1845) and was ordained a deacon and began his ministry in Florida. A year later he was ordained a priest. He served parishes in Texas, Mississippi, and Louisiana before moving to Trinity Church, New York City (1860). In 1867 he was consecrated bishop of Florida, where he remained until his death.

61 'Twas in the Moon of Wintertime

Tune: UNE JEUNE PUCELLE

This hymn is the earliest Canadian hymn in existence and perhaps the earliest of the New World. It is attributed to Father Jean de Brébeuf (1593–1649), a Jesuit missionary who worked among the Huron people (1626, 1633–1649).

His carol is the Christmas story in language the Hurons understood. It was probably sung first in 1641 and each Christmas thereafter until 1649 when the Iroquois invaded Huronia and killed or drove out the Hurons, torturing Father Jean at the stake. Some Hurons escaped to Loretto. A century later another Jesuit priest, Father de Villeneuve, heard the carol and wrote down the words. It was then translated into French as "Jesus est né" and sung in Quebec.

Canadian poet, novelist, playwright, and historian Jesse Edgar Middleton (1872–1960) wrote the English interpretation in 1926. The hymn has had an ecumenical flavor from its very inception.

UNE JEUNE PUCELLE (a young maiden) is a French carol tune from the sixteenth century. Some believe the tune to be closely related to the German tune VON GOTT WILL ICH NICHT LASSEN.

The present setting is a clear example of the influence Native American music has had on other traditions.

62 Bring We the Frankincense of Our Love

Tune: EPIPHANY SONG

Both the text and the tune of this hymn were written by H. Kenn Carmichael while he was associate pastor of Central Presbyterian Church in Lafayette, Indiana.

H. Kenn Carmichael was born in Martins Ferry, Ohio, in 1908 and graduated from Muskingum College (B.A. 1928), the University of Wisconsin (M.A. in Speech, 1930), and the University of Minnesota (Ph.D. in Theater, 1941). He was head of the theater department at Purdue University (1931–1943). From 1943 to 1946, Carmichael served in the U.S. Navy, where he made training films. After his enlistment ended, Carmichael taught at City College, Los Angeles (1947–1954), and then joined Film Production International producing films for denominational stewardship campaigns.

In 1962, Carmichael and his wife were commissioned by the Commission on Ecumenical Mission and Relations (COEMAR) of the United Presbyterian Church U.S.A. as consultants in communications to the Middle East and Africa. After ten years they returned to the United States, where Kenn became associate pastor at Central Church (1972–1979). Since 1979 the Carmichaels have lived at Westminster Gardens, Los Angeles.

Carmichael was Moderator of the Synod of Southern California and Hawaii in 1987. He was also honored as a distinguished alumnus by Muskingum College.

EPIPHANY SONG was composed for this hymn. The arrangement was by Clayton D. Lein, at the request of Carmichael. Measures 9–16 were rearranged by John Weaver for *The Presbyterian Hymnal* (1990). For comments on Weaver, see hymn 565.

63 As with Gladness Men of Old

Tune: DIX

This hymn was written by William Chatterton Dix. He is said to have written it after reading the Gospel lesson for the day while ill in bed. It was published in *Hymns of Love and Joy* (1861) and also in the original edition of *Hymns Ancient and Modern* that same year. Two slight textual changes appearing in the revised edition of *Hymns Ancient and Modern* (1875) met with his approval. The hymn gained prominence as "a work admirable in every respect," when Sir Roundell Palmer mentioned it and Dix in his paper "English Church Hymnody," delivered to the Church Congress at York in 1866. For more on Dix, see hymn 53.

DIX was composed by Conrad Kocher. It was first published in *Stimmen aus dem Reiche Gottes* (1838), where it was set to the text "Treuer Heiland, wir sind hier." The original form of the tune was modified by William Henry Monk when it was used as the setting of Dix's text in *Hymns Ancient and Modern* (1861).

Conrad Kocher (1786–1872) was born in Württemberg, Germany, and studied music in St. Petersburg and Rome. From 1827 to 1865 he was organist and choirmaster at Stiftkirche, Stuttgart. In 1852 he received an honorary degree from the University of Tübingen. Besides his hymn tunes, he composed an oratorio, several operas and sonatas, and a treatise on church music, *Die Tonkunst in der Kirche* (1823).

The tune was titled DIX after it became known as the setting of the present text.

The harmonization is from *The English Hymnal* (1906).

64 De Tierra Lejana Venimos
From a Distant Home

Tune: ISLA DEL ENCANTO

This popular Hispanic Epiphany carol is from Puerto Rico. The English translation is by George K. Evans and Walter Ehret for their collaborative effort *The International Book of Christmas Carols* (1963, 1980). The hymn is a reference to Matthew 2:1–12.

For comments on Evans and Ehret, see hymn 47.

ISLA DEL ENCANTO is a Puerto Rican melody associated with this text.

65 Midnight Stars Make Bright the Sky

Tune: HUAN-SHA-CH'I

This hymn was written by Ching-chiu Yang (1912–1966) in 1930. It was translated by Mildred Kathryn Artz Wiant and first appeared in *Worship Materials from the Chinese* published by the National Council of the Churches of Christ in the U.S.A. (NCC) in 1969. It later appeared in *Hymns of Universal Praise* (1936, rev., 1977).

Mildred Kathryn Artz was born in Lancaster, Ohio, in 1898 and attended Ohio Wesleyan University (B.A. 1920). She married Bliss Wiant (1922) and went to Boston. In 1923 the Wiants moved to Peking, China, where Mildred became associate professor of voice at Yenching University. She was instructor of vocal music at Scarritt College (1942–1946; 1961–1962) and at Chung Chi College, Chinese University of Hong Kong (1963–1965). Many of her translations appeared in the NCC booklet of 1969.

HUAN-SHA-CH'I was composed by Chi-fang Liang in 1934 and appeared in *Hymns of Universal Praise* (1936). The harmonization is by Bliss Wiant (1895–1975), who was educated at Wittenberg College and Ohio Wesleyan University (B.A. 1920), Boston University (M.A. 1936), and Peabody College (Ph.D. 1946). He also studied at Harvard University and Union Theological Seminary, New York City. After ordination (1923), Wiant became head of the music department at Yenching University, Peking (1923–1951). He was pastor of St. Paul's Church, Delaware, Ohio (1953–1955), then minister of music at Mahoning Methodist Church, Youngstown, Ohio. After serving with the Methodist Board of Education, he became director of music at Scarritt College.

66 We Three Kings of Orient Are

Tune: THREE KINGS OF ORIENT

Both text and music of this hymn were composed by John Henry Hopkins, Jr., and included in his *Carols, Hymns, and Songs* (1st ed., 1857).

John Henry Hopkins, Jr. (1820–1891), was born in Pittsburgh, Pennsylvania, and was educated at the University of Vermont (A.B. 1839; M.A. 1845) and General Theological Seminary (B.D. 1850). He served several parishes but distinguished himself in the area of religious music, becoming the first professor of church music at General Theological Seminary (1855–1857). He was also editor of the *Church Journal* (1853–1868). In addition, Hopkins designed stained-glass windows and Episcopal seals and forms. He died near Hudson, New York.

There were four editions of his *Carols, Hymns, and Songs* (1857–1882). He also wrote *Canticles Noted with Accompanying Harmonies* (1866).

THREE KINGS OF ORIENT: The musical introduction is by Robert Stigall for *The Presbyterian Hymnal* (1990). Stigall was born in 1934 in Greensboro, North Carolina, and graduated from Syracuse University (B. Mus. in Organ, 1957) and Union Theological Seminary's School of Sacred Music (M.S.M. 1962). From 1962 to 1963 he served as organist and choir director at the Mount Lebanon Methodist Church, near Pittsburgh, and in 1963 joined the staff of Myers Park Presbyterian Church, Charlotte, North Carolina, where he is director of music and organist. His wife, Anne, is his associate.

67 Brightest and Best of the Stars of the Morning

Tune: MORNING STAR

This Epiphany text was written by Bishop Reginald Heber. It was first published in *The Christian Observer* for November 1811 with five stanzas, the last being the first repeated (this is indicated by the * in *The Presbyterian Hymnal* 1990). Later it was published in a posthumous collection of 1827. The present form of the text is from the *Lutheran Book of Worship* (1978). That committee altered the first line.

Reginald Heber (1783–1826) was born in Malpas, England, and educated at Brasenose College, Oxford, where he won prizes for his poetry. He was ordained in 1807 and became vicar of the family estate at Hodnet, Shropshire. In 1823, Heber was appointed bishop of Calcutta and ordained the first native

Christian there. Heber died suddenly at the end of a day in which he had baptized forty-two people. He wrote all his hymns before he went to India.

MORNING STAR is from the anthem composed by James Proctor Harding for the Gifford Hall Mission, London, in 1892. In 1894 the tune became the setting for Heber's text. It was published in *The Church Hymnal* (1916) edited by Charles Hutchins.

James Proctor Harding (1850–1911) was born in London. He was organist and choirmaster at St. Andrew's Church, Thornhill Square, Islington, London, for thirty-five years. Harding wrote many services for the Gifford Hall Mission, where he and his brother donated their time. He also wrote anthems and children's festival songs.

68 What Star Is This, with Beams So Bright

Tune: PUER NOBIS NASCITUR

The original text was written in Latin by Charles Coffin and included in *Paris Breviary* and *Hymni Sacri Auctore Carolo Coffin*, both published in 1736. It is an Epiphany hymn that has undergone many translations throughout the years. John Julian, in *A Dictionary of Hymnology* (rev. ed., 1907), stated, "In each hymnbook the text is altered, and no two books agree upon the same alterations."

The hymn was translated into English by John Chandler in his *Hymns of the Primitive Church* (1837). For comments on Coffin and Chandler, see hymn 10.

PUER NOBIS NASCITUR is a variant form of PUER NOBIS, a melody found with the Latin original of the hymn "Unto Us a Child Is Born" from a fifteenth-century Trier manuscript. It was adapted by Michael Praetorius in 1609 for the hymn "Geborn ist Gottes Söhnelein." For comments on Praetorius, see hymn 48.

The harmonization is that of George Ratcliffe Woodward. Born in Birkenhead, England, Woodward (1848–1934) was educated at Caius College, Cambridge (B.A. 1872; M.A. 1875). He served several parishes within the Church of England and was recognized as a scholar, linguist, musician, and editor. Among his edited works are *The Cowley Carol Book for Christmas,*

Easter and Ascension Tide (1901, 1902, 1919) and *Piae Cantiones* (1582), 1910. But his *Songs of Syon* (1904, 1910) made a unique contribution to English hymnody. The collection included plainsong melodies, thirteenth- to sixteenth-century metrical tunes, psalm tunes from England, Scotland, and France, as well as tunes from the Lutheran tradition and canticles from the early church. He died in St. Pancras.

69 O Morning Star, How Fair and Bright

Tune: WIE SCHÖN LEUCHTET

This hymn, originally in German "Wie schön leuchtet der Morgenstern," was written by Philipp Nicolai while a pastor in Unna. An unknown "pestilence" had spread so broadly that in seven months thirteen hundred people had died. The pastor's home overlooked the cemetery where up to thirty bodies were buried daily. These events led him to seek comfort in Christ and in the hope of eternal life. One morning there welled forth from the inmost depths of his heart

> this precious hymn of the Savior's love and of the joys of heaven. He was so entirely absorbed in this holy exaltation that he forgot all around him, even his midday meal, and allowed nothing to disturb him in his poetical labors till the hymn was completed—three hours after midday. (John Julian, ed., *A Dictionary of Hymnology* 1:806f.)

The hymn became a favorite "wedding hymn" in Germany. For a biographical sketch of Nicolai, see hymn 17.

Nicolai's text has been altered many times. The English translation by Catherine Winkworth is based on the alteration of Johann Adolf Schlegel (1766) beginning "Wie herrlich strahlt der Morgenstern," which he titled "Longing after union with Jesus, on the model of the old hymn, 'Wie schön leuchtet der Morgenstern.' " "How brightly beams the morning star" by William Mercer (1859) is another popular translation of the text. For comments on Winkworth, see hymn 3.

WIE SCHÖN LEUCHTET was composed by Nicolai for his text and shares its history. The harmonization is by Johann Sebastian Bach (see Hymn 17). He used the tune in Cantatas 1, 36, 37, 49,

61, and 172, one prelude, and included a harmonization in *Choralgesänge.*

70 Christ, When for Us You Were Baptized

Tune: CAITHNESS

The text was written by F. Bland Tucker in 1979 and altered in 1982. It was first published in *The Hymnal 1982.*

F. Bland Tucker (1895–1984) was born in Norfolk, Virginia, and educated at the University of Virginia (A.B. 1914) and Virginia Theological Seminary (B.D. 1920; D.D. 1944). He was rector of Grammer Parish, Brunswick, Virginia (1920–1925); St. John's, Georgetown (1925–1945); and Old Christ Church, Savannah (1951–1967). He served on the Joint Commission on the Revision of *The Hymnal 1940* and *The Hymnal 1982* for the Episcopal Church. A noted hymn writer and translator, he was made a fellow of the Hymn Society of America in 1980.

CAITHNESS was one of thirty-one tunes with harmonizations in the 1635 edition of the Scottish Psalter, *The Psalmes of David in Prose and Meeter.* In that collection it was named CATHNES TUNE. Scholars believe the tune, which received its name from a county in northeast Scotland, to be of Scottish origin. The harmonization is altered from *The English Hymnal* (1906).

71 Lord, When You Came to Jordan

Tune: GENEVAN 130

The text is by Brian Wren. It was written in 1979 for the Church of the Holy Family, Blackbird Leys, Oxford.

The hymn focuses on Jesus' baptism and lifts up the tradition that suggests it was a moment of personal revelation as well as an outward sign of his mission. It asks questions concerning Jesus' inner life and then becomes a prayer on behalf of our being able to see God's work today.

Brian Wren (b. 1936) graduated from New College, Oxford,

in 1960. In 1965 he graduated from Mansfield College and was ordained in the English Congregational Church, now the United Reformed Church, as pastor at Hockley, Essex. In 1970 he began his ecumenical ministry. Wren is a French language scholar and poet. In 1981, Erik Routley (see hymn 218) in conversation with W. Thomas Smith, executive director of the Hymn Society of America, stated that Brian Wren is the most successful English hymn writer since Charles Wesley. (Brian Wren, *Faith Looking Forward*, Foreword; Carol Stream, Ill.: Hope Publishing Co., 1983).

GENEVAN 130: The tune is from the Genevan Psalter (1542), where it is the setting for Psalm 130. It is also known as AU FORT DE MA DÉTRESSE.

72 When Jesus Came to Jordan

Tune: DE EERSTEN ZIJN DE LAATSTEN

The text was written in 1973 by Fred Pratt Green (b. 1903). It was the result of extensive correspondence with Dirk van Dissel, then a divinity student at Trinity College, Melbourne, Australia. It was van Dissel's understanding that the proposed *Australian Hymnbook* would not include liturgical office hymns, a situation that troubled him. He sought a hymn on the baptism of Jesus.

The final version was reviewed by Ian Stratton in The Hymn Society of Great Britain and Ireland's *Bulletin*, January 1981, who said, "Suitable for use at adult baptism . . . must be counted a triumph . . . conscious echoes of the early Christian baptismal liturgies" (Bernard Braley, *The Hymns and Ballads of Fred Pratt Green*, p. 34; Carol Stream, Ill.: Hope Publishing Co., 1982). Green revised the hymn for *The Presbyterian Hymnal* (1990).

DE EERSTEN ZIJN DE LAATSTEN was composed in 1959 by Frederik (Frits) August Mehrtens (1922–1975). It appeared as the setting for "De aarde is vervuld van goedertierenheid" in *Liedboek voor de Kerken* (1973). Mehrtens was a Dutch-born organist and composer of hymn tunes. He was an author, educator, and church music director.

73 Swiftly Pass the Clouds of Glory

Tune: GENEVA

This text was written by Thomas H. Troeger (b. 1945). This is its first appearance in a denominational hymnal. The Lenten text is based on Luke 9:28–36, the Common Lectionary reading for the Second Sunday in Lent, Year C. Troeger, a Presbyterian minister from Cooperstown, New York, is a graduate of Yale University and Colgate Rochester/Bexley Hall/Crozer Theological Seminary, Rochester, New York. He was associate professor of preaching at Colgate Rochester for fourteen years before becoming the first Ralph E. and Norma E. Peck Professor of Preaching and Communication at Iliff School of Theology, Denver, in June 1991. Together with Carol Doran (see hymn 287) he has written two books, *New Hymns for the Lectionary* (1985) and *New Hymns for the Church* (1992).

GENEVA was composed by George Henry Day, a native of New York City. He named it for the town of Geneva, New York, where he was organist and choirmaster at Trinity Episcopal Church from 1935 until his death. It was first published in *The Hymnal 1940.*

George Henry Day (1883–1966) was a choirboy at Trinity Chapel, New York City, where he studied with G. Edward Stubbs. Day was appointed choirmaster at St. Peter's in Chelsea Square (1911) but maintained his position as an assistant auditor of the Gorham Manufacturing Company for two more years. He resigned as assistant auditor, took special courses at Columbia University, and in 1915 graduated from New York College of Music. He served as organist and choirmaster in churches in Youngstown, Ohio; Wilmington, Delaware, where he studied with Edward Shippen Barnes (see hymn 23); and Rochester, New York, before going to Trinity Church. He was awarded a Doctor of Music degree from Lincoln-Jefferson University (1923).

74 Jesus on the Mountain Peak

Tune: MOWSLEY

This text was the second hymn written by Brian Wren. It originally used the word "Christ" instead of "Jesus" and was altered by Wren in 1988 for inclusion in *The Presbyterian Hymnal* (1990). The hymn provides a worshipful atmosphere as one sings of the transfiguration of Jesus Christ. For comments on Wren, see hymn 71.

MOWSLEY was composed by Cyril Vincent Taylor (b. 1907). He attended Magdalen College School, Oxford, in 1926 where he served as a chorister until 1923. In 1929 he graduated from Christ Church, Oxford, and did graduate work at Westcott House, Cambridge. He was ordained a deacon (1931) and priest (1932) in the Church of England. He served as curate of St. Mary's, Hinckley, and St. Andrew's, Kingwood, after which he served fourteen years in religious broadcasting. From 1953 to 1969 he was chaplain and warden of the Royal School of Church Music.

Taylor, a musician as well as a theologian, was one of the editors of the *BBC Hymn Book* (1951), to which he contributed twenty tunes.

75 O Wondrous Sight, O Vision Fair

Tune: DEO GRACIAS

This anonymous fifteenth-century hymn was written for the Feast of Transfiguration. The Latin original was included in the *Sarum Breviary* (1495). The translation by John Mason Neale was published in *The Hymnal Noted* (1851). For comments on Neale, see hymn 4.

DEO GRACIAS is an English melody dating from the fifteenth century. It was composed as the setting for a ballad recalling the success of the British army over the French in Normandy (Agincourt), about 1415. It ended with the words "Deo gracias." When the tune became associated as a hymn setting, its name became DEO GRACIAS.

76 My Song Is Love Unknown

Tune: LOVE UNKNOWN

The text is by Samuel Crossman (1624–1683/4), distinguished as one of the first English poets to write hymns whose content was other than scriptural. He identified himself with the Puritans and was ejected from the Anglican ministry. Later he became a conformist and was appointed one of the king's chaplains. The hymn first appeared in *The Young Man's Meditation* during the plague of 1664.

LOVE UNKNOWN was composed for this text by John Ireland in 1918. It was composed while at lunch with Geoffrey Shaw, who handed a slip of paper to Ireland saying,

> "I want a tune for this lovely poem by Samuel Crossman." The composer took the paper and picked up the menu. After writing on the back of the menu for a few minutes he handed it to Shaw, with the casual remark: "Here is your tune." (Murial Searle, *John Ireland, the Man and His Music* (Tunbridge Wells: Midas Books, 1979)

The chromaticism halfway through the tune (those notes which service the phrase "O who am I") establishes it as Ireland's own.

John Ireland (1879–1962) was born in Bowdon, Cheshire, and educated at the Royal College of Music (1893–1901). The first four years there he spent studying piano. The remaining time he studied with Charles Villiers Stanford (see hymn 264). He became a fellow of the Royal College of Organists in 1895 and in 1905 received his Bachelor of Music degree from Durham University. He was awarded an honorary doctorate from Durham (1932), RAM and FRCM.

Ireland was organist at St. Luke's Church, Chelsea (1904–1926), and taught composition at the Royal College of Music (1923–1939). His published works span fifty years beginning with two string quartets. He composed also for orchestra, choir, solo voice, and piano. His last work was the music score for the film *The Overlanders* (1946–1947). He died at Rock Mill, Washington, Sussex, England.

77 Forty Days and Forty Nights

Tune: AUS DER TIEFE RUFE ICH

The text by George Hunt Smyttan was first published in the *Penny Post,* March 1856, under the title "Poetry for Lent: As Sorrowful, yet always rejoicing." In 1861 a slightly altered form of the text appeared in Francis Pott's *Hymns Fitted to the Order of Common Prayer* and *Hymns Ancient and Modern.*

George Hunt Smyttan (1822–1870) was educated at Corpus Christi College, Cambridge (B.A. 1845), and ordained in 1848. He served as rector of Hawksworth, Notts, from 1850 to his death. His published works include *Thoughts in Verse for the Afflicted* (1849), *Mission Songs and Ballads* (1860), and *Florum Sacra* (1854).

AUS DER TIEFE RUFE ICH was first published in 1676 and has been attributed to both Martin Herbst (1654–1681) and Paul Heinlein (1626–1686). Heinlein (also Hainlein) was one of the famous German family of brass instrument makers. A trumpet and trombone of his survive. He was also a composer and organist in Nuremberg.

The present harmonization was by William Henry Monk (see hymn 10). It appeared in *Hymns Ancient and Modern* (1861). The tune is also called HEINLEIN.

78 Alas! And Did My Savior Bleed

Tune: MARTYRDOM

The hymn text by Isaac Watts was first published in *Hymns and Spiritual Songs* (1707) and later in the enlarged edition (1709).

The last phrase of stanza 1 was altered early on from "for such a worm as I" (which reflected the language of Psalm 22) to "for sinners such as I" (reflecting 1 Tim. 1:15). Watts titled the text "Godly Sorrow Arising from the Sufferings of Christ." The hymn originally had six stanzas but has generally appeared with only four.

For a biographical sketch of Watts, see hymn 40.

MARTYRDOM was composed by Hugh Wilson toward the end of the eighteenth century. It was published in R. A. Smith's *Sacred Music in St. George's Church* (Edinburgh, 1825), where he designated it as an Old Scottish Melody harmonized by himself. The tune later appeared in *The Seraph, a Selection of Psalms and Hymns* (1827) and was attributed to Hugh Wilson. A copyright suit occurred. The outcome determined Wilson the owner of the tune.

Recent studies have suggested MARTYRDOM was derived from

an earlier Scottish folk melody. The tune has also been called FENWICK, INVERNESS, AVON, ALL SAINTS, BOSTAL, and DRUMCLOG.

Hugh Wilson (1766–1824) was born in Fenwick, Scotland, studied mathematics, and worked as a calculator and draftsman throughout his life. He led the psalm singing in the Secession Church.

Robert Archibald Smith (1780–1829) was educated as a musician. He taught music and was precentor and clerk of session at Abbey Church, Paisley, Scotland. He went to Edinburgh as psalmody leader at St. George's Church (1823). Besides *Sacred Music* he compiled the six-volume *The Scottish Minstrel* (1820–1824). He died in Edinburgh.

79 Kind Maker of the World

Tune: A LA VENUE DE NOËL

The Latin of this hymn "Audi, benigne Conditor" is attributed to Gregory the Great and included in his *Works*. In the monastic offices the text was used for Vespers during Lent and in secular rites for Lauds. The present rendering of the text is from *The Hymnal 1982* and is based on John Mason Neale's 1852 translation. The original first line read "O Maker of the world, give ear."

Gregory the Great (I) [c. 540–604] was born to patrician parents and educated in the law. He was a member of the senate and about 570 became the prefect of Rome. After his father's death, he became a Benedictine monk and established six monasteries on his family's land. In 577 he was named a cardinal deacon of Rome and became the pope's representative in Constantinople. In 590 he became pope. Gregory's contributions to the universal church are many. Among them are the establishment of missions in England, revision of the liturgy, the founding or reestablishment of the Roman singing school (Schola Cantorum) and a simplified plainchant. His Gregorian chant became the standard in the Western church. For more on Neale, see hymn 4.

A LA VENUE DE NOËL was composed by an unknown author and first published in Jean Babelon's *Fleurs des noëls* (1535) as the setting of the French carol "A la venue de Noël," which was sung throughout much of France and was found in a manuscript *Livres de Noëls*, which belonged to French king Charles VIII. The collection was compiled sometime prior to 1494.

80 Jesus Walked This Lonesome Valley

Tune: LONESOME VALLEY

This is an American spiritual which rose out of white communities. It portrays the true humanity of Jesus Christ in enduring the trials and temptations of life just as do all other humans. A New Testament allusion may be Hebrews 4:15. The text moves on to make these experiences more personal by saying in stanza 2, "We must walk this lonesome valley" and in stanza 3, "You must go and stand your trial." The hymn is particularly appropriate for the Lenten season.

LONESOME VALLEY is the tune for this text and is also an American spiritual.

81 Lord, Who Throughout These Forty Days

Tune: ST. FLAVIAN

This text by Claudia Frances Ibotson Hernaman was part of *Child's Book of Praise* (1873), where it is designated a Lenten hymn.

The daughter of an Anglican priest, Claudia Ibotson (1838–1898) was born in Surrey and married Rev. J. W. D. Hernaman in 1858. She wrote over one hundred fifty hymns, many of which were for children. She also translated hymns from Latin. Besides the collection already cited, her published works include *Appendix to The Child's Hymn Book* (1874), *Christmas Carol* (1875), *Hymns for Children of the Church* (1878), *Story of Resurrection* (1879), and *Hymns for Little Ones* and *The Altar Hymnal*, both appearing in 1884.

ST. FLAVIAN was first published in John Day's *Psalter* (1562) as the first half of the tune of Psalm 132. The present form of the tune and harmonization is from Richard Redhead's *Ancient Hymn Melodies and Other Church Tunes* (1853). In *Hymns Ancient and Modern* (1861) it was titled REDHEAD 29, but in the revised edition of 1875 it bore the title ST. FLAVIAN.

82 O Lamb of God Most Holy!

Tune: O LAMM GOTTES

This setting of the Agnus Dei was written by Nikolaus Decius about 1541. A version of it appeared in Anton Corvinus' *Christliche Kirchen-Ordnung* (1542).

Decius was born about 1485 in Bavaria. He studied at the University of Leipzig (B.A. 1506) and Wittenberg University (M.A. 1523). Though he was a monk, he was attracted to Luther and became part of the Protestant Reformation in Germany. Decius had Calvinist leanings as well. There is no record of the date or place of his death.

The translation of this text is by Arthur Tozer Russell (1806–1874). He was born in Northampton, England, and educated at St. John's College, Cambridge. In 1829 he was ordained. Russell was vicar of Caxton (1830–1852), St. Thomas (1852–1866), and Wrockwardin Wood (1867–1874).

Russell began his ministry as a High Church Anglican, but after studying St. Augustine's writings, he became a Calvinist. He wrote *Psalms and Hymns, partly Original, partly Selected, for the Use of the Church of England* (1851); *Hymn Tunes, Original and Selected, from Ravenscroft and other Old Musicians* (1840); and *Hymns for Public Worship* (1848). He died in Southwick.

O LAMM GOTTES was adapted by Decius from a plainsong dating from the thirteenth century. Our version of the melody is from the Eisleben *Gesangbuch* (1598) as found in the *Service Book and Hymnal* (1958).

83 O Love, How Deep, How Broad, How High

Tune: DEO GRACIAS

The Latin poem of twenty-three stanzas entitled "Apparuit benignitas" is the source of this hymn attributed to Thomas à Kempis.

Thomas Hammerken (c. 1380–1471) was born at Kempen, near Düsseldorf, to peasant parents and at twelve was sent to study at a poor-scholars house of the Brothers' House of the Brethren of the Common Life in Deventer, where he remained for six years. It was there he became known as Thomas from Kempen (à Kempis). He joined the Brotherhood and moved to the community of St. Agnes, where he was ordained in 1413. He remained there until his death. *The Imitation of Christ*, a devotional classic and one of the earliest books printed, has been attributed to him.

Benjamin Webb and John Mason Neale's translation of stanzas 2, 4, 6, 9, 10, 11, 12, and 23 were included in *The Hymnal Noted*, Part II (1856).

Benjamin Webb (1820–1885) was born in London and educated at St. Paul's School (1838) and Trinity College, Cambridge (B.A. 1842; M.A. 1845). He was ordained in the Church of England in 1843 and spent his ministry as curate of several churches. He became vicar of St. Andrew's, Wells Street, London, in 1862. He was appointed prebend of Portpool in St. Paul's Cathedral (1881), where he remained until his death. He was one of the editors of *The Hymnal Noted, The Hymnary* (1872), and the *Church Quarterly Review* (1881 until his death). For comments on Neale, see hymn 4.

DEO GRACIAS was composed for "The Agincourt Song" (c. 1415). For comments on the tune, see hymn 75. The arrangement by Richard Proulx for *Worship III* (1986) is based on E. Power Biggs' harmonization of the tune prepared for his weekly radio program originating from the Germanic Museum (now Busch-Reisinger Museum) of Harvard University from 1942 to 1958.

Edward George Power Biggs (1906–1977) was born in Westcliff, Essex, and studied at the Royal Academy of Music, London, before emigrating to the United States (1930). He became a citizen in 1937 and pursued a career as an organ recitalist, broadcaster, and recording artist. He is acknowledged as the outstanding organist of his lifetime.

For comments on Proulx, see hymn 573.

84 In the Cross of Christ I Glory

Tune: RATHBUN

The text, loosely based on Galatians 6:14, was written by John Bowring and published in *Hymns: as a Sequel to Matins* (1825). It is the best known of Bowring's hymns. The first line of the hymn is inscribed on his tombstone. For a biographical sketch of the author, see hymn 20.

RATHBUN was composed by Ithamar Conkey in 1849 while organist at Central Baptist Church in Norwich, Connecticut. One Sunday the pastor was preaching a series on "Words on the Cross" and used the hymn "In the Cross of Christ I Glory" to what might be termed a forgettable tune. Because of the rainy weather, only one choir member showed up for the service. In his disappointment Conkey went home and composed a new tune for the text dedicating it to that one faithful choir member, Mrs. Beriah S. Rathbun, soprano soloist.

The tune was first published as the setting for Muhlenberg's "Savior, Who Thy Flock Art Feeding" in H. W. Greatorex's *Collection of Psalm and Hymn Tunes, Chants, and Sentences* (1851).

Ithamar Conkey (1815–1867) was born in Shutesbury, Massachusetts, and was of Scottish ancestry. After his work in Norwich, he went to New York City and served as bass soloist at Calvary Episcopal Church and later bass soloist and choir director of Madison Avenue Baptist Church.

85 What Wondrous Love Is This

Tune: WONDROUS LOVE

The words to this American folk hymn were published about 1811 in a camp meeting songbook, *A General Selection of the Newest and Most Admired Hymns and Spiritual Songs Now in Use* (Lynchburg, Virginia). It also appeared in a Baptist hymnal published in Frankfort, Kentucky.

The text and tune were published together in William Walker's *Southern Harmony* (1843 printing) and later in B. F. White's *The Sacred Harp* (1844).

WONDROUS LOVE first appeared in William Walker's *Southern Harmony* (1843 printing).

When it was published, the name "Christopher" appeared on the page. Some thirty years later Walker published the tune again, crediting the arrangement to James Christopher of Spartanburg, South Carolina. Attempts to relate the tune to the folk song "Captain Kidd" should be discounted.

The harmony is from *Cantate Domino* (1980), the hymnal of

the World Council of Churches. The first edition of *Cantate Domino* was published by the World Student Christian Federation in 1924.

86 When We Are Tempted to Deny Your Son

Tune: PSALM 22

This text was written by David W. Romig and included in *The Worshipbook—Services and Hymns* (1972).

David W. Romig was born in 1926 in New York City and educated at Princeton University (B.A. in History and Humanities, 1948). He graduated from Union Theological Seminary in New York City in 1955. Romig served the Riverdale Presbyterian Church in the Bronx (1952–1957), the Sea and Land Presbyterian Church in the Lower East Side of New York City (1957–1967), and in 1968 became pastor of the Brick Presbyterian Church in Rochester, New York. This church later merged with First and Central churches to become the Downtown Presbyterian Church from which he is honorably retired.

Romig served as chair of the Joint Committee on Worship, which prepared *The Worshipbook* (1970, 1972) from 1962 to 1967. He has written the libretto for the musicals *Joseph the Carpenter* and *Cricket on the Hearth*. He continues to write poetry for modern organ music and has written texts for the compositions of Carol Duran (see hymn 287). The present text was written to help fill a need for more Lenten hymns.

PSALM 22 was composed by Louis Bourgeois for the Genevan Psalter (1542).

Louis Bourgeois (c. 1510–c. 1561) was a French composer and theorist whose major contribution to church music was his adaptations and compositions for the metrical psalms written by Clément Marot and Theodore Beza in Geneva. For a number of years beginning in 1542, Bourgeois wrote, selected, and arranged music for the French psalters. He also published harmonizations of the psalm melodies for four voices as well as more elaborate versions (1547; 1561). His textbook on singing, *Le droit chemin de musique*, the first teaching manual in French on singing and sight-reading, was published in 1550.

Bourgeois was a follower of John Calvin in Geneva and by 1545 was paid to perform the psalms and teach the choristers at

St. Pierre's Church. The next year he worked with the city pastors to derive the list of psalms to be sung at worship. He worked to improve psalm tunes but, ironically, was imprisoned on December 3, 1551, for without a license having "changed the tunes of some printed psalms"—a disturbing action to those who had learned the "old tunes" which had already been printed. The personal intervention of Calvin the next day got him released. Yet the controversy continued and the Genevan City Council ordered the Preface to Bourgeois' "improvements" to eighty-three psalms (49 written by Marot; 34 by Beza) published in Geneva by Jean Crispin (1551) to be burned because the faithful had become disoriented by the new melodies. In the Preface, Bourgeois claimed that not to sing was to be threatened with punishment. Later his alterations were accepted.

Bourgeois ran into further difficulties with the Genevan authorities and by 1560 was in Paris, where his daughter was baptized into the Roman Catholic church. The date of his death is uncertain.

87 The Glory of These Forty Days

Tune: ERHALT UNS, HERR

This hymn has been ascribed to Gregory the Great (see hymn 79), but not without controversy. Some believe it to be of English origin. The oldest existing manuscript of the hymn "Clarum decus jejunii" dates from the eleventh century and is now in the British Museum. It is given in several editions of Gregory's works.

The translation found in *The Presbyterian Hymnal* (1990) is by Rev. Maurice F. Bell for *The English Hymnal* (1906). Bell's original translation contained five stanzas, the final one a doxology:

> Father and Son and Spirit blest,
> To thee be every prayer addrest.
> Who art in threefold Name adored
> From age to age, the only Lord.

Maurice F. Bell (1862–1947), a minister of the Church of England, had three other translations and one original poem included in that collection.

ERHALT UNS, HERR is believed by some to be the work of Martin Luther (see hymn 14). It was first published in Joseph Klug's *Geistliche Lieder* (1543), where it was the setting for "Erhalt uns, Herr, bei deinem Wort" by Luther. The harmonization is by Johann Sebastian Bach, who based Cantata 126 (1725) on the tune. Other names for the tune are READING, SPIRES, WITTENBERG, and PRESERVE US, LORD. For comments on Bach, see hymn 17.

88 All Glory, Laud, and Honor

Tune: VALET WILL ICH DIR GEBEN

This hymn was composed by Theodulph of Orléans about A.D. 820. It was first used as a Palm Sunday processional hymn.

The translation is by John Mason Neale. A version beginning, "Glory, and honour, and laud to Thee, King Christ the Redeemer!" was in *Mediaeval Hymns and Sequences* (1851). Another version beginning, "Glory, and laud, and honour" was included in *The Hymnal Noted* (1854). In 1859, Neale revised the text further for inclusion in *Hymns Ancient and Modern* (1861). For comments on Neale, see hymn 4.

Theodulph of Orléans was born about 750 or 760 in Spain or Italy. He was in a monastery at Florence when discovered by Charlemagne and brought to France in 781 and made abbot of Fleury and bishop of Orléans. He was imprisoned for conspiring against King Louis the Pious. Although legend has it that Theodulph was freed when the king passed the prison and heard him singing this hymn, it is more probable that Theodulph died in prison in 821.

VALET WILL ICH DIR GEBEN: For comments on the tune, see hymn 11.

89 Hosanna, Loud Hosanna

Tune: ELLACOMBE

This text was written by Jennette Threlfall and published in her collection *Sunshine and Shadow* (1873).

Jennette Threlfall (1821–1880) was born in Lancashire and after the premature death of both parents lived with various relatives. She was injured in an accident that left her lame. A later illness left her bedridden. In spite of her circumstances, she maintained a strong faith in God and was known for her cheerfulness. Threlfall was also the author of *Woodsorrel; or Leaves from a Retired Home* (1856).

ELLACOMBE is a variant of AVE MARIA, KLARER UND LICHTER MORGENSTERN, which appeared in *Gesangbuch der Herzogl. Wirtembergischen Katholischen Hofkapelle* (1784). This was a hymnal for use in the private chapel of the Duke of Württemberg. Our version of the tune and its arrangement are from the Appendix to *Hymns Ancient and Modern* (1868), where it was the setting for "Come, Sing with Holy Gladness."

90 Ride On! Ride On in Majesty!

Tune: THE KING'S MAJESTY

This Palm Sunday text was written by Henry Hart Milman and was one of thirteen he contributed to Bishop Reginald Heber's (see hymn 67) collection *Hymns Written and Adapted to the Weekly Church Services of the Year* (1827). All were later published in Milman's own collection *A Selection of Psalms and Hymns* (1837).

Henry Hart Milman (1791–1868), the youngest son of Sir Francis Milman, court physician to King George III, was born in London. He was educated at Brasenose College, Oxford (B.A. 1814; M.A. 1816; D.D. 1849). He became vicar of St. Mary's, Reading (1817), and later professor of poetry at Oxford (1821–1831). He was canon of Westminster and rector of St. Margaret's (1835–1849), and finally dean of St. Paul's Cathedral. As a student, Milman received many awards and honors. As a writer he contributed much to theological studies with a *History of the Jews* (1829), his edition of Edward Gibbon's (1737–1794) *Decline and Fall of the Roman Empire* (1839), a *History of Christianity from the Birth of Christ to the Abolition of Paganism in the Roman Empire* (1840), and a *History of Latin Christianity* (1854–1855). He died near Ascot and is buried at St. Paul's.

THE KING'S MAJESTY was composed as the setting for this text by Graham George. It was published in *The Hymnal 1940.* During choir rehearsal before Palm Sunday, St. Peter's, Sherbrooke, in 1939, George became concerned that the tune WINCHESTER NEW (see hymn 444) did not adequately lift the "tragic trumpets" of Palm Sunday. "At breakfast the next morning I was enjoying my toast and marmalade when the first two lines of this tune sang themselves unbidden into my mind. This seemed too good to miss, so I went to my study, allowed half the tune to complete itself—which it did with very little trouble—and there it was."

Graham George was born in 1912 in Norwich, England, and emigrated to Canada in 1928. He graduated from the University of Toronto (B.Mus. 1936; D.Mus. 1939) and taught at West Hill School, Montreal, for one year and then served in the Canadian Army during World War II. He became professor of music and resident musician at Queen's University in Kingston, Ontario (1946). George studied composition with Paul Hindemith and conducting with Willem van Otterloo (Holland, 1956). Throughout his career he has served as organist of churches and composed choral, orchestral, organ, and piano works as well as film scores. His book *Tonality and Musical Structure* was published in 1970.

91 Ride On! Ride On in Majesty!

Tune: ST. DROSTANE

The text is by Henry Hart Milman. For comments on the text and the author see hymn 90.

ST. DROSTANE was composed by John Bacchus Dykes in 1862. Henry Augustine Smith said about this tune in his book *Lyric Religion*:

> Naturally, other tunes have been used with Milman's text . . . but ST. DROSTANE composed especially for these words, carries them, it seems, with peculiar appropriateness, through awe and grief to the high rapture of redemption. (p. 345; New York: Century Co., 1931)

John Bacchus Dykes (1823–1876) was born in Hull, England, and by the age of ten was the assistant organist at St. John's Church, Hull, where his grandfather was vicar. He studied at Wakefield and St. Catharine's College, Cambridge (B.A. in Classics, 1847) where he cofounded the Cambridge University Musical Society. He was ordained in 1847 as curate of Malton.

For a short time he was canon of Durham Cathedral, then precentor (1849–1862). In 1862 he became vicar of St. Oswald's, Durham. He published sermons and articles on religion but is best known for the over three hundred hymn tunes he composed. Sixty of his tunes were included in the original edition of *Hymns Ancient and Modern* (1861). That same year he was awarded an honorary doctorate from Durham University. He died in Sussex at the age of fifty-three.

92 Beneath the Cross of Jesus

Tune: ST. CHRISTOPHER

This text was written by Elizabeth C. Clephane the year before her death. The hymn was published in the Scottish religious magazine *The Family Treasury* (1872) with the title "Breathings on the Border."

Elizabeth Cecilia Douglas Clephane (1830–1869) was born in Edinburgh and raised in the Free Church of Scotland. After her father's death, the family moved to Melrose, near Abbotsford, the home of Sir Walter Scott. Clephane's hymns were made famous in this country by Ira Sankey.

ST. CHRISTOPHER was composed by Frederick Charles Maker (1844–1927) for this text in the Third Series of the *Bristol Tune Book* (1881 ed.). It was one of seven tunes he contributed to that volume.

Frederick Charles Maker (1844–1927) was born in Bristol, England, where he spent his life. Trained as a chorister at Bristol Cathedral, Maker later served as organist of Milk Street Methodist Free Church, Clifton Downs Congregational Church, and Redland Park Congregational Church (1882–1910). For twenty years Maker was visiting professor of music at Clifton College. He also wrote a number of anthems, the cantata *Moses in the Bulrushes*, and several piano solos.

93 Ah, Holy Jesus

Tune: HERZLIEBSTER JESU

This Lenten hymn was written by Johann Heermann and included in his *Devoti Musica Cordis, Hauss- und Hertz-Musica*

(1630). It is based on Latin meditation number seven of *Meditationes.* The collection is a compilation of writings from the medieval era. At one time Augustine was considered the author. The translation is by Robert Seymour Bridges. It is from the collection *The Yattendon Hymnal* (1895–1899), which Bridges edited with Harry Ellis Wooldridge. The present text form is altered from the *Psalter Hymnal* (1987).

Johann Heermann (1585–1647) was born in Raudten, Silesia, the youngest and only surviving child of five born to his parents. As a child, Heermann was quite ill and his mother vowed if God would spare him, she would dedicate the child's life to the ministry. He was educated at Fraustadt, Breslau, Brieg, and the University of Strassburg. His poor eyesight forced him to discontinue his studies and return home. He was named to the diaconate at Köben and later became pastor in 1611. The town was burned in 1616. His wife died in 1617 and the next year the Thirty Years' War broke out. Heermann ceased preaching in 1634 because of throat trouble. He retired in Lissa, where he died.

Robert Bridges (1844–1930) was born in Walmer, Kent, England. He studied at Corpus Christi College, Cambridge. After two years of traveling, he entered St. Bartholomew's Hospital, where he studied medicine. His dream was to retire from medicine at forty and spend the remaining years writing poetry. Bridges suffered from lung disease and was forced to retire earlier than he intended. He spent the rest of his life studying literature and music. He was appointed poet laureate in 1913, and received the Order of Merit in 1929. He also was awarded honorary doctorates from the University of Michigan, Oxford, St. Andrews, and Harvard.

HERZLIEBSTER JESU was composed by Johann Crüger for *Newes vollkömliches Gesangbuch Augsburgischer Confession* (1640). It has been suggested Crüger may have been influenced by the Genevan Psalter setting of Psalm 23, when composing this tune.

Johann Crüger (1598–1662) was born in Prussia and educated at the Jesuit College at Olmütz and the poetry school at Regensburg. Except for a brief time in 1620 when he went to Wittenberg to study, Crüger spent the years from 1615 to 1622 as a private tutor. In 1622 he became cantor of St. Nicholas' Church in Berlin and a teacher at the Greyfriars' Gymnasium. He held both positions until his death. A distinguished composer and editor, Crüger is remembered mostly for his *Praxis Pietatis Melica* (1644).

94 An Upper Room Did Our Lord Prepare

Tune: O WALY WALY

This hymn was written by Fred Pratt Green (1973) at the request of John Wilson for a text to the English folk melody O WALY WALY. The poetry is written with a meter of 9.8.9.8 reflecting the tune as it was collected and published by Cecil Sharp.

The hymn was published with Wilson's arrangement in *Hymns for Celebration*, the Royal School of Church Music's nondenominational supplement of hymns for Holy Communion, and was sung at the service commemorating the life and work of Mary Wilson (John's wife) in September 1974.

Several attempts have been made to change the text to long meter but the author has denied the request. When used as a hymn for the Lord's Supper, the first two stanzas may be sung before the distribution of the elements and the final two after.

O WALY WALY is an English folk melody first collected and published by Cecil Sharp (1859–1924). He was the most important of the English folk song collectors, gathering 4,977 tunes. He published 1,118 of them and provided accompaniments for 501. His work led to a renewed interest in English art music and gave impetus to composers of the day, including Ralph Vaughan Williams (hymn 6). His influence on Vaughan Williams can be seen throughout *The English Hymnal* (1906).

Among Sharp's publications is *Folk Songs from Somerset* issued in five parts from 1904 to 1909. Sharp was also an authority on the folk dance. During World War I, Sharp visited America gathering tunes and dances of English origin. After his death the tunes were published in a two-volume collection *English Folk Songs from the Southern Appalachians* edited by Maud Karpeles.

The harmonization is by John Weaver for *The Presbyterian Hymnal* (1990). For comments on Weaver, see hymn 565.

95 He Never Said a Mumbalin' Word

The basis for the text of this African-American spiritual is found in Isaiah 53:7:

> He was oppressed, and he was afflicted,
> yet he did not open his mouth;

like a lamb that is led to the slaughter,
and like a sheep that before its shearers is silent,
so he did not open his mouth.

The African-American slaves expressed their admiration for Jesus when he suffered persecution without a word of complaint. James Cone writes, slaves "were deeply moved by the Passion story because they too had been rejected, beaten, and shot without a chance to say a word in defense of their humanity" (*The Spirituals and the Blues*, p. 47; Maryknoll, N.Y.: Orbis Books, 1972, 1991). Silence is seen as evidence of divine strength rather than an inability to speak.

Some versions of the spiritual have as many as ten stanzas. The phrase "The blood came trickalin' down" (stanza 4) also has variant readings. The words "streaming," "a-twinklin'," and "twinkalin' " have all been used to describe the flow of blood from the Savior's wounds.

96 Calvary

This African-American spiritual is ideal for use during Holy Week especially at Good Friday services. Included in *The Presbyterian Hymnal* (1990) are four of the many stanzas traditionally used with this tune.

The composer of the tune is not known but its alternating ascending and descending melodic pattern is characteristic of other African-American music. The arrangement is that of John Wesley Work III from his *American Negro Songs and Spirituals* (1940). For a biographical sketch of Work, see hymn 29.

97 Go to Dark Gethsemane

Tune: REDHEAD 76

The text was written by James Montgomery in 1820. It was published in *The Christian Psalmist* in 1825. By the time it appeared in his *Original Hymns for Public, Private, and Social Devotion* (1853), there was an additional stanza. The title was "Christ Our Example in Suffering." The author had in mind three lessons to be learned by an actual visit to Gethsemane:

how to pray, how to bear the cross, and how to die. For comments on the author, see hymn 22.

REDHEAD 76 was composed by Richard Redhead and appeared in his *Church Hymn Tunes, Ancient and Modern, for Several Seasons of the Church Year* (1853). The tune was named from its location in that collection. The tune is also known as GETHSEMANE because of its association with this text. It has also been known as PETRA and AJALON.

Richard Redhead (1820–1901) was born in Harrow, England, and was a chorister at Magdalen College, Oxford. He was organist first at Margaret Street Chapel, London (1839–1864), and then St. Mary Magdalene, Paddington (1864–1894). Redhead was sympathetic to the Oxford movement and his various collections influenced the church music of that era. With Canon Frederick Oakeley, he edited the Gregorian psalter *Laudes Diurnae* (1843).

98 O Sacred Head, Now Wounded

Tune: PASSION CHORALE

The original Latin poem "Salve caput cruentatum" has been attributed to Bernard of Clairvaux. It contained seven parts each designed to be sung on a different day of the week addressing a different part of Christ's body: feet, knees, hands, sides, breast, heart, and head.

There is much debate as to whether the hymns ascribed to Bernard of Clairvaux (1091–1153) were actually written by him. It is, however, generally agreed that whoever wrote the hymns reflected the type of religious life emulated by Bernard. He brought to religious life a mystic faith and an emotional intensity that enabled him to lead kings, emperors, and popes.

Paul Gerhardt translated the hymn into German as "O Haupt voll Blut und Wunden." It was published in Johann Crüger's *Praxis Pietatis Melica* (1656). For comments on Gerhardt, see hymn 11.

The English text was prepared from the German by James Waddell Alexander. It first appeared in Joshua Leavitt's *The Christian Lyre* (1830).

James Waddell Alexander (1804–1859) received his education at the College of New Jersey (now Princeton University) and theological training at Princeton Theological Seminary. He was later professor of belles-lettres and rhetoric at the college (1833–1844) and of ecclesiastical history, church government and sacred rhetoric at Princeton Seminary (1849–1851). An ordained Presbyterian minister, the son of Archibald Alexander, James served pastorates in New Jersey and New York, including Fifth Avenue Presbyterian Church, both when it was known as Duane Street Church (1844–1849) and again after it was renamed Fifth Avenue (1851–1859). He was the author of many articles and books, and his hymn translations were collected and published posthumously in *The Breaking Crucible and Other Translations* (1861).

PASSION CHORALE was composed by Hans Leo Hassler for the love song "Mein Gmut ist mir verwirret, das macht ein Jungfrau zart," in English "My Heart Is Distracted by a Gentle Maid," from his *Lustgarten neuer teutscher Gesäng, Balletti, Galliarden und Intraden* (1601). It first appeared with the Gerhardt text in *Praxis Pietatis Melica* (1656) and has been associated with the text ever since. For comments on Hassler, see hymn 54.

The harmonization is by Johann Sebastian Bach, who used Hassler's melody five times in the *St. Matthew Passion*, twice in the *Christmas Oratorio*, in five cantatas (24, 135, 153, 159, and 161), and in an organ prelude. For comments on Bach, see hymn 17.

99 Throned Upon the Awful Tree

Tune: ARFON

The text was written by John Ellerton for Good Friday in 1875. It was first published in *Hymns Ancient and Modern* (1875).

John Ellerton (1826–1893) was born in London and educated at Trinity College, Cambridge (B.A. 1849; M.A. 1854). After three curacies he became vicar of Crewe Green (1860) and chaplain to Lord Crewe. He later served as rector of Hinstock (1872), Barnes (1876), and White Roding (1886). Although Ellerton wrote several prose works, he is best known for his work as a hymnologist, hymn writer, editor, and translator.

His edited works include *Hymns for Schools and Bible Classes*

(1859), *Church Hymns* (1871), published by the Society for Promoting Christian Knowledge, and *Notes and Illustrations of Church Hymns* (1881). Ellerton wrote more than fifty hymns and translated others from Latin. They were published in *Hymns, Original and Translated, By John Ellerton, Rector of White Roding* (1888). Some of his hymns were published in Carey Brock's *Children's Hymn Book* (1882), the first Supplement to *Hymns Ancient and Modern* (1889), *Children's Hymns and School Prayers* (1874), and *London Mission Hymn Book* (1885).

ARFON is an anonymous tune that has enjoyed a dual history. It has been claimed by both Wales and France. The French organist and composer Claude Balbastre (1727–1799) used it in his "Recueil de noëls formant 4 suites, harpsichord and pianoforte" (Paris, 1770). The present arrangement and harmonization was by Hugh Davies (1844–1907) for *The English Hymnal* (1906), where it was the setting for Ellerton's text. The tune has also been called NOËL from the carol "Joseph est bien marié."

100 When I Survey the Wondrous Cross

Tune: ROCKINGHAM

Isaac Watts was inspired to write this text after studying Galatians 6:14, "May I never boast of anything except the cross of our Lord Jesus Christ, by which the world has been crucified to me, and I to the world." It was originally sung as a Communion hymn and published in *Hymns and Spiritual Songs* (1707). Watts titled the hymn "Crucifixion to the World by the Cross of Christ. Galatians 6:14." Other scripture references in the hymn are Philippians 3:7, "Yet whatever gains I had, these I have come to regard as loss because of Christ," and Galatians 2:20, "And it is no longer I who live, but it is Christ who lives in me." Matthew Arnold, who believed this to be "the finest hymn in the English language," sang it on his deathbed. For a biographical sketch of Watts, see hymn 40.

ROCKINGHAM was harmonized by Edward Miller and published in *The Psalms of David* (1790) where it was headed "Rockingham, L.M., Part of the Melody Taken from a Hymn Tune." TUNBRIDGE, the tune from which the melody was taken, appeared in *Second Supplement to Psalmody in Miniature* (1783).

Edward Miller (1731–1807) was born in Norwich, England,

and studied under Charles Burney. He received a Doctor of Music degree from Cambridge (1786). He was organist of Doncaster Parish Church from 1756. Among his books are *Elements of Thorough-Bass and Composition* (1804), *The Psalms of David* (1790), and *The Psalms of Watts and Wesley* (1801). Miller died at Doncaster.

101 When I Survey the Wondrous Cross

Tune: HAMBURG

For comments on the text, see hymn 100. For a biographical sketch of Isaac Watts, see hymn 40.

HAMBURG was the first hymn tune composed by Lowell Mason. It was the setting for "Sing to the Lord with Joyful Voice" (1824). The melody is adapted from a Gregorian chant and employs only five notes of the scale. For comments on Mason, see hymn 40.

102 Were You There?

Tune: WERE YOU THERE

This African-American spiritual was first printed in William E. Barton's *Old Plantation Hymns* (1899). It was the first spiritual to be printed in a major denominational hymnal when it appeared in *The Hymnal 1940* of the Protestant Episcopal Church.

WERE YOU THERE: The present harmonization is by Melva Wilson Costen, chair of the Presbyterian Hymnal Committee. For comments on Costen, see hymn 29.

103 Deep Were His Wounds, and Red

Tune: MARLEE

This text was written by William Johnson in 1953 and included in *The Lutheran Companion* the next month. It was later included in the *Service Book and Hymnal* (1958).

Johnson had been studying Isaiah 53:5 and in the "silence and solitude I was able to find the words to express my thoughts about 'His stripes' and 'our healing.' I remember that at the completion of my poem, I had an experience of deep joy and peace."

Johnson was born in 1906 on a farm near Center City, Minnesota. He published two collections of poetry: *Wild Flowers* (1948) and *Bill's Poems* (1969).

MARLEE was composed by Leland Bernhard Sateren as the setting for this text in the *Service Book and Hymnal* (1958). Sateren was born in 1913 in Everett, Washington, and educated at Augsburg College (B.A. 1935) and at the University of Minnesota (M.A. 1943). He was first a public school teacher and later director of music of KUOM, the radio station of the University of Minnesota. He then became professor of music and director of the Augsburg College choir from 1950 until his retirement.

Sateren composed more than three hundred choral works. He was honored by Gettysburg College (D.H.L.) and Lakeland College (D.Mus.), both in 1965.

104 Christ Is Risen! Shout Hosanna!

Tune: HYMN TO JOY

This Easter text was written by Brian Wren in September 1984, for the tune JACKSON NEW by William Rowan. Wren was inspired by the resurrection text "Christ Is Risen, Raise Your Voices" written in the same meter by Frank von Christierson (see hymn 414). For comments on Wren, see hymn 71.

HYMN TO JOY was composed by Ludwig van Beethoven and adopted for use as a hymn by Edward Hodges. For comments on the tune and Hodges, see hymn 464.

105 Because You Live, O Christ

Tune: VRUECHTEN

Shirley Erena Murray was born in Invercargill, New Zealand, in 1931. Educated in the classics, French, and music at Otago

University, she became a teacher of languages. Murray has served as a church organist, pianist, affairs coordinator for Amnesty International in New Zealand, and from 1981–1991 worked in the Labour Party Research Unit in Parliament. Currently she is editor and executive secretary of the New Zealand Hymnbook Trust.

She has written poems and satirical songs as well as hymns. Five of her hymns are included in *The Presbyterian Hymnal* (1990). This is the first appearance of her hymnody in the United States, although some of her hymns have been published in Australia and Great Britain.

VRUECHTEN is a Dutch folk melody from the seventeenth century. It was first associated with the harvest song "De Liefde Voortgebracht." In Joachim Oudaen's *David's Psalmen* (1685) it was the setting for "Hoe groot de Vruechten zijn" for which the tune is named. The harmonization was made by Alice Stuart Parker in 1966 for *The Mennonite Hymnal* (1969). For a biographical sketch of Parker, see hymn 337.

106 Alleluia, Alleluia! Give Thanks

Tune: ALLELUIA NO. 1

Both the text and tune of this contemporary Easter hymn were composed by Donald Fishel (b. 1950) for the Word of God Community in Ann Arbor, Michigan, in the summer of 1971. The hymn is a composite of several of Paul's themes (Rom. 4:24–25; 1 Cor. 15; Gal. 2:20) as well the Easter theme of resurrection. Fishel is a native of Hart, Michigan.

ALLELUIA NO. 1 was composed for this text by Fishel. The arrangement and descant are the result of a collaborative effort by Betty Pulkingham and Fishel, the editors of *Songs for Celebration: Church Hymnal Series IV* (1980).

107 Celebrate with Joy and Singing

Tune: EVELYN CHAPEL

This text by Mary Jackson Cathey was written after a period of meditation and contemplation. About the hymn she says, "I was overwhelmed, again, at what Christ did for all people when He died and then rose from the dead. What a gift He gave!"

Mary Ellen Jackson Cathey (b. 1926) was educated at Winthrop College, Rock Hill, South Carolina (A.B. in Education), Presbyterian School of Christian Education (PSCE), Richmond (M.Rel.Ed.), with additional work at the University of Maryland and PSCE. She began her career as a junior high English teacher in Spartanburg, South Carolina, but soon turned her attention to Christian education. She has served as director of Christian education and/or educational consultant in South Carolina, Maryland, Virginia, and Washington, D.C. Cathey is the winner of two Hymn Society in the United States and Canada contests and has written devotional and educational materials. Josephine Newbury's *More Kindergarten Resources* (1976) contains some of her poetry, and fourteen of her hymns are in Lavon Bayler's *Fresh Winds of the Spirit* (1986). Bayler's book is an inclusive-language resource for the Common Lectionary, Year A. It includes eighty-five new hymns as well as prayers for the various elements of worship.

EVELYN CHAPEL was composed by R. Bedford Watkins (b. 1921) as the setting for the hymn "On This Day of Dedication" for the dedication of Evelyn Chapel (1984) on the campus of Illinois Wesleyan University, Bloomington.

108 Christ Is Alive!

Tune: TRURO

This text by Brian Wren was written in 1968 with a revision of stanza 5 by the author in 1978 and again in 1988. It was written for the Easter worship of Hockley, Essex, just ten days after the assassination of Martin Luther King, Jr. The hymn pictures the resurrected Christ as deeply involved in the life and pain of humanity and not remote from us. For comments on Wren, see hymn 71.

TRURO: For comments on this tune, and on Thomas Williams and Lowell Mason, see hymn 8.

109 Cristo Vive Christ Is Risen

Tune: ARGENTINA (Sosa)

This hymn by the Argentinian Nicolas Martinez (1917–1972) was translated by Fred Kaan for *Cantate Domino* (1974, 1980). The collection published by the World Student Christian Federation (WSCF) as an international ecumenical hymnal is now published by the World Council of Churches.

In 1970, Fred Kaan (b. 1929) became executive of the World Alliance of Reformed Churches after having served in the office of Minister Secretary of the International Congressional Council, an antecedent body. He was the staff person appointed to work with the WSCF to produce *Cantate Domino.* The hymnal's text has one slight alteration from Kaan's original translation.

ARGENTINA (Sosa) was composed by Pablo Sosa in 1960 for the text. Sosa gave it the name CENTRAL. The hymn appears in *The Presbyterian Hymnal* (1990) as in *Cantate Domino*, where the harmonization was altered.

110 Christ Jesus Lay in Death's Strong Bands

Tune: CHRIST LAG IN TODESBANDEN

This hymn by Martin Luther was first included in *Eyn Enchiridion* (Erfurt, 1524). The English translation is by Richard Massie for his collection *Martin Luther's Spiritual Songs* (1854).

Richard Massie (1800–1887) was born in Chester, Cheshire, England, the first of twenty-two children of St. Bride's rector and his wife. Massie devoted himself to translating and publishing hymns from the German, first Luther's and then Karl Spitta's in *Lyra Domestica* (1860, 1864). He died at Pulford Hall, Coddington, Cheshire, one of his family estates.

CHRIST LAG IN TODESBANDEN, which is a reconstruction of CHRIST IST ERSTANDEN (see hymn 112), was published in *Eyn Enchiridion* and in Johann Walther's *Geystliche gesangk Buchleyn* (1524). The harmonization is by Johann Sebastian Bach, who included two settings in *Choralgesänge*, used it as the basis for his Cantata 4 (all seven movements) and Cantata 158, and for several organ preludes. For comments on Bach, see hymn 17.

111 Good Christians All, Rejoice and Sing!

Tune: GELOBT SEI GOTT

The text by Cyril A. Alington was written especially for this tune. It was included in *Songs of Praise* (London, 1931).

Cyril Argentine Alington (1872–1955) was a priest of the Church of England who graduated from Trinity College, Oxford (B.A. 1893; M.A. 1895; D.D. 1917). He was headmaster of Eton College from 1917 to 1933 and dean of Durham after that. Known as a scholar and author, Alington wrote theological books, essays, novels, and poems.

GELOBT SEI GOTT was composed by Melchior Vulpius and is found in *Ein schön geistlich Gesangbuch* (1609). He was the first composer to use the Italian baletto rhythm in hymn tunes, thus introducing a new type of Protestant hymn tune. He is considered the leading composer of hymn tunes between Martin Luther and Johann Crüger.

Born Melchior Fuchs about 1560 (some say 1570), he and a brother Latinized the family name. Vulpius was a German composer, schoolmaster, and musicologist. From 1596 to his death in 1615 he was a teacher at the Latin school and municipal cantor at Weimar.

Vulpius composed nearly two hundred motets and over four hundred hymns along with his other works, all written for Lutheran worship. In addition to *Gesangbuch* (1609), he published *Cantiones sacrae* (1602) and *Kirchengesänge und geistliche Lieder Dr. Luthers* (1604). Some tunes unpublished at the time of his death were collected in the *Cantionale sacrum* (1646).

112 Christ the Lord Is Risen Again

Tune: CHRIST IST ERSTANDEN

The original text beginning "Christus ist erstanden" was written by Rev. Michael Weisse (1480–1534) for the first hymnbook of the Bohemian Brethren entitled *Ein New Gesengbuchlen* (1531). The collection which Weisse edited contained one hundred fifty-five hymns, all either written or translated by him. Weisse was born in Neisse, Silesia, and educated at Krakow University (1504). He was first a priest and then a monk in Breslau before becoming a member of the Bohemian Brethren's House at Leutomischl (1518). He died at Landskron. The translation is by Catherine Winkworth for her *Lyra Germanica* (2nd series, 1858). It was also included in her collection *The Chorale Book for England* (1863). For more on Winkworth, see hymn 3.

CHRIST IST ERSTANDEN is a German folk melody which was used by Weisse as the setting for "Freuen wir uns all in ein." The tune is as it appeared in Klug's *Geistliche Lieder* (1533). It was arranged by Ethel F. Porter in 1958 for the *Pilgrim Hymnal.* She and her husband, Hugh Porter, were the music editors of that collection.

113 Christ the Lord Is Risen Today!

Tune: LLANFAIR

The text was written by Charles Wesley and first published in *Hymns and Sacred Poems* (1739) with the heading "Hymn for Easter." Martin Madan (see hymn 6) altered it for his collection of 1760 and it has been further altered by the Presbyterian Hymnal Committee. For a biographical sketch of Wesley, see hymn 1.

LLANFAIR was composed by Robert Williams. In his manuscript book the tune carries the date July 14, 1817, and the caption BETHEL. The name LLANFAIR can mean the Church of St. Mary. According to Robert McCutchan, in his book *Hymn Tune Names:*

> A village in Montgomery County, Wales, Llanfair's full name is one of the longest words in any language. Llanfairpwllgwyngyllgogerychwyrndrobwllllantysiliogogogoch. . . . The meaning is "Church of St. Mary in a hollow of white hazel near the rapid whirlpool of the Church of St. Tysillio by the red cave." . . . It is the first station on the railway as it enters this county. (p. 94)

Robert Williams (c. 1781–1821) was born on the Island of Anglesey in North Wales. He was born blind and trained as a basket weaver. He was an able singer and composer with the ability to transcribe a tune after hearing it once.

The harmonization is by David Evans (1874–1948). Evans was the music editor and representative of Wales on the revision committee of the *Revised Church Hymnary* (1927). He was born at Resolven, Glamorganshire, and educated at Arnold College, Swansea; University College, Cardiff; and Oxford University (D.Mu. 1895). He was professor of music at University College (1903–1939), and also senior professor at the University of Wales. He was editor of *Y Cerddor*, a Welsh music journal, from 1916 to 1921. Evans died shortly after conducting a *Cymanfa Ganu* (singing festival) near Wrexham.

114 Come, Ye Faithful, Raise the Strain

Tune: AVE VIRGO VIRGINUM

This hymn was written in the middle of the eighth century by John of Damascus. It was used on the first Sunday after Easter (St. Thomas Sunday). The ode originated in an Old Testament canticle "The Song of Moses" from Exodus 15.

John of Damascus was born in Damascus (c. 675–749). He was a student of philosophy and received the title of "Chrysorrhous" (Stream of Gold). He was canonized by both the Greek and Roman churches. Late in his life he was ordained a priest of the church at Jerusalem. Neale described him as the "last but one of the Fathers of the Greek Church, and the greatest of her poets."

The translation is that of John Mason Neale, who published it in an article on Greek hymnology in *Christian Remembrances*, April 1859. In its first English form the hymn had four stanzas, but *The Presbyterian Hymnal* (1990) follows the form of *The Hymnal* (1933) of the Presbyterian Church U.S.A. For comments on the translator, see hymn 4.

AVE VIRGO VIRGINUM was first published in the Bohemian Brethren's *Gesangbuch* (1544). The title of the hymnal was *Ein Gesangbuch der Brüder inn Behemen und Merherrn, Die man auss hass und neyd, Pickharden, Waldenses, . . .* printed by Johann Gunther (1544). The collection was edited by John Horn. The composer is unknown.

115 Come, Ye Faithful, Raise the Strain

Tune: ST. KEVIN

This hymn was written in the middle of the eighth century by John of Damascus. For comments on the text and the author see hymn 114.

ST. KEVIN was composed by Arthur S. Sullivan and was first published in *The Hymnary* (1872).

Arthur Seymour Sullivan (1842–1900) was educated at the Royal Academy of Music and on the continent of Europe where he was a fellow student with Edvard Grieg. He became professor of composition at the Royal Academy in 1866 and also was an organist, choral conductor, and composer. Most of his hymn tunes were written after 1867. Although he composed much serious music, Sullivan is best known for his collaborative efforts with W. S. Gilbert. The two produced comic operas. Both Cambridge and Oxford honored Sullivan with a Doctor of Music degree and he received the Legion of Honor in 1878. He was knighted in 1883.

116 O Sons and Daughters, Let Us Sing!

Tune: O FILII ET FILIAE

The original text of this hymn was written by Jean Tisserand, a fifteenth-century Franciscan (Minorite) monk. The five stanzas presented here (verses 1–4 and 9 of the original poem) form a paraphrase of Matthew 28:1–7.

The hymn, titled "L'aleluya du jour de Pasques," was first published in an untitled booklet between 1518 and 1536, now housed in the Bibliothèque Nationale in Paris. It is written in the form of a trope on the Benedicamus Domino and styled after a folk song with refrain. Tisserand was a preaching friar who founded an order for penitent women and is said to have written a history of members of his order who were martyred in Morocco (1220). He died in Paris in 1494.

The text has been frequently altered since its translation and publication by John Mason Neale in *Mediaeval Hymns and Sequences* (1851). For a biographical sketch of Neale, see hymn 4.

O FILII ET FILIAE, a fifteenth-century French melody, is contemporary with the text and was probably composed as the original melody. The earliest published form of the tune is a four-part setting in *Airs sur les hymnes sacrez, odes et noëls* (Paris, 1623). The earliest printing of the hymn in America was in John Aiken's *Compilation of the Litanies and Vespers, Hymns and Anthems as they are sung in the Catholic Church adapted to the Voice or Organ* (Philadelphia, 1787).

117 O Sons and Daughters, Let Us Sing!

Tune: O FILII ET FILIAE

John Mason Neale's translation of verses 1, 4, 5, 6, 7, and 8 of Jean Tisserand's original poem are presented here. Together they form a paraphrase of John 20:19–29, the Common Lectionary reading for the Second Sunday of Easter, years A, B, and C. Although the hymn may be sung at other times, it is most appropriate on that day. For further comments on the text and the music, see hymn 116.

118 The Day of Resurrection!

Tune: LANCASHIRE

The text was written by John of Damascus as a canon for Easter and has been called the "golden canon" or "the queen of canons." The free translation by John Mason Neale consists of the first eight parts of John's canon. Neale's translation first appeared in *Hymns of the Eastern Church* (1862).

For comments on the author, see hymn 114. For comments on the translator, see hymn 4.

LANCASHIRE was composed by Henry Thomas Smart (1836) as the setting for the text "From Greenland's Icy Mountains" for a missionary meeting at Blackburn, Lancashire, England. The tune was later published in *Psalms and Hymns for Divine Worship* (1867). *The Church Hymnary* (Edinburgh, 1898), edited by

John Stainer, was the first collection to use the present text and tune together. For comments on Smart, see hymns 22 and 417.

119 The Strife Is O'er

Tune: VICTORY

Originally in Latin, "Finita iam sunt praelia," this text is of unknown authorship. Although John Mason Neale claimed it was from the twelfth century, its first appearance was in *Symphonia Sirenum Selectarum, ex quatuor vocibus composita, Ad commodiorem usum Studiosae Juventutis*, published in Cologne in 1695.

The translation is by Francis Pott. It was included in his *Hymns Fitted to the Order of Common Prayer* (1861).

Francis Pott (1832–1909) was born in Southwark, England, and educated at Brasenose College, Oxford (B.A. 1854; M.A. 1857). He was ordained in 1856 and served parishes, ending his career in Northhill, Bedfordshire (1866–1891). He became deaf and was forced to retire in 1891. He died in Kent.

Pott was on the committee for the original edition of *Hymns Ancient and Modern* (1861). He wrote *The Free Rhythm Psalter* (1898).

VICTORY was composed by Giovanni Pierluigi da Palestrina in 1591. William Henry Monk adapted the tune for this text in *Hymns Ancient and Modern* (1861). For comments on Monk, see hymn 543.

Giovanni Pierluigi (c. 1526–1594) was born in Palestrina near Rome and was a chorister at Santa Maria Maggiore, Rome. He returned to his home in 1544 as organist and choirmaster at Santa Agapito. In 1550 the Bishop of Palestrina became pope and shortly thereafter, now Pope Julius III, appointed Giovanni as music director at Cappella Giulia. In 1555 he was admitted to the Cappella Sistina, the pope's official musical chapel. After a succession of popes (three in one year), Palestrina was released from service because he was married. He held several positions from 1555 to 1571. In 1571 he was appointed choirmaster at Cappella Giulia, a position he held the rest of his life.

Palestrina was one of three great composers of the sixteenth century; the other two were Lassus and Byrd. He composed one hundred two masses, four hundred motets, and fifty-six sacred madrigals. His polyphonic techniques continue to be studied by music students. (For a complete listing of Palestrina's works, see Stanley Sadie, ed., *The New Grove Dictionary of Music and Musicians* 14:118–137.

The Alleluias are to be sung only before stanza 1 and after stanza 4.

120 Hail Thee, Festival Day!

Tune: SALVE FESTA DIES

The one-hundred-ten-line Latin poem "Tempora florigero rutilant distincta sereno" by Venantius Honorius Fortunatus is the basis of this hymn. The hymn begins with line 39 of the poem, "Salve festa dies toto venerabilis aevo." Another hymn paraphrase of this text is John Ellerton's "Welcome, Happy Morning."

Venantius Honorius Fortunatus (c. 530–c. 610) was born near Treviso, Italy, and educated at Ravenna and Milan after which he spent his life in Gaul (France) under the influence of Queen Radegunde. He became a monk of the Abbey of St. Croix and was appointed bishop of Poitiers in 599. He died in Poitiers, France.

SALVE FESTA DIES was composed as the setting of this text by Ralph Vaughan Williams for *The English Hymnal* (1906). Originally the tune appeared anonymously but was credited to Vaughan Williams in *Songs of Praise* (1931) and also in *The English Hymnal* (1933).

121 That Easter Day with Joy Was Bright

Tune: PUER NOBIS NASCITUR

The text, originally the Latin "Aurora lucis rutilat," has been ascribed to Ambrose but is not among the twelve undoubted works cited by his Benedictine editors.

The translation is by John Mason Neale and is included in his *Hymnal Noted* (1852) but was altered extensively by the compilers of *Hymns Ancient and Modern* (1861); further alterations have occurred in other hymnals, including *The Presbyterian Hymnal* (1990). For comments on John Mason Neale, see hymn 4.

PUER NOBIS NASCITUR, from a Trier manuscript, was adapted by Michael Praetorius and harmonized by George Ratcliffe Woodward. For more on the tune, see hymn 68.

122 Thine Is the Glory

Tune: JUDAS MACCABEUS

The text of this French hymn "A toi la gloire" was written by Edmond Louis Budry (1884) and published in *Chants Évangéliques* (1885). It was translated into English by Richard Birch Hoyle (1923) for the first edition of *Cantate Domino* (1924).

Edmond Louis Budry (1854–1932) was educated in Lausanne and was pastor in Cully, then pastor of the Free Church, Vevey, Switzerland, a position he held for thirty-five years. He wrote hymns and translated others into French from German, English, and Latin.

Richard Birch Hoyle (1875–1939) was born in Cloughfold and educated at Regent's Park College, London. After serving several churches he became associated with the Young Men's Christian Association during which time he translated over thirty hymns from the French. He came to the United States in 1934 and taught at Western Theological Seminary, Pittsburgh, Pennsylvania. On returning to England in 1936, he became pastor at Kingston-upon-Thames.

JUDAS MACCABEUS was composed by George Frederick Handel. In the oratorio of the same name, it was the setting for "See, the conquering hero comes." The chorus was originally associated with the oratorio *Joshua* (1748) from which it was transferred in 1751. It was first published as a hymn tune in Thomas Butts' *Harmonia Sacra* (1760) as the setting for Charles Wesley's (see hymns 1, 113) "Christ the Lord Is Risen Today!" For comments on Handel, see hymn 59.

123 Jesus Christ Is Risen Today

Tune: EASTER HYMN

The first three stanzas of this hymn are from the fourteenth-century Latin text "Surrexit Christus hodie." It was first published in John Walsh's *Lyra Davidica, or a Collection of Divine Songs and Hymns, partly newly composed, partly translated from the High German and Latin Hymns; and set to easy and pleasant tunes* (1708).

The fourth stanza is a doxology by Charles Wesley from *Hymns and Sacred Poems* (1740). The hymn in its present form appeared in Tate and Brady's *Supplement to the New Version* (1816). For a biographical sketch of Wesley, see hymn 1.

EASTER HYMN is the only surviving tune from *Lyra Davidica* (1708). It is adapted from *The Compleat Psalmodist* (1749).

The descant is from *Hymns Ancient and Modern* (1955). Some names for the tune are THE RESURRECTION, SALISBURY, and WORGAN.

124 Spirit of God, Unleashed on Earth

Tune: KEDRON

This text was written by John W. Arthur for the Inter-Lutheran Commission on Worship and appeared in *Contemporary Worship—4: Hymns for Baptism and Holy Communion* (1972).

John W. Arthur (1922–1980) was born in Mankato, Minnesota. He was educated at Gustavus Adolphus College (B.A., B.Mus. 1944), Augustana Seminary (B.D.), Western Theological Seminary (now Pittsburgh Theological Seminary) (Th.M. 1949). Arthur was ordained into the Lutheran ministry (1946) and served several pastorates. He was a campus minister and administrator for campus ministries in California after which he taught liturgics and was director of worship at Lutheran School of Theology, Chicago (1967–1970). His final pastorate was in Palo Alto, California (1970–1976), from which he retired because of ill health.

Arthur served on the Inter-Lutheran Commission on Worship, the Committee on Common Texts, the Liturgical Conference, and the board of directors of the Center for Contemporary Celebration, and was on the worship committee of the Illinois Synod of the Lutheran Church in America. He wrote several books on worship.

KEDRON has been attributed to Elkanah Kelsay Dare and was published in Amos Pilsbury's *United States Sacred Harmony* (1799). There it was the setting for a stanza of Charles Wesley's "Ye That Pass By, Behold the Man." The title of the tune comes from that hymn which refers to John 18:1, "After Jesus had spoken these words, he went out with his disciples across the Kidron valley."

Originally the melody was in the tenor line. The tune employs a "Scotch snap" in the second musical phrase.

Elkanah Kelsay Dare (1782–1826) was a schoolteacher in Wilmington, Delaware, and the editor of John Wyeth's *Repository of Sacred Music, Part Second* (1813).

125 Come, Holy Spirit, Our Souls Inspire

Tune: VENI CREATOR SPIRITUS

The Latin of this ninth-century hymn was probably written by Rabanus Maurus.

Rabanus Maurus (776–856) was born in Mainz, Germany, and educated at Fulda after which he entered the Benedictine Order. As a deacon (801), he studied under Alcuin, who gave him the name Maurus. He was appointed first head of the school at Fulda (803) and later abbot (822). From 847 until his death he was archbishop of Mainz. He wrote commentaries on the Old and New Testaments as well as *De Universo Libri XXII.*

The translation-paraphrase of this work was by John Cosin for *A Collection of Private Devotions in the Practice of the Ancient Church, Called the Hours of Prayer* (1627). It was later included in *The Book of Common Prayer* (1662). Cosin was involved in the revision.

John Cosin (1594–1672) was born in Norwich, England, and educated at Caius College, Cambridge. After serving briefly as a priest, he fled to France and was chaplain to the English royal family in exile. When the monarchy was restored, Cosin became dean and later bishop of Durham. He died at Westminster.

VENI CREATOR SPIRITUS is a plainsong and was originally the setting for "Hic est dies verus Dei." But it has also been associated with "Veni Creator Spiritus" since the ninth century. The form of the tune here is from *Vesperale Romanum* (1848). The harmonization is by Healey Willan for *The Hymnal 1940*. For a biographical sketch of Willan, see hymn 56.

126 Come, Holy Spirit, Heavenly Dove

Tune: ST. AGNES

The text was written by Isaac Watts and included in *Hymns and Spiritual Songs* (1707) where it was titled "Breathing after the Holy Spirit: or, Fervency of Devotion Desired." The original had five stanzas but much controversy arose surrounding the second:

Look how we grovel here below,
  Fond of these trifling toys:
Our souls can neither fly nor go
  To reach eternal joys.

John Wesley (see hymn 253) altered the hymn to allow for a greater freedom of will and included it in a *Collection of Psalms and Hymns* (1743). At the time of the publication of *The Hymnal* (1933), there were twenty different versions of the text in common usage. The present text is stanzas 1, 3, 4 and 5 of Watts's original with no alterations.

For comments on Watts, see hymn 40.

ST. AGNES was composed by John Bacchus Dykes (1866). For comments on the tune, see hymn 310. For comments on the composer, see hymn 91.

127 Come, O Spirit

Tune: BOUNDLESS MERCY

This text by John A. Dalles is based on Acts 2:1–4. It was his first hymn and was written as a response to a concern of the worship committee of the Wabash Valley Presbytery (1983).

The members wished to highlight the festival of Pentecost within its member churches. Dalles' first choice as a tune for this text was ST. KEVIN (see hymn 115).

John A. Dalles was born in 1954 in Pittsburgh and graduated from Penn State University (B.S. in Architecture, 1976) and Lancaster Seminary (M.Div. 1982). He served as associate pastor of First Presbyterian Church, South Bend, Indiana (1982–1986), before becoming associate pastor of Fox Chapel Presbyterian Church, Pittsburgh. His hymn "O God of Love, Grant Us Your Peace" was a winner in the Hymn Society of America's "Hymns for World Peace" contest (1985) and has been published in the anthology *Singing for Peace* (1986). Another of his prize-winning hymns, "Praise God for Days Long Past" (1991) has been selected for the first Presbyterian Heritage Sunday celebration. It appears in the centennial issue of the *Mission Yearbook for Prayer and Study* (1992).

BOUNDLESS MERCY is from William Caldwell's *Union Harmony,* Maryville, Tennessee (1837). There was only one edition of this collection and Caldwell is listed as composer of forty-two of its tunes. Although some tunes were in existence in the oral tradition, Caldwell harmonized them. He explained:

> Many of the airs which the author has reduced to system and harmonized have been selected from the unwritten music in general use in the Methodist Church, others from the Baptist and many more from Presbyterian taste.

The harmonization is by Hilton Rufty (b. 1909).

128 On Pentecost They Gathered

Tune: MUNICH

The text by Jane Parker Huber was written for the celebration of Pentecost. There are some hymns that mention the person and work of the Holy Spirit but few speak of the Pentecost event as "the birthday of the church."

This hymn contains several direct references to Pentecost from the second chapter of Acts. It ends with hope that the singular event which inspired the disciples to "turn the world upside down" (Acts 17:6) will move modern-day Christians to do the same.

Jane Parker Huber has gained great popularity for her work in presenting fresh texts for traditional hymn tunes. She was born in 1926 of Presbyterian missionary parents in China and spent most of her childhood years on the campus of Hanover College, Indiana, where her father, Albert G. Parker, Jr., was president. Her mother, Katharine McAfee Parker (daughter of Cleland Boyd McAfee; see hymn 527), served on the Board of Foreign Missions, Presbyterian Church U.S.A., and the National Council of Presbyterian Women. Huber attended Wellesley College and graduated from Hanover College (B.A. 1948).

Huber has worked extensively in local churches, with Presbyterian Women and on women's issues with the Social Justice and Peacemaking Ministry Unit of the Presbyterian Church (U.S.A.), and served on the Presbyterian Hymnal Committee. Since 1976 she has been a writer of hymns with inclusive-language texts, mostly set to familiar tunes. Her articles have appeared in *Concern* and *Horizons* magazines, as well as *Reformed Liturgy & Music.* Her hymns are collected in *A Singing Faith* (1987; 73 hymns) and *Fresh Words to Familiar Tunes* (1982; 32 hymns, texts only; 41 hymns with music).

MUNICH is an old German chorale tune from *Neuvermehrtes Meiningisches Gesangbuch* (1693). It was adapted by Felix Mendelssohn. For comments on the tune, see hymn 327. For comments on Mendelssohn, see hymn 31.

129 Come, O Spirit, Dwell Among Us

Tune: EBENEZER

This hymn text was written by Janie Alford in 1979.

Janie Alford (1887–1986) was born in Nashville and attended Hume-Fogg High School. At Watkins Institute in Nashville she studied astronomy, journalism, and income tax. At the University of Tennessee in Nashville, which she attended for one semester, Alford studied library science.

At eighteen Alford went to work to support her mother and sister. She was able to put her nephews through school and worked for over forty years as a medical secretary to a doctor. Alford grew up in the Cumberland Presbyterian Church but transferred to the Moore Memorial Presbyterian Church, which later became the Westminster Presbyterian Church in Nashville. She was a charter member there and started the church's library.

Alford wrote poetry all her life. At the suggestion of Hal Hopson (see hymn 182), she was encouraged to write hymns based on the seasons of the church year. Her *Nine Hymns for the Church Year* appeared in 1979.

EBENEZER (TON-Y-BOTEL) is by Thomas John Williams (1869–1944). It was published in 1890 as a tune from *Llanlyfr Moliant.* It is best known by its alternate name which springs from the legend that it was found in a bottle that washed ashore during a storm onto the Welsh coast. There is no historical fact to support this, however. The melodic sequence is characteristic of many Welsh tunes.

130 Let Every Christian Pray

Tune: LAUDES DOMINI

The text by Fred Pratt Green was, like so many of his texts, written at the request of John Wilson. It was written for Whitsunday 1970 (our Pentecost) and set to the John Dykes Bower (see hymn 489) tune LUDGATE.

The hymn was sung at Westminster Abbey in 1971 at a "Come and Sing" session by Farringtons School. It was first published in *26 Hymns* (1971). Originally the hymn had four stanzas; the third is omitted in *The Presbyterian Hymnal* (1990).

LAUDES DOMINI was composed by Joseph Barnby (1838–1896) for the text "When Morning Gilds the Skies" (hymn 487). It was published in the Appendix to *Hymns Ancient and Modern* (1868). The composer altered the last two measures for *Original Tunes to Popular Hymns* (1869).

Barnby was trained as a chorister at York Minster and eventually held positions as organist. He was precentor at Eton College from 1875 to 1892. He served as conductor of the Royal Choral Society, which premiered Dvořák's *Stabat Mater*, Wagner's *Parsifal* (in concert form), and Bach's *St. Matthew Passion* in England. He was editor of *The Hymnary*

(1872) as well as several other hymn collections. Barnby also served as music adviser to Novello and Company (1861–1867). He died suddenly after conducting a rehearsal of Handel's *Judas Maccabeus.*

131 Wind Who Makes All Winds That Blow

Tune: ABERYSTWYTH

The text is by Thomas H. Troeger. It was written at the request of Father Sebastian Falcone, director of St. Bernard's Institute, Rochester, New York, for a mass celebrating the Holy Spirit. It was first published in *The Christian Ministry,* May 1983.

In *New Hymns for the Lectionary,* a collection of hymns for Year B of the Common Lectionary, Troeger assigned it to be sung on Pentecost. The text is based on Acts 2:1–13. For comments on the author, see hymn 73.

ABERYSTWYTH was composed by Joseph Parry. For comments on the tune, see hymn 20. For comments on the composer, see hymn 303.

132 Come, Great God of All the Ages

Tune: ABBOT'S LEIGH

This hymn text was written by Mary Jackson Cathey in 1987 for the capital cornerstone campaign of the National Presbyterian Church, Washington, D.C. The campaign was undertaken to obtain funds for building maintenance after the General Assembly of the Presbyterian Church (U.S.A.) no longer contributed to the church's upkeep. The original first line read "Come, Great Cornerstone of all the ages." For comments on Mary Cathey, see hymn 107.

ABBOT'S LEIGH was composed by Cyril Vincent Taylor. For comments on the tune, see hymn 461. For a biographical sketch of Taylor, see hymn 74.

133 All Glory Be to God on High

Tune: ALLEIN GOTT IN DER HÖH'

The present text is F. Bland Tucker's 1977 translation of a German hymn by Nikolaus Decius (1522). Decius' version of the Gloria in Excelsis was first published in Low German in the Rostock *Gesang Buch* (1525) and then in High German in Valentin Schumann's *Geistliche Lieder auffs new gebessert und gemehrt* (1539). For comments on Decius, see hymn 82. For comments or Tucker, see hymn 70.

ALLEIN GOTT IN DER HÖH' was adapted by Decius from the tenth-century plainsong melody for the Gloria in Excelsis used by the Roman Catholic Church during Eastertide. He adapted it for this text. The harmonization is that of Hieronymus Praetorius.

Hieronymus Praetorius (1560–1629) was born in Hamburg. He studied organ first with his father, then with Hinrich thor Molen (1573), and later with Albinus Walran (1574–1578). Praetorius was organist at Erfurt (1580–1582). He then became assistant to his father at St. Jacobi. After his father's death he became primary organist, a position he held until his death. He composed masses, motets, and organ works and is considered by many to be the leading German composer of the first quarter of the seventeenth century.

134 Creating God, Your Fingers Trace

Tune: HANCOCK

The text of this hymn was written by Jeffery Rowthorn (1979). Having given his students in a class on contemporary worship (Yale Divinity School) the task of paraphrasing a psalm—something he had never done—Rowthorn decided to write his own paraphrase. The author used present participles to deal with exclusive-language problems and to emphasize a God who is still working in our world. Another interesting aspect of the hymn is the deliberate use of the word "billion" in stanza 4.

Unknown to Rowthorn, the text was entered into a competition on psalm paraphrases conducted by the Hymn Society of America. He learned of the submission when notified his text was one of two winning entries.

Jeffery Rowthorn was born in 1934 in Newport, Gwent, Wales. After service in the Royal Navy, he studied languages at Cambridge University (B.A. and M.A.), and theology at Union Theological Seminary, New York City (M.Div. 1961). He also studied at Cuddesdon Theological College, Oxford, and was ordained a deacon in the Church of England in 1962 and a priest in 1963. In 1968 he became dean of instruction and chaplain at Union Theological Seminary and in 1973 founding member of Yale University's Institute of Sacred Music. At present Rowthorn is bishop suffragan of Connecticut.

He has edited a hymnal supplement for Yale University and is currently the general editor of *A New Hymnal for Colleges and Schools* (1992). In addition, he has published a two-volume collection of litanies. Rowthorn was honored by Berkeley Divinity School with a Doctor of Divinity degree in 1987.

HANCOCK was composed for this text by Eugene W. Hancock. The hymn was brought to the attention of the Presbyterian Hymnal Committee by John Weaver (see hymn 565) after an organist guild meeting where it was played. This is the tune's first appearance in a denominational hymnal.

Eugene W. Hancock (b. 1929), a native of St. Louis, was raised in Detroit. He graduated from the University of Detroit (B.Mus.), University of Michigan (M.Mus.), and the School of Sacred Music of Union Theological Seminary, New York City (D.S.M.). He is professor of music at the Borough of Manhattan Community College, New York City (since 1970), and until 1990 was director of music, West End Presbyterian Church, New York City. He has composed numerous other hymn tunes.

135 God Is One, Unique and Holy

Tune: TRINITY

The text is by Brian Wren and is one of two written after he spent six months working with the Methodist Hymnal text committee. Wren explains the text tries to be faithful and orthodox while avoiding the masculine language of Father-Son. For comments on the author, see hymn 71.

TRINITY was composed especially for this text by Peter Cutts (1983). Erik Routley once described him as

> the most creative composer of hymnody to come out of English Congregationalism. He derives a great versatility from a true sympathy both with music in popular styles and with learned church music. (The *Music of Christian Hymns*, p. 165, col. 2)

Peter Warwick Cutts (b. 1937) is a native of Birmingham, England. He was educated at Clare College, Cambridge (B.A. in Music, 1961; M.A. 1965), and Mansfield College, Oxford (B.A. in Theology, 1963), and has held teaching posts at Huddersfield College, Oastler College, and Bretton Hall College, Wakefield, Yorkshire. He also has held various positions as organist, assistant organist, and music director. His hymn tunes are known throughout the world.

136 Sovereign Lord of All Creation

Tune: GENEVA

This text was written by Stewart Cross (1928–1989) and published in *Worship III* (1986). This Trinitarian hymn originally began with the word "Father." Stanza 2, line 1, read "Jesus Christ, the man for others." Shortly before his death, Cross changed "Father" to "Sovereign" and "man" to "one." His authorized version is presented in *The Presbyterian Hymnal* (1990).

GENEVA was composed by John Henry Day. For comments on the tune and the composer, see hymn 73.

137 We All Believe in One True God

Tune: WIR GLAUBEN ALL' AN EINEN GOTT

This metrical setting of the Apostles' Creed was written in German by Tobias Clausnitzer. It was included in the *Culmbach-*

Bayreuth Gesangbuch (1668). Catherine Winkworth translated the text for her collection *The Chorale Book for England* (1863). The present rendition of the text is from the *Pilgrim Hymnal* (1958). For comments on Clausnitzer, see hymn 454. For comments on Winkworth, see hymn 3.

WIR GLAUBEN ALL' AN EINEN GOTT is an anonymous melody published in the Darmstadt *Kirchengesangbuch* (1699) with Clausnitzer's text. The present arrangement was made by Johann Adam Hiller (1728–1804) for his *Allgemeines Choral-Melodienbuch* (1793).

This tune is not to be confused with the plainsong associated with Luther's text of the same name.

138 Holy, Holy, Holy! Lord God Almighty!

Tune: NICAEA

This text was written by Bishop Reginald Heber for Trinity Sunday and published in *Hymns Written and Adapted to the Weekly Church Service of the Year* (1827). For a biographical sketch of Heber, see hymn 67.

NICAEA was composed by John Bacchus Dykes for this text and published in *Hymns Ancient and Modern* (1861). Dykes named the tune NICAEA because the text expounded the doctrine of the Trinity as found in the Nicene Creed. For a biographical sketch of Dykes, see hymn 91.

The descant was composed by David McKinley Williams in 1948. Williams (1887–1978) was born in Caernarvonshire, Wales, but his parents emigrated to Colorado when he was three months old. He was a choirboy at St. John in the Wilderness' Cathedral, Denver. At thirteen he played organ and directed the choir at St. Peter's Church, Denver. In 1908, Williams became organist at Grace Church Chapel, New York City, but left to study at the Schola Cantorium, Paris. He served two other churches in New York before teaching at both the Juilliard School of Music and Union Theological Seminary, New York City.

Williams was a member of the commission to revise the hymnal of the Episcopal Church and contributed six tunes to *The Hymnal 1940.*

139 Come, Thou Almighty King

Tune: ITALIAN HYMN

This hymn titled "An Hymn to the Trinity" was first found in a tract that also included a hymn by Charles Wesley, "Jesus, Let Thy Pitying Eye." The tract was bound with George Whitefield's *Collection of Hymns for Social Worship* (6th ed., 1757). The author of the hymn is unknown.

ITALIAN HYMN, also known as TRINITY or MOSCOW, was composed by Felice de Giardini for this text and published in *A Collection of Psalm and Hymn Tunes Never published before* (1769). This collection was popularly known as the Lock Collection because it was published by Martin Madan for the benefit of Lock Hospital, Hyde Park, London.

Felice de Giardini (1716–1796) was born in Turin, Italy, and trained as a chorister in Milan. He was a violinist known throughout Europe. He was much less successful managing opera companies and suffered great losses while managing the Italian Opera Company, the Haymarket Comic Opera, London, and later an opera company in Moscow, where he died. His compositions include operas, violin music, and oratorio works.

140 Holy, Holy

Tune: HOLY, HOLY

Both the text and the music of this popular contemporary gospel hymn were composed by Jimmy Owens in 1972 for his musical *Come Together*. The tune is also known as ADORATION.

Owens was born December 9, 1930, in Clarksdale, Mississippi.

141 A Hymn of Glory Let Us Sing

Tune: DEO GRACIAS

The text of this Ascension hymn was written by the Venerable Bede (also Beda and Baeda), with the first line "Hymnum canamus gloriae." The earliest copy of Bede's hymn is an eleventh-century manuscript in the British Museum.

The Venerable Bede (673–735) was born in a village located on the Tyne near what is now Jarrow. He was educated at the sister monasteries of Wearmouth and Jarrow. At nineteen he was ordained deacon by John of Beverley, bishop of Hexham. Ten years later, he was ordained a priest and spent his life contributing to the fields of philosophy, poetry, history, religion, grammar, and scholarship. His hymns (about a dozen) were possibly the first written on English soil.

The translation is from "A Hymn of Glory Let Us Sing" by Elizabeth Rundle Charles from her *Voice of Christian Life in Song* (1858) and "Sing We Triumphant Hymns of Praise" by Benjamin Webb (see hymn 83) from *The Hymnal Noted* (1854).

Elizabeth Rundle Charles (1828–1896) was born in Devonshire and educated at home. She began writing at an early age and through her work became one of the best-known women in England. She made several significant contributions to hymnody which are found in *The Voice of Christian Life in Song; or, Hymn and Hymn-writers of Many Lands and Ages* (1858); *The Three Wakings, and Other Poems* (1859); *The Chronicles of the Schönberg-Cotta Family;* and *Poems* (1867).

DEO GRACIAS was composed for "The Agincourt Song" (c. 1415). For comments on the tune, see hymn 75. For comments on E. Power Biggs, see hymn 83. For comments on Richard Proulx, see hymn 573.

142 All Hail the Power of Jesus' Name!

Tune: CORONATION

This hymn is a composite. The original text by Edward Perronet was published in the *Gospel Magazine* in November 1779. For many years the hymn's authorship was in doubt although John Julian believed it to be Perronet's work. Louis Benson, when examining *Occasional Verses, moral and sacred*, was able to prove the original hymn to be by Perronet (*Studies of Familiar Hymns*, 2nd series, pp. 154–166).

In 1787, John R. Rippon added stanzas of his own while deleting or altering Perronet's original. Rippon's version was first published in *A Selection of Hymns, from the Best Authors intended to be an Appendix to Dr. Watts's Psalms and Hymns* (1787).

Edward Perronet (1726–1792) was born in Kent, England, and was an Anglican priest. He supported the Methodist movement when he found himself at odds with the Anglican Church. Perronet broke with Wesley over the administration of the sacrament of Communion and spent his final days as a Congregational pastor in Canterbury.

John R. Rippon (1751–1836) was born in Devonshire, England, graduated from Baptist College, Bristol, and in 1773 became pastor of the Baptist Church in Carter Lane, Tooley Street, London, where he remained until his death.

CORONATION was composed by Oliver Holden and published in *The Union Harmony, or Universal Collection of Sacred Music* (1793). He wrote the tune for this text just after the birth of his first daughter.

Oliver Holden (1765–1844) was born in Shirley, Massachusetts. A carpenter by trade, he moved to Charlestown at age twenty-one, where he helped rebuild the town after it had been burned by the British. He was a realtor, conducted singing schools, and was a state representative for Massachusetts. In addition to *Union Harmony*, Holden edited several other collections, including *The American Harmony* (1792), *The Massachusetts Compiler* (1795), *Plain Psalmody* (1800), and *The Charlestown Collection of Sacred Songs* (1803).

Holden composed both the text and the tune and trained the choir for the ceremony honoring George Washington's 1789 visit to Boston.

The descant is that of Michael E. Young (1979).

143 All Hail the Power of Jesus' Name!

Tune: DIADEM

For comments on the text by Edward Perronet and John Rippon, see hymn 142.

DIADEM was composed by James Ellor at age nineteen, shortly before he emigrated to the United States in 1838. The tune is widely known throughout South America, where it is the setting for both the Portuguese and Spanish translations of this text.

James Ellor (1819–1899) was an English Methodist layman and hatmaker. He composed the tune and took it to the hat factory in Droylsden the next morning for all the workers to sing.

144 Alleluia! Sing to Jesus!

Tune: HYFRYDOL

This Ascension hymn was written by William Chatterton Dix. It appeared in *Altar Songs* (1867) and was titled "Redemption by the Precious Blood." Of particular interest is the number of titles given to Jesus Christ in stanzas 3 and 4. The first "Bread of angels" is a reference to Psalm 78:25 and an allusion to John 6:32. For comments on Dix, see hymn 53.

HYFRYDOL was composed by Rowland Hugh Prichard (1831). For comments on the tune and the composer, see hymn 2.

145 Rejoice, Ye Pure in Heart!

Tune: MARION

The text was written by Edward Hayes Plumptre for the Peterborough Choral Festival of 1865 and first used in Peterborough Cathedral. Written as a processional hymn it had ten stanzas. Later that year it was published by Novello and Company with special music and then in Plumptre's *Lazarus, and Other Poems* (2nd ed., 1865). It was included in the Appendix to *Hymns Ancient and Modern* (1868) with a change in stanza 1, line 3, from "Your orient banner wave on high" to "Your festal banner wave on high." Today hymnals limit the number of stanzas.

Edward Hayes Plumptre (1821–1891) was born in London and educated at King's College, London, and University College, Oxford. Ordained in 1846, he was chaplain and then professor of New Testament at King's College (1847–1881), after which he was dean of Queen's College and later dean of Wells Cathedral. He was a member of the Old Testament committee for the revision of the Authorized Version of the Bible (1869–1874). Besides his poetic work, his publications include the *Life of Bishop Ken* (1888) and translations of Dante, Sophocles, and Aeschylus.

MARION was composed for this text (1883) by Arthur Henry Messiter and named for his mother. It was sung at Trinity Church, New York City, in 1887, to celebrate the jubilee year of Queen Victoria's succession to the throne of England. Ten years later it was sung at the bicentennial of Trinity Parish.

A native of England, Arthur Henry Messiter (1834–1916) came to the United States in 1863 and became organist of Trinity Church, New York City, in 1867. His male choir, featuring boy sopranos, served as a model for other Episcopal churches. He edited several collections, including the *Psalter* (1889), *Choir Office Book* (1891), and the *Hymnal with Music as Used in Trinity Church* (1893).

146 Rejoice, Ye Pure in Heart!

Tune: VINEYARD HAVEN

The text was written by Edward Hayes Plumptre. For comments on the text, see hymn 145.

VINEYARD HAVEN was composed by Richard Wayne Dirksen. For comments on the tune and the composer, see hymn 206.

147 Blessing and Honor

Tune: O QUANTA QUALIA

The text of this hymn was written by Horatius Bonar and published in *Hymns of Faith and Hope* (3rd series, 1866). The original poem contained eight stanzas beginning "Into the Heav'n of the Heav'ns hath He gone" and was titled "Song of the Lamb." It is based on selected passages from Revelation 4 and 5.

Horatius Bonar (1808–1889) was born and educated in Edinburgh, Scotland. He was ordained into the Church of Scotland in 1837 but left the established church after the disruption of

1843. As a member of the Free Church, Bonar became joint editor of the church paper *The Border Watch*. In 1866 he became pastor of Chalmers Memorial Free Church, Edinburgh, and was elected Moderator of the General Assembly of the Free Church of Scotland (1883). Known as a theologian, poet, and preacher, Bonar authored more than six hundred hymns. The University of Aberdeen honored him with a Doctor of Divinity degree in 1853.

O QUANTA QUALIA is one of several hymn tunes from sixteenth- and seventeenth-century France which represent a modernization in church music. Some of the tunes are metered adaptations of plainsong melodies, while others originated in secular songs. O QUANTA QUALIA was first published in the Paris *Antiphoner* (1681) as the setting for "Fumant Sabaeis." John Mason Neale (see hymn 4) introduced the tune to England. He took a later form of the melody as found in François de la Feillée's *Méthode du plain-chant* (1808) and used it as the setting for his translation of Peter Abelard's "O quanta qualia," "O What Their Joy and Their Glory Must Be," in *The Hymnal Noted* (1851).

148 At the Name of Jesus

Tune: KING'S WESTON

This hymn was written by Caroline Marcia Noel as a processional for Ascension Day and published in *The Name of Jesus and Other Verses for the Sick and Lonely* (enl. ed., 1870). This text is based on Philippians 2:5–11.

Caroline Marcia Noel (1817–1877) was born in London and displayed a gift for poetry very early. For a time she gave up her writing, but at age forty she began writing again. By this point, Noel had been an invalid for five years. Through writing she sought to comfort others. Her first edition of poetry was published in 1861.

KING'S WESTON was composed for this hymn for *Songs of Praise* (1925). For comments on the composer Ralph Vaughan Williams, see hymn 6.

149 The Head That Once Was Crowned

Tune: ST. MAGNUS

This hymn was written by Thomas Kelly and published in *Hymns on Various Passages of Scripture* (1820 ed.). It was based on Hebrews 2:9.

Thomas Kelly (1769–1854) was born in County Queens, Ireland, and educated at Trinity College (B.A. 1789). He studied law at Temple but changed his plans and was ordained in the Church of Ireland. Because of his evangelistic style, he was ordered not to preach, causing him to withdraw from the Established Church and build a number of independent churches. He died at age eighty-five. Kelly wrote 765 hymns, all of which are collected in the 1858 edition of *Hymns on Various Passages of Scripture.*

ST. MAGNUS was composed by Jeremiah Clark and published anonymously in *The Divine Companion* (1709). In that collection it appears immediately following three hymns attributed to Clark and the pieces after it are anthems.

Jeremiah Clark (sometimes Clarke) (1670–1707) was born in London and was a chorister at Chapel Royal under John Blow. He was subsequently organist at Winchester College (1692–1695), St. Paul's, and then the Chapel Royal (1700). Dr. Robert Bridges (see hymn 93) considered Clark "the inventor of the modern English hymn tune." Clark was prone to depression and committed suicide in London.

150 Come, Christians, Join to Sing

Tune: MADRID

This text was written by Christian Henry Bateman and published in *Sacred Melodies for Children* (1843) and then in later editions. It was also published in *Children's Hymnal and Christian Year* (1872). The original first line was "Come, children, join to sing."

Christian Henry Bateman (1813–1889) was born at Wyke near Halifax, England. He studied for the ministry in the Moravian Church and then became minister of Richmond Place Congregational Church, Edinburgh (1843). After successive

Congregational calls, he became a priest in the Church of England. He was curate of St. Luke's, Jersey, and chaplain to the forces (1869–1871), vicar of All Saints, Middlesex (1871–1875), and curate of St. John's, Penymynydd, Hawarden (1877–1884).

MADRID was a popular Spanish folk melody that was arranged for pianoforte by Benjamin Carr and copyrighted in 1825. In 1826 it was published in Philadelphia with the following title: *Spanish Hymn, Arranged and Composed for the Concerts of the Musical Fund Society of Philadelphia, by Benjamin Carr. The Air from an Ancient Spanish Melody. Printed from the Condensed Score of the Society, and Presented to the Composer as a Tribute of Respect and Regard by Some of the Members, his Friends* (Philadelphia, 1826). Montague Burgoyne published the tune in *A Collection of Metrical Versions* (London, 1827). The tune is also known as SPANISH HYMN or SPANISH CHANT.

Benjamin Carr (1768–1831) was born in London and studied with Dr. Samuel Arnold and Charles Wesley II. He emigrated to America in 1793 and the following year became a publisher in both Philadelphia and New York. He was organist of St. Peter's Church, Philadelphia, and also music director of St. Joseph's Roman Catholic Church from 1801. His liturgical works were published in *Masses, Vespers, Litanies, Hymns, Psalms, Anthems & Motets* (1805) for Roman Catholics and the *Collection of Chants and Tunes for the Use of the Episcopal Church in the City of Philadelphia* (1816). In addition Carr wrote operas and piano pieces.

David Evans harmonized this tune for inclusion in the *Revised Church Hymnary* (1927). For a biographical sketch of Evans, see hymn 113.

151 Crown Him with Many Crowns

Tune: DIADEMATA

The text was written by Matthew Bridges. The original poem had six stanzas and was published in *Hymns of the Heart* (2nd ed., 1851) with the following caption: "On his head were many crowns (Revelation 19:12)."

Matthew Bridges (1800–1894) was born in Essex and brought up in the Church of England, but in 1848, under the influence of the Oxford Movement and John Henry Newman, became Roman Catholic. Besides *Hymns of the Heart*, he published a collection *The Passion of Jesus* (1852). He spent much of the remainder of his life in Quebec, Canada, but returned to Devon, England, shortly before his death.

DIADEMATA is the tune most associated with this text. It was composed by George Job Elvey in 1868 for this text and was first published in the Appendix to *Hymns Ancient and Modern* (1868). He named it using the Greek word for crowns (*diademata*).

George Job Elvey (1816–1893) was born in Canterbury, baptized in the Presbyterian Chapel there, and studied under the cathedral organist, whose daughter he later married. He attended the Royal Academy of Music and New College, Oxford (B.Mus. 1838; D.Mus. 1840). At the age of nineteen (1835) he applied for and received King William IV's appointment as organist of St. George's Chapel over such well-known musicians as Samuel Sebastian Wesley (see hymn 442) and Sir George Smart. He served the chapel until 1882, composed anthems and tunes for the church, and taught several members of the royal family. Elvey was knighted in 1871.

152 Earth's Scattered Isles and Contoured Hills

Tune: MEADVILLE

The text of this hymn by Jeffery Rowthorn was commissioned for the American Guild of Organists 1974 convention held in Cleveland, where it was set to a tune by Gerry Hancock. At that meeting, he was approached by Rebecca Borthwick, director of music, First Presbyterian Church, Meadville, Pennsylvania, for permission to have the text used in an anthem being commissioned in honor of the church's one hundred seventy-fifth anniversary. The text was then sent to Walter Pelz, who composed the anthem for choir (stanzas 1–3) and congregation (stanza 4). For more on Rowthorn, see hymn 134.

MEADVILLE was adapted by W. Thomas Jones (b. 1956) from the congregational portion of Walter Pelz's anthem. Jones was a student of Rowthorn's working with him on *Laudamus* (1980), a supplement to *Hymnal for Colleges and Schools* (1956). The request by Rowthorn to name the tune MEADVILLE was honored by both the church and Pelz.

Walter Pelz (b. 1926) was born in Chicago and educated at Concordia Teachers College, River Forest, Illinois (B.S. 1948), and Northwestern University (M.Mus. 1951). After teaching music in the public schools for fourteen years, he became minister of music at Christ Lutheran Church, Minneapolis, and received his Ph.D. from the University of Minnesota (1970). He has been a member of the music faculty of Bethany College, Lindsborg, Kansas, since 1969. There he has directed choirs and conducted the Bethany Oratorio Society, which has performed Handel's *Messiah* annually since 1882.

153 He Is King of Kings

Tune: HE IS KING

This piece is an African-American spiritual richly steeped in biblical imagery. A phrase from a particular scriptural passage, 1 Timothy 6:15–16, serves as the first part of the refrain referring to Jesus Christ as "King of kings, . . . Lord of lords." Images of Christ's kingship are found throughout the hymn text as well as an Old Testament reference to "Canaan ground"—an allusion to the "promised land" of the children of Israel. American slaves had a yearning "to reach that physical *and* spiritual 'promis'd land where all is peace.' " (William B. McClain, *Come Sunday: The Liturgy of Zion*, p. 103). The King has "pitched His tents on Canaan ground" (stanza 2) and in so doing "broke oppressive kingdoms down"—images of particular importance for the slaves who sang this hymn. The repeated phrase "No one works like Him" has direct reference to the power of Christ, but also reminds the slaves of their own enforced labor.

HE IS KING is an African-American spiritual arranged by Joseph T. Jones (1902–1983), an important leader who introduced

curate and then vicar of St. Matthew's Church in Walsall. Darwall composed two volumes of piano sonatas: *A Christmas Hymn and Tune and A Charity Hymn and Tune* and *A Hymn to Which Is Prefixed a Biographical Notice.* He also composed metrical settings for all one hundred fifty psalms in the *New Version of the Psalms of David* (1696). He died at Walsall.

The descant is by Sydney Hugo Nicholson. For a biographical sketch of Nicholson, see hymn 371.

156 You, Living Christ, Our Eyes Behold

Tune: PALACE GREEN

This text was written by Edmund R. Morgan (1888–1979) in 1950 for *Hymns Ancient and Modern* (1955). It was revised by the author in 1973. The hymn refers to Revelation 1:13–15 and alludes to Daniel 7:9–13.

PALACE GREEN was composed by Michael Fleming (b. 1928) in 1958 for the Royal School of Church Music.

157 Jesús Es Mi Rey Soberano
Our King and Our Sovereign, Lord Jesus

Tune: MI REY Y MI AMIGO

Both the text and the music of this Mexican hymn were composed by Vincente Mendoza in 1920.

Vincente Mendoza (1875–1955) was a pastor in the Methodist Church of Mexico. An accomplished musician and hymn writer, he contributed nine original texts to *El Himnario* (1964) and three tunes.

The translation is by George Paul Simmonds for the *Spanish/ English Hymnal* (1968). Simmonds updated his translation in 1989 for inclusion in *The Presbyterian Hymnal* (1990).

George Paul Simmonds died in June 1991 just short of his one hundred first birthday. For many years he served as a Presbyterian missionary to Mexico. In 1964 he edited *El Himnario*, which was to become the most widely used Protestant Hispanic hymnbook of this century. It has been described as mostly a collection of "traditional hymns, old time favorites, translated to Spanish by one of the most prolific translators and composers, a Presbyterian missionary, George Paul Simmonds" (Carlos A. Lopez, "Hymn Singing in the Hispanic Tradition," *Reformed Liturgy & Music*, vol. 21, no. 3 (Summer 1987), pp. 156–157).

Throughout his ministry and particularly in his later years, Simmonds dedicated himself to bringing Hispanic hymnody into the Anglo churches through his publishing company, Cánticos Escogidos, first based in Albuquerque, New Mexico, and later in Duarte, California.

PSALMS

158 The One Is Blest

Tune: DUNFERMLINE

The original of this metrical version of Psalm 1 was published in *The Psalter* (1912). It was altered by the Psalter Task Force of the Presbyterian Church (U.S.A.). *The Psalter* (1912) was the work of a joint committee of churches representing the Reformed tradition in the United States and Canada. Its members were from the Presbyterian Church in the United States of America, the Presbyterian Church in Canada, the Reformed Church in America, the United Presbyterian Church of North America, the Reformed Presbyterian Church, Synod; the Reformed Presbyterian Church, General Synod; the Christian Reformed Church in North America, the Associate Reformed Presbyterian Church, and the Associate Presbyterian Church. The goal was to produce "a version of the psalms which would satisfy modern literary standards and be recognized as the mutual property of the churches."

DUNFERMLINE was first published in Andro Hart's Scottish Psalter, *CL Psalms of David* (1615). This collection of metrical psalms was the first to identify twelve tunes commonly sung by the masses, who for the most part were illiterate. DUNFERMLINE is one of these so-called common tunes and is thought to be the work of John Angus of Dunfermline Abbey. A monk, Angus was precentor at the abbey and sympathized with the Reformation.

Hart was a Scottish bookseller and printer who by 1589 began to import foreign books. His name appeared on the 1601 Dordrecht, Holland, Psalter sold in Scotland. In 1610 he became a publisher in Edinburgh producing Bibles and Psalters as well as books of court poetry. A copy of his 1615 edition bound with one hundred twelve leaves of music manuscript containing four-part harmony dating from 1626 exists.

159 Why Are Nations Raging

Tune: SALZBURG

This paraphrase of Psalm 2 by Fred R. Anderson was written at the request of the Psalter Task Force of the Presbyterian Church (U.S.A.) to be set to the tune SALZBURG. However, when it was published in *Singing Psalms of Joy and Praise* (1986) the decision was made to recommend ABERYSTWYTH as the setting. Originally, the first line read "Why are nations grumbling" but was altered by Anderson for this collection.

Fred R. Anderson was born in San Bernardino, California, in 1941 and attended the University of Arizona before graduating from the University of Redlands, California (B.Mu. 1963). After serving in the Air Force, he attended Princeton Theological Seminary (M.Div. 1973; D.Min. 1981) and was ordained by Palisades Presbytery in 1973. He was pastor of the Pompton Valley Presbyterian Church, Pompton Plains, New Jersey, for five years and from 1978 to 1992 pastor of Pine Street Presbyterian Church, Harrisburg, Pennsylvania. He is now pastor of Madison Avenue Presbyterian Church, New York City.

Anderson wrote his first hymn "The Burning Bush, It Burns" while in Ottawa, Canada, for the 21st General Council of the World Alliance of Reformed Churches in 1982. Later that fall he began metering psalms for the congregation of Pine Street Presbyterian Church. He served as consultant to the Presbyterian Church (U.S.A.)'s task force on the use of psalms in worship (Psalter Task Force) and was a member of the writing team for the denomination's Directory for Worship (1989). The author of many articles, he has also published a collection of metrical psalms, *Singing Psalms of Joy and Praise* (1986).

SALZBURG is attributed to Jacob Hintze in the 1690 edition of *Praxis Pietatis Melica*. It was first published in the 1678 edition as the setting for "Alle Menschen müssen sterben."

Jacob Hintze (1622–1702) was born in Bernau, Germany, and served as town musician in Berlin from 1669 to his death. After Johann Crüger's death he became editor of *Praxis Pietatis Melica* overseeing the twelfth through twenty-eighth editions (1666–1698). He appended sixty-five of his own melodies to the twelfth edition.

The harmonization is a simplified version from Johann Sebastian Bach's *Choralgesänge* as it appeared in *Hymns Ancient and Modern* (1861). For comments on Bach, see hymn 17.

160 PSALM 4

The text of this responsorial psalm is by Brother Anthony Teague. The psalm tone is St. Meinrad VII from the brothers of St. Meinrad Archabbey, Indiana (1973).

Helen L. Wright (b. 1927) wrote the refrain for the Psalter Task Force of the Presbyterian Church (U.S.A.), for which she served as chair. A native of Baltic, Ohio, Helen Wright is a graduate of the College of Wooster with a B.A. degree in English. For some years she served as treasurer and bookkeeper for her husband's medical corporation. Presently she is organist for the Presbyterian Church of Coshocton, Ohio, a position she has held for twenty-four years. Wright served on the Advisory Council for Discipleship and Worship of the United Presbyterian Church U.S.A. prior to the reunion of 1983.

161 As Morning Dawns

Tune: WAREHAM

The text is a new paraphrase of Psalm 5 by Fred R. Anderson. It was first published in *Singing Psalms of Joy and Praise* (1986). For a biographical sketch of Anderson, see hymn 159.

WAREHAM was composed by William Knapp as a setting of Psalm 36:5–10. For comments on the tune, see hymn 421.

Little is known of William Knapp (1698–1768) because the records of the parish where he was born burned in 1762. He was born in Wareham, England, and was probably of German extraction. It is believed he served as organist at Wareham and later at St. James's Church, Poole, where for thirty-nine years he was also parish clerk. Knapp was the author of two collections of hymns: *A Sett of New Psalm-Tunes and Anthems in four parts* (1738) and *The New Church Melody* (1753). He is best known for this tune which Dr. James Moffatt said is "one of the best congregational tunes ever written."

162 O Lord, Our God, How Excellent

Tune: WINCHESTER OLD

The text is a paraphrase of Psalm 8 by Fred R. Anderson and appears in *Singing Psalms of Joy and Praise* (1986). It was an attempt on his part to bridge the gap between ancient Israel and contemporary cosmology. Anderson first encountered the psalm in a choral setting by Howard Hanson. For a biographical sketch of Anderson, see hymn 159.

WINCHESTER OLD was first published in Thomas Este's *Psalmes* (1592). For comments on the tune and the source, see hymn 58.

163 Lord, Our Lord, Thy Glorious Name

Tune: GOTT SEI DANK DURCH ALLE WELT

The text is a metrical version of Psalm 8 from *The Psalter* (1912). The present language is a slight alteration of the original made by the Reformed Church in America's hymnbook committee and appeared in *Rejoice in the Lord* (1985). For comments on *The Psalter* (1912), see hymn 158.

GOTT SEI DANK DURCH ALLE WELT appears in J. A. Freylinghausen's *Geistreiches Gesangbuch* (Halle, 1704). The tune has been known also as BERLIN and CARINTHIA.

Johann Anastasius Freylinghausen (1670–1739), German theologian, was born in Gandersheim, Germany. He studied at the University of Jena (1692). Coming under the influence of Pietist preacher A. H. Franke, whose daughter he later married, he moved to the University of Halle (1695). After many lean years, he was given a post at St. Ulrich's (1715), enabling him to marry. After his father-in-law's death (1727), Freylinghausen became director and pastor of the Halle educational institutions established by Franke.

Freylinghausen's *Geistreiches Gesangbuch* (1704) and its second part *Neues Geistreiches Gesangbuch* (1714) were the most significant pietistic hymnbooks produced. Later bound as one volume (1741), they influenced several hymnals of the established church of the day, most notably Georg Schemelli's

Musikalisches Gesangbuch (1736) for which Johann Sebastian Bach served as music editor.

164 Lord, Who May Dwell Within Your House

Tune: CHESHIRE

This version of Psalm 15 is by Christopher L. Webber. All of Webber's psalms included in *The Presbyterian Hymnal* (1990) are from *A New Metrical Psalter* (1986), which began as a project to enable his parish to sing the psalms in the liturgy. It is Webber's opinion that "Anglican chant and plainsong are no longer familiar to American congregations and the old metrical psalters seem quaint and out-of-date."

His metrical versions are based on the language of the *1979 Book of Common Prayer* of the Episcopal Church. Some alterations to provide more inclusive language were made for the hymnal.

Father Webber is a priest of the Episcopal Church who has served as rector of parishes in the dioceses of Long Island and New York. He spent six years as rector of St. Alban's Church, Tokyo, Japan. He graduated from Princeton University and the General Theological Seminary, where he also served as a fellow and tutor. Webber has been a trustee of the Cathedral of St. John the Divine and the General Theological Seminary as well as a fellow of the College of Preachers in Washington, D.C.

He is currently rector of Christ Church, Bronxville, New York. Webber has had poetry published in various church magazines and is the author of *A Vestry Handbook* and *Meditations on Matthew.*

CHESHIRE first appeared in Thomas Este's *The Whole Booke of Psalmes* (1592), where it is attributed to John Farmer. Little is known about Farmer, who was one of at least twelve composers employed by Este to harmonize the tunes for the collection. Farmer was at one time organist of Christ Church Cathedral, Dublin, and a skilled harmonizer. The tune was introduced first to Presbyterians in *The Hymnal* (1933) under the name CHESHIRE TUNE.

The tune appears as it is found in *Songs of Syon* (1910). For more on Este's *Psalmes,* see hymn 58.

165 When in the Night I Meditate

Tune: ST. FLAVIAN

The paraphrase of Psalm 16 is from *The Psalter* (1912), where it is number 28 bearing the title "Fellowship with God." For comments on the source, see hymn 158.

ST. FLAVIAN was first published in John Day's *Psalter* (1562). For comments on the tune and the source, see hymn 81.

166 The Heavens Above Declare God's Praise

Tune: CAITHNESS

This new metrical paraphrase of Psalm 19:1–6 is by Christopher L. Webber. It was first published in *A Metrical Psalter* (1986). For comments on Webber and the collection, see hymn 164.

CAITHNESS is from the Scottish Psalter (1635) with harmonization from *The English Hymnal* (1906). For comments on the tune, see hymn 70.

167 God's Law Is Perfect and Gives Life

Tune: HALIFAX

This metrical rendering of Psalm 19:7–14 is by Christopher L. Webber. It is from *A New Metrical Psalter* (1986), which attempts to "follow closely the original texts as they are presented in the *Book of Common Prayer*, 1979." According to the Common Lectionary, these verses of Psalm 19 are for use on the Third Sunday after Epiphany, Year C; the Third Sunday in Lent, Year B; and on the Sunday between September 11 and 17, Year A. For comments on Webber, see hymn 164.

HALIFAX is from Handel's oratorio *Susanna* (1748), where it was the setting for the aria "Ask if yon damask rose be sweet." The present arrangement was published in Thomas Butts' *Harmonia Sacra* (c. 1763) with the text "Indulgent Father! How Divine" and titled HALIFAX. The harmonization is by C. Winfred Douglas for *The Hymnal 1940*. For more on Handel, see hymn 59. For comments on Douglas, see hymn 4.

168 Lord, Why Have You Forsaken Me

Tune: CONDITOR ALME SIDERUM

Christopher L. Webber wrote this paraphrase of Psalm 22:1–11. It was published in *A New Metrical Psalter* (1986) to be sung to ELTHAM. The word "ancestors" (stanza 2) was "forefathers" in the original. For comments on Webber, see hymn 164.

CONDITOR ALME SIDERUM is a Sarum plainsong melody (ninth century), harmonized by C. Winfred Douglas. For comments on the tune and a biographical sketch of Douglas, see hymn 4.

169 In the Day of Need

Tune: SAMSON

This metrical paraphrase of Psalm 20 is based on the 1969 rendition by Christopher M. Idle. It is the work of the Psalter Task Force of the Presbyterian Church (U.S.A.) in 1984. Idle's original was written in Peckham, Southeast London, and first published in 1973 in *Psalm Praise.* Idle (b. 1938) is rector of the Parish of Oakley, Norfolk, England.

SAMSON was composed by Norman L. Warren (b. 1934) for the text by Idle. The tune was originally titled IN THE DAY OF NEED, but Warren changed it to SAMSON. It was the setting of the Idle text in *Psalm Praise* (1973).

170 The Lord's My Shepherd, I'll Not Want

Tune: CRIMOND

This paraphrase of Psalm 23 is from the Scottish Psalter (1650), the second metrical Psalter of Scotland. It came into use on

May 1, 1650, and for more than three centuries it has been the authorized metrical text of the psalms in the Church of Scotland. The title of the collection is *The Psalms of David in Meeter: Newly translated, and diligently compared with the original Text, and former Translations: More plaine, smooth and agreeable to the Text, than any heretofore.*

The text, once thought to be the work of Francis Rous, is a composite from several sources, including Zachary Boyd, Thomas Sternhold, Sir William Mure of Rowallan, the Westminster version, and the King James Bible. (For a detailed discussion of the origins of Psalm 23 in the Scottish Psalter (1650), see Millar Patrick, *Four Centuries of Scottish Psalmody*, pp. 103f.)

CRIMOND was composed by Jessie Seymour Irvine (1836–1887) and named for the village in northeast Scotland where she wrote it while her father was pastor. The harmonization is by Thomas Cuthbertson Leithead (T. C. L.) Pritchard (1885–1960), music editor of *The Scottish Psalter* (1929).The setting received worldwide recognition and has gained in popularity since its use in the wedding ceremony of Queen Elizabeth II and Prince Philip, Duke of Edinburgh, in 1947.

171 The King of Love My Shepherd Is

Tune: ST. COLUMBA

The text was written by Henry Williams Baker for the Appendix to *Hymns Ancient and Modern* (1868).

Henry Williams Baker (1821–1877), English baronet and member of the clergy of the Church of England, is best known as chair of the editorial committee of *Hymns Ancient and Modern* (1861). He was born in London, educated at Trinity College (B.A. 1844; M.A. 1847), and ordained in 1844. In addition to *Hymns Ancient and Modern*, he edited or wrote several books, including *Daily Prayers for the Use of Those Who Work Hard; Hymns for the London Mission* (1874); and *Hymns for Mission Services,* collected 1876–1877.

He became vicar of Monkland (1851), where he remained until his death. As Baker lay dying, his last words were the third stanza of this hymn:

Perverse and foolish oft I strayed,
But yet in love He sought me,
And on His shoulder gently laid,
And home, rejoicing, brought me.

ST. COLUMBA is a tune of Irish origin and was first published in Dr. George Petrie's (1789–1866) collection of old Irish airs (1855) with the caption, "an Irish hymn sung at the dedication of a chapel, county Londonderry." Charles Villiers Stanford (see hymn 264) published a *Complete Collection of Irish Music as noted by George Petrie* (1902).

The tune is named for St. Columba, who brought Christianity to Ireland and incidentally was the first to report sighting the Loch Ness monster.

172 My Shepherd Will Supply My Need

Tune: RESIGNATION

This is the Isaac Watts version of Psalm 23. It was published in a collection by Watts entitled *The Psalms of David Imitated in the Language of the New Testament, and Applied to the Christian State and Worship* (1802).

The language of the lyrics, though inspired by the Psalms and following their general thought, is pure Watts. His collection was first published in the United States by Benjamin Franklin in 1729. For a biographical sketch of Watts, see hymn 40.

RESIGNATION is an American folk hymn tune which first appeared in William Walker's *Southern Harmony* (1835). The harmonization is by Dale Grotenhuis. For comments on Grotenhuis, see hymn 201.

173 PSALM 23

This paraphrase of Psalm 23 was written in 1984 for the Psalter Task Force of the Presbyterian Church (U.S.A.) by Robert J. Moore, a member of the task force. It was first published in *A Psalm Sampler* (1986).

Robert J. Moore was born in Phoenix in 1952 and received his education at Arizona State University (B.A. 1973; M.S.W. 1992) and San Francisco Theological Seminary (M.Div. 1977). He is an ordained Presbyterian minister and served as associate pastor of Westminster Presbyterian Church, Sacramento, California (1978–1980), First Presbyterian Church, Roswell, New Mexico (1980–1982), and Christ Presbyterian Church, Tucson, Arizona (1983–1990), before returning to graduate school.

The refrain and psalm tone were composed by Joseph Gelineau in 1959 and were first used with Gelineau's French translation of Psalm 23. The present setting was published with the 1963 English translation commonly known as The Grail.

Joseph Gelineau (b. 1920), a French Jesuit, was a member of the translation committee for *La Bible de Jerusalem* (1959). He worked with the Psalter in an effort to reproduce the Hebrew rhythm patterns in French. In 1963, Ladies of the Grail produced an English psalter compatible with the French Psalmody of Gelineau. By so doing, The Grail was able to use tones and refrains composed by Gelineau.

Gelineau is the leader in reviving psalm singing in the Roman Catholic Church. He and his associates at the Centre Nationale de Pastorale Liturgique in Paris

> set their texts to chant-like melodies wherein the accented syllables occur at a steady pulse, in keep[ing] with the rhythmic nature of the original psalms. The usual form is that of verse and antiphon (a recurring "refrain")—a form of psalmody now becoming familiar to us Protestants. The antiphon often is more melodic than the verses, and thus is more conducive to singing by a congregation. A choir or soloist may sing the verses. (Myron Braun, *Companion to the Book of Hymns Supplement*, p. 70; Nashville: Discipleship Resources, 1982.)

174 The Lord's My Shepherd

Tune: DOMINUS REGIT ME

This metrical paraphrase of Psalm 23 is by Jane Parker Huber for *The Presbyterian Hymnal* (1990). For a biographical sketch of Huber, see hymn 128.

DOMINUS REGIT ME was composed by John Bacchus Dykes for Henry Williams Baker's text "The King of Love My Shepherd Is" (see hymn 171). They were published together in the Appendix to *Hymns Ancient and Modern* (1868). DOMINUS REGIT ME is Latin for "The Lord rules me." The tune is also known as CECILIA. For comments on Dykes, see hymn 91.

175 The Lord's My Shepherd, All My Need

Tune: EVAN

This rendering of Psalm 23 is by Christopher L. Webber for *A New Metrical Psalter* (1986). For comments on Webber, see hymn 164.

EVAN was composed by William Henry Havergal in 1846 for Robert Burns's poem "O Thou Dread Power, Who Reign'st Above." The arrangement and harmonization were made by Lowell Mason in 1850. He used the first, second, seventh, and eighth lines of the original as a psalm setting and titled it EVA in *New Carmina Sacra.* For comments on Mason, see hymn 40.

William Henry Havergal (1793–1870) was born in High Wycombe, Bucks, and educated at Merchant Taylor's School, London, and St. Edmund Hall, Oxford (B.A. 1815; M.A. 1819). He was ordained in 1816 and held several curacies before becoming rector of St. Nicholas, Worcester (1845), and honorary canon of Worcester Cathedral. In 1860 he retired to Shareshill. Havergal began composing cathedral music in the 1830s, winning the Gresham Prize Medal in 1837. His *Old Church Psalmody* (1847) drew attention to the classical school of church music and introduced the German chorale into English use. He published two volumes of sermons and *A History of the Old Hundredth Psalm Tune* (1854) as well as the periodical *Our Own Fireside.* He died at Leamington, Warwicks.

176 The Earth and All That Dwell Therein

Tune: CAITHNESS

The text is a metrical paraphrase of Psalm 24 from *The Psalter* (1912). In 1986, the Psalter Task Force of the Presbyterian

Church (U.S.A.) altered the text slightly. For comments on the source of the text, see hymn 158.

CAITHNESS was first published in the Scottish Psalter of 1635. The harmonization is altered from *The English Hymnal* (1906). For comments on the tune, see hymn 70.

177 PSALM 24

Tune: PROMISED ONE

This metrical setting of Psalm 24 is by Arlo D. Duba. It was published in *A Psalm Sampler* (1986). Duba wanted people who sang it to get the double message of the advent of the Lord (stanzas 1–3) and the triumphal entry (stanzas 4–7). It is Duba's hope that people will use the first three stanzas for the season of Advent and the last four on Palm Sunday. The refrain is by Rev. Willard F. Jabusch (1966).

A native of South Dakota, Arlo Dean Duba (b. 1929) was educated at the University of Dubuque, Iowa (B.A. 1952), and Princeton Theological Seminary (B.D. 1955; Ph.D. 1960). He did postgraduate work at The Liturgical Institute, Paris, France (1968–1969). An ordained Presbyterian minister (1955), Duba has spent most of his ministry in higher education, first as assistant professor of religion and chaplain, Westminster Choir College, Princeton, New Jersey (1957–1968), then as director of the chapel, director of admissions and lecturer in liturgics at Princeton Theological Seminary (1969–1982). From 1982–1992 Duba was university vice-president and dean of the Theological Seminary, University of Dubuque, Iowa. Four of his psalm paraphrases are in *The Presbyterian Hymnal* (1990).

PROMISED ONE is an Israeli folk melody arranged by John Ferguson (1973). It was published as the setting for "The King of Glory Comes" by Jabusch in *Sing to God* (1984).

John Ferguson was born in Cleveland, Ohio, in 1941 and educated at Oberlin College Conservatory of Music (B.Mus.), Kent State University (M.A.), and Eastman School of Music of the University of Rochester, New York (D.M.A.). He was music editor for *The Hymnal* of the United Church of Christ (1974) and simultaneously served as professor of music at Kent State

University and organist and choir director at Kent United Church of Christ. In 1978 he became organist at Central Lutheran Church, Minneapolis. Presently, Ferguson is professor of organ and church music at St. Olaf College, Northfield, Minnesota.

178 Lord, to You My Soul Is Lifted

Tune: GENEVAN 25

This new metrical rendering of Psalm 25 is by Stanley Wiersma (1930–1986) for the *Psalter Hymnal* (1987) of the Christian Reformed Church.

GENEVAN 25 was first published in the Genevan Psalter (1551), where it was the setting for Psalm 25. The tune is attributed to Louis Bourgeois. For comments on Bourgeois, see hymn 86.

The 1985 harmonization is by Howard Slenk (b. 1931) for the *Psalter Hymnal* (1987), to which he contributed twelve harmonizations. Slenk serves as editorial consultant to *Reformed Worship: Resources in Music and Liturgy*, a quarterly publication of the Christian Reformed Church in North America.

179 God Is My Strong Salvation

Tune: CHRISTUS, DER IST MEIN LEBEN

The text is by James Montgomery, who is ranked among the most important hymn writers in the English language. This metrical setting of Psalm 27 appeared in his *Songs of Zion* (1822). For comments on the author, see hymn 22.

CHRISTUS, DER IST MEIN LEBEN was composed by Melchior Vulpius as the setting for the anonymous German chorale of the same name. It was included in his *Ein schön geistlich Gesangbuch* (1609). The tune was used by Johann Sebastian Bach as the basis of Cantata 95, *Christus, der ist mein Leben*, and is the subject of two harmonizations in his *Choralgesänge*. The tune is known by several other names, including MEIN

LEBEN, BREMEN, HEIDELBERG, VULPIUS, and LINCOLN. For comments on Vulpius, see hymn 111.

180 The God of Heaven

Tune: GLORY

This paraphrase of Psalm 29 was written by Michael A. Perry in 1973. Perry recommended two word changes from the original poem. In stanza 1, line 2, "his" was changed to "whose" and in stanza 2, line 3, "Sear" to "The." For more on Perry, see hymn 602.

GLORY was composed by Norman L. Warren (b. 1934) for the text. The text and music were first published in *Psalm Praise* (1973).

181 Come Sing to God

Tune: ELLACOMBE

This paraphrase of Psalm 30 was written by Fred R. Anderson for use in Pine Street Presbyterian Church, Harrisburg, Pennsylvania. It was published as a five-stanza hymn in *Singing Psalms of Joy and Praise* (1986). The original first stanza, printed below, was deleted from *The Presbyterian Hymnal* (1990).

I will extol your name, O Lord,
  For you have rescued me.
You have not let my foes rejoice.
  You give me victory.
O Lord, my God, I cried for help,
  You saved me from the pit,
Restoring me to daily life,
  Among the saints to sit.

For a biographical sketch of Anderson and comments on the source, see hymn 159.

ELLACOMBE appeared in *Gesangbuch der Herzogl. Wirtembergischen Katholischen Hofkapelle* (1784). For comments on the tune, see hymn 89.

182 PSALM 31:9–16

This modern English language translation of Psalm 31:9–16 was prepared by Ladies of the Grail, England. For more on the Grail translation, see hymn 173.

The refrain and music were composed for the chapel services at Duke University and included in *The Psalms* (1983).

Hal H. Hopson was born in 1933 and educated at Baylor University, Waco, Texas (B.Mus.), and Southern Theological Seminary, Louisville, Kentucky (M.S.M.). Presently he is music ministry consultant, Preston Hollow Presbyterian Church, Dallas. Hopson has served on the church music faculties of Westminster Choir College, Princeton, New Jersey, and more recently at Scarritt Graduate School, Nashville. He has published more than nine hundred works, including compositions for organ, harpsichord, congregation, and anthems for children's, youth, and adult choirs. His compositions have been performed at many national music events and his cantata *God with Us* was performed on National Public Radio.

Hopson is active as a conductor and clinician, having conducted choral festivals and workshops in the United States and Europe. His biography is included in *The International Who's Who in Music* (Cambridge, England). Hopson is active in several professional organizations and has served on the national boards of the Presbyterian Association of Musicians and the Choristers Guild. As a member of the American Society of Composers, Authors, and Publishers, Hopson has received an annual award for several consecutive years. He also served on the Psalter Task Force of the Presbyterian Church (U.S.A.).

183 In You, Lord, I Have Put My Trust

Tune: IN DICH HAB' ICH GEHOFFET

This paraphrase of Psalm 31 was written by Adam Reissner (also Reusner). It was first published in *Form und Ordnung Gystlicher Gesang und Psalmen*, Augsburg (1533), and later in Wackernagel's collection. The translation is by Catherine Winkworth and appeared in *The Chorale Book for England* (1863).

Adam Reissner (1496–c. 1575) was born in Mündelsheim, Swabian Bavaria, and educated at Wittenberg. He later studied

Hebrew and Greek under Johann Reuchlin, a noted language scholar and writer (1521). Reissner was private secretary to Georg von Frundsberg until the latter's death (1528), then moved to Strassburg, and was apparently living at Frankfurt am Main at the time of his death. For comments on Winkworth, see hymn 3.

IN DICH HAB' ICH GEHOFFET was published as the setting for this text in Georg Sunderreiter's *Himmlische Harfen*, Leipzig (1573) and Nuremberg (1581).

184 How Blest Are Those

Tune: ES FLOG EIN KLEINS WALDVÖGELEIN

Fred R. Anderson wrote this paraphrase of Psalm 32 and included it in *Singing Psalms of Joy and Praise* (1986). He intended the text be set to EWING or MUNICH (see hymn 128). For a biographical sketch of Anderson, see hymn 159.

ES FLOG EIN KLEINS WALDVÖGELEIN was harmonized by George Ratcliffe Woodward from a seventeenth-century Memmingen manuscript. Woodward's harmonization was first published in *Songs of Syon* (1904). For comments on Woodward, see hymn 68.

185 PSALM 33

This psalm is classified by scholars as a hymn that was probably sung at the Autumn Festival in ancient Israel. While it is difficult to date the original hymn, many believe it to be postexilic. The text is from the New Revised Standard Version of the Bible (1989). It has been versified to coincide with the natural break in the Hebrew text by Robert C. Dentan. The psalm may be read responsively or chanted. Dentan was a member of the committee of translators for the New Revised Standard Version. Bruce M. Metzger, chair of the revision committee, wrote:

> The New Revised Standard Version of the Bible is an authorized revision of the Revised Standard Version, published in

> 1952, which was a revision of the American Standard Version, published in 1901, which, in turn, embodied earlier revisions of the King James Version, published in 1611.

The translation committee is a continuing body, ecumenical in nature. Thirty men and women, representing various Protestant denominations, Roman Catholic, Eastern Orthodox, and one Jewish scholar serve on the committee.

The psalm tone was composed by Laurence Bevenot for Ampleforth Abbey. It was published in *Worship III—Lectionary Accompaniment/Cantor Book* (1987), where it is the tone for Psalm (32) 33 for use in the Common Lectionary reading for the Second Sunday in Lent or the Fifth Sunday of Easter, Year A. The text of the refrain is from the Ladies of the Grail translation of the Psalms (1963). The setting is by Richard Proulx (see hymn 573) for *Worship III*. For comments on The Grail, see hymn 173.

186 Thy Mercy and Thy Truth, O Lord

Tune: TALLIS' ORDINAL

This paraphrase of Psalm 36 was number 94 in *The Psalter* (1912). In that volume it had an additional stanza that read:

> The workers of iniquity
> Are fallen utterly;
> They shall not triumph in their pride,
> Or drive my soul from Thee.

For comments on *The Psalter* (1912), see hymn 158.

TALLIS' ORDINAL was composed by Thomas Tallis and appeared in Matthew Parker's *The Whole Psalter translated into English Metre, which contayneth an hundred and fifty Psalmes* (c. 1567) as the setting for "Come, Holy Ghost."

Not much is known of Thomas Tallis' (1505–1585) early life. He was born probably in Kent and was organist at Dover's Benedictine Priory (1532). He also served at St. Mary-at-Hill Church (1537–1538). He moved to Waltham Abbey (1538) and Canterbury Cathedral (1541). Beginning with Henry VIII, Tallis served under four separate English monarchs, both Church of England and Roman Catholic. This fact alone stands as tribute to his musical ability and good sense. In 1575, Elizabeth I granted him and William Byrd exclusive rights to print and publish music in England. Tallis produced a wide range of secular and sacred music. (For a complete listing of Tallis' works, see Stanley Sadie, ed., *The New Grove Dictionary of Music and Musicians*, 18:541f.)

187 PSALM 34:9–22

The text of this responsorial psalm was written by Helen L. Wright in 1984 for the Psalter Task Force of the Presbyterian Church (U.S.A.). For a biographical sketch of Wright, see hymn 160.

St. Meinrad VIII is a psalm tone from the brothers of St. Meinrad Archabbey, Indiana (1973).

The refrain is by Robert E. Kreutz. For comments on Kreutz, see hymn 521.

188 Fret Not for Those Who Do Wrong Things

Tune: CULROSS

This metrical paraphrase of Psalm 37:1–10 is by Christopher L. Webber. The present form of the text was originally printed as two hymns in *A New Metrical Psalter* (1986). Our stanzas 1–3 were one text (no. 87) and our 2–5 another (no. 88). In the interest of inclusiveness, Webber offered slight alterations in the present stanzas 2 and 5. For comments on Webber, see hymn 164.

CULROSS was originally found in the Scottish Psalter (1635). The arrangement and harmonization are from *The English Hymnal* (1906).

189 As Deer Long for the Streams

Tune: ROCKINGHAM

This metrical rendering of Psalm 42:1–7 is by Christopher L. Webber. It was first published in *A New Metrical Psalter* (1986). Psalm 42 is the Common Lectionary reading for Easter Vigil, Years A, B, C, and Proper 6, Year C. For comments on Webber, see hymn 164.

ROCKINGHAM appeared in *Second Supplement to Psalmody in Miniature* (1783) and was harmonized by Edward Miller. For comments on the tune and harmonization, see hymn 100.

190 PSALM 42

This psalm marks the beginning of the subdivision known as Book II of the Psalms. It is a lament, possibly written by a cultic official ejected by Nehemiah during the fifth century B.C. For comments on the translation, see hymn 185. The refrain is by Joseph Gelineau for Ladies of the Grail, England (1963). For comments on Gelineau, see hymn 173.

As presented in *The Presbyterian Hymnal* (1990), the psalm may be read responsively or chanted.

The psalm tone was composed by Douglas Mews for the International Committee on English in the Liturgy. In *Worship III* (1986) it is one of the recommended tones for Psalm 42 (41) coupled with the Gelineau refrain.

191 God Is Our Refuge and Our Strength

Tune: WINCHESTER OLD

The text is a metrical paraphrase of Psalm 46 adapted from selection 128 of *The Psalter* (1912) (see hymn 158). It was altered by Jane Parker Huber, a member of the Psalm subcommittee for *The Presbyterian Hymnal* (1990). For a biographical sketch of Huber, see hymn 128.

WINCHESTER OLD was first published in Thomas Este's *Psalmes* (1592). For comments on the tune and the source, see hymn 58.

192 God, Our Help and Constant Refuge

Tune: MICHAEL

The text is a paraphrase of Psalm 46 by Fred R. Anderson from his collection *Singing Psalms of Joy and Praise* (1986). It was written at the request of the Psalter Task Force of the Presbyterian Church (U.S.A.). MICHAEL was the intended setting of the text. For a biographical sketch of Anderson, see hymn 159.

MICHAEL is a tune by Herbert Howells. It was composed in memory of his son who at nine died of spinal meningitis. Howells mourned the death for over three years. Anderson wrote that the circumstances surrounding the composition of the music "had significant meaning for me as I worked with this classic text of hope in the midst of strife and pain."

Herbert Norman Howells (1892–1983) was born in Gloucester and at a young age decided he wanted to compose. He won a scholarship to the Royal College of Music, where he studied with Charles Villiers Stanford (see hymn 264) and Charles Wood. In 1920 he began teaching composition at the Royal College, a position he held until after his eightieth birthday. He was the director of music at St. Paul's Girls' School, Hammersmith (1936–1962), and in 1950 he was appointed King Edward VII Professor of Music at London University.

Among his many compositions are *Hymnus Paradisi* (1938), a requiem for soloists, choir, and orchestra; *King David* (De la Mare) (1921); and "Take Him, Earth, for Cherishing" (*Motet on the Death of President Kennedy*) (1964).

Howells received an honorary doctorate from Oxford (1937), the Collard Life Fellow of the Worshipful Company of Musicians, Commander of the Order of the British Empire (1953), and Champion of Honor (1972).

193 PSALM 46

This psalm is classified as a "Song of Zion." It was probably sung at the great Autumn Festival in ancient Israel. The psalm is best known by Martin Luther's paraphrase "Ein' feste Burg ist unser Gott" (see hymn 260).

For comments on the present form of the text, see hymn 185. The psalm may be read responsively or chanted.

The accompaniment for psalm tone 8-g is by Richard Proulx (1975). The refrain is by Dom A. Gregory Murray for Ladies of the Grail, England (1963). Murray was born in 1905 and is a Benedictine monk at Downside Abbey, Bath, England. He has served as the major musical influence on English Catholic hymnody during his lifetime. Many of his tunes appear in the *Westminster Hymnal* (1940). For comments on Proulx, see hymn 573. For more on Ladies of the Grail, see hymn 173.

194 Peoples, Clap Your Hands!

Tune: GENEVAN 47

This new paraphrase of Psalm 47 is by Joy F. Patterson, a member of the Presbyterian Hymnal Committee.

Joy F. Patterson was born in 1931 in Lansing, Michigan, to a Congregational family. She became a Presbyterian at the age of twelve. She is a graduate of the University of Wisconsin (B.A. 1953; M.A. 1957). A lifelong poet, she began writing hymns in 1975, and in 1982 she became one of seven winners of the Hymn Society of America's competition "Hymns for the Whole Family of God" (see hymn 337).

Patterson, an elder in First Presbyterian Church, Wausau, Wisconsin, served as a member of the Advisory Council on Discipleship and Worship from 1980 to 1985. She attributes her interest in hymnody and poetry to her maternal grandmother, Ella Blachly Andrews, who, as an infant during the Civil War, sat in the choir loft with her mother. Although many of her forebears were poets, Patterson is the only hymn writer. She has written more than thirty hymns.

GENEVAN 47 gets its name from the psalm to which it was set in the Genevan Psalter (1551). The tune is attributed to Louis Bourgeois. For more on Bourgeois, see hymn 86. The harmonization is that of Claude Goudimel (1564).

Claude Goudimel (c. 1505–1572) was born in southern France and wrote many secular and religious works. Some scholars believe he opened a public school of music in Rome before being converted to Protestantism around 1560. He began to compose settings for the Psalter even before his conversion since the psalms were used in the Roman Catholic Church as well as in Protestant churches. Goudimel produced three settings of the Genevan Psalter (1564; 1568; 1551–1566). His third psalter, published in eight volumes of from eight to ten pieces each, presented psalm tunes in three- to eight-part motets. It was incomplete at the time of Goudimel's death in

Lyons, France, during the St. Bartholomew's Day Massacre of 1572 when thousands of Protestants were killed.

195 Have Mercy on Us, Living Lord

Tune: PTOMEY

This metrical version of Psalm 51 written by Fred R. Anderson was first published in *Singing Psalms of Joy and Praise* (1986). He intentionally set it to Hal Hopson's tune PTOMEY. Hopson exercised considerable influence on Anderson's early work and encouraged him by giving him a number of hymn tunes to use as settings. For a biographical sketch of Anderson, see hymn 159.

PTOMEY was composed by Hal H. Hopson in 1983 and first matched with the text "From Thee All Skill and Science Flow" by Charles Kingsley (1871). The tune is named for Rev. K. C. Ptomey, who at the time was pastor of Westminster Presbyterian Church, Nashville, where Hopson was music director. For a biographical sketch of Hopson, see hymn 182.

196 PSALM 51

This translation of Psalm 51 is from Ladies of the Grail. It appeared in their 1985 version of The Grail and is not found in the 1963 version. For more on Ladies of the Grail, see hymn 173.

The refrain and psalm tone are by David Clark Isele from *Praise God in Song* (1979), where they were used with a translation by Rev. Massey H. Shepherd, Jr., of the Church Divinity School of the Pacific.

The psalm as it appears in *The Presbyterian Hymnal* (1990) is from *A Psalm Sampler* (1986).

197 My Soul in Silence Waits for God

Tune: CHESHIRE

According to the author, Fred R. Anderson, this metrical version of Psalm 62 is a reworking of number 161 in *The Psalter*

(1912). While the images are similar, the language has been extensively changed for the contemporary church. Anderson began the work at the request of the Psalter Task Force of the Presbyterian Church (U.S.A.). The hymn is published here for the first time. For a biographical sketch of Anderson, see hymn 159.

CHESHIRE appeared in Este's *Psalmes* (1592) and then in *Songs of Syon* (1910). For comments on the tune and the source, see hymn 164.

198 O God, You Are My God

Tune: ST. BRIDE

This metrical version of Psalm 63 was written by Christopher L. Webber. It was published in *A New Metrical Psalter* (1986). About his version of the psalms Webber has said:

> A metrical version of the Psalter may not be a "translation" in the strict sense, but it does offer new words and music with which God's word may be sung by more people. At the least, such a fuller use of psalmody should lead to a deeper understanding of the meaning of redemption as we respond to it in worship.

For comments on Webber, see hymn 164.

ST. BRIDE was composed by Samuel Howard and first published in William Riley's *Parochial Harmony* (1762) where it was the setting for Psalm 130 and titled "St. Bridget's Tune, by Saml Howard." The tune gets its name from St. Bride's Church, which is named for St. Bridget's (or St. Bride's) Well, a spring supposedly possessing miraculous healing powers.

Samuel Howard (1710–1782) was born and died in London. He was a chorister in the Chapel Royal and later sang tenor for Handel (1732–1735). He was organist at both Clement Danes and St. Bride's Church, Fleet Street. He received a Doctor of Music degree from Cambridge (1769). Howard composed mostly secular theater music. However, he helped William Boyce prepare the three-volume anthology *Cathedral Music* (1760–1773) and wrote several hymn tunes.

199 O Lord, You Are My God

Tune: ALBERTA

This text was paraphrased from Psalm 63 by John G. Dunn in 1983. Dunn is principal and musical director of the Boston Archdiocesan Choir School at St. Paul's, Cambridge, Massachusetts.

ALBERTA was composed by William Henry Harris (1883–1973) in 1930. Harris was an English organist and composer who was born in London and won an organ scholarship to the Royal College of Music in 1899. While assistant organist at Lichfield Cathedral, he taught harmony at Birmingham and the Midland Institute. In 1923 he joined the Royal College of Music as professor of organ and harmony and remained there until 1953. From 1933 to 1961 he was organist at St. George's Chapel, Windsor Castle. Harris was director of musical studies at the Royal School of Church Music from 1956 to 1961. Harris wrote music for the coronations of 1937 and 1953 but is also remembered for his setting of Francis Thompson's *The Hound of Heaven* (1919).

200 To Bless the Earth

Tune: CHRISTUS, DER IST MEIN LEBEN

This paraphrase of Psalm 65 is number 171 in *The Psalter* (1912) where it appears in three stanzas of eight lines. In that collection it is titled "God in Nature." The present text is altered from stanzas 2 and 3 of the original. For more on the source, see hymn 158.

CHRISTUS, DER IST MEIN LEBEN: For comments on the tune, see hymn 179. For comments on the composer, Melchior Vulpius, see hymn 111.

201 Praise Is Your Right, O God, in Zion

Tune: GENEVAN 65

This new metrical version of Psalm 65 was made by Stanley Wiersma (1930–1986) for the *Psalter Hymnal* (1987) of the Christian Reformed Church.

GENEVAN 65 is from the Genevan Psalter (1543). It was harmonized by Dale Grotenhuis for the *Psalter Hymnal* (1987). Grotenhuis (b. 1931) served on the revision committee for that work and is on the faculty of Dordt College in Sioux Center, Iowa.

202 PSALM 67

This psalm of thanksgiving is probably postexilic. The exact setting of its origin is debated. One possible explanation is the Feast of Tabernacles, which like the psalm looks to both past and future blessings from God. In its present form the psalm may be read responsively or chanted. For comments on the translation, see hymn 185.

The psalm tone is by Laurence Bevenot, originally for Ampleforth Abbey. The refrain is by Marie Kremer for *Worship III—Lectionary Accompaniment/Cantor Book* (1987). Psalm 67 is the Common Lectionary reading for the Sixth Sunday of Easter, Year C.

203 God of Mercy, God of Grace

Tune: IMPACT

This metrical paraphrase of Psalm 67 was written by Henry F. Lyte. The hymn was first published in *The Spirit of the Psalms* (1834). In 1984 the text was altered by the Psalter Task Force of the Presbyterian Church (U.S.A.).

Henry Francis Lyte (1793–1847) was born in Kelso, Scotland, and was a gifted writer, winning three poetry prizes while a student at Trinity College, Dublin. He had intended to be a physician but was led into the Christian ministry. He was ordained in 1815 and served small parishes throughout his ministry. He died at Nice while recuperating from tuberculosis. He also published *Tales on the Lord's Prayer in Verse* (1826) and *Poems, Chiefly Religious* (1833).

IMPACT was composed in 1973 by David G. Wilson (b. 1940) for the Church Pastoral Aid Society, London. It was published in *A Psalm Sampler* (1986) as the setting for Lyte's text.

204 PSALM 72

This is a royal psalm which was probably written in the preexilic era. It is one of several that came to be known as messianic by both the Jewish tradition and the early church. The psalm may be read responsively or chanted.

For comments on the source of the text, see hymn 185.

The psalm tone was composed by Laurence Bevenot for the use of Ampleforth Abbey (1986). The refrain was composed by John Schiavone (1975).

205 All Hail to God's Anointed

Tune: ROCKPORT

This text by James Montgomery is a metrical setting of Psalm 72. It was written as an ode and sung at a British Moravian settlement on Christmas Day in 1821. The next year Montgomery recited the hymn at a missionary meeting in the Pitt Street Wesleyan Chapel in Liverpool, where it was heard by Dr. Adam Clarke. Clarke was so impressed by the hymn he included it in his *Commentary on the Bible* (1822). It was also included in Montgomery's *Songs of Zion* (1822). The original first phrase was altered in 1984 from "Hail to the Lord's anointed" to "All hail to God's anointed." For comments on the author, see hymn 22.

ROCKPORT was composed in 1938 by T. Tertius Noble. It was named for the city of Rockport, Massachusetts, where Noble died.

Thomas Tertius Noble (1867–1953) was born in Bath, England, educated at the Royal College of Music, and was a noted composer and organist. He founded the York Symphony in 1898 and revived the York Music Festivals. He came to the

United States and served as organist and choir director at St. Thomas Church, Fifth Avenue, New York City (1912–1947), where he established an Anglican musical tradition at the church.

206 O Hear Our Cry, O Lord

Tune: VINEYARD HAVEN

This paraphrase of Psalm 80 was written by Fred R. Anderson. It appeared in *Singing Psalms of Joy and Praise* (1986). Anderson wrote the poem intending that it would be sung to MARION (see hymn 145). He says:

> The refrain of that tune was exceptionally well suited to the poem's refrain "O come, Lord, come, restore and save us now." The committee's choice of VINEYARD HAVEN was a surprise. And yet, now I prefer Dirksen's tune even more than the one to which the test was originally written.

For a biographical sketch of Anderson, see hymn 159.

VINEYARD HAVEN was composed by Richard Wayne Dirksen and appeared on a leaflet in 1974. He wrote it as a processional for the installation of the Archbishop of the National Cathedral, Washington, D.C. It was the setting of "Rejoice, Ye Pure in Heart!" (see hymn 146). In only three years the popularity of the tune led to its inclusion in three hymnals. Today this tune, which Erik Routley called the "American ABBOT'S LEIGH," is included in most hymn collections.

Richard Wayne Dirksen (b. 1921) is canon precentor of Washington's National Cathedral.

207 How Lovely, Lord

Tune: MERLE'S TUNE

This paraphrase of Psalm 84 is by Arlo D. Duba. While serving on the Psalter Task Force of the Presbyterian Church (U.S.A.) in 1984, Duba was struck by the fact that metered versions of the psalm did not seem to carry with them the understanding of God's house being a wonderfully pleasing place in which to be. He thought of the peace and tranquillity represented in Johannes Brahms' "How Lovely Is Thy Dwelling Place" and left the room humming MERLE'S TUNE. Duba recalls, "Once I had the first line the rest of the paraphrase just came to me." For a biographical sketch of Duba, see hymn 177.

MERLE'S TUNE was composed by Hal H. Hopson for Michael A. Perry's paraphrase of the Song of Zechariah in 1983. For more on the tune, see hymn 602.

208 PSALM 84

Most scholars believe this psalm to be part of the Feast of Tabernacles celebrating the kingship of God. As such it may be understood as a Song of Zion. The present versification may be read responsively or chanted. For comment on the translation, see hymn 185.

The psalm tone was prepared by Chrysogonus Waddell for the use of Gethsemani Abbey in Kentucky. The refrain was composed by A. Gregory Murray (see hymn 193) for Ladies of the Grail (1963). For comments on the source, see hymn 173.

209 My Song Forever Shall Record

Tune: ST. PETERSBURG

The original source of this metrical rendering of Psalm 89 is *The Psalter* (1912). There it appeared as numbers 241 and 242. *The Presbyterian Hymnal* text is a composite of those texts as it appeared in *The Hymnbook* (1955) set to the tune ST. PETERSBURG. Our stanza 1 is stanza 1 plus the first two phrases of stanza 2 of *The Psalter*, number 241. Our stanza 2 is stanza 1 of number 242 and the first two poetic lines of stanza 4 of number 242. Stanza 3 uses the first two phrases of stanza 8 plus all of stanza 9 of number 241 in the original and stanza 4 uses number 242, stanza 2, and the last poetic lines of stanza 3. For more on *The Psalter* (1912), see hymn 158.

ST. PETERSBURG is adapted from the 1822 mass composed by Dimitri Bortniansky (also Bortnyansky). In the choral book of Johann Heinrich Tscherlitzky (1825) the tune was used as the setting of "Ich bete an die Macht der Liebe." Tscherlitzky titled it ST. PETERSBURG after the church and city where he was organist.

Dimitri Stepanovitch Bortniansky (1751–1825) was born in Glukhov, Ukraine, and when just eight years old was admitted to the imperial choir school where he is thought to have studied with Galuppi. He later studied in Italy for a ten-year period. While there, he wrote his first operas. In 1779, Bortniansky returned to Russia, where he was appointed Kapellmeister to the imperial court. Paul I appointed him music director in 1796. His compositions have influenced later Russian composers, particularly Rachmaninoff and Tchaikovsky. Bortniansky composed seven operas as well as other vocal and instrumental music. In 1881, Peter Tchaikovsky edited Bortniansky's sacred works amassing ten volumes. Bortniansky died in St. Petersburg.

210 Our God, Our Help in Ages Past

Tune: ST. ANNE

The text is a metrical version of Psalm 90:1–5 by Isaac Watts. It was published in *The Psalms of David* (1719) under the title "Man Frail, and God Eternal." About this hymn John Julian wrote, "It is undoubtedly one of his finest compositions and his best paraphrase."

John Wesley (see hymn 253) altered the first line to read "O God" for his *Collection of Psalms and Hymns* (1737). The original has been restored here. However, the Presbyterian Hymnal Committee altered the fourth stanza to read "Soon bears us all away" from "Bears all her sons away" for inclusiveness.

For a biographical sketch of Watts, see hymn 40.

ST. ANNE was attributed to William Croft. It was first published anonymously in Tate and Brady's *A Supplement to the New Version of the Psalms* (6th ed., 1708) as the setting for "As Pants the Hart for Cooling Streams" (Psalm 42). The name of the tune comes from St. Anne's Church, Soho, where Croft was organist from 1700 to 1711. The tune proved a favorite of musicians. Handel (see hymn 40) used it in his anthem "O Praise the Lord" (1734) and J. S. Bach (see hymn 17), in his Fugue in E-flat Major ("St. Anne's Fugue") at the end of his Catechism chorales for organ.

William Croft (1678–1727) was born a few miles southeast of Stratford-on-Avon, England. He was a chorister in the Chapel Royal and was a student of John Blow. In 1708 he succeeded Blow as organist of Westminster Abbey. He received his Doctor of Music degree from Oxford University in 1713.

His publication *Musica Sacra* (1724) is the first example of English church music in score. Previously, choirs used part books. With Henry Purcell, Croft wrote a burial service which was the best of its time. Today Croft is best remembered for his hymn tunes.

211 Lord, You Have Been Our Dwelling Place

Tune: LOBT GOTT IN SEINEM HEILIGTUM

Fred R. Anderson wrote this paraphrase of Psalm 90 for use in Pine Street Presbyterian Church, Harrisburg, Pennsylvania. The congregation sings it to PENTECOST or ROCKINGHAM OLD. It was published twice in 1986: in *A Psalm Sampler*, with the present setting, and in *Singing Psalms of Joy and Praise*, with four suggested tunes. For a biographical sketch of Anderson, see hymn 159.

LOBT GOTT IN SEINEM HEILIGTUM was composed by Heinrich Schütz, and published in *Psalmen Davids, in Teutsche Reimen gebrachte durch D. Cornelium Beckern* (1628). The so-called Becker Psalter is numbers 97a–256a in W. Bittinger's catalog *Schütz-Werke-Verzeichnis: Kleine Ausgabe* (1960).

Heinrich Schütz (baptized Oct. 9, 1585–1672) was the greatest German composer of the seventeenth century and the first to reach international prominence. His influence was felt for more than two centuries after his death.

In 1598, after hearing the young Henrich (as Schütz signed himself) sing, the Landgrave Moritz of Hessen-Kassel began a campaign to have the boy study at Kassel. In 1599, Christoph Schütz took his son to the landgrave's seat, where he served as a choirboy and pursued his education showing particular facility in Greek, Latin, and French. After he lost his treble voice, he set out for the University of Marburg, where he studied law. But under the sponsorship of the landgrave, Heinrich went to Venice (1609) and studied with Giovanni Gabrieli until Gabrieli's death in 1612. In 1613 he returned to Germany, once again studying law while serving as organist to the landgrave. He was lent to Johann Georg I of Saxony (1614) and subsequently became director of the chapel, a position he held the rest of his life. The untimely death of his wife after six years of marriage (1625) led him to devote himself to the composition of church music. After several petitions Schütz was granted leave to study with Claudio Monteverdi and once again set out for Venice. For much of his life the Thirty Years' War obstructed his work, and he spent time moving from court to court in Europe, finally settling in Dresden in 1641, where he died.

212 Within Your Shelter, Loving God

Tune: ABBEY

This text was written by John G. Dunn in 1982. For a biographical sketch of Dunn, see hymn 199.

ABBEY is one of the twelve common tunes from the Scottish Psalter, *CL Psalms of David* (1615). This collection was the work of Andro Hart (d. 1621), a Scottish bookseller and printer. It was the first psalter to name tunes.

213 God, Our Lord, a King Remaining

Tune: BRYN CALFARIA

This metrical version of Psalm 93 was written by John Keble.

John Keble (1792–1866) was born in Fairford and educated first at home and then Oxford (B.A. at age eighteen). He remained at Oxford as a tutor and examiner. He was ordained (1816) and served with his father at Fairford until the latter's death (1835). He married that same year and moved to Hursley, where he was vicar the remainder of his life. According to Cardinal Newman it was the "Assize Sermon" Keble preached at Oxford in 1833 that started the Oxford Movement. Although Keble was a leader in the Tractarian movement, unlike Newman and Pusey, he never left the Church of England. The profits from his book *The Christian Year* (1827) were used to rebuild the church at Hursley. He wrote other books, one hundred hymns, and twelve volumes of sermons. He also translated several hymns.

BRYN CALFARIA was composed by William Owen (1852) and was published in *Y Perl Cerddorol*, vol. 2 (1886). For another harmonization of the tune and a biographical sketch of the composer, see hymn 154.

214 O Come and Sing Unto the Lord

Tune: IRISH

This versification of Psalm 95 is from *The Psalter* (1912), where it is number 256. In *The Hymnbook* (1955) the original text was altered to remove the word "Jehovah" in the first line of stanzas 1 and 3. Jane Parker Huber made further alterations of stanzas 3 and 4 in *The Presbyterian Hymnal* (1990). The original is printed below:

3. Jehovah is a mighty King,
   Above all gods His throne;
   The depths of earth are in His hand,
   The mountains are His own.
4. To Him the spacious sea belongs,
   He made its waves and tides;
   And by His hand the rising land
   Was formed, and still abides.

IRISH: The source of this tune is *A Collection of Hymns and Sacred Poems,* Dublin (1749). In Caleb Ashworth's *Collection of Tunes,* Part 1 (1775), compiled for J. Buckland of London, it appears as selection number 31 and is given the name IRISH TUNE. The only known copy of this book is in the Warrington Collection housed at Pittsburgh Theological Seminary, Pennsylvania. Some scholars believe the tune to be connected with John Wesley. There are those who say Wesley edited the Dublin collection when in Ireland in 1749.

215 Come, Sing with Joy to God

Tune: TO GOD WITH GLADNESS

This paraphrase of Psalm 95 was written by Arlo D. Duba for the Psalter Task Force of the Presbyterian Church (U.S.A.). It was specifically written with this tune in mind. Psalm 95 celebrates the enthronement of God as King and refers to the testing (*massah*) of God by the Israelites (see Ex. 17:1–7). For more on Duba, see hymn 177.

TO GOD WITH GLADNESS was composed by David Clark Isele for *Worship* (1979). For comments on Isele, see hymn 196.

216 O Sing a New Song to the Lord

Tune: GONFALON ROYAL

The hymn text is a paraphrase of Psalm 96 by Charles Hutchison Gabriel and is a departure from his usual hymn writing.

Charles Hutchison Gabriel (1856–1932) was born in Wilton, Iowa. He was one of the most prolific gospel song writers of his day. He served as music editor of Homer Rodeheaver's Publishing Company, now known as Word Music, from 1912 until his death. Gabriel edited more than one hundred fifty collections of religious music, including gospel songbooks, Sunday school songbooks, male and treble voice chorus books, children's songbooks and cantatas, Christmas cantatas as well as numerous books on musical instruction, and began several singing schools all without the benefit of any formal music education or lessons.

It has been estimated that Gabriel was involved in the writing of more than eight thousand gospel songs. Like most early gospel writers he wrote both text and music for his hymns. He died in Los Angeles.

GONFALON ROYAL was composed by Percy Carter Buck as a setting for "The Royal Banners Forward Go" for the boys at Harrow School, where he served as director of music (1902–1927). Gonfalon is an old Norman-English word meaning "banner." The present form of the music is from the *Revised Church Hymnary* (1927).

Percy Carter Buck (1871–1947) was trained in organ and

served as organist of Worcester College, Oxford, Wells Cathedral, and Bristol Cathedral. He was professor of music at Trinity College, Dublin, from 1910 to 1920. In 1925 he was appointed King Edward Professor of Music at the University of London and also taught at the Royal College of Music. He was knighted in 1937.

He wrote several volumes, including *The Scope of Music*, and with MacPherson edited *The English Psalter* (1925) and singly edited *The Oxford Song Book* (1929) and *The Oxford Nursery Song Book* (1934). He was considered a leader in English music education.

217 O Sing a New Song

This is an antiphonal setting of Psalm 96. The text was paraphrased by Helen L. Wright, the chair of the Psalter Task Force of the Presbyterian Church (U.S.A.) in 1983. Hal H. Hopson, also a member of that task force, composed the tune and refrain. It was first published in *A Psalm Sampler* (1986). For a biographical sketch of Wright, see hymn 160. For more on Hopson, see hymn 182.

The refrain is to be sung once by a solo voice (cantor) or choir and then repeated by the congregation. Then the cantor or choir continue to sing the versicles and at the appropriate time the congregation sings the refrain. The refrain is to be sung when the (*R*) appears in the text.

218 New Songs of Celebration Render

Tune: RENDEZ À DIEU

This paraphrase of Psalm 98 was written in 1972 by Erik Routley. It was published in *Ecumenical Praise* (1977) and *Cantate Domino* (1980). The text as presented here was slightly altered from the original by the Psalter Task Force of the Presbyterian Church (U.S.A.) in 1984.

Erik Routley (1917–1982) was born in Brighton, England, and educated at Magdalen College, Oxford (B.A. 1940); Mansfield College (B.Div. 1946); and Oxford (D.Phil. 1952). He was ordained and became pastor of Dartford Congregational Church in 1943. He served churches in Edinburgh (1959) and Newcastle-upon-Tyne (1967) before coming to the United States as visiting professor and director of music, Princeton Theological Seminary, January 1975. In September 1975 he became professor of church music at Westminster Choir College, Princeton, New Jersey, and in 1978 became director of the chapel. Regarded as one of the most influential persons in English and American church music during the twentieth century, Routley lectured and published extensively. Among his many writings are *The Church and Music: An Enquiry Into the History, the Nature and the Scope of Christian Judgment of Music* (1950; enl. 1967); *An Historical Study of Christian Hymnology: Its Development and Discipline* (1952; pub. as *The Music of Christian Hymnody*, 1957); *The English Carol* (1958); and *A Panorama of Christian Hymnody* (1979). For a complete bibliography, see Robin A. Leaver and James H. Litton, eds., *Duty and Delight: Routley Remembered* (Carol Stream, Ill.: Hope Publishing Co., 1985), pp. 243f. He died while leading a church music seminar in Nashville.

RENDEZ À DIEU was composed or adapted by Louis Bourgeois (1543). It was published in the Strassburg Psalter of 1545, and a revised version appeared in the Genevan Psalter (1551). Routley's text was written for this tune. For more on Bourgeois, see hymn 86.

219 To God Compose a Song of Joy

Tune: KEDDY

The hymn began as a translation of Psalm 98 by Ruth C. Duck for a Hebrew language class. She then paraphrased it for a class in hymnody at Boston University School of Theology.

Born in 1947, Ruth C. Duck was educated at Southwestern-at-Memphis University, now Rhodes College (B.A. 1969), Chicago Theological Seminary (M.Div. 1973), and Boston University School of Theology (Th.D. 1989). She received an honorary Doctor of Divinity degree from Chicago Theological Seminary (1983).

Ordained in the United Church of Christ in 1973 she has served churches in Wisconsin, Illinois, and Massachusetts. Presently, she is assistant professor of worship at Garrett-Evangelical Theological Seminary, Evanston, Illinois. She has edited or co-edited several books, including *Everflowing Streams: Songs for Worship* (1981), *Bread for the Journey: Resources for Worship* (1981), *Flames of the Spirit: Resources for Worship* (1985), and *Touch Holiness: Resources for Worship* (1990).

KEDDY was composed by Edwin R. Taylor for the text "O God, Your Hand Is Guiding Us" by Beulah Keddy and is named for her. Taylor's tune was first sung on May 3, 1987, at the Fenton United Methodist Church in Michigan at the church's one hundred fiftieth anniversary celebration.

220 All People That on Earth Do Dwell

Tune: OLD HUNDREDTH

This metrical version of Psalm 100 by William Kethe was published in the Anglo-Genevan Psalter (1561) and Day's *Psalter* (1562) where the spelling of "folck" (i.e., folk) was changed to "folke." In the original text, stanza 1, line 3, read "him serve with fear" but the Scottish Psalter (1650) changed the word "fear" to "mirth" because the biblical psalm contains the phrase "Serve the Lord with gladness." That collection also changed stanza 2, line 1, from "The Lord you know is" to "Know that the Lord."

Although little is known of William Kethe (active 1555–1593), he was a Scotsman who fled to the Continent during the reign of Mary, was chaplain to the English soldiers at Havre under the Earl of Warwick (1563 and again in 1569), and contributed twenty-five texts to the Anglo-Genevan Psalter. His texts were included in the Sternhold and Hopkins Psalter (1562). He was also one of the translators of the *Geneva Bible.* He lived in England as rector of Childe Okeford in Dorsetshire from 1561 until his death in 1608.

OLD HUNDREDTH was composed or adapted by Louis Bourgeois for *Trente quatre pseaumes de David* (1551) as the setting for Theodore Beza's versification of Psalm 134, "Or sus, serviteurs du Seigneur." In Day's *Psalter* (1562) the tune was associated with Kethe's text and the two have been linked ever since, hence the name OLD HUNDREDTH. Several variations in the rhythm and harmonization of the tune are in common usage. For comments on Bourgeois, see hymn 86.

221

Tune: OLD HUNDREDTH (*Fauxbourdon*)

This setting of OLD HUNDREDTH with the melody in the tenor was composed by John Dowland for Thomas Ravenscroft's *The Whole Booke of Psalmes* (1621).

It is not certain where John Dowland (1563–1626) was born. Arguments have been made for London, Westminster, and Dublin, but he himself attested to the year. Dowland went to Paris in 1580 and returned sometime around 1584. He was educated at Christ Church, Oxford (B.Mus. 1588), Cambridge (B.Mus., date unknown), and from 1622 given the title "Doctor" although the institution is unknown. He is considered one of the outstanding English composers and lutenists of his day. Dowland contributed musical settings to Thomas Este's *The Whole Booke of Psalmes* (1592) as well as to Thomas Ravenscroft's *The Whole Booke of Psalmes* (1621). He died in London.

222 PSALM 103

This psalm has been classified by many scholars as an individual thanksgiving psalm in the form of a hymn. It was written in the late postexilic era. The psalm may be read responsively or chanted. For comments on the translation, see hymn 185.

The psalm tone and refrain were composed by Richard Proulx (1975) and published in the Psalter section of *Worship III* (1986). For more on Proulx, see hymn 573.

223 O My Soul, Bless Your Redeemer

Tune: STUTTGART

This metrical paraphrase of Psalm 103 first appeared as "O My Soul, Bless God the Father" in *The Book of Psalms*, published by the United Presbyterian Church of North America (1871). It was altered slightly for *The Worshipbook—Services and Hymns* (1972). The committee further altered it for inclusion in *The Presbyterian Hymnal* (1990).

STUTTGART, originally in Witt's *Psalmodia Sacra* (1715), appears here as published in *Hymns Ancient and Modern* (1861). For further comments on the tune, the original source, and an additional harmonization, see hymn 1.

224 Bless the Lord, My Soul and Being

Tune: RUSTINGTON

The text by Fred R. Anderson was originally intended to be used with Beethoven's HYMN TO JOY (see hymn 464), but according to Anderson "the tune RUSTINGTON gives the text a new dimension." The text was first published in *Singing Psalms of Joy and Praise* (1986) with the first line reading "Bless the Lord, with all my being." For a biographical sketch of Anderson, see hymn 159.

RUSTINGTON was composed by C. Hubert H. Parry and first appeared in *The Westminster Abbey Hymn-Book* (1897) as the setting for the text "Praise the Rock of Our Salvation" by Benjamin Webb (see hymn 83). The tune is named for the town of Rustington, Sussex, England, where Parry lived toward the end of his life.

Charles Hubert Hastings Parry (1848–1918) was born in Bournemouth and died in Rustington. He studied with George Elvey (see hymn 151) and obtained a Bachelor of Music degree from Oxford while still at Eton. He received a Bachelor of Arts degree in composition from Exeter College, Oxford (1870), after which he studied with Edward Dannreuther, who introduced him to Wagner's music.

In addition to his many compositions he contributed to the 1877 edition of George Grove's *Dictionary of Music and Musicians.* Parry was a member of the staff of the Royal College of Music (1883) and succeeded Grove as its director in 1894. He succeeded John Stainer (see hymn 509) as professor of music at Oxford in 1900, a position he resigned in 1908. He made several lasting contributions to the study of music history, including *The Art of Music* (1893); the third volume of the Oxford History of Music, *The Music of the Seventeenth Century* (1902); and the critical biography *Johann Sebastian Bach: The Story of the Development of a Great Personality* (1909). Most of his songs were collected in twelve volumes of *English Lyrics* (1885–1920). Parry was granted honorary doctorates in music from Cambridge (1883), Oxford (1884), and Dublin (1891) and a Doctor of Civil Law degree from Durham University (1894). He was knighted in 1898.

225 Praise the Lord!

Tune: LAUDATE PUERI

This paraphrase of Psalm 113 is by Marjorie Jillson and was included in *Five Hymns* (1973). She gives Heinz Werner Zimmermann (see below) credit for the first stanza; she wrote the remaining three.

Marjorie Jillson was born in 1931 in Detroit and graduated from the College of Wooster, Ohio (B.A. in Religion, 1953). She was employed in various secretarial positions by the U.S. Government, Washington, D.C. She returned to Detroit and worked as a dental secretary (1973–1980) until she became ill. A member of Grosse Point Memorial Presbyterian Church, Jillson wrote the texts for *Three Simple Melodies* (1972) and *Five Hymns* (1973). The music for both collections was composed by Zimmermann.

LAUDATE PUERI was composed by Heinz Werner Zimmermann for this text. Zimmermann was born in 1930 in Freiburg, Germany, and began composing at age sixteen. He studied at Heidelberg Church Music Institute and received a state diploma for composition and theory from State Music Academy in Freiburg. He was appointed lecturer in theory and composition at Heidelberg (1954–1963). In 1963, he was appointed principal of Spandau Church Music School, Berlin, where he also teaches composition. He has lectured in both Great Britain and the United States. In 1967, Zimmermann was granted an honorary doctorate by Wittenberg University, Springfield, Ohio. He has composed many works especially for choir with varied instrumental accompaniments. His compositions contain what Zimmermann calls "Polystylistic polyphony, i.e., the attempt to combine established contrapuntal techniques, the vocal character of Distler and the rhythms of jazz."

226 Sing Praise Unto the Name of God

Tune: GENEVAN 36

This paraphrase of Psalm 113 by Fred R. Anderson was originally set to the tune MELITA in *Singing Psalms of Joy and Praise* (1986). The text was somewhat altered in *A Psalm Sampler* (1986) and set to GENEVAN 36 (incorrectly titled GENEVAN 113) in that collection. Anderson was unhappy with what he considered "the sampler's distorted rhyme scheme which made the hymn almost unsingable" and agreed to rework the text for *The Presbyterian Hymnal* (1990) and set it to GENEVAN 36. For a biographical sketch of Anderson, see hymn 159.

GENEVAN 36 was composed by Matthäus Greiter and first published in the *Strassburger Kirchenampt* (1525). In Calvin's (see hymn 457) *Aulcuns Pseaumes et cantiques mys en chant* (1539) it is the setting for Psalms 36 and 68. The tune is also known as GENEVAN 68. A truncated form of the tune appears under various names, including OLD 113TH, O MENSCH, BEWEIN', and LUCERNE (see hymn 253).

Matthäus Greiter (c. 1495–1550), German composer and cantor, was born in Aichach and educated at Freiburg University, where it is believed he studied theology. He became a monk and cantor at Strassburg Minster but in 1524 was persuaded to become a Protestant. He married and on October 8, 1524, became a citizen of Strassburg. He taught music at the Gymnasium Argentinense (1538) while continuing at the minster, now in Protestant hands. Charged with adultery in 1546, he lost most of his appointments and reverted to Catholicism in 1549. In 1550 he was reinstated as cantor and music teacher at Strassburg Minster which was once again Roman Catholic. He died of the plague. Greiter published the primer *Elemantale musicum* (1544).

227 Not Unto Us, O Lord of Heaven

Tune: MEADVILLE

This metrical rendering of Psalm 115 was first published in *The Psalter* (1912) (no. 308), where it had five stanzas. *The Presbyterian Hymnal* (1990) contains the first three stanzas from the earlier collection. The language has been slightly altered from the original.

MEADVILLE was composed by Walter Pelz and adapted by W. Thomas Jones. For comments on the tune and the composer, see hymn 152.

228 O Thou, My Soul, Return in Peace

Tune: MARTYRDOM

This metrical rendering of Psalm 116 is a composite. Stanzas 1 and 2 are from the *Murrayfield Psalms* (1950). The remaining four stanzas are from *The Psalter* (1912) (no. 313). Stanza 4 of the original has been omitted. The composite was published in *Rejoice in the Lord* (1985) for the Reformed Church in America. A few additional alterations were made by the Presbyterian Hymnal Committee.

MARTYRDOM: For comments on the tune, the composer Hugh Wilson, and Robert Smith, see hymn 78.

229 From All That Dwell Below the Skies

Tune: LASST UNS ERFREUEN

The hymn is a paraphrase of Psalm 117 by Isaac Watts. The original hymn had two stanzas (our stanzas 1 and 3, unaltered). Its present form is from the *York Pocket Hymn Book* (1781) edited by Robert Spence, a Methodist class leader and bookseller from York. For a biographical sketch of Watts, see hymn 40.

LASST UNS ERFREUEN is from *Ausserlesene Catholische Geistliche Kirchengesäng* (1623). The composer is not known but the first line of the melody and the first line of the sixteenth-century tune VERZAGE NICHT, DU HÄUFLEIN KLEIN (see GENEVAN 36, hymn 226, and OLD 113TH, hymn 253) by Matthäus Greiter are the same.

The present harmonization is by Ralph Vaughan Williams for *The English Hymnal* (1906), where it was the setting for "Ye Watchers and Ye Holy Ones" (see hymn 451).

230 This Is the Day the Lord Hath Made

Tune: NUN DANKET ALL' UND BRINGET EHR'

This paraphrase of Psalm 118 by Isaac Watts was first published in *The Psalms of David* (1719), where he headed it "Hosanna; The Lord's Day; or Christ's Resurrection, and Our Salvation." Watts's intention was for it to be sung on Easter Day or on Sundays. The text was altered slightly for inclusion in *The Presbyterian Hymnal* (1990). For a biographical sketch of Watts, see hymn 40.

NUN DANKET ALL' UND BRINGET EHR' was composed by Johann Crüger as the setting for Paul Gerhardt's "Nun danket all' und bringet Ehr' " in the second edition of *Praxis Pietatis Melica* (1647). Forty-five editions of *Praxis* were published in Berlin and twelve or more editions came from Frankfurt in the one hundred years following 1640. For a biographical sketch of Crüger, see hymn 93.

231 PSALM 118:14–24

Psalm 118 concludes the "Egyptian Hallel" (Psalms 113–118) and according to the Mishnah it was first used during the Feast of Tabernacles. Traditionally Psalms 113–118 were sung at the annual feasts, including Passover. Psalms 113–114 were sung before the meal and 115–118 after it. In the Common Lectionary, Psalm 118:14–24 is recommended for use on Easter Day each year. For comments on the translation, see hymn 185. The psalm may be read responsively or sung.

The refrain is by A. Gregory Murray for the Grail publication of 1963. The psalm tone was composed by Laurence Bevenot for use at Ampleforth Abbey (1986). For comments on Murray, see hymn 193. For more on Ladies of the Grail, see hymn 173.

232 PSALM 118:19–29

In the Common Lectionary, Psalm 118:19–29 is recommended to be read or sung on Palm Sunday each year. For further comments on the psalm, its tone by Laurence Bevenot, and refrain by A. Gregory Murray, see hymn 231.

233 Blest Are the Uncorrupt in Heart

Tune: RICHMOND

Fred R. Anderson wrote this paraphrase of Psalm 119:1–16 for his congregation at Pine Street Presbyterian Church in Harrisburg, Pennsylvania. It was published in *Singing Psalms of Joy and Praise* (1986). According to Anderson, stanza 5 represents his "struggle with Trinitarian language, especially the search for metaphors to describe the first person of the Trinity without traditional masculine imagery." For a biographical sketch of Anderson, see hymn 159.

RICHMOND was composed by Thomas Haweis and appeared in *Carmina Christo; or Hymns to the Saviour. Designed for the use and comfort of those who worship the Lamb that was slain* (1792). In that collection it was the setting of "O Thou from Whom All Goodness Flows." It was adapted by Samuel Webbe, Jr., in 1808 and named for his friend Leigh Richmond, rector of Turvey, Bedfordshire, England. The tune is also known as CHESTERFIELD and SPA FIELDS CHAPEL.

Thomas Haweis (1734–1820) was born at Truro, Cornwall, and studied for a career in medicine. He later studied for the ministry at Christ Church, Oxford, and Magdalen Hall. In 1757 he became curate of St. Mary Magdalen's Church, Oxford. He was assistant chaplain under Martin Madan at St. Luke's Hospital, then rector of All Saints, Aldwinkle (1764), and chaplain to Lady Huntingdon's chapel (1768). He died at Bath. Some of his other works include *A History of the Church, A Translation of the New Testament*, and *A Commentary on the Holy Bible.*

Samuel Webbe, Jr. (1770–1843), adapted the tune. He was organist at Paradise Street Unitarian Church, Liverpool (1798). Later he succeeded his father as organist at the Spanish Ambassador's Chapel, London (1817), and then St. Nicholas' Church and St. Patrick's Roman Catholic Chapel, Liverpool.

234 I to the Hills Will Lift My Eyes

Tune: DUNDEE

The text is a metrical setting of Psalm 121 from *The Psalter* (1912) where it is number 344. It was slightly altered by the Presbyterian Hymnal Committee. For comments on the source, see hymn 158.

DUNDEE is one of the twelve common tunes in Andro Hart's Scottish Psalter, *CL Psalms of David* (1615), where it is named FRENCH. In Thomas Ravenscroft's *The Whole Booke of Psalmes* (1621) it is called DUNDY and indexed as Scottish.

235 With Joy I Heard My Friends Exclaim

Tune: GONFALON ROYAL

The hymn is a metrical version of Psalm 122 (no. 350) from *The Psalter* (1912). The text was slightly altered for *The Presbyterian Hymnal* (1990). For comments on the source, see hymn 158.

GONFALON ROYAL is by Percy Carter Buck. For comments on Buck and the tune, see hymn 216.

236 Now Israel May Say

Tune: OLD 124TH

This metrical rendering of Psalm 124 is from *The Psalter* (1912) where it is number 353. In that collection it bears the heading

"Divine Deliverance." In *The Hymnbook* (1955) the phrase "Our only help is in God's holy name" was substituted for "Our only help is in Jehovah's Name." *The Presbyterian Hymnal* (1990) contains one additional alteration. "Cruel foes" in stanza 1 has been substituted for "cruel men."

OLD 124TH is from the Genevan Psalter (1551), where it is the setting for Psalm 124. Though many arrangements of the tune are available, the present one is from *The Hymnal* (1933), which is a slight modification of the arrangement in *The English Hymnal* (1906). It is said that when the Duke of Savoy was defeated in his attack against Geneva, December 12, 1602, the grateful people sang Psalm 124 to this tune.

237 When God Delivered Israel

Tune: SHEAVES

This paraphrase of Psalm 126 was written by Michael A. Saward (b. 1932) and first published in *Psalm Praise* (1973). Originally stanza 2, line 2, read "Could not deny his power" instead of "that power."

SHEAVES was the setting for this text in *Psalm Praise* (1973). The music was composed by Norman L. Warren (b. 1934).

238 Unless the Lord the House Shall Build

Tune: BOURBON

This metrical version of Psalm 127 was first published in *The Psalter* (1912). It was number 359 titled "Conscious Dependence on God." The language has been updated.

BOURBON was attributed to the little-known composer Freeman Lewis. It was published in *Columbian Harmony* (1825). Lewis (1780–1859), who was born in Uniontown, Pennsylvania, was a surveyor and musician. His collected tunes were published in *The Beauties of Harmony* (1813; 2nd ed., 1816; 3rd ed., 1818).

The harmonization is by John Leon Hooker (b. 1944) for *The*

Hymnal 1982, where it is the setting for "Take Up Your Cross, the Savior Said."

239 How Happy Is Each Child of God

Tune: WINCHESTER OLD

This text is a paraphrase of Psalm 128 by Dwyn M. Mounger. While a pastor in Valdosta, Georgia, Mounger tried to remain faithful to the Common Lectionary's choice of Psalms and scripture lessons for Sundays. There were psalms that *The Hymnbook* (1955) did not have either to be read responsively or to be sung. He and his associate began to paraphrase the psalms and set them to familiar tunes. This text was one of those paraphrases. It became a favorite of the congregation and was sung on Christian Family Sunday every year.

Dwyn M. Mounger was born in 1938 in Jackson, Mississippi, and was educated at Belhaven College, Jackson, Mississippi (B.A. 1960), Mississippi State University (M.A. 1961), Princeton Theological Seminary (M.Div. 1965), and Union Theological Seminary, New York City (M.Phil., Ph.D. 1976). From 1961 to 1962, Mounger was a Fulbright Scholar studying at the Free University of Amsterdam, Netherlands. He has served churches in Georgia and North Carolina before accepting his present call as pastor of Central Presbyterian Church, Anderson, South Carolina (1990). Mounger has written articles, dramas, and vignettes for presbyteries and synods of the Presbyterian Church (U.S.A.). This is the first of his hymns to be published in a denominational hymnal.

WINCHESTER OLD was first published in Thomas Este's *Psalmes* (1592). For additional comments on the tune and the source, see hymn 58.

240 Out of the Depths

Tune: AUS TIEFER NOT

This versification of Psalm 130 is by Martin Luther. Four stanzas were in circulation in 1523 and published in *Etlich Christlich lider Lobgesang uñ Psalm* (1524) and set to the tune

ES IST DAS HEIL. The second stanza was expanded to two stanzas and appeared in Johann Walther's *Geystliche gesangk Buchleyn* (1524) set to the present tune. The English translation is by Richard Massie from his English translation of *Martin Luther's Spiritual Songs* (1854). For comments on Massie, see hymn 110.

Martin Luther (1483–1546) was born to peasant parents in Eisleben and educated at the University of Erfurt (M.A.) after which he became an Augustinian monk (1505). He was ordained into the priesthood (1507) and the following year sent to Wittenberg for graduate study in theology (D.D. 1512). There he also lectured on the Bible. Luther protested after Pope Leo X authorized the selling of indulgences in 1517. He was excommunicated in 1520 after burning a papal bull requiring him to recant his beliefs. In 1521 he was summoned to Worms and after refusing to change his position was banned. While traveling back to Wittenberg, Luther's friend Elector Frederick placed him in protective custody, taking him to Wartburg. There he translated the New Testament from Greek into German. He returned to Wittenberg (1522), developed a German Mass, and wrote hymns for his followers' use. He died at Eisleben at age sixty-three.

AUS TIEFER NOT has been attributed to Luther and as noted above was associated with the text from early times. The present harmonization is that of Johann Sebastian Bach (see hymn 17) for his Cantata 38 (c. 1740).

241 Behold the Goodness of Our Lord

Tune: CRIMOND

This paraphrase of Psalm 133 was written by Fred R. Anderson and included in *Singing Psalms of Joy and Praise* (1986). In 1983 during a board meeting of the journal *Reformed Liturgy & Music*, word came to the members that the presbytery which was needed to ratify the reunion of the Presbyterian Church U.S. and the United Presbyterian Church U.S.A. had just voted in the affirmative.

The action moved Anderson to write this paraphrase which the board members, who represented the former two streams now reunited, sang to the tune CRIMOND as part of the final worship. The hymn was then sung at the opening Communion service of the reunion assembly in Atlanta in 1983. For a biographical sketch of Anderson, see hymn 159.

CRIMOND was composed by Jessie Seymour Irvine. The harmonization is by T. C. L. Pritchard. For comments on the tune, see hymn 170.

242 Come, All You Servants of the Lord

Tune: DANBY

This paraphrase of Psalm 134 by Arlo D. Duba was written after hearing the tune DANBY which was brought to the attention of the Psalter Task Force of the Presbyterian Church (U.S.A.) by Kenneth E. Williams (see hymn 548). It was first published in *A Psalm Sampler* (1986). For comments on Duba, see hymn 177.

DANBY is a traditional English folk melody. It was the hymn setting for Samuel Longfellow's " 'Tis Winter Now," in *The English Hymnal* (1906). In that volume it was harmonized by Ralph Vaughan Williams. *The Presbyterian Hymnal* (1990) setting is that of Arthur Hutchings for the International Committee on English in the Liturgy. Hutchings' harmonization was first published in *Resource Collection of Hymns and Service Music for the Liturgy* (1981).

243 We Thank You, Lord, for You Are Good

Tune: WAS GOTT TUT

This metrical version of Psalm 136 was written by John G. Dunn and submitted to the Presbyterian Hymnal Committee by the Psalter Task Force of the Presbyterian Church (U.S.A.). For comments on Dunn, see hymn 199.

WAS GOTT TUT was composed by Severus Gastorius. The harmonization is from the *Common Service Book* (1917). For comments on the tune and the composer, see hymn 284.

244 Let Us with a Gladsome Mind

Tune: MONKLAND

John Milton wrote this paraphrase of Psalm 136 while a student at St. Paul's School, London. He was fifteen. It was first published in the *Poems of Mr. John Milton, both English and Latin* (1645). The text has been altered from the original which contained twenty-four two-line stanzas with the refrain "For His mercies aye endure, Ever faithful, ever sure." The present stanzas reflect Psalm 136:1, 7–9, 25, 26.

John Milton (1608–1674), an English Puritan, was born in London and educated at Christ's College, Cambridge (B.A. 1628; M.A. 1632). He spent several years with his father in Horton, Buckinghamshire, where he wrote *Il Penseroso* and *L'Allegro.* While touring France (1638) he met with the imprisoned Galileo. He returned to England and opened a school at Aldersgate Street and in 1649 was appointed Latin Secretary to the Council of State of Oliver Cromwell, a position he held for ten years. Having suffered from weak eyes all his life, at age forty-four he became totally blind. His greatest literary works *Paradise Lost* (1667), *Paradise Regained* and *Samson Agonistes* (both 1671) were dictated to others in this later period.

His contributions to hymnody are limited to nineteen psalm paraphrases. One is included here.

MONKLAND was first published in Johann A. Freylinghausen's *Geistreiches Gesangbuch* (1704) with no composer credit. It appeared in John Lees' edited work *Hymn Tunes of the United Brethren* (Manchester, 1824). The present harmonization is that of John Bernard Wilkes (1785–1869) for *Hymns Ancient and Modern* (1861).

Wilkes titled the tune MONKLAND after the village in Hertfordshire, where he was the organist and Sir Henry Williams Baker (see hymn 171) was the pastor.

245 By the Waters of Babylon

Verse 1 of Psalm 137 is the text of this three-part canon set to a traditional Jewish melody. The asterisk at the beginning of each musical line indicates where the next voice is to enter. An alternate version of the text is also popular:

By the flood of Babylon,
we sat down and wept,
when we remembered thee, O Zion.

The melody-only hymn is especially appropriate for children and youth.

246 By the Babylonian Rivers

Tune: KAS DZIEDAJA

This metrical paraphrase of Psalm 137 is by Ewald Bash (b. 1924). It first appeared in *Songs for Today* (1964) published by the Youth Department of the American Lutheran Church (now Evangelical Lutheran Church in America).

KAS DZIEDAJA is a Latvian melody harmonized by Geoffrey Laycock (b. 1927) for this text in the *New Catholic Hymnal* (London, 1971). Together with Anthony Petti, a professor of English in Canada, he edited the collection. Laycock is director of music at a teachers college in Norwich.

247 I Will Give Thanks with My Whole Heart

Tune: HERR JESU CHRIST

This version of Psalm 138 is by Christopher L. Webber and was first published in *A New Metrical Psalter* (1986). The original texts of stanzas 3 and 5 were written in the third person. Webber revised those stanzas for *The Presbyterian Hymnal* (1990). He also changed the phrase "hostile wrath" in stanza 4 to "my foe's wrath." For more on Webber, see hymn 164.

HERR JESU CHRIST first appeared in *Cantionale Germanicum* (1628). It received its name when used with the text "Herr Jesu Christ, dich zu uns wend," in *Cantionale Sacrum* (2nd ed., 1651). One tradition traces the tune to John Huss. The arrangement is by Johann Sebastian Bach, who wrote four organ settings in *Orgelbüchlein* as well as the harmonization in *Choralgesänge.* For comments on Bach, see hymn 17.

248 You Are Before Me, Lord

Tune: SURSUM CORDA (SMITH)

This paraphrase of Psalm 139 is by Ian Pitt-Watson. He wrote the text in 1973 and revised it extensively in 1989. The new "authorized version" appears in *The Presbyterian Hymnal* (1990).

Ian Pitt-Watson was born in 1923 and currently is professor of preaching and practical theology at Fuller Theological Seminary, Pasadena, California.

SURSUM CORDA was composed by Alfred Morton Smith as the setting for Henry Montagu Butler's meditation on the Sursum corda "Lift Up Your Hearts" in the Episcopal *Hymnal 1940.*

Alfred Morton Smith (1879–1971) was born in Jenkintown, Pennsylvania, and studied at the University of Pennsylvania (B.S. 1901) and Philadelphia Divinity School (B.D. 1905; S.T.B. 1911). An Episcopalian, Smith was ordained a deacon (1905) and a priest (1906). After a short time in Philadelphia and Long Beach, California, he served at St. Matthias Church, Los Angeles, for ten years. He was a chaplain in the U.S. Army during World War I, returning to Philadelphia in 1919, where he spent the remainder of his career. He retired in 1955. In 1963, Smith moved to Druim Moir, Chestnut Hill, Pennsylvania, and in 1968 to Brigantine, New Jersey, where he remained until his death.

249 O Lord, Make Haste to Hear My Cry

Tune: CANNONS

This metrical setting of Psalm 141 first appeared as number 386 in *The Psalter* (1912). The present text is the first four stanzas of the original with the archaic language removed.

CANNONS was composed by George Frederick Handel (c. 1750) and was originally used with Charles Wesley's text, "Sinners, Obey the Gospel Word." It is one of three tunes by Handel which were published as settings for Wesley's text by Samuel Wesley in 1826. The other tunes are FITZWILLIAM with "O Love Divine, How Sweet Thou Art" and GOPSAL with "Rejoice, the Lord Is King." The originals are in the Fitzwilliam Museum, Cambridge. For comments on Handel, see hymn 59.

250 When Morning Lights the Eastern Skies

Tune: ST. STEPHEN

This metrical rendering of Psalm 143 appears here as published in *The Psalter* (1912) (no. 391). That collection used selected stanzas from the original versification of the Wesleyan Methodist Conference (1904).

ST. STEPHEN was composed by William Jones (1789). For comments on the tune and the composer, see hymn 390.

251 Your Faithfulness, O Lord, Is Sure

Tune: WINCHESTER NEW

This paraphrase of Psalm 145:13–21 is by Joy F. Patterson. When the Presbyterian Hymnal Committee was unable to find a paraphrase suitable, Patterson wrote one. These verses of the psalm emphasize God's providence and care for all creation. For comments on the author, see hymn 194.

WINCHESTER NEW is from *Musikalisches Handbuch* (1690). For comments on the tune, see hymn 444. The harmonization is by William Henry Monk (1847). For comments on Monk, see hymn 543.

252 O Lord, You Are My God and King

Tune: JERUSALEM

This metrical setting of Psalm 145:1–13 is an altered form of number 397, "The Greatness and Grace of God" in *The Psalter* (1912). Joy F. Patterson altered it in 1989 for *The Presbyterian Hymnal* (1990). For comments on Patterson, see hymn 194. For comments on the source, see hymn 158.

JERUSALEM was composed by C. Hubert H. Parry in 1916. The sacred choral song, based on William Blake's (1757–1827) *Jerusalem,* was written for unison voices and orchestra. For a biographical sketch of Parry, see hymn 224.

The harmonization by Richard Proulx was prepared for *Worship III* (1986). For comments on Proulx, see hymn 573.

253 I'll Praise My Maker

Tune: OLD 113TH

This metrical paraphrase of Psalm 146 was written by Isaac Watts and published as number 360 in *The Psalms of David Imitated in the Language of the New Testament* (1719). It was adapted by John Wesley for *Collection of Psalms and Hymns. Charles Town. Printed by Lewis Timothy* (1736–1737). Wesley handed out the hymn to the congregation during the last worship he conducted. He sang the first two stanzas just two days before his death and on the day he died, Wesley was heard trying to sing the hymn but was only able to repeat the words "I'll praise, I'll praise." For a biographical sketch of Watts, see hymn 40.

John Wesley (1703–1791) was born in the parsonage at Epworth, Lincolnshire, England, and educated at Charterhouse (1714–1720) and Christ Church, Oxford (B.A. 1724; M.A. 1726). He was ordained (1725), elected a fellow of Lincoln College, Oxford (1726), and then returned to assist his father as curate of Epworth and Wroot. From 1729 to 1735, Wesley taught at Oxford. He and his brother Charles traveled as missionaries of the Society for the Propagation of the Gospel to Georgia. Disheartened, he returned to England (1737) and was influenced by the Moravian Peter Böhler. Present at a Moravian meeting when one of them read the preface to Luther's *Epistle to the Romans*, Wesley stated:

> About a quarter before nine, while he was describing the change which God works in the heart through faith in Christ, I felt my heart strangely warmed. I felt I did trust in Christ, Christ alone, for salvation; and an assurance was given me, that He had taken away *my* sins, even *mine*, and saved *me* from the law of sin and death.

The course of Wesley's life was changed that day and he preached more sermons, published more books, and made more converts than any other evangelist of his day. It is estimated Wesley traveled 250,000 miles on horseback and preached some 40,000 sermons. He died in London.

OLD 113TH is an abridged version of GENEVAN 36 and is attributed to Matthäus Greiter. In German hymnals the tune is titled O MENSCH, BEWEIN' and is associated with the text "O Mensch, bewein' dein' Sünde gross." During the eighteenth century the tune was shortened to its present form and became known as

LUCERNE. For more on the tune and the composer, see hymn 226.

The harmonization is by V. Earle Copes for *The Book of Hymns* (1964) for which he was a consultant.

V. Earle Copes was born in 1921 in Norfolk, Virginia, and educated at Davidson College, North Carolina (B.A. 1940), and Union Theological Seminary, New York City (M.S.M. 1944; B.D. 1945). An ordained Methodist minister, he has served as minister of music in several churches. He was on the faculty of Hendrix College, Conway, Arkansas; Cornell College, Mount Vernon, Iowa; and Wright State University, Dayton, Ohio. He was music editor for the General Board of Education of the Methodist Church in Nashville and editor of *Music Ministry*. Copes is a member of the promotion committee of the Hymn Society in the United States and Canada.

254 PSALM 146

This psalm is classified as a hymn and in later Jewish worship was used in daily morning prayer. Together with Psalms 145, 147–150 it is considered a Hallel psalm. For information on the translation of the text, see hymn 185. The psalm may be read responsively or sung.

The psalm tone and refrain were prepared for *Worship III* (1986) by Howard Hughes and John Schiavone.

255 Now Praise the Lord

Tune: ST. ANNE

The text is a new metrical paraphrase of Psalm 147 by Fred R. Anderson set to ST. ANNE. It was first published in *Singing Psalms of Joy and Praise* (1986), where it included a seventh stanza focusing on the Trinity.

> Sing Praise to God, the source of life,
> Sing praise to God the Son.
> Sing praise to God's life-giving power,
> Forever three in one.

For a biographical sketch of Anderson, see hymn 159.

ST. ANNE was composed by William Croft. It appeared in *A Supplement to the New Version of the Psalms* (1708). For comments on the tune and the composer, see hymn 210.

256 Let the Whole Creation Cry

Tune: SALZBURG

The text was written by Stopford A. Brooke and first published in *Christian Hymns* (1881), where it is noted as an "Invitation to Praise God. An imitation of Psalm 148."

Stopford Augustus Brooke (1832–1916) was born in Letterkenny, Donegal, Ireland, and educated at Trinity College, Dublin (B.A. 1856; M.A. 1858). He took Holy Orders and was curate of St. Matthew's Marylebone (1857–1859), Kensington (1860–1863), and then chaplain to the British Embassy in Berlin (1863–1865). He became minister of St. James Chapel, London (1866–1875), and Bedford Chapel (1876). His liberal views led him to secede from the Anglican Church in 1880 after which he chose to remain independent from any denominational ties. His published works include *Life and Letters of the Late F. W. Robertson* (1865), *Theology in the English Poets* (1874), and *Primer of English Literature* (1876). He died at Surrey.

SALZBURG, attributed to Jacob Hintze, harmonized by J. S. Bach, appears as in *Hymns Ancient and Modern* (1861). For more on the tune, see hymn 159.

257 Give Praise to the Lord

Tune: LAUDATE DOMINUM

This text is a paraphrase of Psalm 149 from *The Psalter* (1912) number 407. It was altered by the Psalter Task Force of the Presbyterian Church (U.S.A.) in 1984.

LAUDATE DOMINUM was composed by C. Hubert H. Parry about 1915. For a biographical sketch of Parry, see hymn 224.

258 Praise Ye the Lord

This text of Psalm 150 was adapted from the Revised Standard Version of the Bible (1952, 1971) by J. Jefferson Cleveland in 1981. It was published in *The Upper Room Worshipbook* (1985).

J. (Judge) Jefferson Cleveland (1937–1986) was a musician, composer, hymnologist, and editor of several collections for the United Methodist Church. He had a particular expertise in the field of African-American music. This is demonstrated in *Songs of Zion*, a 1981 collection he edited with Verolga Nix.

The music, as composed by Cleveland, may be sung as a solo with the congregation singing the refrain.

TOPICAL HYMNS

259 A Mighty Fortress Is Our God

Tune: EIN' FESTE BURG

This hymn based on Psalm 46, with the exception of stanza 1, lines 1 and 2 by Martin Luther and translated by Frederick Henry Hedge, is the work of Omer Westendorf. When a friend returned from a funeral expressing the joy of singing the Protestant Martin Luther's "A Mighty Fortress," Westendorf reread Psalm 46. He found Luther's hymn differed from the ideas expressed by the psalmist. So he wrote a new paraphrase under the pseudonym of J. Clifford Evers. It was published in the *People's Mass Book* (1964). For comments on Luther, see hymn 240. For comments on Hedge, see hymn 260.

Generally acknowledged as the person most responsible for introducing ecumenical hymnody to the American Roman Catholic Church, Omer Westendorf (b. 1916), is a lifelong resident of Cincinnati. He has a Bachelor of Arts degree in Music and received his Master of Arts degree from the College-Conservatory of Music, University of Cincinnati (1950). In 1936 he became choirmaster and organist at St. Bonaventure Church, one block from his home, a position he held for over forty years.

A chance meeting with a choir member (Mr. Aerts) from the Frauenkirche, Maastricht, Holland, during World War II, changed Westendorf's life and the music life of American Roman Catholics forever. Aerts introduced Westendorf to the music of the Mass by the Dutch composers Nieland and Andriessen. After the war Westendorf sent for catalogs and samples of the Mass from many European countries. He founded World Library of Sacred Music as the American distributor of these European music firms (1950). In 1955 his company produced the first Roman Catholic hymnal in the United States, *The People's Hymnal*. It contained eighty-five hymns. In the nine years between 1955 and 1964 he published five different hymnals. Using the pseudonyms J. Clifford Evers, Mark

Evans, and the People's Hymnal Committee, Westendorf included his own hymns. After Vatican Council II his hymnals were in greater demand, and the *People's Mass Book* (1964) sold over two million copies. He changed the name of the company to World Library Publications and added choral and organ music to the company's output. Since his retirement he continues to write hymns and assists the editorial staff of World Library (see hymn 521).

EIN' FESTE BURG (rhythmic) was composed by Martin Luther. For comments on the tune, see hymn 260. The harmonization is by Hans Leo Hassler as it appears in *The Hymnal 1982*. For a biographical sketch of Hassler, see hymn 54.

260 A Mighty Fortress Is Our God

Tune: EIN' FESTE BURG

This hymn, text and tune, was written by Martin Luther in 1529. It is based on Psalm 46. Generally thought to have been composed for the Diet of Speyer, it soon became the rallying cry of the Protestant Reformation. Luther sang it daily at Coburg. By 1900 over eighty translations were being used, and today there are more than two hundred versions in common usage. For comments on Luther, see hymn 240.

The present translation is that of Frederick Henry Hedge. It appeared in W. H. Furness' *Gems of German Verse* (1852) and Hedge's *Hymns for the Church of Christ* (1853).

Frederick Henry Hedge (1805–1890) was born in Cambridge, Massachusetts, and educated in Germany and at Harvard University (1825). He entered Harvard Divinity School and befriended Ralph Waldo Emerson, father of the transcendental movement. Hedge was ordained a Unitarian minister in 1829 and served congregations in West Cambridge; Bangor, Maine; Providence, and Brookline, Massachusetts. His major work *Prose Writers of Germany* was written when he was in Bangor. He taught ecclesiastical history and German at Harvard University from 1857 to 1882.

EIN' FESTE BURG (isometric), composed by Luther for this text, may have been his adaptation of a Gregorian melody. It is believed to have appeared first in Joseph Klug's *Geistliche Lieder* (1529), but no copy of that volume exists today. The earliest printed version of the hymn is in *Kirche gesang, mit vil schönen Psalmen vnnd Melodey, gantz geendert uñ gemert* (1531). The harmonization is by Johann Sebastian Bach, who used the tune in Cantata 80.

The tune is popular with other composers as well. Felix Mendelssohn used it in the *Reformation Symphony* (1830), Richard Wagner in "Kaisersmarsch" (1871), and Giacomo Meyerbeer in the opera *Les Huguenots* (1836). For comments on Bach, see hymn 17.

261 God of Compassion, in Mercy Befriend Us

Tune: O QUANTA QUALIA

The text was written by John James Moment, a member of the committee to compile *The Hymnal* (1933).

Moment (1875–1959) was born in Orono, Ontario, Canada, and educated at Princeton University (B.A. 1896) and Hartford Theological Seminary (B.D. 1906). He began his career as a teacher at Lawrenceville School, New Jersey (1898–1904), then served several New Jersey pastorates until moving to the Crescent Avenue Presbyterian Church, Plainfield, New Jersey, in 1918, where he remained until his retirement.

O QUANTA QUALIA from Paris *Antiphoner* (1681) appears as in La Feillée's *Méthode du plain-chant* (1808). For comments on the tune, see hymn 147.

262 God of the Ages, Whose Almighty Hand

Tune: NATIONAL HYMN

This hymn is typically known from its first line as "God of Our Fathers, Whose Almighty Hand." The Presbyterian Hymnal Committee altered this first phrase to "God of the ages, whose almighty hand," following the pattern set in most denominational hymnals today.

The author of the text, Daniel Crane Roberts (1841–1907) was born in Bridgehampton, Long Island, New York, and was ordained in the Protestant Episcopal Church (1866). He was a private in the Civil War and graduated from Kenyon College (1857). He served parishes in Vermont, Massachusetts, and for more than twenty years was vicar of St. Paul's Church, Concord, New Hampshire.

In a letter to Louis F. Benson, Roberts recounted how he came to write this text.

> The hymn was written in 1876 for a celebration of the Centennial "Fourth" of July, and sung at Brandon, Vermont, to the tune called "Russian Hymn," set to "Rise, crowned with light" in our Hymnals. When our General Convention appointed a Commission to revise the Hymnal, I sent it, without my name, promising to send the name if the hymn were accepted. It was accepted, and printed anonymously in the report of the Commission. Before the Hymnal was printed, the Rev. Dr. Tucker, late of Troy, editor of our best musical Hymnal, and Mr. George William Warren, organist of St. Thomas' Church, New York, were appointed a committee to choose a hymn for the centennial celebration of the adoption of the Constitution. They selected this hymn, then anonymous, and, wanting a tune, Mr. Warren composed a tune to which it has since been set in the "Tucker" Hymnal. Subsequently it was selected as the "Recessional" at the "Bi-Centenary" of Trinity Church, New York City. (Louis F. Benson, *Studies of Familiar Hymns*, 2nd series, p. 122.)

The hymn was first included in the Protestant Episcopal *Hymnal* (1892).

NATIONAL HYMN appeared in the *Hymnal for the Episcopal Church* (1894). It was composed by George William Warren (1828–1902) for Roberts' text.

Warren was born in Albany, New York, and served Albany churches as organist. He became organist of Trinity Church in New York City (1860) and later at St. Thomas' Church in New York, during which time his tunes composed for the St. Thomas' choir drew crowds to the church. At his funeral service, no music was played and no organ sounded to indicate there was no longer anyone to lead the music at St. Thomas'.

263 Immortal, Invisible, God Only Wise

Tune: ST. DENIO

This text was written by Walter Chalmers Smith and included in *Hymns of Christ and the Christian Life* (1867). It appeared in a slightly revised form in W. Garrett Horder's *Congregational Hymns* (1884). Stanza 4, line 1, is as it appears in *The Hymnal 1982* of the Episcopal Church.

Walter Chalmers Smith (1824–1908) was born in Aberdeen, Scotland, and was educated at the University of Aberdeen and New College, Edinburgh. He was ordained in 1850 and served churches in London, Glasgow, and Edinburgh. He was Moderator of the Free Church of Scotland in 1893 in its fiftieth anniversary year. He died at Kinbuck, Perthshire.

Among Smith's publications are *The Bishop's Walk* (1860), *North Country Folk* (1883), *Poetical Works, Olrig Grange* (1872), *Borland Hall* (1874), *Hilda Among the Broken Gods* (1878), and *A Heretic and Other Poems* (1891).

ST. DENIO, also known as JOANNA, is a Welsh folk melody from the early nineteenth century. It was adapted as a hymn tune in John Roberts' *Caniadau y Cyssegr* (1839).

264 When in Our Music God is Glorified

Tune: ENGELBERG

The hymn text is by Fred Pratt Green, who has been credited with starting the twentieth century's hymn explosion. It was written at the request of John Wilson, who wanted a hymn for a Festival of Praise or choir anniversary set to ENGELBERG. The text appeared on the front cover of the Hymn Society of America's journal *The Hymn* in the summer of 1973. For a biographical sketch of Green, see hymn 72.

ENGELBERG is by Charles Villiers Stanford (1852–1924), prominent conductor and composer. Most of his work was in festival music. It was orginally composed for the 1904 edition of *Hymns Ancient and Modern* with the text "For All the Saints." But ENGELBERG lost its status with the hymn text when *The English Hymnal* (1906) printed "For All the Saints" to the new Ralph Vaughan Williams tune SINE NOMINE. Then ENGELBERG was introduced into American hymnody with the text "All Praise to Thee, for Thou, O King Divine." Wilson points out that the tune should never be sung without the composer's special Amen, which contains the climax of the melody, the one and only fourth-space E in the melody line.

265 Great God, We Sing That Mighty Hand

Tune: WAREHAM

This text was written by Philip Doddridge. It is from Job Orton's collection of Doddridge's texts, *Hymns Founded on Various Texts in the Holy Scriptures* (1755). The caption to the hymn reads "Help obtained from God. Acts 26:22. For the New Year."

Philip Doddridge (1702–1751) was born in London and was one of twenty children. Since he was orphaned at an early age, the Duchess of Bedford offered to send him to Cambridge, but the offer contained the obligation to become an Anglican priest. Instead, he attended the nonconformist academy in Kibworth and became a nonconformist minister. A supporter of John Wesley and George Whitefield and a friend of Isaac Watts, Doddridge wrote more than four hundred hymns. All were published after his death from tuberculosis.

In addition to his hymns, Doddridge wrote the *Rise and Progress of Religion in the Soul* and *The Family Exposition.*

WAREHAM was composed by William Knapp. For comments on the tune, see hymn 421. For comments on the composer, see hymn 161.

266 Thank You, God, for Water, Soil, and Air

Tune: AMSTEIN

This text by Brian Wren was written in 1973 for *New Church Praise* (1975). The hymn makes a statement about ecological issues from a Christian viewpoint. It was set to the tune ALTHROP in *Ecumenical Praise* (1977). For comments on the author, see hymn 71.

AMSTEIN was composed by John Weaver for this text at the request of the Presbyterian Hymnal Committee. He named the tune after Rev. Charles A. Amstein, associate pastor of Madison Avenue Presbyterian Church, New York City, where Weaver is the organist and music director. For comments on the composer, see hymn 9.

267 All Things Bright and Beautiful

Tune: ROYAL OAK

The text was written by Cecil Frances Humphreys Alexander for the children of her Sunday school class to teach them the various truths of the Apostles' Creed. It illustrates the first phrase of the creed "I believe in God the Father Almighty, Maker of heaven and earth." The hymn was first published in her *Hymns for Little Children* (1848). For a biographical sketch of the author, see hymn 49.

ROYAL OAK is an English folk melody first published in the *Dancing Master* (1686). It was adapted as the setting for this text by Martin Shaw in *Song Time* (1915). The present harmony is that of David Hugh Jones for *The Hymnbook* (1955). For comments on Shaw and Jones, see hymns 12 and 28, respectively.

268 God, Who Stretched the Spangled Heavens

Tune: HOLY MANNA

This hymn by Catherine Arnott Cameron was first found in *Contemporary Worship—1* (1969), a supplement published by the Inter-Lutheran Commission on Worship.

Cameron said the hymn was "written over a period of several months at a time when I was experiencing a new sense of direction, growth, and creativity in my life. I wrote it to go with the tune 'Austria' " (as quoted by Marilyn Kay Stulken in *Hymnal Companion to the Lutheran Book of Worship*, p. 488).

Cameron was born in Canada in 1927 but is now a U.S. citizen. She is on the faculty of the University of La Verne in

California, where she teaches social psychology. She is married and has two children.

HOLY MANNA first appeared as the setting for "Brethren, We Have Met to Worship" in William Moore's collection, *The Columbian Harmony* (1825). All that is known of Moore is that he lived in Wilson County in the District of West Tennessee. He claimed this tune as well as seventeen others as his own.

The harmonization is by Charles Anders (b. 1929).

269 O God of Bethel, by Whose Hand

Tune: DUNDEE

The text was written by Philip Doddridge to complement a sermon on Genesis 28:20–22, "Jacob's Vow," which he preached on January 16, 1737. It was included in *Hymns Founded on Various Texts in the Holy Scriptures*, published posthumously in 1755. The collection contained the author's alteration of the first line to read "O God of Jacob, by whose hand." The present form of the hymn is from John Logan's alteration of 1781. For comments on Doddridge, see hymn 265.

John Logan (1748–1788) acted as an editor of other people's texts which at times he credited as his own. Ordained in the Church of Scotland, Logan was forced to leave the active ministry because of his "intemperate ways." He spent the remainder of his life in London.

DUNDEE appears in the Scottish Psalter (1615). For comments on the tune, see hymn 234.

270 O God, in a Mysterious Way

Tune: DUNDEE

The text was written by William Cowper in 1773 after he attempted suicide while living at Olney. This, the last hymn Cowper wrote, was first published in John Newton's *Twenty-six Letters on religious Subjects; to which are added Hymns* (1774).

William Cowper (1731–1800) was born in the rectory at

Berkhampstead, educated at Westminster, and admitted to the bar (1754). Cowper's life was overshadowed by periodic depressions which led to several hospitalizations.

He was known as a satirist and poet. Together with John Newton (see hymn 280) he wrote *Olney Hymns* (1779). His greatest poetic work was *The Task* (1783). He died at East Dereham.

DUNDEE: This setting of the tune first appeared in Thomas Ravenscroft's edited work *The Whole Booke of Psalmes* (1621). Included were 105 common psalm tunes in four-part settings with the melodies in the tenor voice. Ravenscroft contributed 55 of the musical settings.

Thomas Ravenscroft, English composer, editor, and theorist (c. 1592–c. 1635) was a chorister at St. Paul's Cathedral and graduated from Cambridge's Pembroke Hall (B.Mus. 1605), although some authorities say 1607. In 1609, *Pammelia* and *Deuteromelia*, two important collections of English rounds, were published. Ravenscroft was the editor. The round "Three Blind Mice" first appeared in *Deuteromelia*. Another of his collections, *Melismata, Musical Phansies, Fitting the Court, Citie and Countrey Humours*, was published in 1611. His *Briefe Discourse* (1614) was an attempt to revive the musical notation of the previous century. Ravenscroft was music master of Christ's Hospital from 1618 to 1622.

271 Many and Great, O God, Are Thy Things

Tune: LACQUIPARLE

This hymn, commonly known as "Dakota Hymn," was written by Joseph R. Renville and included in his edited hymnal *Dakota Odowan* (1842). Renville used Jeremiah 10:12–13 as a basis for his text, originally in the Dakota language.

Joseph R. Renville (1779–1846), a fur trader, who was half Dakota and half French, was instrumental in having a mission established at Lac qui Parle where he had his trading post. The American Board of Commissioners for Foreign Missions commissioned the mission site (located in western Minnesota) and Dr. Thomas Williamson, a physician, and Stephen Riggs, Presbyterian and Congregational missionaries, established the mission.

The translation-paraphrase is by Francis Philip Frazier, a Congregational pastor. A full-blooded Sioux, born in a tepee, Frazier (1892–1964) was educated at Santee Indian School, Yankton College Academy, and Mt. Hermon School. He entered Dartmouth College but left to join the U.S. Army. Later he graduated from Oberlin College (1922) and Chicago Theological Seminary (B.Div. 1925). He was ordained in 1926 and returned to minister to his people. At the time of his death he was supervisor of the Sioux Indian Mission of Standing Rock Reservation. Frazier was honored with the Indian Achievement Award (1958), by Oberlin College (1960), and by Dartmouth College (D.D. 1964).

LACQUIPARLE is a traditional Native American Dakota tune adapted by Renville for his text. The tune was first printed in the 1879 edition of *Dakota Odowan*, edited by Renville's son, John (see hymn 355).

The harmonization is by James R. Murray, composer and music editor. For a biographical sketch of Murray, see hymn 25.

272 God of the Sparrow

Tune: ROEDER

The text by contemporary Lutheran pastor, editor, poet, and hymn writer Jaroslav J. Vajda was composed in 1983 for the one hundred tenth anniversary of Concordia Lutheran Church of Kirkwood, Missouri. Born in 1919 of Czechoslovakian parentage, Vajda began writing poetry at eighteen and made his first translation from the Slovak at age twenty-one. The author has a fascination for the "proper and effective" motivation for Christian service. He believes this hymn provides an opportunity to ask why and how God's creatures are to perform service.

Vajda is known for his use of new images and irregular meters as well as the strong theological thrust of his hymns. His collected hymns were published as *Now the Joyful Celebration: Hymns, Carols, and Songs* (1987). In addition to writing hymns, Vajda has several volumes of translated works. His texts have been published in both the United States and Czechoslovakia. (See "An Interview with Jaroslav Vajda," *The Hymn*, vol. 39, no. 2 [April 1988], pp. 7–9.)

ROEDER was written by Carl Flentge Schalk for this text. Schalk was born in Des Plaines, Illinois, on September 26, 1929. He served on the editorial advisory committee of Concordia Publishing House and was editor of *Church Music*. In addition to his hymn tunes, Schalk is known for his choral and instrumental works.

273 O God the Creator

Tune: KASTAAK

The text of this hymn was written by Native Americans Elizabeth Bess Haile and Cecil Corbett as the theme song of the 1977 Indian Youth Conference, Tulsa, Oklahoma. The hymn was captioned "A New Song on the Four Themes." It was published in the Charles Cook Theological School's periodical *Indian Quest*, Fall 1977. Originally the text was set to the tune ONE IN THE SPIRIT.

Elizabeth Haile has been active in the work of the Presbyterian Church (U.S.A.) in a variety of capacities, many relating to work with Native Americans. Her daughter, Holly Haile Smith, is the first Native American woman ordained in the PC(USA). Haile lives on the Shinnecock reservation in Southhampton, Long Island, New York.

Cecil Corbett is a graduate of the University of Dubuque Theological Seminary and has served as pastor for Native American congregations. He was also president of the Charles Cook Theological School in Tempe, Arizona, where many Native American students are educated and trained.

KASTAAK was composed by Joy F. Patterson for this text when it became clear the tune to which it was set originally could not be included in the collection. She named the tune KASTAAK for Sofia Porter, a Native American member of the Presbyterian Hymnal Committee, because Kastaak is the Americanized form of her birth name. Porter, originally from Sitka, Alaska, lives in the State of Washington. For more on Patterson, see hymn 194.

274 O God of Earth and Space

Tune: LEONI

Written in 1980 by Jane Parker Huber, the text praises God for all the gifts provided in creation. She says, "God's care is also a providence that extends beyond material things into the realm of the spirit, where God has just as wonderfully provided music, thought, art, faithfulness, love, and justice" (Jane Parker Huber, *A Singing Faith*, p. 109; Philadelphia: Westminster Press, 1987).

The hymn was winner for best original text by Trinity Lutheran Seminary, Columbus, Ohio, 1981, as part of its one hundred fiftieth anniversary celebration. It alludes to the creation story in Genesis 1 and various psalms.

For a biographical sketch of Huber, see hymn 128.

LEONI, also known as YIGDAL, was introduced into Christian worship around 1770. The story goes that Thomas Olivers (1725–1799), a Wesleyan minister, attended Great Duke's Place Synagogue, Alegate, London, and heard Meyer Lyon (Leoni) sing the *Yigdal* (long doxology) and was impressed with the melody. Lyon (1751–1797), a cantor and accomplished musician of his day, transcribed the melody for Olivers, who in turn named the tune LEONI. Lyon died in Kingston, Jamaica, where he was hazan in the English and German Synagogue from 1787 to 1797.

275 God of Our Life

Tune: SANDON

This hymn was written by Hugh Thomson Kerr in 1916 for the fiftieth anniversary of the Shadyside Presbyterian Church, Pittsburgh, where Kerr was pastor. It was then published in *The Church School Hymnal for Youth* (1928).

Hugh Thomson Kerr (1871–1950) was born in Canada and educated at the University of Toronto and Western Theological Seminary (now Pittsburgh Theological Seminary). He was ordained in 1897 and served in Hutchinson, Kansas, and Chicago before going to Shadyside in 1913. Kerr was Moderator of the General Assembly of the Presbyterian Church U.S.A. in 1930.

SANDON was the tune for which Hugh Thomson Kerr wrote the text. Charles Henry Purday composed SANDON for "Lead, Kindly Light, Amid the Encircling Gloom" and published it in *The Church and Home Metrical Psalter and Hymnal* (1860).

Charles Henry Purday (1799–1885) was born in Folkestone, England. He was a vocalist and sang at the coronation of Queen Victoria. He conducted the psalmody at Crown Court, Scots Church, Covent Garden. He authored *Copyright, a Sketch of Its Rise and Progress* (1877) as part of his attempt to reform the copyright laws. He died in London.

The harmonization is by John Weaver for *The Presbyterian Hymnal* (1990). For comments on Weaver, see hymn 565.

276 Great Is Thy Faithfulness

Tune: FAITHFULNESS

This text is one of the few gospel hymns that address God specifically. It was written by Thomas Obediah Chisholm and is based on Lamentations 3:22–23. It was first published in Runyan's (see below) private song pamphlets.

Thomas Obediah Chisholm (1866–1960) was born in a log cabin near Franklin, Kentucky, and at sixteen taught in the country school, where he received his education. He became associate editor of a weekly, *The Franklin Favorite* (1887). After experiencing a conversion during a revival meeting conducted by H. C. Morrison, he moved to Louisville, Kentucky, to become editor and business manager of Morrison's *Pentecostal Herald.* Chisholm was ordained into the Methodist ministry when he was thirty-six. Shortly after his ordination, his health failed and he moved to Winona Lake, Indiana (1909), and then Vineland, New Jersey, where he opened an insurance office. He began writing poetry and in 1923 sent a number of poems to William M. Runyan, a friend and colleague in ministry. He retired from the insurance business in 1953 and moved to a Methodist retirement home in Ocean Grove, New Jersey. Chisholm wrote more than twelve hundred sacred poems.

FAITHFULNESS was composed by William Marion Runyan for this text at the request of Chisholm. He wrote that the poem held such an appeal he prayed his tune might "carry its message in a worthy way."

William Marion Runyan (1870–1957) was a Methodist minister and music editor, long associated with the Moody Bible Institute. He grew up in Kansas and was ordained at twenty-one. He served several pastorates totaling twelve years. In 1903, Runyan was appointed evangelist for the Central Kansas Methodist Conference. For a time, he was associated with John Brown University, in Arkansas, and Hope Publishing Company. He died at the age of eighty-seven.

277 O God, Our Faithful God

Tune: O GOTT, DU FROMMER GOTT

This hymn originally in German was written by Johann Heermann and titled "A Daily Prayer." It was published in *Devoti Musica Cordis, Hauss- und Hertz-Musica* (1630). The translation is by Catherine Winkworth for her *Lyra Germanica* (1858). The text appears here as in *The Worshipbook—Services and Hymns* (1972). For comments on Heermann, see hymn 93. For comments on Winkworth, see hymn 3.

O GOTT, DU FROMMER GOTT was first published in *Neu ordentlich Gesangbuch* (Hanover, 1646). The sharps were added in the Lüneburg *Gesangbuch* (1665). The tune and text appeared together in Hamburg (1690). The harmonization was by Johann Sebastian Bach for the Choral Partita of the same name. Within fifteen years of the Heermann's text appearance three tunes became associated with it. WAS FRAG' ICH NACH DER WELT appears at hymn 278. The other was an earlier version of the tune MUNICH (see hymn 128). For comments on Bach, see hymn 17.

278 Our God, to Whom We Turn

Tune: WAS FRAG' ICH NACH DER WELT

The text was written by Edward Grubb (1854–1939) and published in *The Light of Life: Hymns of Faith and Consolation*

(1925). Grubb was an English Quaker. The present setting includes four of the five stanzas from *The Hymnbook* (1955).

WAS FRAG' ICH NACH DER WELT was composed by Ahasuerus Fritsch and included in *Himmels-Lust und Welt-Unlust* (1679), where it was the setting for Johann Jacob Schütz's "Die Wollust dieser Welt." Later the tune became associated with Wolfgang Dessler's "Was frag' ich nach der Welt" in the Darmstadt *Geistreiches Gesangbuch* (1698). The harmonization was by Johann Sebastian Bach for his August 6, 1724 worship. In addition he used the tune in four of his cantatas (45, 64, 94, 133).

Ahasuerus Fritsch (1629–1701) was born in Mücheln, Germany, where his father was the mayor. These were wartimes and the family had to move frequently to avoid the soldiers. Fritsch was educated at the Halle Gymnasium and later in Jena (D.L. 1661). He was a tutor for some time and then served as chancellor of the university and president of the consistory of Rudolstadt. The tune is also known as DARMSTADT and O GOTT, DU FROMMER GOTT.

For comments on Bach, see hymn 17.

279 Lord of Our Growing Years

Tune: LITTLE CORNARD

This hymn was written by David Mowbray (b. 1938) in 1982.

LITTLE CORNARD was written in 1915 by Martin Shaw (1875–1958) and included in *Additional Tunes and Settings for Use at St. Mary's Primrose Hill* (1915). It was named after the village in Suffolk, England, where Shaw spent his honeymoon. When it was published, Shaw was organist at St. Mary's, Primrose Hill, where Percy Dearmer (see hymn 459) was vicar. For more on Shaw, see hymn 12.

280 Amazing Grace, How Sweet the Sound

Tune: AMAZING GRACE

This hymn was written by John Newton for the people of Olney, Buckinghamshire, England, where he was a pastor.

John Newton (1725–1807) was born in London and at age eleven went to sea with his father. His mother had died when he was six. By age seventeen he was in the British Royal Navy assigned to a man-of-war. After serving as a sailor on a slave ship, he became a captain, transporting Africans to port where they could be sold for the best price. In 1748 he was caught in a storm at sea and experienced a spiritual awakening. Later he left the sea and became responsible for checking incoming ships for contraband.

At age forty Newton was ordained in the Church of England despite his lack of formal education. In 1782 he went to St. Mary Woonoth Church, London, where he remained the rest of his life. Newton and William Cowper (see hymn 270) were responsible for *Olney Hymns* (1779).

Newton wrote his own epitaph which reads:

JOHN NEWTON
CLERK
ONCE AN INFIDEL AND LIBERTINE
A SERVANT OF SLAVES IN AFRICA
WAS
BY THE RICH MERCY OF OUR LORD AND SAVIOUR
JESUS CHRIST
PRESERVED, RESTORED, PARDONED,
AND APPOINTED TO PREACH THE FAITH
HE HAD LONG LABORED TO DESTROY

The present fifth stanza, erroneously credited to John P. Rees, is actually the tenth stanza of "Jerusalem, My Happy Home" as printed in Richard and Andrew Broaddus' *A Collection of Sacred Ballads* (1790). The collection was published almost forty years before Rees was born.

The first stanza has been translated into five Native American languages and appears in *The Presbyterian Hymnal* (1990) as in *The United Methodist Hymnal* (1989).

AMAZING GRACE, also known as NEW BRITAIN, was first printed in *Virginia Harmony* (1831). Although its origin is unknown, some believe it to be based on an African melody.

The arrangement of the tune is by Edwin Othello Excell (1851–1921). It was published in *Make His Praise Glorious* (1900).

281 Guide Me, O Thou Great Jehovah

Tune: CWM RHONDDA

William Williams, known as the "Sweet Singer of Wales" and "the Isaac Watts of Wales" wrote this text, full of biblical imagery. It was published in his *Alleluia* (1745).

William Williams (1717–1791) was born at Cefn-y-Coed, in the parish of Llanfair-y-bryn near Llandovery (1717) and ordained a deacon in the Church of England (1740). Williams soon became identified with the Calvinist Methodist movement. For over fifty years he traveled throughout Wales preaching. His wife, a singer, often traveled with him. He wrote more than eight hundred hymns in Welsh and another hundred in English. He died at Pantycelyn.

The earliest translation was by Peter Williams (no relation, 1722–1796) of Carmarthen and published in *Hymns on Various Subjects* (1771). Williams accepted part of Peter Williams' translation, added a stanza, and printed it on a leaflet captioned "A Favorite Hymn sung by Lady Huntingdon's Young Collegians *Printed by the desire of many Christian friends.* Lord, give it thy blessing!"

CWM RHONDDA was written by John Hughes for a *Cymanfa Ganu* (singing festival) at Capel Rhondda, Pontypridd, Wales. It is named for the principal coal town in Glamorganshire. Sources differ as to the date of its composition; some say 1905, others 1907. The tune was used as the setting of James Montgomery's "Angels, from the Realms of Glory" (hymn 22) in the Calvinist Methodist Church of America's bilingual hymnal (1918).

John Hughes (1873–1932) was born at Dowlais, Wales, and grew up in Llantwit Vardre, Glamorganshire. He was active in the Salem Baptist Church and succeeded his father as deacon and precentor.

282 If Thou but Trust in God to Guide Thee

Tune: WER NUR DEN LIEBEN GOTT

Both the German text and the musical setting of this hymn were composed by Georg Neumark. The hymn was published in his *Fortgepflanzter musikalisch-poetischer Lustwald* (Jena, 1657).

Neumark had set out to attend the University of Königsberg and on his way was robbed of all his possessions, except his prayer book and a little money. Schooling was now out of the question. In his darkest hour he was offered the job of tutor for Judge Stephen Henning. The appointment made it possible for him to save the money needed to attend the university. "On that very day I composed [this hymn] to the honor of my beloved Lord. . . . I certainly had cause enough to thank the divine compassion for such unlooked for grace." The hymn is based on Psalm 55:22–23.

Georg Neumark (1621–1681) was born in Thuringia and received his education at the University of Königsberg, where he studied law and poetry. He was court poet, librarian, and registrar to Duke Wilhelm II and later was secretary of the archives. He became blind during his last months of life.

The English translation, by Catherine Winkworth, was published in *Lyra Germanica* (1st series, 1855) with the first two lines reading "Leave God to order all thy ways, And hope in Him whate'er betide thee." In *The Chorale Book for England* (1863) she revised the hymn. It now began "If thou but suffer God to guide thee." That line has been further revised for *The Presbyterian Hymnal* (1990). For comments on Winkworth, see hymn 3.

WER NUR DEN LIEBEN GOTT was published with the text. Johann Sebastian Bach used the tune in eight of his cantatas (21, 27, 84, 88, 93, 166, 179, and 197) as well as in choral and organ settings. In former Presbyterian hymn collections this tune was known as NEUMARK.

283 God Marked a Line and Told the Sea

Tune: KEDRON

This hymn text based on Genesis 2:4b–9 was written by Thomas H. Troeger. Although there are many times throughout the church year this hymn may be sung, it was specifically written to be used on the First Sunday in Lent, Year A, of the Common Lectionary. Other scripture references evident in the hymn are Genesis 2:15–17 and Job 38:8–11. For comments on Troeger, see hymn 73.

KEDRON is attributed to Elkanah Kelsay Dare and appears as in Pilsbury's *United States Sacred Harmony* (1799). For comments on the tune, see hymn 124.

284 O God, What You Ordain Is Right

Tune: WAS GOTT TUT

The German original of this text "Was Gott tut, das ist wohlgetan" is by Samuel Rodigast. He wrote it for a personal friend who at the time was quite ill. It is based on Deuteronomy 32:4 and was published the next year in *Das Hannoversche Gesangbuch* (1676). The Prussian Frederick William III counted this hymn among his favorites and at his command it was sung at his funeral. The hymn has some similarities to an earlier hymn by Johann Michael Altenburg (1584–1640).

Samuel Rodigast (1649–1708) was born in Gröben and attended the University of Jena (M.A. 1671), where he was appointed adjunct in philosophy (1676). He was co-rector of the Greyfriars Gymnasium, Berlin (1680–1698). Although offered many professorships, he continued at the Gymnasium, becoming sole rector in 1698. He remained there until his death.

The translation by Catherine Winkworth appeared in *Lyra Germanica* (2nd series, 1858). She altered her translation in *The Chorale Book for England* (1863). In former Presbyterian collections the first line read, "Whate'er my God ordains is right." That line and others were altered from third person to second person for *The Presbyterian Hymnal* (1990). For comments on Winkworth, see hymn 3.

WAS GOTT TUT was composed by Severus Gastorius (1646–1682) for this text which Rodigast had written for him during a period of illness. Gastorius was cantor at Jena in 1675. The tune first appeared with the text in *Ausserlesenes Weimarisches Gesangbuch* (1681). The present harmonization from the 1917 *Common Service Book* of the United Lutheran Church (now Evangelical Lutheran Church in America) has appeared in previous Presbyterian collections. The tune was used by Johann Sebastian Bach (see hymn 17) in Cantatas 12, 69, 75, 98, 100, 144, and one of his wedding cantatas.

285 God, You Spin the Whirling Planets

Tune: AUSTRIAN HYMN

Written by Jane Parker Huber for the 1979 National Meeting of United Presbyterian Women, whose theme was "In the Image of God." The hymn was number 1 in the song booklet *Creation Sings* (Geneva Press, 1979) where it was titled "In God's Image."

The author relates the thrill of seeing "the words projected onto screens on the huge stage; there was the text as I had written it and, alongside it a translation into Spanish by Nanin Braulio of Puerto Rico" (Jane Parker Huber, *A Singing Faith*, p. 108; Philadelphia: Westminster Press, 1987).

The creation story, especially Genesis 1:26–27, served as the focus of the hymn. For a biographical sketch of Huber, see hymn 128.

AUSTRIAN HYMN was the tune chosen by Jane Parker Huber because the opening night of the national meeting featured a rendition of Franz Joseph Haydn's *Creation.* The tune by Haydn was written for the birthday of the Austrian emperor Franz den Kaiser in February 1797, at the request of the prime minister.

Haydn was inspired to write a national anthem for his people after having heard "God Save the King" at Westminster Abbey (1791). The melody appears to be a variant of a Croatian folksong "Vjatvo rano se ja vstanem."

The composer enjoyed the hymn so much he used it as the subject of the second movement of the String Quartet, Opus 76, No. 3 in C. Some say he played this piece last before his death.

The son of a wheelwright and brother of Johann Michael, Franz Joseph Haydn (1732–1809) was a choirboy in St. Stephen's Cathedral, Vienna, for ten years. After a few years of free-lance composing he became Kapellmeister to Prince Paul Anton Esterházy (1761). He received a Doctor of Music degree from Oxford in 1791.

Through the financial backing of the royal family (some thirty years) Haydn was able to achieve great strides as a composer. "Papa" Haydn, as he was known even to his students, wrote 108 symphonies, 398 folk song arrangements, 126 baritone trios, 68 string quartets, 14 masses, and 23 sacred songs as well as operas, sonatas, cantatas, oratorios, and other music. (For a complete listing of Haydn's works, see Stanley Sadie, ed., *The New Grove Dictionary of Music and Musicians* 8:328f.)

Haydn, a devout Christian, was grateful to God for his talent. He prefaced all his compositions with the words "In nomine Domini" and ended them with "Laus Deo."

286 Give to the Winds Thy Fears

Tune: ST. BRIDE

The original German hymn began "Befiehl du deine Wege." It was written by Paul Gerhardt while he was in his first pastorate at Mittenwald (1656). He began each of the twelve stanzas with a word from Luther's translation of Psalm 37:5. Gerhardt named it "Hymn of Trust." For more on Gerhardt, see hymn 11.

John Wesley first heard this hymn sung by the Moravians while traveling to America. The translation was included in the hymnbook Wesley compiled for the colonists in Georgia, where he was living. His Journal entry for May 7, 1737 read, "translated six hymns from the German while on a journey to another plantation." For more on Wesley, see hymn 253.

ST. BRIDE appears here with an altered rhythm from the original by Samuel Howard. For more on the tune and the composer, see hymn 198.

287 God Folds the Mountains Out of Rock

Tune: REVISION

This text was written by Thomas H. Troeger (1985) for the Common Lectionary reading for the Eighteenth Sunday after Pentecost, Year B. For a biographical sketch of Troeger, see hymn 73.

REVISION is by Carol Ann Doran (b. 1936). Since 1975 Doran has taught at Colgate Rochester/Bexley Hall/Crozer Theological Seminary in Rochester, New York, where she is currently associate professor of church music and director of community worship and the pastoral music program.

Doran graduated from West Chester State University, Pennsylvania (B.S.) and the Eastman School of Music at the University of

Rochester, New York (M.M.; D.M.A.). She has served as organist and director of choirs at the Episcopal Church of the Incarnation in Penfield, New York, and the Twelve Corners Presbyterian Church in Rochester, New York (1964–1969). Her published works include *A History of Music in the Episcopal Church*, with William H. Petersen (1987), and with Thomas Troeger, *New Hymns for the Lectionary: To Glorify the Maker's Name* (1987) and *Open to Glory: Renewing Worship in the Parish* (1983). Her hymn tunes have appeared in several recent denominational hymnals.

288 I Sing the Mighty Power of God

Tune: ELLACOMBE

This text by Isaac Watts was first published in his *Divine and Moral Songs for the Use of Children* (1715), where it was titled "Praise for Creation and Providence." This was the first hymnal written exclusively for children. Of the volume he wrote:

> Children of high and low degree, of the Church of England or dissenters, baptized in infancy or not, may all join together in these songs. And as I have endeavored to sink the language to the level of a child's understanding, and yet to keep it, if possible, above contempt, so I have designed to profit all, if possible, and offend none.

Sometimes the hymn appears with the word "Almighty" instead of "Mighty." For more on Watts, see hymn 40.

ELLACOMBE appeared in *Gesangbuch der Herzogl. Wirtembergischen Katholischen Hofkapelle* (1784). For comments on the tune, see hymn 89.

289 O God of Every Nation

Tune: LLANGLOFFAN

This text was written by William Watkins Reid, Jr., in 1958. It won first prize in a hymn-writing contest cosponsored by the Hymn Society of America and the National Council of Churches' Department of International Affairs. It was published in the Hymn Society's *Twelve New World Order Hymns* and sung by the six hundred delegates at the Fifth World Order Study Conference, Cleveland, Ohio, November 18–21, 1958. The text was revised slightly for inclusion in *The Worshipbook—Services and Hymns* (1972).

William Watkins Reid was born in New York City in 1923 and educated at Oberlin College (B.A.) and Yale Divinity School (B.D.). He served in the Army Medical Corps from 1943 to 1945 and for eight months was a prisoner of war in Germany. Reid is an ordained Methodist minister. With the exception of a summer in North Dakota, his entire career has been in Pennsylvania churches.

LLANGLOFFAN is from Daniel Evans' *Hymnau a Thonau*, the harmonization as in *The English Hymnal* (1906). For comments on this Welsh folk melody, see hymn 15.

290 God Created Heaven and Earth

Tune: TŌA-SĪA

This hymn of unknown authorship originally came from Amoy, China. The 1981 translation is by Boris and Clare Anderson, English missionaries to Taiwan. Concerning the hymn the Andersons wrote:

> It is a great pleasure to us that this Taiwanese hymn, which we have sung so often in Taiwan in the past, will now be available to more people. The tune is magnificent, and I-to's harmonization wonderfully compact and economical, so we are grateful if our translation has provided a slipway for its launch into wider waters.

TŌA-SĪA is a melody from the Malayo-Polynesian tribes, the Pi-po tribe, who were the original inhabitants of Taiwan. It was harmonized by I-to Loh in 1963. He revised the harmonization in 1982.

291 O God of Earth and Altar

Tune: LLANGLOFFAN

The present text is a composite. The original hymn was written by G. K. Chesterton for *The Commonwealth*, the journal of the

Christian Social Union, and later appeared in *The English Hymnal* (1906). The alterations to stanza 2 and the new stanza 3 were written by Jane Parker Huber at the request of Lewis Mudge, for the final worship of the Life and Mission Statement Consultation held at Mo Ranch in 1985. About the alterations, Huber said she attempted to keep the force and

> clarity of the Chesterton text and to incorporate contemporary concerns about the church's mission in the world, in the second stanza, "lies of tongue and pen" became "lies of pen and voice" that "make our hearts rejoice" instead of "comfort cruel men." The third stanza puts the ideas of the original author into contemporary language: unity and action for peace and justice under God's guidance and leadership. The alterations were completed in less than a couple of hours . . . in time for the closing service.

Gilbert Keith Chesterton (1874–1936) was born in Kensington (London) and was known as an author, journalist, and poet. He was educated at St. Paul's School and the Slade School of Art, London. He began his career as an art critic whose articles appeared in *The Spectator* and *The Bookman*. From there he went on to become one of the most versatile and provocative journalists of his day. He maintained a lecture series while dictating more than fourteen thousand words a week, in addition to his writing efforts. Chesterton fell under the influence of Hilaire Belloc and like Belloc became an advocate for the England of the Middle Ages. In 1922 he separated from the Church of England and became Roman Catholic. He died at Topmeadow, Beaconsfield, England. Among his many writings are the Father Brown mysteries and *Short History of England* (1917).

For a biographical sketch of Huber see hymn 128.

LLANGLOFFAN is from Daniel Evans' *Hymnau a Thonau*, the harmonization as in *The English Hymnal* (1906). For comments on this Welsh folk melody, see hymn 15.

292 All Beautiful the March of Days

Tune: FOREST GREEN

The text was written by Frances Whitmarsh Wile (1878–1939). She was approached by her pastor Dr. William Channing Gannett and Dr. Frederick Lucian Hosmer, who knew of her poetic ability, to write a hymn about the "spiritual values of winter" for inclusion in their collection *Unity Hymns and Carols* (enl. ed., 1911).

The hymn suggests that winter has a beauty of its own. It recalls the activities of winter and the promises it brings. The final stanza is a paraphrase of Psalm 19:1–4.

FOREST GREEN, an English folk melody, was arranged by Ralph Vaughan Williams. For comments on the tune, see hymn 43.

293 This Is My Father's World

Tune: TERRA BEATA

This text by Maltbie D. Babcock is part of a much longer poem in the collection *Thoughts for Everyday Living* published shortly after his death.

Maltbie Davenport Babcock (1858–1901) was born in Syracuse, New York, and educated at Syracuse University (1875) and Auburn Theological Seminary. He was ordained to the Presbyterian ministry and held pastorates in Lockport, New York, and Baltimore before succeeding Henry van Dyke (see hymn 305) at New York City's Brick Presbyterian Church. He was there only eighteen months when he died while visiting Naples, Italy.

TERRA BEATA was adapted from an English folk song by Franklin L. Sheppard, who learned it as a child from his mother. The tune appears to be a modified form of RUSPER, published as the setting of "Come Unto Me, Ye Weary" by William Chatterton Dix (see hymn 53) in *The English Hymnal* (1906). It was harmonized (1953) for *The Hymnbook* (1955) and altered (1988).

Franklin L. Sheppard (1852–1930) was born in Philadelphia and educated at the University of Pennsylvania (B.A. 1872). In 1875 he moved to Baltimore to supervise his father's foundry. There he became active in the Presbyterian Church U.S.A. He became president of the Board of Publication and Sabbath-School Work and was instrumental in the construction of the Witherspoon Building in Philadelphia, which for many years housed the denomination's publications unit. Sheppard edited the church school hymnal *Alleluia* (1915) and was a member of the revision committee for *The Hymnal* (1911). He died in Germantown, Pennsylvania.

294 Wherever I May Wander

Tune: NEW ENGLAND

This children's hymn was written by Ann B. Snow in 1959. It was published in *Songs and Hymns for Primary Children* (1963) by Westminster Press for the United Presbyterian Church U.S.A.

NEW ENGLAND is a folk melody from New England. The present arrangement was first published by the Unitarian Universalist Association.

295 O God of Love, O God of Peace

Tune: DU MEINER SEELEN

The text was written by Henry Williams Baker for inclusion in the original volume of *Hymns Ancient and Modern* (1861) with the caption "In Times of Trouble."

Baker may have produced this hymn to fill a void in the hymnal, but he certainly had reason to pray for peace. Italy was in the midst of a civil war which involved France, Austria, and the Papal States; England and France were at war; and in the United States civil war had recently broken out. For comments on Baker, see hymn 171.

DU MEINER SEELEN was first published in *Cantica Spiritualia* (1847).

296 Camina, Pueblo de Dios
Walk On, O People of God

Tune: NUEVA CREACIÓN

Cesáreo Gabaráin is the author and composer of this contemporary Spanish hymn which has become a favorite among Hispanics in the Americas. Gabaráin (1936–1991), a native of Mondragon, Spain, was a Roman Catholic parish priest and then monsignor in Madrid. He was the Spanish chaplain to Pope Paul VI and was granted the title emeritus shortly before his death in April 1991. Some of his hymns have been translated into over forty languages.

The English translation is by Rev. Dr. George Lockwood (1987) for *The United Methodist Hymnal* (1989). Lockwood was born in 1946 and has been a missionary to Costa Rica. He has pastored Spanish-speaking congregations in both Arizona and California and served on the editorial committee for the Methodist hymnal supplement *Celebremos II*. In addition, Lockwood has traveled throughout Central and South America interviewing church musicians and gathering new hymns from both Spanish and Portuguese cultures which he then presents at conferences and workshops.

297 O Lord of Every Shining Constellation

Tune: VICAR

This text was written by Albert F. Bayly (1950) and appeared in his first collected volume, *Rejoice, O People* (1951).

Albert Frederick Bayly (1901–1984) was born in Sussex, England, and educated at St. Mary Magdalen School, St. Leonards, and Hastings Grammar School. He studied to be a shipwright at the Royal Dockyard School, Portsmouth, and then received a Bachelor of Arts degree from London University. He was ordained in 1929 after studying for the ministry at Mansfield College, Oxford, where he graduated in 1928. Bayly served Congregational churches in Whitley Bay, Morpeth, Burnley, Swanland (East Yorkshire), Eccleston (St. Helens, Lancashire), and Thaxted (Essex) from 1929 to 1972.

Bayly was made a fellow of Westminster Choir College, Princeton, New Jersey (1972), and honored at Westminster Abbey in 1978. His hymns were published in several volumes: *Rejoice, O People* (1951); *Again I Say, Rejoice* (1967); *Rejoice Always* (1971); and *Rejoice in God* (1977).

VICAR was composed by V. Earle Copes in 1963 for *The Book of Hymns* (1964, 1966) of the United Methodist Church. It was the setting for "Hope of the World" by Georgia Harkness (see hymn 360). For a biographical sketch of Copes, see hymn 253.

298 There's a Wideness in God's Mercy

Tune: IN BABILONE

This hymn was written by Frederick William Faber and is part of a longer hymn "Souls of Men, Why Will Ye Scatter?" first published in *Oratory Hymns* (1854).

Frederick William Faber (1814–1863) was born in Yorkshire, England, to Calvinist parents. He was educated at Balliol and University colleges, Oxford (B.A. 1836; M.A. 1839). He was strongly influenced by John Henry Newman and was ordained an Anglican deacon in 1837 and a priest in 1839. After a brief service to the Church of England, he, like many others in the Oxford movement, became a Roman Catholic priest in 1846. Faber founded a branch of Newman's order, the Priests of the Congregation of St. Philip Neri (1849). He died at Brompton. Faber wrote one hundred fifty hymns, all after his conversion to Roman Catholicism.

IN BABILONE is a Dutch melody that appeared in *Oude en Nieuwe Hollantse Boerenlities en Contradansen* in the early eighteenth century. It was harmonized by Julius Röntgen and was published in *The English Hymnal* (1906). Röntgen's own collection *Old Dutch Peasant Songs and Country Dances Transcribed for the Piano* (1912) also contained the piece.

Julius Röntgen (1855–1933) was born in Leipzig and studied there. He then traveled to Amsterdam in 1877, where he became a professor at the Amsterdam Conservatory and then conductor of the Society for the Advancement of Musical Art in 1886. From 1918 to 1924 he was director of the conservatory, retiring to compose. He died at Utrecht.

299 Amen, Amen

This African-American spiritual chronicles the life of Jesus Christ from birth to resurrection. The congregational (choral) "Amens" serve as the foundation for the solo narrative and should be sung as affirmations of the leader's (soloist's) freely improvised message.

Modulating by half steps after each stanza can increase the intensity of the spiritual's story.

The traditional African-American tune was arranged by Nelsie T. Johnson (b. 1912) for *The Presbyterian Hymnal* (1990). It is an example of the traditional singing of the spiritual, particularly in Southeastern America. Johnson was born in Greer, South Carolina, where she resides. She is a retired schoolteacher who continues to serve as choir director, organist, and pianist for Presbyterian churches in the Greenville and Spartanburg, South Carolina, area. She was frequently the accompanist for Rev. Joseph T. Jones (see hymn 153) as he led music for Presbyterian gatherings.

300 Down to Earth, as a Dove

Tune: PERSONENT HODIE

The text was written by Fred Kaan to preserve the tune PERSONENT HODIE in the event the text "Personent hodie" ("On This Day Earth Shall Ring," hymn 46) ever fell out of use. According to Kaan, his use of the phrase "In the house there is bread" in stanza 3 is to remind the singer that the word "Bethlehem" means "house of bread" (*The Hymn Texts of Fred Kaan*, p. 21; Carol Stream, Ill.: Hope Publishing Company, 1985).

The text and tune were published for general use in *The Canadian Hymnbook.*

PERSONENT HODIE is from *Piae Cantiones* (1582) and arranged by Gustav Theodore Holst (1924). For comments on the tune, see hymn 46. For comments on Holst, see hymn 36.

301 Lord Jesus, Think on Me

Tune: SOUTHWELL

This hymn was originally written in Greek. It is one of the last ten odes written by Synesius of Cyrene. The translation-paraphrase was made by Allen William Chatfield and appeared in his *Songs and Hymns of the Earliest Greek Christian Poets* (1876).

Synesius (c. 370–c. 414) was born in Cyrene and studied under Hypatia the Neo-Platonist. He was a friend of Augustine of Hippo. He was appointed bishop of Ptolemais, Cyrene, around 410, but was allowed to keep his wife.

Allen William Chatfield (1808–1896) was born at Chatteris, Cambridgeshire, England, and studied at Trinity College, Cambridge (B.A. 1831). He was ordained by the Church of England and was vicar of Stotfold, Bedfordshire (1833–1847), before becoming vicar of Much-Marcle, Herefordshire. He served there until his death.

SOUTHWELL was the setting for Psalm 45 in Daman's *Psalmes of David in English Meter, with Notes of Foure Parts Set Unto Them by Guilielmo Daman, for John Bull, to the vus of the godly Christians for recreatying them selues, in stede of fond and unseemely Ballades*, printed by John Day (1579). Many of the tunes in this collection were from earlier Psalters: Anglo-Genevan Psalter (1556), English Psalter (1562), Scottish Psalter (1564). Daman was unhappy with the simple harmonies he had created and tried to destroy the copies.

Guilielmo Daman (also William Damon) was born in Liège about 1540. A register of aliens living in London in 1571 indicated that one "William de Man" was brought to England in 1565 to serve Lord Buckhurst. Later he was the organist at the Chapel Royal for Queen Elizabeth I. An inventory of his possessions was made in the presence of his widow in 1591.

302 I Danced in the Morning

Tune: SIMPLE GIFTS

This hymn was written by Sydney Carter and has become his most famous song. It uses an American Shaker melody which is often sung to " 'Tis a Gift to Be Simple." Carter adapted it and harmonized it for this text.

Sydney Carter was born in Camden, London, in 1915 and was educated at Christ's Hospital and Balliol, Oxford, where he studied to be a teacher. During World War II he joined the Friends' Ambulance Unit in Greece and served in the Middle East for two years. Later, he became a script writer and lecturer.

Carter is a leader in the church folk song movement. His hymns are collected in *9 Ballads or Carols* (1962) and *Green Print for Song* (1973).

SIMPLE GIFTS is a Shaker tune deriving from the Shaker movement which originated during an English revival in 1747. The name "Shaker" came from the shaking that occurred during the stress of the spiritual exaltation the members experienced in their meetings. Shakers in England and America lived in communities, separate from the rest of society. They rose at a common hour, were uniformly dressed, ate meals together, and those in the "Senior order" maintained common property.

303 Jesus, Lover of My Soul

Tune: ABERYSTWYTH

The text was written by Charles Wesley in 1740. This hymn is often regarded as his best. Yet it did not appear in an official Methodist hymnal until nine years after his death. His brother John Wesley, founder of the Methodist movement, opposed the hymn's use in public worship. For a biographical sketch of Charles Wesley, see hymn 1.

The story goes that Charles was inspired to write these words when a dove flew to him as protection from a hawk. Another story describes a seabird that took refuge from a storm in his room. There is also the tale that he wrote the hymn after his escape from an angry mob. In reality, Wesley wrote this hymn shortly after his conversion. It was included in the 1740 collection *Hymns and Sacred Poems.* The hymn was originally intended to be used "in time of Prayer and Temptation."

ABERYSTWYTH was composed by Joseph Parry in 1879. The tune was originally published set to another text. It became associated with "Jesus, Lover of My Soul" in Parry's cantata *Ceridwen.* The tune is named for a Welsh Sea resort on Cardigan Bay. Parry was born in Wales in 1841. He moved with his family to Danville, Pennsylvania, in 1854. As an adult he moved back to Wales, where he remained until his death in 1903.

304 Jesus Loves Me!

Tune: JESUS LOVES ME

The text was written by Anna Bartlett Warner for her novel *Say and Seal* (c. 1859). The main characters of the novel were a dying child Johnny Fax, his Sunday school teacher John Linden, and Linden's fiancée, Faith Derrick. Toward the end of the book, Linden carries the child and sings to him what has now become the familiar children's hymn.

Anna (1820–1915) and Susan Warner were daughters of a New York lawyer who between them wrote more than seventy books. Every Sunday afternoon from their home, Good Crag, located on Constitution Island in the Hudson River, West Point, New York, they taught a Bible class to the cadets of West Point (the home was willed to West Point and is now a national shrine). The sisters were buried with full military honors which recognized the contribution they made to the lives of young military officers.

Anna Warner published two hymn collections: *Hymns of the Church Militant* (1858) and *Wayfaring Hymns, Original and Translated* (1869). She died at ninety-five near the spot where she was born.

JESUS LOVES ME was composed by William Batchelder Bradbury as the setting for this text in his collection *The Golden Shower* (1862).

William Batchelder Bradbury (1816–1868) was born in York, Maine, but moved to Boston at fourteen to study with Sumner Hill. He enrolled in Lowell Mason's choir and Boston Academy. At Mason's urging, he held music classes in Machias, Maine, and later at St. John's, New Brunswick.

In 1841, Bradbury became organist at Baptist Tabernacle, New York City, and held annual children's music festivals as a way of introducing music into New York public schools. The last twenty years of his life were dedicated to composition and compiling collections of sacred and secular music. His publications include *The Jubilee* (1858), *Fresh Laurels*, and the Golden series.

305 Jesus, Our Divine Companion

Tune: PLEADING SAVIOR

The text written by Henry van Dyke in 1909 was altered in 1910 for the collection *Hymns of the Kingdom of God*, edited by Henry Sloane Coffin and Ambrose White Vernon. The theme of Christ's presence among the workers is van Dyke's attempt to restore vitality to the Christian life. Although not in *The Hymnal* (1933), it has enjoyed popularity in more recent hymnals. It was first set to PLEADING SAVIOR in *The Hymnal 1940* of the Protestant Episcopal Church.

Henry van Dyke (1852–1933) was born in Germantown, Pennsylvania. He was educated at Princeton University (A.B. 1873; A.M. 1876) and Princeton Theological Seminary (B.D. 1877). He also studied at the University of Berlin for a year prior to being ordained as a minister in the Presbyterian Church U.S.A. (1879). He served as pastor of the Brick Presbyterian Church, New York City (1883–1900), after which he became professor of English literature at Princeton University. There he became good friends with Woodrow Wilson, president of the university. In 1913, then–U.S. President Wilson appointed van Dyke as minister to the Netherlands and Luxembourg, a position he held until 1917. After the United States entered World War I, van Dyke volunteered for active duty becoming a lieutenant commander in the Naval Chaplain Corps. From 1923 on, he lived in his beloved home "Avalon" in Princeton, New Jersey, devoting himself to literary endeavors.

Van Dyke served as editor of *The Book of Common Worship* (1905), and it was his motion at the General Assembly of 1928 that led to its revision in 1931. He also served on the advisory committee on *The Hymnal* (1933).

Throughout his life, van Dyke received many honors, including a Doctor of Civil Law degree from Oxford University.

PLEADING SAVIOR is an American folk melody popularized as a camp-meeting tune. It was first published in Joshua Leavitt's *Christian Lyre* (1830) as the setting for the text "Now the Savior Stands A-pleading," also "Now Behold, the Savior Pleading," hence the name. In 1855 the tune appeared as PLYMOUTH in Henry Ward Beecher's *Plymouth Collection.* The hymn tune gained popularity in England and was renamed SALTASH when it began appearing in English collections. The harmonization of the tune is by Richard Proulx and is as it appears in *The Hymnal 1982*. For comments on Proulx, see hymn 573.

306 Fairest Lord Jesus

Tune: CRUSADERS' HYMN

This text has been traced to the Jesuits in Münster. A handwritten copy from 1662 and a published collection from the Münster Gesangbuch (1677) date its origin. The original had five stanzas and began "Schönster Herr Jesu." There was an altered version published in *Schlesische Volkslieder* (Leipzig, 1842).

This translation first appeared in Richard Storrs Willis' *Church Chorals and Choir Studies* (1850). It was slightly altered for *The Presbyterian Hymnal* (1990). Another translation by Dr. Joseph A. Seiss beginning "Beautiful Savior! King of Creation" was published in *The Sunday School Book* of the American Lutheran General Council (Philadelphia, 1873).

CRUSADERS' HYMN was published in the Leipzig collection *Schlesische Volkslieder* (1842) with the altered text mentioned above. In the preface to the collection, Hofmann, the editor, stated, "In the summer of 1836 I visited a friend in Westphalia. Toward evening I heard the haymakers singing—I made inquiries. They sang folk songs which seemed to me worthy of being collected." How far back this melody goes cannot be determined. It is sung by all classes and all ages.

307 Fight the Good Fight

Tune: DUKE STREET

This hymn based on 1 Timothy 6:12 is by John S. B. Monsell. It was included in his *Hymns of Love and Praise for the Church's Year* (1863). He published eleven poetry books which included his more than three hundred hymns.

The son of the Archdeacon of Londonderry, John Samuel Bewley Monsell (1811–1875) was born in St. Columb's, Londonderry, Ireland, and educated at Trinity College, Dublin (B.A. 1832; LL.D. 1856). He was ordained a deacon in 1834 and priest in 1835. He was chaplain to Bishop Mant, and the rector of Ramoan. He went to England in 1853 and became vicar of Egham, Surrey, and later rector of St. Nicholas, Guildford. He died of injuries received when he fell off the roof of his church, which was in the process of being rebuilt. The hymn was introduced to Americans in *The Episcopal Hymnal 1889* and the Presbyterian *Hymnal* (1895). The present text is slightly altered from the original.

DUKE STREET was composed by John Hatton and first appeared in *A Select Collection of Psalm and Hymn Tunes by the late Henry Boyd, teacher of Psalmody* (Glasgow, 1793), where it was the setting for Joseph Addison's paraphrase of Psalm 19. In 1805 it was published in William Dixon's *Euphonia* with the name DUKE STREET and attributed to John Hatton. Hatton, a Presbyterian, was born in Warrington, England (date unknown), and lived in Lancaster, England, in the village of St. Helen's on Duke Street. He died in 1793.

308 O Sing a Song of Bethlehem

Tune: KINGSFOLD

Written by Louis Benson (1899), this hymn is one of the best poetic portrayals of the life of Christ. Using four geographical areas, the hymn lifts up stages in Jesus' life. In Bethlehem there shone a light that continues today. In Nazareth flowers bloomed and today these flowers bring beauty into the believer's life. The peace that came over Galilee still brings peace to the believer. Calvary's redeeming power is adequate to meet today's needs.

Louis FitzGerald Benson (1855–1930) was born in Philadelphia, where he died. He was educated at the University of Pennsylvania in law, a career he abandoned after seven years. He entered Princeton Theological Seminary and was ordained to the Presbyterian ministry in 1886. After a six-year pastorate at Church of the Redeemer in Germantown, he became editor of several hymnals authorized by the General Assembly of the Presbyterian Church U.S.A., including *The Hymnal* (1895). He also served on the committee that prepared *The Book of Common Worship* of the Presbyterian Church in the U.S.A. (1905) and on the revision committee of that volume.

Benson lectured in liturgics at Auburn Seminary, in hymnology at Princeton Theological Seminary, and wrote several books on hymnody. Among these are *The Best Church Hymns, Studies of Familiar Hymns, The Hymnody of the Christian Church,* and *The English Hymn.* His hymnological library, thought to be one of the world's most valuable private collections, was given to Princeton Seminary when he died.

KINGSFOLD is a traditional English melody first published by Lucy Etheldred Broadwood and J. A. Fuller Maitland in their *English Country Songs* (1893). There it was the setting for "Dives and Lazarus." It appeared in *The English Hymnal* (1906) arranged and harmonized by Ralph Vaughan Williams as the setting for "I Heard the Voice of Jesus Say." The tune was first used with the present text in *The Hymnary* (1927) of the United Church of Canada. It was named for a village in Surrey, where Vaughan Williams heard a variant of the tune. The Irish know the tune as THE STAR OF COUNTY DOWN. For a biographical sketch of Vaughan Williams, see hymn 6.

309 Of the Father's Love Begotten

Tune: DIVINUM MYSTERIUM

The Latin text "Corde natus ex Parentis" was written by Aurelius Clemens Prudentius. He was the most prolific and prominent author of early sacred Latin poetry.

A native of Spain, Aurelius Clemens Prudentius (348–c. 413) was educated in imperial schools where he studied the Latin poets Horace and Virgil. He became a law student and twice a magistrate before being appointed to court office by Theodosius. At age fifty-seven he renounced the world and retreated to a life of poverty, seclusion, and writing.

The hymn was translated by John Mason Neale (1854) as "Of the Father Sole Begotten," and revised by Henry Williams Baker for *Hymns Ancient and Modern* (1861). Baker also included a translation of the Doxology in the hymn.

For comments on Neale and Baker, see hymns 4 and 71, respectively.

DIVINUM MYSTERIUM is a plainsong melody used by Neale for his translation of "Corde natus ex Parentis" in the collection *The*

Hymnal Noted (1851). There it was captioned "Melody from a manuscript at Wolfenbutel of the XIIIth century."

More than likely the source of the tune was *Piae Cantiones Ecclesiasticae et Scholasticae* (1582). The collection was used by Thomas Helmore, music editor of *The Hymnal Noted.* For comments on Helmore, see hymn 9.

The harmonization is by C. Winfred Douglas for *The Hymnal 1940* of the Episcopal Church. For comments on Douglas, see hymn 4.

310 Jesus, the Very Thought of Thee

Tune: ST. AGNES

This hymn is taken from the Latin poem "Jesu dulcis memoria" (see hymn 510), which has been attributed to Bernard of Clairvaux (1091–1153). For comments on Bernard of Clairvaux, see hymn 98.

The text was translated by Edward Caswall (1848) and was included in his *Lyra Catholica* (1849). The translation has been slightly altered for *The Presbyterian Hymnal* (1990). For comments on Caswall, see hymn 51.

ST. AGNES was composed by John Bacchus Dykes as the setting of this text in Rev. J. Grey's *A Hymnal for Use in the English Church*, with accompanying tunes (1866). The title was originally ST. AGNES, DURHAM, named for the thirteen-year-old Roman martyr of the fourth century. For comments on Dykes, see hymn 91.

311 We Meet You, O Christ

Tune: NORMANDY

This text by Fred Kaan was written as a result of the preparation of a script for the British Broadcasting Company television series "Seeing and Believing," in 1966. The show was to be broadcast on the twenty-fifth anniversary of the destruction of the city of Plymouth, England, in a German air raid. A photograph of the ruins of St. Andrew's Church served as the theme for the program. The photograph showed an apple tree growing out of the rubble which had once been a house of worship.

Kaan titled the hymn "The Tree Springs to Life." It was sung in the broadcast by English folksinger Len Pearcy to a melody by Philip Humphreys. For more on Kaan, see hymn 109. This text has been set to several tunes, including Erik Routley's DURHAM 72 and Pablo Sosa's BOSSEY. The setting here is from *Hymnal Supplement* (1984).

NORMANDY is a Basque carol harmonized by George Mims in 1979. Mims (b. 1938) served as music editor for *Songs for Celebration: Church Hymnal Series IV* (1980). He is organist and choirmaster of Church of the Redeemer, Episcopal, in Houston, Texas.

312 When Jesus Wept

Tune: WHEN JESUS WEPT

Both the text and the music of this canon were composed by William Billings and appeared in the *New England Psalm Singer* (1770), a collection of one hundred twenty vocal compositions. This competely American collection was the first of its type and also the first music book to contain tunes by a single American composer.

William Billings (1746–1800) was born in Boston and was apprenticed to a tanner. He became an inspector of tanned leather, chalking his early tunes on the walls of the bark mill.

Billings was physically limited. He had sight in only one eye, a withered arm, one leg shorter than the other. He became known as a voice teacher and composer. His singing school at Stoughton, Massachusetts, begun in 1774, became the Stoughton Musical Society, the oldest society of its kind still in existence (1786).

Billings compiled and published five additional collections of church music: *The Singing Master's Assistant* (1778), *Music in Miniature* (1779), *The Psalm Singer's Amusement* (1781), *The Suffolk Harmony* (1786), and *The Continental Harmony* (1794). In addition, Billings introduced the bass viol and pitch pipe into church choirs.

313 Come Down, O Love Divine

Tune: DOWN AMPNEY

This hymn was written by Bianco da Siena. It was part of an eight-stanza poem included in *Laudi Spirituali del Bianco da Siena* edited and published by Telesforo Bini (1851).

The English translation is by Richard Frederick Littledale and included in his *People's Hymnal* (1867).

Bianco was born at Anciolina in Val d'Arno. His date of birth is unknown. He entered the Order of Jesuates, an unordained order that followed the rule of St. Augustine. He lived for some time in Venice and died there in 1434.

Richard Frederick Littledale (1833–1890) was born in Dublin, Ireland, and educated at Bectine Hense Seminary and Trinity College (B.A. 1858; M.A. 1858; LL.B. and LL.D. 1862), and received the Doctor of Civil Law degree from Oxford (1862). He was ordained a deacon in 1856 and a priest in 1857. Littledale was forced to retire from parish ministry in 1861 because of ill health and spent the remainder of his life writing. He published works on theology, history, liturgy, and hymnology. He compiled *Carols for Christmas and Other Seasons* (1863) and *The Altar Manual* (1863–1877).

DOWN AMPNEY was composed for this text by Ralph Vaughan Williams for *The English Hymnal* (1906). It was named for his birthplace near Cirencester, Gloucestershire. For a biographical sketch of Vaughan Williams, see hymn 6.

314 Like the Murmur of the Dove's Song

Tune: BRIDEGROOM

This text was written by Carl P. Daw, Jr., in 1982. Daw was born in Louisville, Kentucky, in 1944 and presently serves as vicar-chaplain at St. Mark's Episcopal Chapel at the University of Connecticut. He has written over thirty hymn texts, among the most popular being "Surely It Is God Who Saves Me" and the present text. He is recognized for contributing outstanding paraphrases of the Psalms and many of his hymns have yet to be published.

BRIDEGROOM was composed by Peter Cutts in 1969. For a biographical sketch of Cutts, see hymn 135. This tune was first published in *100 Hymns for Today* (1969).

315 Every Time I Feel the Spirit

Tune: PENTECOST

This African-American spiritual demonstrates the belief that communion with God is a spirit-filled encounter involving the total person. African Americans have always had an understanding of a God who could be felt. Under the power of the Spirit, one is moved to pray, preach, sing, or witness.

PENTECOST: Melva Wilson Costen adapted Joseph T. Jones' arrangement of this spiritual for inclusion in *The Presbyterian Hymnal* (1990). The syncopated rhythm invites total involvement of singers. Costen cautions:

> Care should be taken not to assume that participants should "clap" or otherwise "beat" the rhythm in order for the song to be authentically rendered! This could provide a gradual acceleration of the tempo and momentum which could distort the sacredness and intentionality of the jubilant music.

For comments on Costen and Jones, see hymns 29 and 153, respectively. For more on the African-American singing experience, see Melva W. Costen, "Singing Praise to God in African American Worship Contexts," in Gayraud Wilmore, ed., *African American Religious Studies: An Interdisciplinary Anthology* (Durham, N.C.: Duke University Press, 1989), pp. 392–403.

316 Breathe on Me, Breath of God

Tune: TRENTHAM

This text was written by Edwin Hatch and published in the pamphlet *Between Doubt and Prayer* (1878). It later appeared in *Towards Fields of Light* (1890).

Edwin Hatch (1835–1889) was born in Derby and educated

at King Edward's School, Birmingham, and Pembroke College, Oxford (B.A. 1857). He became a member of the Church of England, taking holy orders in 1859, and ministered for three years in London's East End before becoming professor of classics at Trinity College, Toronto, Canada, and rector of Quebec High School (1859–1867). Hatch returned to England and served as vice-principal of St. Mary's Hall and then held several other faculty positions at Oxford University. His Bampton Lectures, "On the Organization of Early Christian Churches," were translated into German by Adolf von Harnack, the leading authority on the subject in that day. Hatch was engaged in producing a *Concordance to the Septuagint and Other Greek Versions of the Old Testament* at the time of his death. The project was subsequently finished by H. A. Redpath and published in 1897.

TRENTHAM was composed by Robert Jackson in 1894 and was published in *Sacred Leaflets.* The tune is named after the small village of Trentham in Staffordshire, England.

Robert Jackson (1842–1914) was born in Oldham, Lancashire, England, and studied at the Royal Academy of Music. He was organist at St. Mark's Church, London, and on the death of his father, Jackson took his position as organist and choirmaster at St. Peter's Church, Oldham. Jackson and his father between them served the same St. Peter's Church for almost ninety years.

317 Holy Ghost, Dispel Our Sadness

Tune: GENEVA

This hymn for Whitsuntide was written by Paul Gerhardt and appeared in Johann Crüger's *Praxis Pietatis Melica* (3rd ed., 1648). John Christian Jacobi's translation "O Thou Sweetest Source of Gladness" first appeared in his *Psalmodia Germanica*, Part 2 (1725). In the 1732 edition the text was extensively altered. The text was altered again to read "Holy Ghost dispel our sadness" by Augustus Montague Toplady and published in the *Gospel Magazine* (1776). For a biographical sketch of Gerhardt, see hymn 11.

John Christian Jacobi (1670–1750) was born in Germany and appointed keeper of the Royal German Chapel, St. James

Palace, London (1708). He held the position until his death. He was responsible for the English translation and publication of several collections of German hymns.

GENEVA was composed by John Henry Day. For comments on the tune and the composer, see hymn 73.

318 Gracious Spirit, Holy Ghost

Tune: ANDERSON

This hymn text is a paraphrase of 1 Corinthians 13 by Christopher Wordsworth. It first appeared in *The Holy Year* (1st ed., 1862).

Christopher Wordsworth (1807–1885) was born at Lambeth, where his father was parish minister. He was educated at Winchester and Trinity College, Cambridge (degree, 1830), where he had a distinguished record and was later employed as a classical lecturer and the public orator for the university (1836). He became a parish priest for nineteen years before becoming bishop of Lincoln (1869), where he served for more than fifteen years and to within a few months of his death. He was the nephew of the poet laureate William Wordsworth.

Wordsworth wrote much, including a commentary on the entire Bible. His *The Holy Year* contained hymns for all seasons of the church year and for every phase of the seasons as indicated in the rubrics of *The Book of Common Prayer*. He saw hymns as a means of teaching Christian doctrine and held it to be "the first duty of a hymn-writer to teach sound doctrine, and thus to save souls." He sought materials for hymns in scripture, ancient Christian writings, and the poetry of the early church.

ANDERSON was composed by Jane Manton Marshall in 1985 for this text and published in *Hymnal Supplement, II* (1987). For comments on Marshall, see hymn 340.

319 Spirit

Both the text and the tune of this contemporary hymn were written by James K. Manley in 1975 while he was working toward his Doctor of Ministry degree at Claremont School of

Theology under Professor John Cobb. After he completed the rough draft of his paper, he felt the "prodding and pushing" of the Holy Spirit as both a "comforter and challenger."

James K. Manley was born in 1940 in Holyoke, Massachusetts, and was educated at Whittier College (1962), Pacific School of Religion (M.Div. 1966), and Claremont School of Theology (D.Min. 1976). He was pastor of the Niles United Church of Christ, Fremont, California (1966–1968). He served the Mid-Pacific Institute Prep School (1968–1978). Then Manley became pastor of a United Church of Christ church in San Marino, California (1978–1988). Since 1988, Manley has been pastor of Foothills United Church of Christ in Los Altos, California.

The full accompaniment for the hymn was published in *Sing to God: Songs and Hymns for Christian Education* (Christian Education: Shared Approaches, 1984).

Manley's original text included the phrase "goaded your people" in the second stanza. The Presbyterian Hymnal Committee changed the phrase to "gifted your people." Several printings of *The Presbyterian Hymnal* (1990) include this change. Manley has since requested the original be restored.

320 The Lone, Wild Bird

Tune: PROSPECT

The text of this hymn was written by Henry Richard McFadyen (also MacFayden) when he was a field worker for the Presbytery of Nashville. He wrote it for a national hymn-writing contest of *The Homiletic and Pastoral Review*. In a letter to William Chalmers Covert in 1934, McFadyen wrote, "The hymn was written on a quiet Sunday afternoon in the fall or winter of 1925 and sent to the *Review*. It was forgotten until I was surprised with an announcement that I had been awarded the third prize in the contest." It was first published in 1927 and later in *The Hymnal* (1933), where the original first line read "The lone, wild fowl."

Henry Richard McFadyen (1877–1964) was born in Beaden County, North Carolina, and was pastor of the Presbyterian Church in Pinetops, North Carolina.

PROSPECT is an American folk melody arranged and harmonized by David N. Johnson. It first appeared in *Twelve Folksongs and*

Spirituals (1968), compiled and arranged by Johnson. For a biographical sketch of Johnson, see hymn 458.

321 Holy Spirit, Truth Divine

Tune: SONG 13

This text was written by Samuel Longfellow and first published in his *Hymns of the Spirit* (1864), where it was subtitled "The Holy Spirit Desired." The present text was altered by the Presbyterian Hymnal Committee. A stanza of the original was deleted and there is a phrase change in stanza 4, line 2, from "King within my conscience reign" to "Make my conscience wholly Thine."

Samuel Longfellow (1819–1892) was born in Portland, Maine, and educated at Harvard College (B.A. 1839) and Divinity School (B.D. 1846). He was ordained a Unitarian minister and served churches in Fall River, Massachusetts (1848–1853); Brooklyn, New York (1853–1860); and Germantown, Pennsylvania (1878–1882). The intervening years he spent as a free-lance preacher, writer, and editor. His intermittent pastorates were caused largely by poor health. Longfellow moved to "Craigie House" to write the *Life of Henry Wadsworth Longfellow* (1886), his older brother, and *Final Memorials of H. W. Longfellow* (1887).

With Samuel Johnson, a friend from seminary, he edited *A Book of Hymns for Public and Private Devotion* (1846) and *Hymns of the Spirit* (1864). Longfellow also published *Vespers* (1859) and *A Book of Hymns and Tunes* (1860; rev., 1876).

SONG 13 was composed by Orlando Gibbons for the text "O My Love, How Comely Now" from the Song of Songs. It was published in George Wither's *Hymns and Songs of the Church* (1623). For a biographical sketch of Gibbons, see hymn 385.

322 Spirit of the Living God

Tune: LIVING GOD

Both the text and the tune of this hymn were written by Daniel Iverson (1890–1977). The story is told that George C. Stephans was conducting a revival in Orlando, Florida, in the spring of 1926. His friend Rev. Daniel Iverson, a Presbyterian U.S. pastor from Lumberton, North Carolina, came and spent a few days with him. Iverson was extremely moved by the sermon he heard on the Holy Spirit and wrote the hymn that day, sharing it with his friends. E. Powell Lee, Stephans' music director, introduced the piece that night. Lee continued to spread the hymn through his work with Southern Baptist churches and through the Home Mission Board in Atlanta. The hymn was published in 1935 by Moody Press.

Iverson spent his ministry serving churches in Georgia, North and South Carolina, and Florida. After his retirement in 1951, Iverson moved to Montreat, near Asheville, North Carolina, where he died.

323 Loving Spirit

Tune: OMNI DIE

The text was written by Shirley Erena Murray (b. 1931) and published in her booklet *In Every Corner Sing* (1987). For comments on Murray, see hymn 105.

OMNI DIE, of unknown authorship, was the setting for the *Marienlied* "Omni die dic Mariae" in David Gregor Corner's *Gross Catholisch Gesangbuch* (2nd ed., 1631). The collection contained hymns from new sources, including Jesuit hymnals published at Cologne (1623, 1625), Mainz (1628), Würzburg (1628), Heidelberg (1629), and Amberg (1629), Protestant hymn writers, and hymns Corner labeled "Incerti Authoris."

David Gregor Corner (1581–1648) was born in Hirschberg, Silesia (now Jelenia Góra, Poland) and studied in Prague (M.A. 1609), Graz, and Vienna (Th.D. 1624; Ph.D.). He was first a priest and then a Benedictine monk at Göttweig (1625), where he was prior and later abbot. In 1638 he became rector of the University of Vienna and a leader in the Counter-Reformation.

The harmony is that of William Smith Rockstro (Rackstraw). Born in Surrey, Rockstro (1823–1895) studied with John Purkis and Sterndale Bennett and Felix Mendelssohn (see hymn 31) at Leipzig Conservatory (1845–1846). An authority on early music, he wrote textbooks on harmony and music history and several biographies, including *The Life of G. F. Handel* (1883), *Mendelssohn* (1884), and with H. S. Holland, *Memoir of Jenny Lind-Goldschmidt* (1891) and *Jenny Lind the Artist* (1893).

324 Open My Eyes, That I May See

Tune: OPEN MY EYES

The author and composer of this hymn, Clara Scott (1841–1897), was born in Elk Grove, Illinois. For much of her life she taught music in the Ladies' Seminary at Lyons, Iowa. Scott wrote many pieces for voice and instruments, including *The Royal Anthem Book* (1882), the first collection of anthems published by a woman. She died at Dubuque, Iowa.

The phrase "Open my eyes" is drawn from Psalm 119:18.

325 Spirit Divine, Attend Our Prayers

Tune: NUN DANKET ALL' UND BRINGET EHR'

The text was written by Andrew Reed for a worship service organized by the London Board of Congregational Ministers. The service, held on Good Friday, was titled the "Day of Solemn Prayer and Humiliation." It was to promote a revival of religion in the British churches.

Born in Butcher Row, London, Andrew Reed (1787–1862) was educated at Hackney College and entered the family's watchmaking business. He was ordained a minister in the Congregational Church of England and served New Road Chapel, St. George's-in-the-East. Under his leadership the church grew and a new edifice was built named Wycliffe Chapel. Also a philanthropist, Reed founded six welfare institutions. When urged by his son to write his autobiography Reed stated, "I was born yesterday, I shall die tomorrow, and I must not spend today telling what I have done, but in doing what I may for Him who has done all for me." Yale University granted him an honorary doctor's degree.

Reed wrote twenty-one hymns. They were first published

anonymously in *Hymn Book* (1825) and later (1842) with his name attached.

NUN DANKET ALL' UND BRINGET EHR' is by Johann Crüger. For more on the tune, see hymn 230. For a biographical sketch of Crüger, see hymn 93.

326 Spirit of God, Descend Upon My Heart

Tune: MORECAMBE

This hymn by George Croly was first published in *Psalms and Hymns for Public Worship* (1854) and later in *Lyra Britannica* (1867).

George Croly (1780–1860) was born in Dublin, Ireland, and attended the University of Dublin (M.A. 1804; D.L. 1831). He was ordained and served until age thirty in Ireland, then moved to London and devoted himself to literary works. In 1835 he returned to active ministry and served two yoked churches, St. Stephen's, Walbrook, and St. Benedict's, Sherehob. In 1854 he prepared his collection at the request of the congregation. He died suddenly in London.

MORECAMBE was composed by Frederick Cook Atkinson (1841–1897) for "Abide with Me: Fast Falls the Eventide" (1887). It was named for Morecambe Bay not far from Bradford. Chorister and assistant organist at the Cathedral of Norwich, Atkinson was educated at Cambridge (B.A. 1867). He held several organist positions before being called to Norwich Cathedral.

327 O Word of God Incarnate

Tune: MUNICH

The text was written by William Walsham How. It was written for the first supplement to *Psalms and Hymns* (1867). The present text form is from the Christian Reformed Church's *Psalter Hymnal* (1987).

William How (1823–1897) was born in Shrewsbury, educated there and at Wadham College, Oxford (B.A. 1845). He was ordained in 1846 and held successive positions as curate of St. George and of Holy Cross at Shrewsbury, rector of Whittington, rural dean of Oswestry, canon of St. Asaph, and chaplain of the English Church at Rome. He became bishop suffragan in London and bishop of Wakefield (1888).

How wrote all his hymns while in the parish of Whittington (1858–1871). In addition to his hymn writing, he authored several books for the Society for Promoting Christian Knowledge. How was joint editor of several hymnals: *Psalms and Hymns* (1854), Supplement to *Psalms and Hymns* (1867), and *Church Hymns* (1871). He died while on vacation in Ireland.

MUNICH is from the German hymnal *Neuvermehrtes und zu Übung Christliche Gottseligkeit eingerichtetes Meiningisches Gesangbuch* (1693) as the setting of the text "O Gott, du frommer Gott" (hymn 277). It appeared in a variety of forms and by the nineteenth century was known throughout Europe. The tune was named for the German city of Munich.

The present form is by Felix Mendelssohn, who adapted and harmonized the melody in the oratorio *Elijah* (1847) as the setting for "Cast Thy Burden Upon the Lord." For comments on Mendelssohn, see hymn 31.

328 All Praise to God for Song God Gives

Tune: SACRED SONG

This hymn text was written by Carlton C. Buck. Buck was born in Salina, Kansas, in 1907 and educated at the Biola Institute, Whittier College, Los Angeles Bible Seminary (B.S.M. 1946), and San Gabriel College (M.A. 1950). He was ordained in the Christian Church in 1934 and served First Christian Church, Arlington, California, for five years. He then served three other California churches before becoming pastor of First Christian Church, Eugene, Oregon, from 1960 until his retirement. Buck wrote three books as well as many hymns, poems, and meditations.

SACRED SONG was commissioned by the First Presbyterian Church, Orange, California. It was composed by Dale Wood for this text in 1986.

Dale Wood was born in Glendale, California, in 1934 and at

age thirteen was the winner of a nationwide contest sponsored by the Luther League. His first anthem was published in 1951 when Wood was organist at Hope Lutheran Church in Hollywood, California. He was educated at Los Angeles City College (two years) and then Los Angeles Institute for the Arts. He was organist at Eden Lutheran Church, Riverside, California, and the Episcopal Church of St. Mary the Virgin in San Francisco (1968–1976). Wood has been a consultant for several hymnals and contributed to the Inter-Lutheran Commission on Worship and the Choristers Guild. He spends his time in his home in The Sea Ranch, California, as a composer and editor.

329 Break Thou the Bread of Life

Tune: BREAD OF LIFE

This text was written by Mary Artemisia Lathbury for the Chautauqua Literary and Scientific Circle in the summer of 1877. It was published in *Chautauqua Carols* (1878).

Mary Artemisia Lathbury (1841–1913) was born in Manchester, New York, and devoted her life to art and writing. She was once editor for the *Methodist Sunday School Union* and was a partner with Methodist Bishop John H. Vincent in the promotion of Chautauqua. She died in East Orange, New Jersey.

BREAD OF LIFE was composed by William Fiske Sherwin for this text that same summer and has enjoyed a parallel history.

William Fiske Sherwin (1826–1888) was born in Buckland, Massachusetts, and at fifteen became a student of Lowell Mason (see hymn 40). For a time he taught school and then taught voice at the New England Conservatory of Music. He was music director for Chautauqua's choir and music editor for two music publishing companies. He died in Boston.

330 Deep in the Shadows of the Past

Tune: SHEPHERDS' PIPES

Brian Wren wrote this text in 1973 for *New Church Praise* (1975). He says the hymn "tells the story of the Bible in a manner acceptable to different beliefs about its inspiration." The "Bible as the 'classic model' of and for the Christian faith" drawn from James Barr's *The Bible in the Modern World* (1973) served as the basis for the hymn. The first three stanzas illustrate the biblical story and the fourth describes its compilation and emphasizes the comfort and strength a believer gains from this "working model for our faith." For comments on Wren, see hymn 71.

SHEPHERDS' PIPES was written by Annabeth McClelland Gay in 1952 as the setting for "The Lord Is Rich and Merciful" in the *Pilgrim Hymnal* (1958).

Every Christmas the Gays sent an original Christmas song to their friends. In 1952 it was Annabeth's turn to compose the music for which her husband would supply the words. "This tune 'dropped out of the blue' one evening while I was at the piano. Bill said, 'Sounds like shepherd pipes,' and ran for the Bible dictionary to see if such were used by the shepherds in Palestine. The words came quickly for him" (Albert C. Ronander and Ethel K. Porter, *Guide to the Pilgrim Hymnal*, p. 258).

Annabeth McClelland Gay was born in 1925 in Ottawa, Illinois, where her father was the pastor of the Presbyterian church. She was educated at Knox College (B.M.E. 1947) and Union Theological Seminary's School of Sacred Music, New York City (M.S.M. 1949). She has been choir director in the various churches her husband has served as pastor.

331 Thanks to God Whose Word Was Written

Tune: WYLDE GREEN

This text by R. T. Brooks was written in 1954 for the triple Jubilee of the British and Foreign Bible Society and set to LAUDA ANIMA (see hymn 478).

Reginald Thomas Brooks was born in London in 1918 and educated at the London School of Economics and St. Catherine's and Mansfield colleges, Oxford. After serving as a Congregational minister in Skipton and Bradford, England, he became producer of the Religious Broadcasting Department of the British Broadcasting Company Television.

WYLDE GREEN was composed by Peter Cutts and appeared in *The Methodist Hymnal* (1964, 1966) as the setting for "God Is Love, by Him Upholden." It was the first of his tunes to be published in a denominational hymnal. For a biographical sketch of Cutts, see hymn 135.

332 Live Into Hope

Tune: TRURO

The text is by Jane Parker Huber (b. 1926) for United Presbyterian Women's National Meeting at Purdue University in July 1976. It is based on Luke 4:16–20.

The team planning worship wanted a hymn that expounded the Luke passage, was written in inclusive language, raised one's spirits even in difficult situations, and was familiar enough to be sung with enthusiasm when first heard. They were unsuccessful in their search and Huber, sensing TRURO to be a perfect vehicle for the words "Live Into Hope," sat down and wrote her first hymn. Originally there were twelve stanzas, today there are four. With this text Jane Parker Huber found a new vocation (Jane Parker Huber, *A Singing Faith*, p. 126; Philadelphia: Westminster Press, 1987). For a biographical sketch of the author, see hymn 128.

TRURO: For comments on the tune, Thomas Williams, and Lowell Mason, see hymn 8.

333 Seek Ye First

Tune: LAFFERTY

The first stanza of this "biblical song" was composed by Karen Lafferty (b. 1948) in 1972. It won immediate popularity among youth and young adult groups. Matthew 6:33 and 7:7 provide the biblical basis for the text. The present arrangement is from *The Hymnal for Worship and Celebration* (1986).

Lafferty wrote the hymn after attending a Bible study where "Seek ye first the kingdom of God" (Matt. 6:33, KJV) was studied. When she returned home she composed the melody for the stanzas on her guitar. Lafferty calls this "a song in which people can put God's desire for their lives above their own."

Stanza 2, of unknown authorship, has also become an essential part of the song.

LAFFERTY is also known as SEEK YE FIRST. Originally the tune was in the key of E-flat.

334 When Israel Was in Egypt's Land

Tune: GO DOWN MOSES

This African-American spiritual is part of the collection of Fisk University and appeared in *Jubilee Songs* (1872). It is a song of deliverance from oppression showing the parallels between Israel's slavery in Egypt and the African Americans' bondage in the United States.

GO DOWN MOSES is the African-American tune that has traditionally been associated with this text. The arrangement is by Melva Wilson Costen for *The Presbyterian Hymnal* (1990). For comments on Costen, see hymn 29.

335 Though I May Speak

Tune: O WALY WALY

This text is a paraphrase of 1 Corinthians 13 by Hal Hopson for his anthem "The Gift of Love" (1972). It appeared in *Hymnal Supplement* (1985) as a unison hymn. In that collection the setting was Hopson's adaptation of O WALY WALY, which he titled THE GIFT OF LOVE. For comments on Hopson, see hymn 182.

O WALY WALY is an English folk melody harmonized by John Weaver. For comments on the tune, see hymn 94. For comments on Weaver, see hymn 565.

336 As a Chalice Cast of Gold

Tune: INWARD LIGHT

This text was written by Thomas H. Troeger in 1984. It is based on Mark 7:1–8, 14–15, 21–23 and was written for the Common Lectionary reading for the Fifteenth Sunday after Pentecost, Year B. For a biographical sketch of Troeger, see hymn 73.

INWARD LIGHT was composed for this text by Carol Doran. For a biographical sketch of Doran, see hymn 287.

337 Isaiah the Prophet Has Written of Old

Tune: SAMANTHRA

The text, one of seven winners of the Hymn Society of America's 1982 competition, was written by Joy F. Patterson. She chose Isaiah 11 as a basis for the hymn as a way of contrasting what life should and will be when "God's earthly kingdom shall come" with the present reality of life for many of the world's people. For comments on Patterson, see hymn 194.

SAMANTHRA, an American folk melody, was first printed in *Sacred Harp* (1835). The 1961 arrangement is by Alice Parker and Robert Shaw as the setting for "His Voice as the Sound" recorded by the Robert Shaw Chorale. There is one deviation from the original melody in the ninth measure. Parker and Shaw retained the fifth of the chord in the soprano and allowed the melody to move to the alto for one note, thereby retaining the four-part harmony.

Alice Stuart Parker, American composer, arranger, and conductor, was born in 1925 in Boston. She was educated at Smith College and Juilliard School of Music. She was an arranger for the Robert Shaw Chorale (1948–1967) and conductor at the Mennonite Church Center, Laurelville, Pennsylvania (1961–1970). Since 1951 she has taught music privately.

Parker's compositions include several operas as well as works for chorus and orchestra, chorus and woodwinds, and chorus and organ. Together with Robert Shaw, Parker has arranged folk songs, hymns, and carols. She is the author of a dictionary of music and *Creative Hymn Singing*. She has received awards and honors throughout the United States and is listed in *Who's Who of American Women*; *World Who's Who of Women*, and the *Dictionary of International Biography*.

Robert Lawson Shaw was born in 1916 in Red Bluff, California. As a student at Pomona College, Claremont, California, he directed the glee club. His work impressed Fred Waring, who persuaded him to establish the Fred Waring Glee Club (1938–1948). In 1941, Shaw founded the Collegiate Chorale (New York) and in 1946 made his debut with the NBC Symphony Orchestra. He was director of the choral department at the Juilliard School of Music and the Berkshire Music Center. He founded and conducted the Robert Shaw Chorale (1948–1966).

In 1943 the National Association of Composers and Conductors named Shaw "America's greatest choral conductor." In 1965 at Christmas in Cleveland he conducted Handel's *Messiah*, noting in the program that it was "not necessary to continue to pay homage to George II by rising for the 'Hallelujah' chorus" (Stanley Sadie, ed., *The New Grove Dictionary of Music and Musicians* 17:235).

338 Kum ba Yah

This African-American spiritual stresses the presence of God. William B. McClain, in *Come Sunday: The Liturgy of Zion* (p. 113), writes:

> Black people have always trusted in Jesus' promise in Matthew 18:20 that, "where two or three are gathered together in my name, there am I in the midst of them." As the slaves met for worship, often under the cover of darkness, first on their agenda was to invoke the presence of the Lord by softly and reverently chanting "Kum Ba Yah" (this being the earlier slaves' rendition of the English words, "Come By Here").

While this is often used as a children's hymn, it is appropriate also for all ages.

The tune is African in origin.

339 Be Thou My Vision

Tune: SLANE

This hymn text is from an ancient Irish poem, "Rob tu mo bhoile, a Comdi cride" dating from around A.D. 700. The text was translated by Mary E. Byrne and included in the journal *Erin* (vol. 2, 1905). The versification was by Eleanor Hull and included in the *Poem Book of the Gael* (1912).

Mary Elizabeth Byrne (1880–1931) was born in Ireland and graduated from the National University of Ireland in 1905. She was honored with the Chancellor's Gold Medal at the Royal University and was a member of the Royal Irish Academy. She was the coauthor of the *Old and Mid-Irish Dictionary.*

Eleanor Henrietta Hull (1860–1935), an Irish author and researcher, was founder of the Irish Text Society. The text has been altered for *The Presbyterian Hymnal* (1990).

SLANE is an ancient Irish ballad named for Slane, a hill near Tara, Ireland. In the fifth century, it was at Slane where the first fires of Easter were lighted by St. Patrick as a challenge to King Laoghaire. The tune was included in Patrick W. Joyce's *Old Irish Folk Music and Songs* (1901), where it was the setting for "With My Love Come on the Road."

The harmonization is by David Evans for the *Revised Church Hymnary* (1927). For a biographical sketch of Evans, see hymn 113.

340 Eternal Light, Shine in My Heart

Tune: JACOB

The Latin text of this hymn is from a prayer attributed to Alcuin (c. 735–804). Born in Northumbria, he was educated at the Cathedral school in York, where he spent most of his life. He became master of the school in 766 and at the time of his death was abbot of the monastery of St. Martin at Tours. Alcuin was a counselor and cultural adviser to Charlemagne (c. 780 for a time, permanently 793) and inspired the Carolingian Renaissance. He revised the Roman lectionary in Gaul and composed votive masses. He is also credited with the introduction of the Feast of All Saints.

The paraphrase is by Christopher Idle (b. 1938), contemporary English hymn writer and rector of the Parish of Oakley, Norfork. His text first appeared in *Hymns for Today's Church* (1982). Idle was a member of the text committee of that publication.

JACOB was composed by Jane Manton Marshall (b. 1924) at the request of Sarah Jacob's parents for their daughter's confirmation at First Methodist Church, Richardson, Texas. Marshall is a native Texan and graduate of Southern Methodist University. She is on the faculty of Perkins School of Theology, Southern Methodist University, Dallas. A noted composer of choral music as well as hymn tunes, Marshall chaired the task force that prepared the *Supplement to the Book of Hymns* (1982) and was a consultant to the Language/Theology Subcommittee of the Hymnal Revision Committee of the United Methodist Church.

341 Whak Shil Hahn Nah Eh Kahn Jeung
Blessed Assurance, Jesus Is Mine!

Tune: ASSURANCE

This popular gospel song is by Fanny Jane Crosby (1820–1915), one of the most prolific writers of gospel music. She was born in South East, Putnam County, New York, and died in Bridgeport, Connecticut. It is estimated Fanny Crosby wrote more than eight thousand gospel song texts during her life. She was blind.

During much of her life while under contract to a music publisher, Crosby wrote three new hymns a week. She used more than two hundred pen names in addition to her own. A number of original texts are still being discovered. Visiting ministers frequently suggested themes for which they wanted a new song. In other instances, musician friends would compose the music and ask Crosby for the words.

Crosby wrote about her life in *Memories of Eighty Years* (1906). On Crosby's tombstone are words from Mark 14:8 spoken by Jesus: "She hath done what she could."

The text is also given in Korean in *The Presbyterian Hymnal* (1990) because of the great popularity of this piece among Korean congregations. The transliteration was done by Myung Ja Yue (1989).

ASSURANCE was written by Phoebe Palmer Knapp (1839–1908), an amateur musician and wife of the founder of the Metropolitan Life Insurance Company. She was a close friend of Fanny Crosby's. One day Mrs. Knapp played this melody and asked Crosby, "What does this tune say?" She responded immediately, "Why, that says: 'Blessed Assurance, Jesus Is Mine' " (Kenneth W. Osbeck, *101 Hymn Stories*, p. 43. See Bernard Ruffin, *Fanny Crosby*; Philadelphia: Pilgrim Press, 1976). Knapp herself published more than five hundred gospel songs, including "Open the Gates of the Temple."

342 By Gracious Powers

Tune: INTERCESSOR

The text by Fred Pratt Green is based on Dietrich Bonhoeffer's "New Year 1945," a letter he wrote to his friends while imprisoned by Hitler's army. It was smuggled out of prison and appeared in Bonhoeffer's *The Cost of Discipleship.*

Green's original text had five stanzas and was set to music by Joseph Gelineau, the French priest known for his psalm settings (hymn 173). As a hymn, the fifth stanza has been omitted and the text is usually sung to INTERCESSOR.

INTERCESSOR was the setting for Ada Rundall Greenaway's text "O Word of Pity" in *Hymns Ancient and Modern* (1904). The tune was composed by C. Hubert H. Parry. For a biographical sketch of Parry, see hymn 224.

343 Called as Partners in Christ's Service

Tune: BEECHER

This text was written by Jane Parker Huber (1981) for the Women's Breakfast at the General Assemblies of the United Presbyterian Church U.S.A. and the Presbyterian Church U.S. held concurrently in Houston, Texas.

The partnership of women and men in the church was on the author's mind as she penned these words. She was thinking of the fiftieth anniversary of the ordination of women as elders (1980) and the twenty-fifth anniversary of women ordained to the ministry of Word and Sacrament. Today, the concept of partnership has broadened to include people graduating from seminary, those planning ordination and installation services, couples planning their marriage, and clergy couples serving the same congregation. For a biographical sketch of Huber, see hymn 128.

BEECHER was composed by John Zundel and was first published in *Christian Heart Songs* (1870). The tune was written in the popular mode of the day reflecting both the influence of Thomas Hastings and Lowell Mason. It was named for Henry Ward Beecher, pastor of Plymouth Church, Brooklyn.

John Zundel (1815–1882) was born and educated in Hochdorf, Germany, but spent much of his career in the United States. He was organist at First Unitarian Church, Brooklyn, New York, and St. George's Church, New York City, before beginning his thirty-year music ministry (1850) at Plymouth Church, Brooklyn.

Zundel and Beecher became close friends and together published *The Plymouth Collection* (1855). In addition Zundel published several other works, including *The Choral Friend* (1852) and *Christian Heart Songs* (1870). When he retired he returned to Germany, where he died in July 1882.

344 Christ of the Upward Way

Tune: SURSUM CORDA (Lomas)

This text was written by Walter John Mathams as a hymn for youth around 1915 and was published in *The Church School Hymnal for Youth* (1928). It is loosely based on Philippians 3:14. Louis Benson indicated that personal correspondence with Mathams revealed the words "Lord, I am here" are "based upon a scholastic custom of answering class roll call with the Latin word '*Adsum*' " (William Chalmers Covert and Calvin Weiss, eds., *Handbook to The Hymnal,* p. 300).

Walter John Mathams (1853–1932) was born in London and, after a time as a sailor, entered Regent's Park Baptist College in 1874. He was pastor of Preston, Lancashire, but because of ill health spent time in Australia. He returned to England in 1883 and served two churches before becoming chaplain to armed forces in Egypt. In 1905, Mathams was ordained as a Church of Scotland minister. He served congregations in Orkney and Inverness.

Mathams is the author of *At Jesus' Feet* (1876), *Fireside Parables* (1879), and *Sunday Parables* (1883).

SURSUM CORDA was composed by George Lomas for "I Lift My Heart to Thee, Savior Divine" and published in *The Bristol Tune Book* (1876).

George Lomas (1834–1884) was born in England and was a volunteer organist for twenty-five years before becoming a professional musician. He received his Bachelor of Arts degree in music at age forty-five, only five years before his death.

345 Dear Lord and Father of Mankind

Tune: REST

The text of this hymn employs stanzas 12, 13, 14, 16, and 17 of the seventeen-stanza poem "The Brewing of Soma" by John Greenleaf Whittier written in 1872. Soma is an intoxicating drink made from honey and milk used by the priests of the Hindu god Indra during their worship. The poem likens the revivals and camp meetings of Whittier's day to that worship. Whittier's understandings of true Christian worship are represented in the hymn portion of the poem. The text appears unaltered with a suggested first line for those choosing to use inclusive language.

John Greenleaf Whittier (1807–1892) was born in Haverhill, Massachusetts, to Quaker parents and had little formal education. Deeply influenced by his faith and the poetry of Robert Burns, Whittier began to write poetry in his teens. His sister Mary sent one poem to William Lloyd Garrison, publisher of the Newburyport *Free Press*, who published it and then urged Whittier's father to have the young man educated. Whittier attended Haverhill Academy for two years and through the help of Garrison was appointed editor of *The American Manufacturer* (1828) and later the *New England Weekly Review* (1830). With the death of his father (1831), Whittier was forced to return to the family farm for five years. In 1836 he was appointed secretary of the American Antislavery Society and moved to Philadelphia, where he edited the *Pennsylvania Freeman.*

Whittier returned to New England in 1840 and in 1847 became corresponding editor of the *National Era.* He wrote the hymn for the opening celebration of the Centennial Exhibition in Philadelphia (1876) and authored several collections of poetry, including *The Panorama and Other Poems* (1856) and *Occasional Poems* (1865). He is best remembered for *Snowbound* (1866). Whittier, one of the first to suggest its formation, considered himself a founder of the Republican Party. He died in Hampton Falls, New Hampshire.

REST was composed for this text by Frederick Charles Maker and published in G. S. Barrett and Edward John Hopkins' *Congregational Church Hymnal* (1887). (On Hopkins, see hymn 539.) For comments on Maker, see hymn 92.

346 Christ, You Are the Fullness

Tune: ARIRANG

The text is a versification of Colossians 1:15–18 and 3:1–4, 15–17 by Bert Polman (b. 1945). Polman served on the revision committee for the *Psalter Hymnal* (1987) of the Christian Reformed Church. He is associate professor of music at Redeemer College, Ancaster, Ontario, Canada, and a member of Immanuel Christian Reformed Church, Hamilton, Ontario. He is also a member of the Hymn Society in the United States and Canada's Executive Committee, which is responsible for research.

ARIRANG is an adaptation of a popular Korean folk melody. There are more than seventy versions of the tune in common usage depending on locality. The harmonization is by Dale Grotenhuis for the *Psalter Hymnal* (1987). For comments on Grotenhuis, see hymn 201.

347 Forgive Our Sins as We Forgive

Tune: DETROIT

This text based on Matthew 6:12, "Forgive us our debts, as we also have forgiven our debtors," was written by Rosamond E.

Herklots and first appeared in the parish magazine of St. Mary's Church, Bromley, Kent (1966). It was subsequently published (1969) in both *Hymns and Songs* (supplement to the British *Methodist Hymnbook*) and *100 Hymns for Today* (supplement to *Hymns Ancient and Modern*). Speaking of this text the author relates:

> The idea of writing the "Forgiveness" hymn came to me some years ago when I was digging up docks in a long neglected garden. Realizing how these deeply-rooted weeds were choking the life out of the flowers in the garden, I came to feel that deeply-rooted resentments in our lives could destroy every Christian virtue and all joy and peace unless, by God's grace, we learned to forgive.

For comments on Herklots, see hymn 35.

DETROIT appeared anonymously in *Supplement to Kentucky Harmony* (1820) and *Virginia Harmony* (1831). In William Walker's *Southern Harmony* (1835) there is a credit to "Bradshaw." The harmonization is by Margaret W. Mealy (b. 1922) and was published in *The Hymnal 1982.*

348 Christian Women, Christian Men

Tune: HUNTSVILLE

The text of this hymn was written in 1985 by Dorothy Diemer Hendry. This is its first appearance in a hymnal. Hendry was born in 1918 in Excelsior Springs, Missouri, and educated at Central Missouri State University, Warrensburg (B.A.), and Columbia University, New York City (M.A.). She presently lives in Huntsville, Alabama, where she taught English and for nineteen years served as chair of the English department at Huntsville High School. In addition to her teaching, Hendry was an editor with Harcourt Brace Jovanovich. Together with her sister, Emma Lou Diemer, she has published other works, including a Christmas cantata *The Holy Child* (1990).

HUNTSVILLE was composed by Emma Lou Diemer for this text and named for Huntsville, Alabama, where her sister Dorothy lives. Diemer was born in 1927 in Kansas City, Missouri, and educated at Yale School of Music (B.Mus. and M.M.) and Eastman School of Music (Ph.D.). She was professor of theory and composition at the University of Maryland (1965–1970) and since 1971 at the University of California, Santa Barbara. Diemer has served as organist for the Lutheran Church of the Reformation, Washington, D.C. (1962–1971), and in Santa Barbara at First Church of Christ, Scientist (1973–1984), and since 1984 at First Presbyterian Church.

Diemer has received many awards, including a Fulbright scholarship to study in Belgium, Creative Arts grants from the universities of Maryland and California, a certificate of merit from Yale, and commissions from many musical organizations. She has composed music for orchestra, band, chamber ensemble, organ, piano, chorus, vocal solos, as well as hymn settings.

349 Let All Who Pray the Prayer Christ Taught

Tune: CHESHIRE

The text of this hymn by Thomas H. Troeger was written in 1985 and first appeared in *New Songs of Praise 2* (1986). It is an exposition of Matthew 6:9.

CHESHIRE first appeared in Este's *Psalmes* (1592). For comments on the tune and its source, see hymn 164.

350 Fill My Cup

Tune: FILL MY CUP

Both the text and the music to this contemporary gospel hymn were written by Isaiah Jones, Jr. Jones composed the refrain at a friend's house as he entertained himself at the piano. The stanzas were completed two days later. The hymn began as a personal prayer of appeal for his life to overflow with God's love, but now he sees it as a prayer for the church.

Isaiah Jones, Jr., was born in 1940 in St. Louis and educated at California State University, Los Angeles (B.A. 1972); Talbot Theological Seminary, La Mirada (M.Div. 1977); and San Francisco Theological Seminary (D.Min. 1989). He was associate minister for Christian education at First Presbyterian Church, Los Angeles (1979–1987). In addition, from 1985 to

1987 he was associate pastor at St. Paul's Presbyterian Church, Los Angeles. Since 1987 he has been pastor of the Community Presbyterian Church, Los Angeles. Jones has written more than one hundred hymns and religious songs and "Fill My Cup" has been recorded by more than fifteen singing groups. The Gospel Music Academy named him "best songwriter of the year" (1973), and his hymn "God Has Smiled on Me" from the film *Clara's Song* was nominated for a Grammy award.

351 Give to Me, Lord, a Thankful Heart

Tune: GATESCARTH

This text was written by the English scholar and musician Caryl Micklem in 1973.

(Thomas) Caryl Micklem (b. 1925) was raised in Oxford, where his father was chaplain and tutor of Mansfield College. He is a nephew of the theologian Nathaniel Micklem. Caryl was educated at Mill Hill, New College, and Mansfield College, Oxford. He was ordained a Congregational (later United Reformed Church) minister in 1949 and became pastor at Oundle, Northants (1949–1953), Banstead, Surrey (1953–1958), Kensington Chapel, London (1958–1978), and St. Columba's United Reformed Church, Oxford, in 1978. Micklem has chaired the Hymnody Group of the United Reformed Church and is active in hymn societies, on boards, and with publications. He has edited several books of prayers and was a contributor to *New Church Praise* (1975). His versatility as a writer is seen in his compositions of both text and music which have been appearing in British hymn collections since 1951. He also writes texts and tunes for children.

GATESCARTH was composed by Caryl Micklem for this text. It appeared in *New Church Praise* (1975).

352 Great Are Your Mercies, O My Maker

Tune: SONG OF THE HOE

This hymn was published in *Hymns of Universal Praise* (1936), a collection of six major denominations in China. It contained more than four hundred hymns of Western Christendom translated into Chinese. Also included were sixty-two hymns by Chinese Christians and seventy-two tunes of Chinese origin.

In 1953, Frank W. Price selected and translated twenty-three of those Chinese hymns in *Chinese Christian Hymns* for the Educational Department of World Missions of the Presbyterian Church U.S.

Tzu-chen Chao (1888–1979) was considered one of the most brilliant Chinese theologians of the twentieth century. He was educated at the Missionary Council in Jerusalem and Madras. He was one of the six vice-presidents of the World Council of Churches at its inaugural meeting in Amsterdam in 1948. Chao was dean of the School of Religion of Yenching University from 1928 to 1956. The school's name was changed in 1953 to Yenching Union Theological Seminary.

Frank W. Price (1895–1974) was a Presbyterian missionary to China for thirty years. In 1952, after having been in detention by the Communists for three years, he returned to the United States and became director of the Missionary Research Library at Union Theological Seminary in New York City until his retirement in 1961.

SONG OF THE HOE is a Chinese folk tune that was harmonized by W. H. Wong (b. 1917) for the revised edition of *Hymns of Universal Praise* (1977).

353 Great God, Your Love Has Called Us Here

Tune: DAS NEUGEBORNE KINDELEIN

The hymn written by Brian Wren (1973) is dedicated to Erik Routley. The opening address of stanzas 1, 3, and 5, "Great God" was originally "Lord God"; it was altered by the author (1988) for inclusion in *The Presbyterian Hymnal* (1990).

According to Wren, the text is a restatement in contemporary terms of Charles Wesley's hymn "And Can It Be That I Should Gain." Themes addressed in Wren's hymn concern God's gracious love, societal sin, and Christian hope.

Wren wrote the text for Erik Routley's tune ABINGDON, which had been the setting of Wesley's text in *Congregational Praise.*

He hoped those who preferred SAGINA with the Wesley text would appreciate and sing ABINGDON.

DAS NEUGEBORNE KINDELEIN was the setting for Cyriacus Schneegass' text "Das neugeborne Kindelein" ("The Newborn Child") in Vulpius' *Ein schön geistlich Gesangbuch* (Jena, 1609). It is one of thirty-one tunes in the two-volume collection attributed to Vulpius. For comments on the composer, see hymn 111.

354 Guide My Feet

Tune: GUIDE MY FEET

Hebrews 12:1–2, "And let us run with perseverance the race that is set before us, looking to Jesus the pioneer and perfecter of our faith," serves as the basis for this African-American spiritual. The tune is from the spirituals collected by Willis Laurence James (1900) and harmonized by Wendell Phillips Whalum (1932–1987). Whalum asserts, "The *Bible,* more than any other one source, provided the textual material for the religious music which is at the base of Black hymnody" ("Black Hymnody" *Review and Expositor*, vol. 70, no. 3 [Summer 1973], p. 341).

Whalum, a noted author and conductor, was educated at Morehouse College, Atlanta, and the University of Iowa (Ph.D.). He was head of the music department at Morehouse and directed the glee club. Whalum was the first African American to serve as choral clinician at the Presbyterian Association of Musicians' Worship and Music Conference in Montreat, North Carolina.

355 Wotanin Waste Nahon Po
Hear the Good News of Salvation

Tune: NETTLETON

John B. Renville (c. 1840–c. 1890) was a Native American Dakota, the first to be ordained to the Presbyterian ministry. He thrived in the latter half of the nineteenth century after being licensed and ordained in 1865. Renville served as pastor of the

Ascension Church on the Lake Traverse Reservation at Sisseton, South Dakota, from 1870 to 1890.

The hymn first appeared in the 1879 edition of *Dakota Odowan* (The Dakota Hymnal) where it is attributed to Renville. The hymnal was edited by him and continues in popular use among Native Americans today.

A literal translation of the hymn was made by Emma Tibbets, Native American (Dakota), for the book *The Gift Is Rich* (Friendship Press, 1955). The metrical version of the text was rendered by Jane Parker Huber (see hymn 128) for *The Presbyterian Hymnal* (1990).

Born in 1905, Tibbets and her husband served as United Church of Christ missionaries to the Dakota people until their retirement.

NETTLETON is an American folk hymn. Folk hymns became part of the rural singing school because of their publication in numerous shape note tune books. It was originally published in John Wyeth's *Repository of Sacred Music, Part Second*, in Harrisburg, Pennsylvania (1813), under the tune name HALLELUJAH. The text to which it was set is "Come, Thou Fount of Every Blessing" (see hymn 356). It appeared in duple meter and with some melodic changes from our present-day hymnal versions.

356 Come, Thou Fount of Every Blessing

This text was written by Robert Robinson about 1758 and was included in *A Collection of Hymns Used by the Church of Christ in Angel-Alley, Bishopsgate* (1759). It was later included with the tune NETTLETON in John Wyeth's *Repository of Sacred Music, Part Second* (1813).

Robert Robinson (1735–1790) was born in Norfolk, England, and became a barber. After attending an evangelistic service of George Whitefield's, he began to work for the evangelical revival. In 1758, Robinson became a minister of the Chapel at Mildenhall, Norfolk. He then became pastor of the Baptist Church in Cambridge. Although he had no formal education, he learned French and Latin and wrote several books, including a *History of the Baptists* (1790). He died in Birmingham.

This text should be sung to NETTLETON found at hymn 355.

357 O Master, Let Me Walk with Thee

Tune: MARYTON

The hymn text was written by Washington Gladden and published in the magazine *Sunday Afternoon* (1879), for which Gladden served as editor. He titled the hymn "Walking with God."

Washington Gladden (1836–1918) was born in Pottsgrove, Pennsylvania, and graduated from Williams College in 1859. He studied theology and became a Congregational minister, serving first in New York, then in Massachusetts, where he was pastor in Springfield (1874–1882), and finally in Columbus, Ohio (1882–1918), where he died.

Gladden wroted and preached on social and civic issues. Some of his writings include *The Christian Way* (1877), *The Christian Pastor* (1898), *Christianity in Socialism* (1905), and *The Labor Question* (1911). Gladden was associate editor of *The Pilgrim Hymnal* (1904). He received honorary degrees from the University of Wisconsin, Roanoke College, and the University of Notre Dame.

MARYTON was composed for "Sun of My Soul, Thou Savior Dear" in *Church Hymns with Tunes* (1874). This tune was the deliberate choice of Gladden for his text and he always discouraged any other settings.

Henry Percy Smith (1825–1898) was born in Malta and educated at Balliol College (B.A. 1848; M.A. 1850). He became a priest in the Church of England and the first curate at Eversley, Hants (1849–1851). He then served St. Michael's, York (1851–1868), and became vicar of Great Barnton, Suffolk (1868–1882). Later Smith was chaplain at Cannes and then canon of Gibraltar. He died in Hampshire.

358 Help Us Accept Each Other

Tune: BARONITA

This text by Fred Kaan was inspired by a Bible study written for the Cumberland Presbyterian Church by Mrs. Jackie Mattonen. Mrs. Mattonen served for several years as a member of the Executive Committee of the World Alliance of Reformed Churches, for which Kaan served as staff from 1968 to 1978.

Several biblical references are present in the hymn: Romans 15:7 in stanza 1; John 3:21, Ephesians 4:15, and Matthew 18:21 in stanza 3.

BARONITA was composed by Doreen Potter in 1975 especially for this text in *Break Not the Circle* (1975). According to Kaan, the appearance of this hymn in *Cantate Domino* (1980) occurred only after copyright clearance could not be obtained for another hymn. He writes, "It so happened that my 'Hymn on acceptance' was just of the right length to fill the two blank pages that needed filling" (Fred Kaan, *The Hymn Texts of Fred Kaan*, p. 55; Carol Stream, Ill.: Hope Publishing Co., 1985). The hymn was used by Church Women United in the 1983 World Day of Prayer service.

359 More Love to Thee, O Christ

Tune: MORE LOVE TO THEE

This hymn by Elizabeth Payson Prentiss was written at a time of personal sorrow. In 1856 she wrote most of the hymn at one sitting. It was not until thirteen years later that she added a final stanza to the hymn at the urging of her husband, Dr. George L. Prentiss, professor of homiletics at Union Theological Seminary, New York City. The hymn was printed in leaflet form and distributed to friends.

Elizabeth Payson Prentiss (1818–1878) was born in Portland, Maine, and began writing poems at age sixteen. Some of her poetry was published in *The Youth's Companion*. She became a schoolteacher, first in Portland, Maine, then in Ipswich, Massachusetts, and Richmond before she married. She died in Dorset, Vermont. This is the only one of her one hundred twenty poems that has survived.

MORE LOVE TO THEE was composed as a setting for this text by William Howard Doane in 1870 after he saw the printed text.

William Howard Doane (1832–1915) was born in Preston, Connecticut, and joined his father's cotton manufacturing business. He later represented the business in Chicago and then Cincinnati. There he became head of a large woodworking plant. In 1862, Doane turned to composing when, after a serious illness, he was influenced by Fanny Crosby (see hymn 341).

Doane wrote more than twenty-three hundred songs, ballads, and cantatas. Much of his music was composed for the Moody-Sankey revivalist team. Doane was honored with the Legion of Honor of the French government and received an honorary Doctor of Music degree from Denison University. He died in South Orange, New Jersey.

360 Hope of the World

Tune: DONNE SECOURS

Georgia Harkness wrote this text in 1954 during the Second Assembly of the World Council of Churches held in Evanston, Illinois. The Hymn Society of America published it the same year in *Eleven Ecumenical Hymns*.

Georgia Elma Harkness (1891–1974) was born in Harkness, New York, and educated at Cornell University (B.A. 1912) and Boston University (M.A. 1920; M.R.E. 1920; Ph.D. 1923). She was ordained a Methodist minister (1926) and did postgraduate work at Harvard University, Yale University, and Union Theological Seminary, New York City. She taught philosophy at Elmira College in New York (1922–1927) and at Mount Holyoke College for two years. She became professor of applied theology at Garrett Theological Seminary (1939–1950) and was the first woman in the United States to become a full professor in a theological seminary. From 1950 to 1961 she was professor of applied theology at the Pacific School of Religion in Berkeley, California. She traveled extensively and taught in the Philippines and Japan besides being very active in the Methodist Church, particularly in the Methodist Commission on World Peace. Harkness wrote thirty-seven books, including *John Calvin: The Man and His Ethics* (1931), *Prayer and the Common Life* (1947), *Christian Ethics* (1957), *The Ministry of Reconciliation* (1971), and *Women in Church and Society* (1972).

DONNE SECOURS was composed or adapted by Louis Bourgeois for Clément Marot's version of Psalm 12 in the Genevan Psalter (1551). For more on the Genevan Psalter, see hymn 194. For more on Bourgeois, see hymn 86.

361 How Firm a Foundation

Tune: FOUNDATION

The text first appears in John Rippon's *A Selection of Hymns* (1787). Rippon, an English Baptist, became famous and wealthy by publishing a hymnbook containing a collection of texts by Watts and "A Selection of the Best Authors." In the first edition of *Selections*, the hymn was attributed to one "K———." Later reprints credited the text to Kn and Keen. The precentor, that is the person who lined out the hymns to be sung, in Rippon's church, one R. Keene, wrote the tune to which the text was first set. Many have concluded that he also wrote the text. For comments on John Rippon, see hymn 142.

Selections won immediate popularity in the United States and within three years Baptists in Philadelphia reprinted "How Firm a Foundation." Shortly thereafter the entire collection was reprinted in New York. Interestingly, the Established Church in England has never included this hymn in its collections.

The hymn is actually a poetic sermon. The first stanza speaks of the foundation of Christian life as being rooted in God's Word. The subsequent stanzas are paraphrases from both the Old and New Testaments.

FOUNDATION is an American folk melody originally entitled PROTECTION. (The American folk tradition matched popular folk tunes with hymn texts from the Evangelical Revival movement. Many of these tunes undergo harmonic changes to fit conventional harmonies.) It is a pentatonic tune written for this text. They first appeared together in Joseph Funk's *Genuine Church Music* (Winchester, Virginia, 1832). Later editions of Funk's book are still being published under the name *New Harmonia Sacra.*

362 I Love the Lord, Who Heard My Cry

This hymn text was written by Isaac Watts and published in *The Psalms of David* (1719). It is a paraphrase of Psalm 116. For a biographical sketch of Watts, see hymn 40.

The tune is an African-American spiritual which has become popular as the setting of the text. In fact, the text and tune are so well matched that some have mistaken Watts's lyrics for a spiritual.

The harmonization is by Richard Smallwood (1975).

363 I Want Jesus to Walk with Me

Tune: SOJOURNER

The words of this African-American spiritual indicate that slaves viewed life as a pilgrimage from bondage into the promised land. They identified strongly with Jesus, who, born on the fringe of society, became the burden bearer of the downtrodden and oppressed. The spiritual demonstrates that Jesus is the only one able to walk with the pilgrim through all the trials and troubles of life.

African Americans are quick to point out the text is "not a request but an affirmation that Jesus will walk with them." Other stanzas associated with this spiritual speak of the experiences of those faithful who have gone before as a basis for this affirmation: "He walked with my mother, he'll walk with me."

364 I Sing a Song of the Saints of God

Tune: GRAND ISLE

This text was written by Lesbia Scott and was "meant for use on Saints' days, to impress the fact that sainthood is a living possibility today." It was not intended for publication but instead was written for Scott's own children. It was later published in *Everyday Hymns for Children* (1929).

Lesbia Scott was born in 1898 in London and educated at Panen's Croft School in Sussex. In addition to her hymns, Scott wrote religious dramas. Among these are *Malta Cathedral Nativity Play* (1931), *That Fell Arrest* (1937), and *Then Will She Return* (1946).

GRAND ISLE was composed by John Henry Hopkins, the nephew of John Henry Hopkins, Jr. (see hymn 66). It appeared with Scott's text in *The Hymnal 1940.*

John Henry Hopkins (1867–1945) was the son of a clergyman and grandson of a bishop. He was educated at the University of Vermont and General Theological Seminary, where he was organist. He served several churches in the Midwest and became rector of the Church of the Redeemer in Chicago in 1910. Hopkins was on the tune committee for *The Hymnal 1940.*

The tune is named for Grand Isle, Vermont, the place where Dr. Hopkins lived after his retirement and until his death.

365 Jesus, Priceless Treasure

Tune: JESU, MEINE FREUDE

This text was written by Johann Franck in 1650. It was modeled on the song, "Flora, meine Freude, Meiner Seele Weide" found in Heinrich Albert's *Arein*, Part IV (1641). The hymn was first published in Johann Crüger's *Praxis Pietatis Melica* (1653).

Franck was a major seventeenth-century hymn writer, ranking only behind Paul Gerhardt (see hymn 11) in importance. He wrote one hundred ten hymns which helped mark a movement in German church music away from the "church song" to a more personal and almost mystical type of poetry. This text is a clear example of this type of writing.

Johann Franck (1618–1677) was born in Guben, Brandenburg, Germany, and educated at the University of Königsberg, the sole German university not disrupted by the Thirty Years' War. He became a lawyer and eventually mayor and a representative of his province to the Diet of Lower Lusatia.

This translation is from Catherine Winkworth's *The Chorale Book for England* (1863). For comments on Winkworth, see hymn 3.

JESU, MEINE FREUDE was used as the tune for this text in Crüger's *Praxis Pietatis Melica* (1653).

The harmonization is by Johann Sebastian Bach (1723), who used this tune in his Cantatas 12, 64, 81, and 87. Bach also prepared organ works employing the tune. They are found in *Orgelbüchlein* and Miscellaneous Preludes. For more on Bach, see hymn 17.

366 Jesus, Thy Boundless Love to Me

Tune: ST. CATHERINE

The text is John Wesley's translation of Paul Gerhardt's hymn "O Jesu Christ, mein schönstes Licht." This hymn, written in 1653, was first published in Johann Crüger's *Praxis Pietatis Melica* (1653). John Julian reports that J. A. Bengel had the hymn sung while celebrating Holy Communion on his deathbed and that J. Lange's wife was comforted by it during her last hours.

Wesley first heard this hymn sung by the Moravians while on a voyage to America. The story is told that Wesley needed the support of this text because he was a misfit. The translation was included in *Hymns and Sacred Poems* (1739), Wesley's first collection for the Georgia colonies.

For comments on the author, see hymn 11. For comments on the translator, see hymn 253.

ST. CATHERINE was composed by Henri Frederick Hemy and included in *Crown of Jesus Music*, Part II (1864). It served as the setting for "Sweet Saint Catherine, maid most pure." The tune is named for Catherine of Alexandria, a Christian martyr of the fourth century. The last eight measures were added by James George Walton in *Plainsong Music for the Holy Communion Office* (1874). In England the tune is known as TYNEMOUTH.

Henri Frederick Hemy (1818–1888) was born in Newcastle upon Tyne, England, to German parents. He was church organist at St. Andrew's Roman Catholic Church and professor of music at Tynemouth, as well as St. Cuthbert's College, Durham. He was the author of a book on piano playing, *Royal Modern Tutor for the Pianoforte* (1858).

James George Walton (1821–1905) was born in Lancashire, England, and little is known of him besides the collection cited above.

367 Jesu, Jesu, Fill Us with Your Love

Tune: CHEREPONI

This Ghanaian folk hymn was translated into English by Tom Colvin in 1969. It has enjoyed wide acceptance and appears in many hymnals. In stanza 2, the original translation read "Neighbors are black and white," but the Presbyterian Hymnal Committee requested the phrase be changed to "Varied in color and race." For comments on Colvin, see hymn 55.

CHEREPONI is a Ghanaian folk melody associated with the text. Colvin adapted the tune for use with the English language (1963). Jane Marshall arranged the tune (1982). For comments on Marshall, see hymn 340.

368 I've Got Peace Like a River

This text with its tune is an African-American spiritual. The text portrays peace, joy, and love as like a river, a fountain, and an ocean. It conveys a sense of the moving, refreshing vastness of God's presence. Most directly it picks up the language of Galatians 5:22 as love, joy, and peace are cited as the first three in the list of the "fruit[s] of the Spirit."

369 I'm Gonna Live So God Can Use Me

Tune: I'M GONNA LIVE

This African-American spiritual affirms a righteous life as the response to the gospel message. Melva Wilson Costen suggests that the retention of "gonna" as a contracted form of "going to" reflects "the continuing use of the traditional dialect."

I'M GONNA LIVE is the African-American melody to which this text is sung. The arrangement is by Wendell Whalum. For a biographical sketch of Whalum, see hymn 354.

370 Just as I Am, Without One Plea

Tune: WOODWORTH

The text was written by Charlotte Elliott (1789–1871), who was born in Clapham, England, and died in Brighton. In 1821 as a result of illness Elliott became a permanent invalid. The hymn was written in 1834 while the rest of the family was preparing for a bazaar to raise funds to build a school at St. Mary's Hall for the daughters of the poorer clergy of Brighton. It was published in the second edition of *The Invalid's Hymn Book* (1836).

For many years a casual remark made by César Malan (1822), an evangelist from Geneva, has been credited as the origin of this text. He told her, "Come as you are, a sinner, to the Lamb of God that taketh away the sin of the world." Elliott considered the moment as her spiritual birthday and celebrated it yearly. The two developed a close friendship that continued throughout the next forty years.

Concerning the hymn, her brother wrote, "In the course of a long ministry, I hope I have been permitted to see some fruits of my labors; but I feel far more has been done by a single hymn of my sister's."

WOODWORTH was composed by William Batchelder Bradbury for the text "The God of Love Will Sure Indulge" in *Psalmistra* (1849). For comment on Bradbury, see hymn 304.

Thomas Hastings was the first to set the Bradbury tune to the Elliott text. The harmonization is from *The Hymnbook* (1955).

371 Lift High the Cross

Tune: CRUCIFER

This hymn is Michael Robert Newbolt's revision of the earlier text by George William Kitchin. It was first published in the Second Supplement to *Hymns Ancient and Modern* (1916).

George William Kitchin (1827–1912) was born in Suffolk, England, where his father was rector of St. Stephen's, Ipswich. He graduated from Christ Church, Oxford (1846), and in 1863 became censor and tutor at Oxford. He was ordained into the Anglican clergy and appointed dean of Winchester (1883), dean of Durham (1894), and chancellor of Durham University (1909). He published works of biography, history, and archaeology.

Michael Robert Newbolt (1874–1956) was educated at St. John's College, Oxford (B.A. 1895; M.A. 1912), and ordained an Anglican priest in 1900. He served various English parishes as well as being principal of the Missionary College, Dorchester (1910–1916); perpetual curate of St. Michael and All Angels,

Brighton (1916–1927); and canon of Chester Cathedral (1927–1946). In 1946 he received a license of officiate in the diocese of Oxford.

CRUCIFER was composed for this text by Sydney Hugo Nicholson in 1916.

Sydney Hugo Nicholson (1875–1947) was born in London and educated at New College, Oxford (M.A.; D.Mus.). He served as organist for a parish church before becoming organist at Eton College in 1903 and the next year, assistant organist at Carlisle Cathedral. In 1908 he became organist of Manchester Cathedral and in 1918 moved to Westminster Abbey. In 1927 he resigned this post to found the School of English Church Music at St. Nicholas College, Chislehurst, where he remained until his death. This school became the Royal School of Church Music in 1945 and moved to Canterbury, and in 1954 to Addington Palace, Croydon.

In 1913, Nicholson became music editor of *Hymns Ancient and Modern* under W. H. Frere and in 1928, proprietor—the first layperson to hold that post. From 1938 to 1947 he was chair of the proprietorship. Nicholson published various forms of church music as well as works, including *Church Music, a practical handbook* (1927); *Quires and Places where they sing* (1932); *Peter—The Adventures of a Chorister* (1944); and with George L. H. Gardner, *A Manual of English Church Music* (1923). In 1938, he toured the United States. Also in that year, he was knighted in recognition of his services to church music.

The descant for this tune is by Richard Proulx and composed for *Worship III* (1986). For comments on Proulx, see hymn 573.

372 Lord, I Want to Be a Christian

Tune: I WANT TO BE A CHRISTIAN

The origin of this African-American spiritual has been traced to a "Presbyterian environment" in Virginia during the ministry of Samuel Davies (1748–1759). In a personal letter (January 1991), Melva Wilson Costen wrote:

> New converts were required to ask permission to be admitted into the community of faith, and spent time as catechumens in preparation for questions which would admit them as candidates for Baptism.

The use of the language "in-a my heart" from earlier publications not only reflects traditional usage, but captures the intentionality of the creators of this Spiritual. The depth of the longing to be like Jesus, to be more loving, to be more holy, and thus be a Christian deep down within one's total being is best expressed "in-a my" rather than merely "in my" heart.

I WANT TO BE A CHRISTIAN shares the text's history.

373 Kahm Kahm hahn Bom Sanaoon Lonely the Boat

Tune: BAI

This text was written in 1921 by Whalrahm Kim, who was depicting the destiny of Korea under Japanese rule from 1910 to 1945. Korea is a lonely boat on a stormy sea. It is a patriotic prayer written by a Korean feminist and educator. We have come to know her as Helen Kim. A literal translation of the first phrase is: "Dark was the night on the Sea."

The transliteration was by Samuel Yun in 1989. Hae Jong Kim (b. 1935) translated the hymn. The versification was by Hope C. Kawashima for *The United Methodist Hymnal* (1989).

BAI (The Little Ship) was composed in 1967 by Tonghoon Lee (also known as Dong Hoon Lee) for the Korean hymnal.

374 Lord, Make Us Servants of Your Peace

Tune: DICKINSON COLLEGE

The text is a new English paraphrase of a hymn credited to Francis of Assisi. Written during the early years of his life, this poem has become popular in recent years and has been set to music by several contemporary composers.

The present paraphrase is by Father James Quinn, a Jesuit priest. Quinn has made the hymn corporate by pluralizing the first person pronouns. In addition, he has substituted "Jesus Christ" for "O divine master" (stanza 3).

Born in Assisi, Giovanni Francesco Bernardone (1181/2–1226), better known as Francesco, or Francis, was the son of a wealthy cloth merchant. His mother taught him songs in French, Provençal, and Italian. In school he learned Latin. He served in the Assisi-Perugia war and was imprisoned for about a year.

Sometime later, while visiting the ruins of St. Damian's Chapel, Francis heard the voice of Jesus from a crucifix asking him to repair the church. He went home, gathered the cloth from his father's warehouse and sold it and the horse. His father publicly disinherited him before civil authorities and the bishop. Francis handed over all his possessions saying, "From henceforth I desire to say nothing else than 'Our Father who art in heaven.' " He rebuilt three churches and formed the Third Order of Brothers and Sisters of Penance (1212). He died at forty-five, and two years later was canonized by Pope Gregory IX (see hymn 455).

DICKINSON COLLEGE was composed in 1962 by Lee Hastings Bristol, Jr., and named for Dickinson College, from which he received one of his eleven honorary doctoral degrees in 1959.

Lee Hastings Bristol (1923–1979) was born into the Bristol-Myers family and for some time was associated with that concern as director of public relations for its products division. He resigned the family business to become president of Westminster Choir College, Princeton, New Jersey. Bristol was active as an Episcopal lay reader and licensed to preach. He was also president of the Laymen's Movement for a Christian World.

Bristol was educated at Hamilton College, Clinton, New York (A.B. 1947), and Trinity College of Music in London (1947). He had an active career of civic activities, professional memberships, musical contributor, and composer of anthems, collections, and organ compositions.

Bristol wrote *Hymns for Children & Grownups* (with Harold W. Friedell, 1952) and edited the 1971 supplement to *The Hymnal 1940* titled *More Hymns and Spiritual Songs* (1971; enl. 1977).

375 Lord of All Good

Tune: TOULON

This text was written for Eccleston Congregational Church's Christmas Fair of 1962 by Albert Frederick Bayly, who was then the pastor. It was first printed in *Again I Say, Rejoice* (1967). For a biographical sketch of Bayly, see hymn 297.

TOULON is a truncated form of OLD 124TH (see hymn 236), which was first published in the Genevan Psalter (1551).

376 Love Divine, All Loves Excelling

Tune: HYFRYDOL

The text was written by Charles Wesley and was first published in *Hymns for those that Seek, and those that have Redemption* (1747). For a biographical sketch of the author, see hymn 1.

HYFRYDOL was composed by Rowland Hugh Prichard (1831). For comments on the tune and the composer, see hymn 2.

377 Tú Has Venido a la Orilla

Lord, You Have Come to the Lakeshore

Tune: PESCADOR DE HOMBRES

This hymn was written by Cesáreo Gabaráin in 1979. He had traveled to Galilee and was moved by the experience of being at the seaside where some of the disciples had been called. Upon his return to Spain he wrote this text. It is a reminder that Christ still calls disciples today. Gabaráin told others this was the favorite Spanish hymn of Pope Paul VI. For more on Gabaráin, see hymn 296. The translation is by Gertrude Suppe, George Lockwood, and Raquel Achón (1988).

PESCADOR DE HOMBRES was composed by Gabaráin for his text. The harmonization is by Skinner Chávez-Melo and was first published in *Albricias* (1987), the Spanish hymnal of the Episcopal Church.

Skinner Chávez-Melo (1944–1992) was born in Mexico City but spent most of his life in the United States. He was educated at Eastern Nazarene College (B.Mus. 1968) and Union Theological Seminary School of Sacred Music (M.S.M. 1971). Skinner taught at Manhattan School of Music (1974–1979) and then at Mannes College of Music (1979–1985), both in New York City. Since that time Chávez-Melo has edited *Albricias* (1987), *Albricias II* (1992), and *The Altar Book* (1990) for the Episcopal Church and *Songs of Hope and Peace* (1988) for the United Church of Christ. When he died he was working on a Spanish Methodist hymnal.

378 Make Me a Captive, Lord

Tune: ST. BRIDE

This hymn by George Matheson was first published in his only poetic work *Sacred Songs* (1890). He titled it "Christian Freedom."

George Matheson (1842–1906) was born in Glasgow, Scotland, and attended the University of Glasgow (B.A. 1861; M.A. 1865). He was pastor of Innellan in Argyllshire (1868–1886) and then St. Bernard's Parish Church in Edinburgh, where he remained until 1899. Although Matheson was blind, he was an author and poet due to the devotion of his sister. His books include *Aids to the Study of German Theology, Can the Old Faith Live with the New?, Representative Men of the Bible*, and *Studies in the Portrait of Christ*. However, he is best known for his hymn "O Love That Wilt Not Let Me Go" (see hymn 384).

ST. BRIDE was composed by Samuel Howard. For comments on the tune and the composer, see hymn 198. The harmonization is by David Evans for the *Revised Church Hymnary* (1927). For comment on Evans, see hymn 113.

379 My Hope Is Built on Nothing Less

Tune: SOLID ROCK

The text of this hymn was written by Edward Mote. When telling of this hymn he stated that "one day it came into my mind as I went to labor to write a hymn on the 'Gracious Experience of a Christian.' " The hymn was first sung at the bedside of a dying parishioner and met with such instant favor that it was printed as a leaflet, and then inserted in the *Spiritual Magazine.* It was published in the collection *Hymns of Praise* (1836), where it was titled "The Immutable Basis of a Sinner's Hope."

Rev. Edward Mote (1797–1874) was born in London, where his parents owned a pub. According to him, his parents were not God-fearing people and he attended a school that did not allow Bible reading. At sixteen he became an apprentice cabinetmaker. His employer took him to hear John Hyatt preach, which Mote pointed to as the beginning of his conversion. He studied for the ministry and was pastor of Horsham Baptist Church for twenty-six years (some sources read twenty-one) until his death.

His hymns are collected in *Hymns of Praise, A New Selection of Gospel Hymns, Combining All the Excellences of Our Spiritual Poets, with many originals* (1836).

SOLID ROCK was composed by William Batchelder Bradbury in 1863 for this text and was published in *The Devotional Hymn and Tune Book* (1864), the only Baptist hymnal published in the United States during the Civil War. For comments on Bradbury, see hymn 304.

380 O Christ, the Healer

Tune: ERHALT UNS, HERR

This text was written by Fred Pratt Green in 1969, during deliberations concerning the supplement to the *Methodist Hymnbook* of Great Britain known as *Hymns and Songs.* The group felt that a hymn addressing mental healing needed to be included.

Fred Pratt Green spent most of the night struggling with this theme while trying to sleep. The next day he produced the first draft of this hymn which he titled "A Prayer for Wholeness." The last phrase of stanza 3 was amended to read "Unconscious pride resists or shelves" at the suggestion of Brian Frost, then director of the Notting Hill Ecumenical Centre, London.

The hymn is used at the Ipswich St. Raphael Club for Handicapped Persons as their own St. Raphael hymn. The original last poetic phrase, "Shall reach, and shall enrich mankind" was altered to "Shall reach the whole of humankind" by the author for *The Hymns and Ballads of Fred Pratt Green.*

ERHALT UNS, HERR first appeared in Joseph Klug's *Geistliche Lieder* (Wittenberg, 1543). Some authorities believe Luther composed it. It seems to be patterned after a twelfth-century plainsong melody, "Veni, Redemptor gentium." The tune is known by several other names, including SPIRES and WITTENBERG.

The harmonization is that of Johann Sebastian Bach, who based his Cantata 126 on the tune. For comments on Bach, see hymn 17.

381 O Come Unto the Lord

Tune: KOREA

This text was written in 1943 by Young tāik Chun. It was translated by Steve S. Shim for the Korean-English Hymnbook Publication Commission in 1976. The text was adjusted for English-speaking singers by Joy F. Patterson for *The Presbyterian Hymnal* (1990).

Shim, a Presbyterian minister, was the first executive of Hanmi Presbytery, the nongeographical Korean Presbytery of the Presbyterian Church (U.S.A.).

KOREA was composed by Chai Hoon Park (also Tai Jun Park) in 1949 when asked by a student at Yonsei University to write a hymn for the student to take to an international youth meeting in India. The original text was "Precious Love of the Lord."

Park was born in Korea and educated at Union Christian College, Pyengyang, Korea (1921); Tusculum College, Greeneville, Tennessee (1933); Westminster Choir College, Princeton, New Jersey (B.Mus. 1935; M.Mus. 1936), and the College of Wooster, Ohio (D.Mus. 1952). He was professor of music at Union Christian College (1936–1938) and professor, then dean, of Yonsei University (1948–1965). Park was president of both the Music Association of Korea and the Federation of Church Music.

382 Somebody's Knocking at Your Door

Tune: SOMEBODY'S KNOCKIN'

This African-American spiritual is based on Revelation 3:20, "Listen! I am standing at the door, knocking; if you hear my voice and open the door, I will come in to you and eat with you, and you with me." The slaves often felt the word of Christ to be directed at them. Joseph Washington said that in this spiritual there is a "sense of drama, an appeal to emotion and a highly personal demand, fundamentals of the existential decision embodied in the community of faith" (William B. McClain, *Come Sunday: The Liturgy of Zion*, p. 117).

SOMEBODY'S KNOCKIN', an African-American spiritual, was arranged for *The Presbyterian Hymnal* (1990) by Joy F. Patterson, a member of the Presbyterian Hymnal Committee. For a biographical sketch of Patterson, see hymn 194.

383 My Faith Looks Up to Thee

Tune: OLIVET

The text was written by Ray Palmer while he was teaching at a girls school in New York City. In his account of its writing Palmer states, "These stanzas were born out of my own soul with very little effort . . . 'Oh, bear me safe above, A ransomed soul!' . . . the thought that the whole work of redemption and salvation was involved in those words . . . brought me to a degree of emotion that brought abundant tears." He copied the stanzas into a morocco-covered notebook he always carried with him.

Ray Palmer (1808–1887) was born in Little Compton, Rhode Island. He was the son of a judge who taught him his elementary education at home. At thirteen, he went to Boston and became a clerk in a dry goods store before attending Andover Academy and Yale University. While in Boston, Palmer attended Park Street Congregational Church, where he received his call to ministry. To support himself while studying theology he taught part-time in a girls school in New York City. Once ordained (1835), he spent fifteen years in a pastorate in Bath,

Maine, and fifteen in Albany, New York. From 1865 until his retirement in 1878 he was Secretary to the Congregational Union of New York. He then moved to Newark, New Jersey, where he died in 1887.

Palmer was the first American hymnist to introduce his translations of Latin texts to this country.

OLIVET was composed by Lowell Mason as the setting of Ray Palmer's text. The story goes that Mason, having met Palmer while the latter was visiting a friend in Boston, asked him if he knew any hymn texts that Mason could put in a new hymnal he and Thomas Hastings were compiling. Palmer showed Mason the notebook where he had written the text of this hymn.

Shortly afterward, Mason wrote to Palmer, "Mr. Palmer, you may live many years and do many good things, but I think you will be best known to posterity as the author of 'My Faith Looks Up to Thee.' " The hymn was first published in *Spiritual Songs for Social Worship* (1831).

The tune remains one of Mason's best-known original tunes. For comments on Mason, see hymn 40.

384 O Love That Wilt Not Let Me Go

Tune: ST. MARGARET

This text was written by George Matheson. He wrote:

> The hymn was composed in the manse of Innellan on the evening of June 6, 1882. . . . It was the day of my sister's marriage and the rest of my family were staying overnight in Glasgow. Something had happened to me which was known only to myself, and which caused me the most severe mental suffering. The hymn was the fruit of that suffering. . . . I had the impression rather of having it dictated to me by some inward voice. . . . I am quite sure that the whole work was completed in five minutes. . . . It never received at my hands any retouching or correction. (H. Augustine Smith, *Lyric Religion*, p. 300; New York: Appleton-Century-Crofts, 1931.)

It was first published in *Life and Work*, the record of the Church of Scotland (1883) and *The Scottish Hymnal* (1885). For more on Matheson, see hymn 378.

ST. MARGARET was composed by Albert Lister Peace for this text in *The Scottish Hymnal* (1885).

Albert Lister Peace (1844–1912) was born in Huddersfield, England, and by age nine was organist at Holmfirth Parish Church, Yorkshire. He served four churches before his appointment to Glasgow Cathedral (1879). In 1897 he went to St. George's Hall, Liverpool, where he remained until his death. He served as editor of *The Scottish Hymnal* (1885), *Psalms and Paraphrases with Tunes* (1886), *The Psalter with Chants* (1888), and *The Scottish Anthem Book* (1891).

385 O God, We Bear the Imprint of Your Face

Tune: SONG 1

The text was written by Shirley Erena Murray and first published in her collection *In Every Corner Sing* (1987), where it is titled "A Hymn About Racism." In the Foreword to that work Murray writes, "Singing our faith in the present tense means having to stock some corners of the Christian household with new themes. For me, human rights and racism . . . need singing about, and words to sing are hard to find." For comments on Murray, see hymn 105.

SONG 1 is one of seventeen tunes (so Groves) composed by Orlando Gibbons for George Wither's collection *Hymnes and Songs of the Church* (1623). It was composed for a hymn based on Exodus 15, "Now shall the praises of the Lord be sung." The tune was revived and harmonized by Ralph Vaughan Williams for *The English Hymnal* (1906).

Orlando Gibbons (1583–1625) was born at Oxford and was chorister at King's College, Cambridge, from 1596 to 1598. He was educated at Cambridge (B.Mus. 1606) and Oxford (D.Mus. 1622). The Chapel Royal Cheque Book in an entry dated May 19, 1603, lists Gibbons as one agreeing to conditions of services under the new king, James I. He was organist at the Chapel Royal from about 1605 and also organist of Westminster Abbey from 1623. Gibbons died of a stroke at Canterbury, where he had gone to prepare the music for King Charles' reception of his bride, Queen Mary of France.

386 O for a World

Tune: AZMON

This text was written by Sister Miriam Therese Winter in 1987 and has enjoyed wide circulation within ecumenical bodies. It was first published in *The Presbyterian Hymnal* (1990).

Dr. Winter is professor of liturgy, worship, and spirituality at Hartford Seminary, Connecticut. She is a member of the Medical Mission Sisters, Philadelphia.

AZMON was composed by Carl G. Gläser in 1828. It was a German tune introduced into this country by Lowell Mason in *The Modern Psalmist* (1839) as the setting of "Come, Let Us Lift Our Joyful Eyes." Mason arranged the tune and named it "*azmon,*" the Hebrew word for "fortress."

Carl Gotthelf Gläser (1784–1829) was born in Weissenfels, Germany. His father was his first music teacher. Later he was a chorister at St. Thomas School, Leipzig, and studied violin with Bartholomeo Campagnoli, the famous Italian master.

After a short time of studying law he settled in Barmen and taught piano, violin, and voice, directed choruses, and managed his own music store. He also composed various motets, chorales, and instrumental music.

For comments on the arranger Lowell Mason, see hymn 40.

387 Savior, Like a Shepherd Lead Us

Tune: BRADBURY

The text was written by Dorothy Ann Thrupp for inclusion in the fourth edition of *Hymns for the Young* (1836).

Dorothy Ann Thrupp (1779–1847) was born and died in Paddington Green, London. She was the editor of the series *Hymns for the Young* (1830–1836) compiled for the Religious Tract Society. Her earlier hymns were published in Mrs. Herbert Mayo's *Selection of Hymns and Poetry for the use of Infant Schools and Nurseries*, 1838 (the third edition of the collection changed the title to *A Selection of Hymns and Poetry of Infant and Juvenile Schools and Families).* Other of her texts were published in W. Carus Wilson's *Friendly Visitor* and his *Children's Friend* under the pseudonym Iota.

BRADBURY was composed by William Batchelder Bradbury as a setting for this text. He included it in a collection of Sunday school songs published in 1859. For comments on Bradbury, see hymn 304.

388 O Jesus, I Have Promised

Tune: ANGEL'S STORY

For comments on the text by John Ernest Bode, see hymn 389.

ANGEL'S STORY was composed by Arthur Henry Mann as the setting for "I Love to Hear the Story Which Angel Voices Tell" by Emily Huntington Miller in *The Methodist Sunday School Hymnal* (London, 1881). The tune is known also as SUPPLICATION and WATERMOUTH.

Arthur Henry Mann (1850–1929) was born in Norwich, England, and was a chorister in Norwich Cathedral. He was educated at Oxford (B.Mus. 1874; D.Mus. 1882). In 1876, after several organist positions, he became organist and choirmaster of King's College, Cambridge, where he remained the rest of his life. Mann revolutionized the music there transforming the choir from the worst of the three choirs maintaining daily services to the most famous Anglican choir in the world. He was music editor of *The Church of England Hymnal* (1895).

Mann was an authority on Handel. In 1894, Mann and Ebenezer Prout found the original wind parts to *Messiah* which he used to reconstruct the score. The oratorio was performed the following year. He was a fellow of King's College and received an honorary Master of Music degree from Cambridge.

389 O Jesus, I Have Promised

Tune: NYLAND

The hymn was written by John Ernest Bode for his children's (two boys and a girl) confirmation at Castle Camps Church. It originally read "O Jesus, We Have Promised," and contained six stanzas. The four presented here are those in common usage.

The text was first published in leaflet form (1868) and then in the *Appendix to Psalms and Hymns* (1869), both by the Society for Promoting Christian Knowledge.

John Ernest Bode (1816–1874) was born in St. Pancras, London, England, and educated at Eton, Charterhouse, and Christ Church, Oxford (B.A. 1837; M.A. 1840). After graduation he was a tutor for six years and then entered the Anglican ministry (1847). He served three parishes: Westwell, Oxfordshire, and Castle Camps; and published three volumes of verse. Only this hymn has survived.

NYLAND is a tune from the Finnish Province of Nyland. It was published in the Appendix to *Suomen Evankelis Luterilaisen Kirken Koraalikirja* (1909).

The tune was introduced into English hymnody by David Evans, who adapted and harmonized it for Anna Waring's text "In Heavenly Love Abiding" for the *Revised Church Hymnary* (1927). For more on David Evans, see hymn 113.

390 O Savior, in This Quiet Place

Tune: ST. STEPHEN

The text by Fred Pratt Green was written at the request of St. Barnabas Counseling Centre, Norwich, where it was first sung in June 1974. It has become widely used at healing services. Erik Routley called the hymn "a little gem," and John Wilson commented on the readability of the text.

There is a slight alteration in the text as presented in *The Presbyterian Hymnal* (1990). The original poem began "Here Master" instead of "O Savior."

ST. STEPHEN was composed by William Jones. It was named after Jones' favorite saint. The tune first appeared at the end of the book *Ten Church Pieces for the Organ with Four Anthems* (1789), set to Psalm 23. It is sometimes known as NAYLAND or NEWINGTON.

William Jones (1726–1800), English cleric, writer, and composer, was educated at Charterhouse and Oxford. After several curacies he was named perpetual curate to Nayland from 1777.

Interested in both music and science, Jones was a controversial figure. His *Essay on the First Principles of Natural Philos-*

ophy (Oxford, 1762) led to Oxford's rescinding his Master of Arts degree. He later was awarded the degree from Sidney Sussex College, Cambridge, in 1782. Jones' writings include *A Treatise on the Art of Music; in which the Elements of Harmony and Air are practically considered* (Colchester, 1784).

391 Take My Life

Tune: HENDON

The text was written by Frances Ridley Havergal at Areley House (1874) and was published in *Loyal Responses* (1878; musical ed., 1881) and *Life Chords* (1880) as well as a leaflet called both "Confirmation" and "Self-Consecration." The history of the hymn is in Havergal's manuscripts. She wrote:

> Perhaps you will be interested to know the origin of the consecration hymn "Take My Life." I went for a little visit of five days. There were ten persons in the house, some unconverted and long-prayed-for, some converted but not rejoicing Christians. He gave me the prayer, "Lord, give me all in this house!" And He just *did.* Before I left the house, everyone had got a blessing! The last night of my visit . . . I was too happy to sleep, and passed most of the night in renewal of my own consecration, and these little couplets formed themselves and chimed in my heart one after another till they finished with "Ever, only, *all* for Thee."

Havergal later wrote a book, *Kept for the Master's Work*, based on the hymn.

Frances Ridley Havergal (1836–1879) was born in Worcestershire, England, and educated in England and Düsseldorf, Germany. She was a poet, musician, linguist, and Bible student. Many of her hymns were printed in leaflets, which were transferred to several volumes: *Ministry of Song* (1869), *Under the Surface* (1874), and *Loyal Responses* (1878). After her death they were collected into one volume by her sister. Frances Havergal had a lifelong correspondence with Fanny Crosby (see hymn 341).

HENDON was composed by Henri A. César Malan in 1827 and probably named after a hill located a few miles northeast of St. Paul's Cathedral, London.

Henri A. César Malan (1787–1864) was born and educated in Geneva, Switzerland. He was ordained in the Reformed Church but was dismissed because he preached against the formalism and spiritual apathy there. He became an independent, building his own church.

The writer of many hymns and tunes, he published *Chants de Sion* for the Evangelical Society and the French Reformed Church. Lowell Mason was the first American to publish the tune in a collection.

392 Take Thou Our Minds, Dear Lord

Tune: HALL

This hymn text was written in 1918 by Dr. William Hiram Foulkes after his friend Calvin W. Laufer, humming a tune, approached him at the Stony Brook, Long Island, train station and said:

> "Dr. Foulkes, we need a devotional hymn for the young people that will challenge their hearts and minds. It has occurred to me that you might be in a mood to write a few verses for such a hymn." We then hummed the tune together so that I remembered it. As I went in on the train that morning, the words of the first three stanzas came to me almost spontaneously. That evening, as I recall it, I handed them to Dr. Laufer, and he gave them the musical setting of this simple but lovely melody. . . . Several years later [1920], at a young people's conference at Blairstown, the words of the fourth stanza came to my mind as a fitting summary for the other three; so it is found in the later editions of the hymn. (William Chalmers Covert and Calvin Weiss Laufer, eds., *Handbook to The Hymnal*, p. 266)

Foulkes was born in Quincy, Michigan, and graduated from the College of Emporia, Kansas (1897), and attended the Presbyterian Theological Seminary in Chicago (now McCormick Theological Seminary). He then studied under the Barnardine Orme Smith Fellowship at New College, Edinburgh. He became pastor of several Presbyterian Church U.S.A. congregations before becoming General Secretary of the Board of Ministerial Relief and Sustentation (1913–1918), then chair of the New Era

Movement. Foulkes was a member of the General Council of the denomination and was Moderator of the General Assembly in 1937.

HALL was composed by Rev. Calvin W. Laufer at a youth conference that met at the College of Emporia, Kansas, but he had no text in mind. It was first published in *Conference Songs* (1918) with Foulkes' text. The original name of the tune was STONY BROOK, but Laufer and Foulkes together agreed to name the tune after William Ralph Hall.

Calvin Weiss Laufer (1874–1938) was born in Brodheadsville, Pennsylvania, and educated at Franklin and Marshall College (B.A. 1897; M.A. 1900) and Union Theological Seminary, New York City (1900). After a brief time in the pastorate, he became field representative for the Presbyterian Board of Publication and Sunday School Work (1914–1924) and later at the Board of Christian Education (1925–1938).

Laufer was assistant editor of *The Hymnal* (1933) and associate editor of the *Handbook to The Hymnal* (1935). Among his many publications are *Junior Church School Hymnal* (1927), *The Church School Hymnal for Youth* (1928), *Primary Worship and Music* (1930), and *Hymn Lore* (1932). He died in Philadelphia.

393 Take Up Your Cross, the Savior Said

Tune: BOURBON

This hymn was written by Charles W. Everest when he was nineteen. It was published in his *Visions of Death and Other Poems* (1833).

Charles William Everest (1814–1877) was born in East Windsor, Connecticut, and graduated from Trinity College, Hartford (1838). He was ordained into the Episcopal priesthood (1842) and served as rector at Hampton, Connecticut, his entire ministry (1842–1873). He died in Waterbury, Connecticut. With one alteration, the text appears as in *The Hymnal 1982*.

BOURBON was composed by Freeman Lewis. For comments on tune and composer, see hymn 238. The harmonization is by John Leon Hooker (1984).

394 There Is a Balm in Gilead

Tune: BALM IN GILEAD

This is a popular African-American spiritual responding to the questions in Jeremiah 8:22, "Is there no balm in Gilead? Is there no physician there?" It provides an answer of hope and encouragement. As James Cone wrote, "Hope, in the black spirituals, is not a denial of history. Black hope accepts history, but believes that the historical is in motion, moving toward a divine fulfillment" (*The Spirituals and the Blues*, p. 86; Maryknoll, N.Y.: Orbis Books, 1972, 1991).

BALM IN GILEAD is an African-American tune taking its name from this text. The present arrangement is altered from Melva Wilson Costen (1989). For comments on Costen, see hymn 29.

395 Piedad

Take Pity, Lord

Tune: PIEDAD

Both the text and the tune of this hymn are by Marcelino Montoya. It was first published in *El Himnario* (1964), a collection of hymns for use by Spanish-speaking people in North, Central, and South America. The collection was made possible by the Council on Spanish American Work and the Rodeheaver Company.

Hispanic congregations commonly sing this hymn after the prayer of confession or before the sacrament of the Lord's Supper. The translation is by Rev. George P. Simmonds for the *Spanish/English Hymnal* (1968). For comments on Simmonds, see hymn 157.

PIEDAD, composed by Marcelino Montoya, was harmonized by Norman Parish, Jr. (b. 1932), and arranged by George P. Simmonds (1964).

396 O for a Closer Walk with God

Tune: CAITHNESS

The text was written by William Cowper (1769) for his Olney housekeeper and friend Mrs. Unwin, who was ill at the time. About the hymn he wrote:

> She is the chief of blessings I have met with in my journey since the Lord was pleased to call me. . . . I began to compose the verses yesterday morning before daybreak but fell asleep at the end of the first two lines; when I awaked again, the third and fourth were whispered to my heart in a way which I have often experienced.

The hymn was first published in Conyer's *Collection of Psalms and Hymns* (1772). In the *Olney Hymns*, Book I (1779), it bore the heading "Walking with God" based on the scripture, "And Enoch walked with God" (Gen. 5:24). For a biographical sketch of Cowper, see hymn 270.

CAITHNESS was from the Scottish Psalter (1635) with harmonization from *The English Hymnal* (1906). For comments on the tune, see hymn 70.

397 O for a Closer Walk with God

Tune: DALEHURST

The text was written by William Cowper (1769). For comments on the text, see hymn 396. For a biographical sketch of Cowper, see hymn 270.

DALEHURST was composed by Arthur Cottman (1842–1879) and was first published in his *Ten Original Tunes* (1874) and two years later in *The Bristol Tune Book*. It was probably named for a homestead or estate. Cottman studied for a career in law but for much of his life he had an interest in sacred music.

398 There's a Sweet, Sweet Spirit

Tune: SWEET, SWEET SPIRIT

This gospel hymn was composed by Doris Mae Akers during her time as choir director of the Skypilot Church, Los Angeles. It was the choir's custom to pray together before the service, but this particular morning she asked them to pray again because she felt they had not prayed enough. The choir prayed with renewed vigor and she was reluctant to stop the prayers so she notified the pastor about the "prayer service" taking place. Finally Akers told the choir they would have to go into worship. "I hate to leave this room and I know you hate to leave, but you know we do have to go to the service. But there is such a sweet, sweet Spirit in this place." She explains:

> Songwriters always have their ears open to a song. The song started "singing" to me. I wanted to write it down, but couldn't. I thought the song would be gone after the service. Following the dismissal I went home. The next morning to my surprise, I heard the song again, so I went to the piano and wrote.

One of ten children, Doris Mae Akers was born in 1922 in Brookfield, Missouri. She wrote her first gospel song at age ten and has written more than three hundred gospel songs. She now lives in Columbus, Ohio.

399 We Walk by Faith and Not by Sight

Tune: DUNLAP'S CREEK

This hymn was written by Henry Alford. It was included in *Psalms and Hymns, adapted for the Sundays and Holidays throughout the year* (1844) and *Year of Praise* (1867).

Henry Alford (1810–1871) was born in London and educated at Trinity College, Cambridge (1832). He was ordained as curate of Ampton, and served as vicar of Wymeswold and Quebec College, and finally as dean of Canterbury Cathedral from 1857 until his death.

At the age of six he wrote a life of Paul and at ten a pamphlet *Looking Unto Jesus the Believers' Support Under Trials and Afflictions.* Alford compiled his first hymnbook at eleven and openly dedicated his life to God on the flyleaf of his Bible at sixteen: "I do this day, in the presence of God and my own soul, renew my covenant with God, and solemnly determine henceforth to become his, and to do his work as far as in me lies."

Alford's literary efforts extended to poetry and hymn writing, but he was best known for his Greek scholarship. He labored for twenty years to produce a four-volume edition of the Greek Testament with notes. It became a standard critical commentary.

DUNLAP'S CREEK was composed by Samuel McFarland, who flourished around 1816. The harmonization is that of Richard Proulx for *Worship III* (1986). For comments on Proulx, see hymn 573.

400 Pues Si Vivimos
When We Are Living

Tune: SOMOS DEL SEÑOR

The first stanza of this hymn was circulated orally in Mexico. Its author is unknown. The remainder of the hymn is by Roberto Escamilla (b. 1931).

Stanza 1 was translated by Elise Shoemaker Eslinger (b. 1942) for *Celebremos II*, Spanish/English supplement to *The Book of Hymns* of the United Methodist Church. George Lockwood translated the remaining stanzas. The hymn is presented as it appears in *The United Methodist Hymnal* (1989). For a biographical sketch of Lockwood, see hymn 296.

SOMOS DEL SEÑOR has been associated with the text from the beginning. A Spanish melody, it is meant to be sung with guitar accompaniment.

401 When Will People Cease Their Fighting?

Tune: RUSTINGTON

Constance Cherry wrote this hymn in 1983. It was a winning entry for the "Pens Into Plowshares Award" competition sponsored by the Trinity Presbyterian Church, Harrisonburg, Virginia. This is its first appearance in a hymnal.

A native of Charlotte, Michigan, Constance Cherry (b. 1953) grew up in the United Brethren in Christ Church, where her father is a minister. She is a graduate of Huntington College (B.A. 1975) and Bowling Green University (M.M. 1982). Cherry was organist and choir director at a United Brethren in Christ church in Michigan (1975–1977), Presbyterian churches in Van Wert (1977–1980) and Chillicothe, Ohio (1982–1986), before becoming director of music at St. Mark's Church, Findlay, Ohio (1986). She was consecrated to the United Methodist Diaconal ministry, and her title was changed to Diaconal Minister of Music (1990). Another of her hymns "Proclaim New Hope Through Christ, Our Lord" was winner of the Presbyterian Men's Association competition for a theme song for one of their national gatherings.

RUSTINGTON was composed by C. Hubert H. Parry. For comments on the tune and the composer, see hymn 224.

402 Now Praise the Hidden God of Love

Tune: DICKINSON COLLEGE

The text by Fred Pratt Green was written in 1975 as an entry for a competition sponsored by the Hymn Society of America. The category was for a hymn that could be sung by Christians and non-Christians in later life. It fills a void, for there are very few hymns that feature the subject of aging.

DICKINSON COLLEGE was written by Lee Hastings Bristol, Jr. (1962). For comments on the tune and the composer, see hymn 374.

403 Jin Shil Ha Shin Chin Goo What a Friend We Have in Jesus

Tune: CONVERSE

There are differences of opinion about the circumstances surrounding the writing of this text by Joseph Scriven. One story tells of the sudden death of his bride-to-be the night before their wedding. Another says the hymn was sent to Scriven's mother in Dublin, Ireland, as a source of comfort when she was seriously ill. When Ira Sankey asked about the hymn's origin, Scriven said he had composed it for his mother.

The hymn was included in Sankey's *Gospel Hymns Number One* (1875) and was also published in Horace Hastings' *Social*

Hymns, Original and Selected (Boston, 1865). This hymn is extremely popular in Korea and at the request of Korean Presbyterians it appears in *The Presbyterian Hymnal* (1990) in Korean as well as English. The transliteration was done by Myung Ja Yue.

Joseph Scriven (1819–1886) was born in Seapatrick, Ireland, and attended Trinity College, Dublin. At twenty-five he emigrated to Canada and settled at Port Hope, Ontario. He was heavily influenced by the Plymouth Brethren and from that time on became a philanthropist, giving freely of his money and even his own clothing. He was considered an eccentric and was known as the man who "saws wood only for poor widows and sick people who cannot pay" (Ira Sankey, *My Life and Sacred Songs*, p. 279).

Scriven's poems were published in *Hymns and Other Verses* (1869). He drowned in Race Lake, Buneley, Canada. Whether his death was accidental or suicide no one knows, but Scriven's neighbors built a monument to his memory.

CONVERSE was composed by Charles Crozat Converse in 1868. It was included in *Silver Wings* (1870).

Charles Crozat Converse (1832–1918) was born in Warren, Massachusetts, and studied at Leipzig Conservatory and then at the Law School in Albany, New York, from which he graduated in 1861. He practiced law in Erie from 1875 and composed a number of hymn tunes and larger works. Converse declined a Doctor of Music degree from Cambridge but in 1895 received a Doctor of Law degree from Rutherford College.

Converse wrote many articles under the pen name Karl Reden. He is best remembered for his tune associated with this text. He died in Highwood, New Jersey.

The tune is known elsewhere as ERIE and WHAT A FRIEND.

404 Precious Lord, Take My Hand

Tune: PRECIOUS LORD

This hymn was written by Thomas A. Dorsey, the most influential figure in the gospel song movement, when his first wife died in 1932. It has become the most popular black gospel song ever written, largely due to its use by Martin Luther King, Jr., in the civil rights movement.

"Georgia Tom" Dorsey was born in Villa Rica, Georgia, in 1899 and died on January 23, 1993, in Chicago. The son of a revivalist preacher, Dorsey moved to Atlanta (1910) and was influenced by blues pianists. In 1932 he became choral director of the Pilgrim Baptist Church, Chicago, a position he held for forty years. He was also president of the National Convention of Gospel Choirs and Choruses. Dorsey was principal composer of *Gospel Pearls* (1921).

PRECIOUS LORD was composed by George N. Allen (1812–1877) in 1842 but has received its popularity through its association with this text. Thomas Dorsey adapted and arranged the tune for the text.

405 What Does the Lord Require

Tune: SHARPTHORNE

This hymn by Albert Frederick Bayly (1949) is based on Micah 6:6–8. Verse 8 provides the first line of the hymn, "What does the LORD require of you but to do justice, and to love kindness, and to walk humbly with your God?"

The hymn is one of a series based on themes from the Old Testament prophets to which Bayly added a Christian message. It was published in *Rejoice, O People* (1951). The text appears in *The Presbyterian Hymnal* (1990) as published in *The Hymnal 1982* of the Protestant Episcopal Church. For a biographical sketch of Bayly, see hymn 297.

SHARPTHORNE was composed as the setting for this text by Erik Routley in 1968. For a biographical sketch of Routley, see hymn 218.

406 Why Has God Forsaken Me?

Tune: SHIMPI

Bill (W. L.) Wallace, author of this hymn text, is a New Zealand Methodist minister who has served in less affluent housing areas for the last twenty years. He has expressed his dreams through hymns, poems, and sculpture as well as in experimental projects such as the formation of ten Methodist–Presbyterian Union congregations in the Dunedin area. This was one of the first nonhierarchical team ministries in New Zealand.

Currently Wallace is a part-time minister of the Hornby Methodist Circuit, Christchurch, and part-time coordinator of the Hornby Community Care Center, which he helped establish. This project marked the first occasion in New Zealand for wide cooperation among government and voluntary agencies, service clubs and Anglican, Roman Catholic, Methodist, and Presbyterian churches.

Wallace's hymns are collected in *Something to Sing About: Hymns and Reflections in Search of a Contemporary Spirituality*, published by the Joint Board of Christian Education of Australia and New Zealand (1981). Since this collection he has written more than fifty-five other hymns.

This hymn was produced for the funeral resource pack of the New Zealand Methodist Church.

SHIMPI was specially composed by Taihei Sato of Japan in 1981 for this piece. Sato was a fellow participant with Bill Wallace in the Asian Consultation on Liturgy and Music organized by the Christian Conference of Asia. The consultation was held in Manila in December 1980.

407 Cuando el Pobre
When a Poor One

Tune: EL CAMINO

This hymn is a result of the combined efforts of J. A. Olivar and Miguel Manzano. The text is a paraphrase of Jesus' parable of the great judgment recorded in Matthew 25:31–46. There is a suggestion of the road to Emmaus story (Luke 24:13–35) in the refrain. Both Olivar and Manzano are former priests from Madrid, Spain. Since Vatican Council II, they have collaborated on many hymns for Spanish-singing congregations.

The translation is by George Lockwood for *The United Methodist Hymnal* (1989). For a biographical sketch of Lockwood, see hymn 296.

EL CAMINO was composed by the team of Olivar and Manzano. The arrangement was by Alvin Schutmaat. For a biographical sketch of Schutmaat, see hymn 432.

408 Where Cross the Crowded Ways of Life

Tune: GERMANY

The hymn was written by Frank Mason North at the request of Professor Caleb Winchester, a member of the Joint Commission for *The Methodist Hymnal* (1905). Winchester had met North at the Methodist headquarters in New York City and asked him to write a hymn with a missionary theme. North protested he was not capable of writing hymns but promised to try. It appeared first in *The Christian City* (1903), which North edited. Its second appearance was in the hymnal.

Frank Mason North (1850–1935) was born in New York City and educated at Wesleyan University (B.A. 1872; M.A. 1875; Honorary D.D. 1894; Honorary D.L. 1919). He was ordained a Methodist minister (1873) and served churches in Florida, New York, and Connecticut before becoming editor of *The Christian City* and secretary to the New York City Missionary Society of the Methodist Episcopal Church (1892–1912). He then served as corresponding secretary to the Board of Foreign Missions of the Methodist Church. He died at Madison, New Jersey.

GERMANY was first published in William Gardiner's *Sacred Melodies from Haydn, Mozart, and Beethoven adapted to the best English Poets and Appropriated to the use of the British Church* (6 vols., 1812–1815). It was attributed to Beethoven. When asked, Gardiner was unable to point out where in the works of Beethoven he found it.

William Gardiner (1770–1853) was born in Leicester, England, and became an assistant in his father's manufacturing business. He was a musician at heart and introduced England to many German hymns. Among his writings are *The Music of Nature* (1832), *Music and Friends: or Pleasant Recollections of a Dilettante* (1838–1853), *Sights in Italy* (1847), and a translation of Marie-Henri Beyle's *Lives of Haydn and Mozart.* He was eighty-four when he died at Leicester.

The tune is also known as WALTON.

409 Wild and Lone the Prophet's Voice

Tune: ABERYSTWYTH

The text by Carl P. Daw, Jr., was published in 1989. For comments on Daw, see hymn 314.

ABERYSTWYTH was composed by Joseph Parry and published in 1879. For comments on the tune and the composer, see hymns 20 and 303, respectively.

410 Yee Jun Ae Joo Nim Eul Nae Ka Mol La When I Had Not Yet Learned of Jesus

This hymn was composed on the basis of the parable of the talents (Matt. 25:14–30). It emphasizes faithfulness to the Lord.

Yongchul Chung wrote the text in 1967. It was translated and transliterated from Korean into English by Samuel Yun in 1989 and his translation paraphrased by Jane Parker Huber for *The Presbyterian Hymnal* (1990). For a biographical sketch of Huber, see hymn 128.

The tune is by Yoosun Lee.

411 Arise, Your Light Is Come!

Tune: FESTAL SONG

This text by Ruth C. Duck was written for a collection of hymns adapted for inclusive language for the Ecumenical Women's Center of Chicago in 1974. Duck explains, "I was working on adapting 'Rise Up, O Men of God,' when this new hymn text came to me, as if the new wine of the faith I wanted to express would not fit into the old wineskin of the earlier text." It was the first of her texts to appear in a denominational hymnal, *Rejoice in the Lord* (1985) and one of two in *The Presbyterian Hymnal* (1990). For comments on the author, see hymn 219.

FESTAL SONG is a tune by William Henry Walter. It was the setting for William Hammond's "Awake and Sing the Song" in John Ireland Tucker's *The Hymnal with Tunes Old and New* (1872).

William Henry Walter (1825–1893) was born in Newark, New Jersey, and was organist at both a Presbyterian and an Episcopal church there. From 1842 on he served various Episcopal churches in New York City and finally became organist at Trinity Chapel, Columbia University, in 1865. The university had granted him an honorary Doctor of Music degree in 1864.

Walter wrote masses, service music, and anthems, but is best known for FESTAL SONG. Other publications include *Manual of Church Music* (1860), *Chorals and Hymns, Hymnal with Tunes Old and New, Selections of Psalms with Chants* (1857), *The Common Prayer with Ritual Song* (1868).

412 Eternal God, Whose Power Upholds

Tune: FOREST GREEN

This text by Henry Hallam Tweedy was the 1928 winner of the Hymn Society of America's competition for missionary hymns. There were more than one thousand manuscripts submitted. According to Albert E. Bailey in *The Gospel in Hymns* (p. 576), Tweedy's thesis is that in God's nature we find a justification for mission. "God is the reality behind all phenomena, physical or spiritual; He is love, truth, beauty, righteousness, and benevolence."

Henry Hallam Tweedy (1868–1953) was born in Binghamton, New York, and educated at Phillips Andover Academy, Yale University, Union Theological Seminary, New York City, and the University of Berlin. A Congregationalist minister, he served Plymouth Church, Utica, New York (1892–1902), and South Church, Bridgeport, Connecticut (1902–1909), before becoming professor of practical theology at Yale Divinity School (1909–1937). The study of hymnals in common use led him to write his own texts.

FOREST GREEN, an English folk melody, was arranged by Ralph Vaughan Williams. For comments on the tune, see hymn 43.

413 All Who Love and Serve Your City

Tune: CHARLESTOWN

Erik Routley wrote this, his first hymn text, in 1966 while in residence with poets and composers in the Scottish Churches House in Dunblane. He was asked to compose a piece of music but began thinking about the recent riots of Oakland, California. He had also been looking for a text for BIRABUS, a tune by Peter Cutts (see hymn 135 for comments on Cutts). Routley began writing and this hymn was the result. For a biographical sketch of Routley, see hymn 218.

CHARLESTOWN is an American folk melody published in Amos Pilsbury's *United States Sacred Harmony* (1799). It was harmonized by Carlton R. (Sam) Young (1964) for *The Book of Hymns* (1964, 1966). In that collection it was the setting for "Cross of Jesus, Cross of Sorrow." Young's harmonization employs the melody as it appeared in Stephen Jenks and Elijah Griswold's *American Compiler of Sacred Harmony, No. 1* (1803).

Carlton Raymond Young (b. 1926) was born in Hamilton, Ohio, and received his education from the University of Cincinnati College of Music (B.M.Ed. 1950) and Boston University School of Theology (B.Sac.T. 1953). Ordained in 1953, he served churches in Ohio as minister of music until becoming editor and director of music publications at Abingdon Press (1959–1964). He was associate professor (1964), later professor (1970) of church music at Perkins School of Theology and School of Arts, Southern Methodist University, Dallas. In 1975, Young became professor of church music and director of the church music education Master of Arts program at Scarritt College, Nashville, where he now serves as director of the Foundation for the Arts. Young was editor of *The Book of Hymns* (1964, 1966), later known as *The Methodist Hymnal* (1966) and *The United Methodist Hymnal* (1989). He was coauthor of the *Companion to the Hymnal: A Handbook to the 1964 Methodist Hymnal* (1970). Young has composed more than one hundred choral works and serves as editorial consultant to Hope Publishing Company (since 1971). Ohio Northern University granted him an honorary Doctor of Music degree in 1969.

414 As Those of Old Their Firstfruits Brought

Tune: FOREST GREEN

Written in 1960, this text by Frank von Christierson was first published in *Ten New Stewardship Hymns* (1961) by the Hymn Society of America. It is well-known as an anthem arranged by Austin Lovelace (see hymn 507). The original first line, "As men of old their first fruits brought" was altered by Christierson to "As saints of old their first fruits brought" for the *Lutheran Book of Worship* (1978). The word "those" in the text presented here is from *The Hymnal 1982*. On this text Christierson wrote: As pastor of two small churches,

> with small memberships and great financial needs, I have been deeply concerned with stewardship, also because I am deeply concerned about missions and the outreach of the church to "all the world," also because stewardship is a very important phase of the Christian life. No one is deeply Christian until he [she] is a "good steward."

Born on Christmas Day (1900) in Lovisa, Finland, in a house previously owned by Jan Sibelius, Frank von Christierson came to the United States with his parents when he was five. He is a graduate of Stanford University (B.A. 1926; M.A. 1930) and San Francisco Theological Seminary (B.D. 1929). He was pastor of Calvary Presbyterian Church in Berkeley, California, for fourteen years and founding pastor of United Presbyterian churches in North Hollywood and Citrus Heights. After retiring, he served as interim of several churches before becoming assistant pastor of First Presbyterian Church, Roseville, where he is now pastor emeritus. He served the greater church as moderator of San Francisco and Los Angeles presbyteries, vice-moderator of the Synod of California, Utah and Nevada, and chaired committees in several presbyteries. His hymn "Eternal God, Thy Children Bow" was chosen as the official hymn of the Temple of Religion and the Tower of Peace, Golden Gate International Exposition, San Francisco (1939). Christierson's hymns have appeared in seven major denominational hymnals here and in England and have been translated into Norwegian and Portuguese. He was made a fellow of the Hymn Society of America in 1982. In 1984 two of his hymns were sung in the Queen's Chapel at Oxford University.

FOREST GREEN, an English folk melody, was arranged by Ralph Vaughan Williams. For comments on the tune, see hymn 43.

415 Come, Labor On

Tune: ORA LABORA

The text is by Jane Laurie Borthwick and was published in *Thoughts for Thoughtful Hours* (1857). Originally the hymn had seven stanzas but several of them have fallen into disuse.

Known primarily as a translator, Jane Laurie Borthwick, a member of the Free Church of Scotland, along with her sister Sarah Borthwick Findlater (see hymn 15), published four volumes titled *Hymns from the Land of Luther* (1854–1862). Their translations rank second only to Catherine Winkworth's (see hymn 3) in quality.

Jane Laurie Borthwick (1813–1897) was born in Edinburgh, Scotland, where she spent her life. She devoted herself to religious and social work always maintaining a deep interest in home and foreign missions.

Using the initials H.L.L., she wrote prose works and hymns, many of which were collected and published in *Thoughts for Thoughtful Hours.*

ORA LABORA was written by Thomas Tertius Noble in 1918. It was first published in *The New Hymnal*, 1916 (music edition, 1918). The tune was composed especially for unison singing. For comments on the composer, see hymn 205.

416 Christ Is Made the Sure Foundation

Tune: WESTMINSTER ABBEY

The author of this Latin hymn which begins "Angularis fundamentum" is unknown. It has been dated variously from the sixth to the eighth centuries. It is based on several passages from scripture: 1 Peter 2:5; Revelation 21; and Ephesians 2:20. In most medieval rites the hymn was used for the dedication of a church. The hymnal translation is by John Mason Neale and was included in his *Mediaeval Hymns and Sequences* (1851). It was altered in 1861 and again in 1972.

WESTMINSTER ABBEY was written by Henry Purcell (1659–1695) and derives its name from Westminster Abbey, London. Purcell was one of the greatest composers of the Baroque era and one of the greatest English composers of all time. His boyhood was spent as a chorister in the Chapel Royal, where he began composing at the age of eight. In 1679 he succeeded John Blow as organist of Westminster Abbey, a position he retained until his death. He was buried in Westminster Abbey's north aisle adjoining the organ.

The tune as it appears was adapted for use in *The Hymnal 1982.*

417 Christ Is Made the Sure Foundation

Tune: REGENT SQUARE

For comments on the seventh-century Latin text translated by John Mason Neale, see hymn 416.

REGENT SQUARE was composed by Henry Thomas Smart (1813–1879), son of Henry Smart, violinist and music publisher. He served as music editor of the *Chorale Book* (1865) and *The Presbyterian Hymnal* (Edinburgh, 1877). He contributed materials to *Hymns Ancient and Modern* (1861) and *Psalms and Hymns for Divine Worship* (London, 1867). After he became completely blind at age fifty-two, he dictated all his compositions to his daughter. The tune is named for Regent Square Church, the English Presbyterian Church located in London.

418 God, Bless Your Church with Strength!

Tune: ICH HALTE TREULICH STILL

This text was written in 1984 by John A. Dalles (b. 1954) for the one hundred fiftieth anniversary of First Presbyterian Church, South Bend, Indiana, where he was associate pastor. Rather than a hymn that could only be used as an anniversary piece, he chose to write a general hymn with a primary focus on the changing world of the twentieth century and a Christian response to those changes. Dalles originally wrote the text with the tune DIADEMATA (see hymn 151) in mind. This is the hymn's first appearance in a hymnal. For a biographical sketch of Dalles, see hymn 127.

ICH HALTE TREULICH STILL appeared first in George Christian Schemelli's *Musikalisches Gesangbuch* (1736). This was a collection of sacred songs he commissioned Johann Sebastian Bach to edit. The composer of the melody of ICH HALTE TREU-

LICH STILL is unknown. Many believe it and others from the collection to be by Bach himself. The selections were all scored for "basso continuo" and melody only. Almost a century later, the edition of George Wüllner (1832–1902) contained the four-part harmony present in most modern hymn collections. For comments on Bach, see hymn 17.

419 How Clear Is Our Vocation, Lord

Tune: REPTON

The text was written by Fred Pratt Green in 1981. It was the result of Erik Routley's request for new text to Parry's REPTON, and a letter from the joint director of music at University United Methodist Church, Austin, Texas, for a hymn on vocation.

On receipt of Green's first draft, Russell Schulz-Widmar, music director of the Austin church, was critical of two words. They were "own" in the sense of "acknowledge," and "mark" meaning "take note of." He wrote, "Both these of course have long histories in hymnic diction but I do see them being removed from American hymnals by editors who believe they are becoming obscure." Green altered "own" to "learn" in stanza 1 and "We mark your saints, how they become" to "We marvel how your saints become" in stanza 3. The text appears in *The Presbyterian Hymnal* as it was published in *Rejoice in the Lord* (1985).

REPTON was composed by C. Hubert H. Parry for his oratorio *Judith* in 1888. For a biographical sketch of the composer, see hymn 224.

420 God of Grace and God of Glory

Tune: CWM RHONDDA

This text was written by Harry Emerson Fosdick for the opening of Riverside Church, New York City, in 1930. The hymn was sung at the dedication services in February 1931 and was published in *Praise and Service* (1932). Fosdick sought to make the church ecumenical, serving the needs of different social classes and ethnic groups.

Harry Emerson Fosdick (1878–1969) attended Colgate University (A.B. 1900), Union Theological Seminary, New York City (B.D. 1904), and Columbia University (A.M. 1908). After ordination he was pastor of First Baptist Church, Montclair, New Jersey (1904–1905). He taught homiletics (1908–1915) and practical theology (1915–1946) at Union Theological Seminary. From 1919 to 1926 he was preacher and associate minister of First Presbyterian Church, New York City. Fosdick accepted the call of Park Avenue Baptist Church, later renamed Riverside after the congregation moved to its present location overlooking the Hudson River. He served the church for twenty years until his retirement in 1946. He wrote thirty-two books and pioneered in radio preaching and pastoral counseling. He died in Bronxville, New York, at age ninety-one.

CWM RHONDDA was composed by John Hughes. For comments on the tune and the composer, see hymn 281.

421 The Church of Christ in Every Age

Tune: WAREHAM

The text by Fred Pratt Green was written in 1969. Its theological emphasis is on the church as partner in Christ's ministry. It was first published in *26 Hymns* (1971). The text as it appears today is the result of the committee compiling the *Lutheran Book of Worship* (1978). The members asked permission to remove a stanza and to place the second stanza last. Green came to prefer the changes.

WAREHAM was composed by William Knapp in 1738. Again it was the Lutheran hymnal committee who first set WAREHAM to Fred Pratt Green's text. He agreed although he prefers HERONGATE. The Presbyterian Hymnal Committee chose to retain the Lutheran marriage since WAREHAM has a long history in Presbyterian hymn collections.

The tune first appeared in Knapp's *A Sett of New Psalm Tunes and Anthems in Four Parts* (London, 1738). It was composed for the sacrament of the Lord's Supper as the setting for Psalm 36:5–10.

There are two harmonizations of WAREHAM in *The Presbyte-*

rian Hymnal (1990). For more on the tune and the composer, see hymn 161.

422 God, Whose Giving Knows No Ending

Tune: BEACH SPRING

The text by Robert Lansing Edwards (b. 1915) was written for the Hymn Society of America's 1961 competition for stewardship hymns. It was one of ten chosen as winners of the competition and was published in *Ten New Stewardship Hymns* (1961).

BEACH SPRING first appeared in B. F. White and Elisha James King's *Sacred Harp,* published in Philadelphia (1844). The tune is attributed to White. The present harmonization is that of James H. Wood (1958).

423 Jesus Shall Reign Where'er the Sun

Tune: DUKE STREET

This Isaac Watts text was first published in his *Psalms of David Imitated in the Language of the New Testament* (1719) as part two of his paraphrase of Psalm 72. He titled it "Christ's Kingdom Among the Gentiles." For more on Watts, see hymn 40.

DUKE STREET was composed by John Hatton. For comments on the tune and the composer, see hymn 307. The descant was composed by David McKinley Williams and published as selection number 1 in the *St. Thomas Church Descant Book* (1959). For a biographical sketch of Williams, see hymn 138.

424 O Jesus Christ, May Grateful Hymns Be Rising

Tune: CHARTERHOUSE

Bradford Gray Webster's hymn was chosen by the Hymn Society of America as its first choice of the hymns submitted for the

Convocation on Urban Life in America in 1954. This convocation was called by the Council of Bishops of the Methodist Church. The hymn appeared in *Five New Hymns on the City* published for the occasion and was included in *Contemporary Worship—1* (1969). *The Australian Hymn Book* (1977) included the hymn in its ecumenical collection.

Bradford Gray Webster was born in 1898 in Syracuse, New York, and attended Amherst College before serving in World War I. He graduated from Boston University School of Theology (1925) and served as a Methodist minister for forty years in New York state.

This hymn expressed Webster's deep concerns about modern urban society and city life.

CHARTERHOUSE was composed by David Evans for the *Revised Church Hymnary* (1927). For comments on Evans, see hymn 113.

425 Lord of Light, Your Name Outshining

Tune: ABBOT'S LEIGH

This hymn was written by Howell Elvet Lewis for *The Congregational Hymnary* (1916). It was written to declare that "in doing God's will, active co-operation is as much needed as humble resignation."

Howell Elvet Lewis (1860–1953) was born in Wales and educated at the University of Wales (M.A. 1906) and the Presbyterian College in Carmarthenshire. He was ordained into the Congregational ministry and held various pastorates before becoming pastor of the Welsh Tabernacle, King's Cross, London (1904–1940). Lewis was one of the earliest members of the Hymn Society of Great Britain and Ireland and served on the editorial committee of *The Congregational Hymnary* (1916). He wrote several books of poetry, devotions, and sermons. He died at Penwith.

ABBOT'S LEIGH was composed by Cyril Vincent Taylor. For comments on the tune, see hymn 461. For comments on Taylor, see hymn 74.

426 Lord, Speak to Me, That I May Speak

Tune: CANONBURY

The text was written by Frances Ridley Havergal in 1872 during a stay at Winterdyne, in Bewdley, near Birmingham, England. It was first published as one of William Parlane's musical leaflets with the title "A Worker's Prayer. 'None of us liveth to himself.' Romans 14:7." It was published in *Under the Surface* (1874) and *Life Mosaic* (1879). For a biographical sketch of the poet, see hymn 391.

CANONBURY is an arrangement of Robert Schumann's "Nachtstücke in F, Opus 23, No. 4" (1839). It was first published in Jones's *Book of Common Worship.*

Writing about his experiences on March 15, 1839, Schumann said, "I used to rack my brains for a long time, but now I scarcely ever scratch a note. It all comes from within, and I often feel as if I could go playing straight on without ever coming to an end."

Robert Schumann (1810–1856) was born in Saxony and devoted his life to music, first as a concert pianist, a career shortened because of a finger injury, and later as a composer. He wrote in a fine lyrical style for solo voice, chorus, strings, orchestra, piano, and organ. He was the first to recognize the genius of Chopin and Brahms. He attempted suicide in 1854 and at his request spent his last two years in an asylum near Bonn.

427 Lord, Whose Love Through Humble Service

Tune: BLAENHAFREN

This hymn by Albert Frederick Bayly was included in *Seven New Social Welfare Hymns* for the Second National Conference on Churches and Social Welfare, October 23–27, 1961, published by the Hymn Society of America. For a biographical sketch of Bayly, see hymn 297.

BLAENHAFREN is a Welsh hymn melody. The tune is apparently named for a farm or homestead.

428 We Give Thee but Thine Own

Tune: SCHUMANN

The text was written by William Walsham How (c. 1858) for the offertory. It was first published in T. B. Morrell and How's *Psalms and Hymns* (1864). For a biographical sketch of the author, see hymn 327.

SCHUMANN is a tune that appeared in Lowell Mason and George Webb's *Cantica Laudis* (1850). In that collection the tune was named WHITE and was the setting for "Thou Shalt, O Lord, Descend, and All Thy Kingdoms Bless." The caption indicated that it was an arrangement of an unidentified piece by Robert Schumann. For comments on Schumann, see hymn 426.

Cantica Laudis was an effort to take melodies of great composers and adapt them for choir and congregation in order to develop an appreciation for music among the people.

429 Lord, You Give the Great Commission

Tune: ABBOT'S LEIGH

The text was written by Jeffery W. Rowthorn at the request of the graduating class of Yale Divinity School in 1978. It was sung at the baccalaureate service.

In stanza 3 the original phrase "Let your priests, for earth's true glory," which Rowthorn intended to indicate the "priesthood of all believers," was thought by many to speak of the ordained office so he accepted the variant reading "Let us all, for earth's true glory." This text has enjoyed wide acceptance ecumenically. Rowthorn chose the tune ABBOT'S LEIGH as the setting because of its close proximity to his birthplace. For a biographical sketch of Rowthorn, see hymn 134.

ABBOT'S LEIGH was composed by Cyril Vincent Taylor, former warden of the Royal School of Church Music. It is considered by many to be his finest tune. It is named for the village Abbot's Leigh, where it was composed in 1941. For comments on the tune, see hymn 461. For comments on Taylor, see hymn 74.

430 Come Sing, O Church, in Joy!

Tune: DARWALL'S 148TH

The text was written by Brian Dill in 1988 for a competition held by the Presbyterian Church (U.S.A.) Bicentennial Committee. The theme of the bicentennial year (June 1988–June 1989) was "Celebrate the Journey." Dill's hymn was the first-place winner and was designated "The Bicentennial Hymn."

Brian Dill was born in 1949 in Springfield, Ohio, and educated at Ohio State University (1971) and Pittsburgh Theological Seminary (M.Div. 1974). An accomplished musician, he is presently pastor of Meadowview Presbyterian Church, Louisville, Kentucky.

DARWALL'S 148TH was composed by John Darwall. For comments on the tune and the composer, see hymn 155.

431 O Lord, You Gave Your Servant John

Tune: ST. PATRICK'S BREASTPLATE

This text by Joy F. Patterson was written in 1988 to address life in the inner city. There are not many hymns that speak to the indifference of Christians as they observe some dimensions of the inhumanity of city life. Patterson uses John's vision in Revelation as a means of contrasting the present conditions with future realities of Christ's presence. For comments on the author, see hymn 194.

ST. PATRICK'S BREASTPLATE is an Irish folk melody usually linked to *Atomriug indiu*, "I Bind Unto Myself Today" ("I Sing as I Arise Today," *The Worshipbook*, 1972, hymn 428). It appeared in George Petrie's *Collection of Irish Music* (1903), edited by Charles Villiers Stanford, who adapted the tune for that volume. For comments on Stanford, see hymn 264.

432 Canto de Esperanza
Song of Hope

Tune: ARGENTINA

The text was written by Alvin L. Schutmaat in 1984 and first published in the *Mission Yearbook for Prayer and Study,* that year.

Alvin L. Schutmaat (1921–1987) was born in Holland, Michigan, attended Hope College, and then transferred to the University of Michigan (B.A. 1942; M.A. 1951). He attended McCormick Theological Seminary (B.D. 1945), and New College, Edinburgh, Scotland (Ph.D. 1957). Schutmaat also studied Latin American literature and education.

In 1945, Schutmaat was appointed by the Board of Foreign Missions of the Presbyterian Church U.S.A., and assigned to Colombia, South America. He remained there for fifteen years, after which he served as coordinator of the Colegio Americano in Caracas, Venezuela, until 1972. While maintaining a residence in Venezuela, Schutmaat became interim director of the International Christian Center for the Arts, Theological Community of Mexico (1971–1978), turning over his responsibilities to a Latin American colleague in January 1979. At the time of his death, he taught theology and music at the Presbyterian Seminary of Bogotá and was consultant and teacher at the Latin American Biblical Seminary, Costa Rica. He and his wife, Pauline, also a musician, founded the Presbyterian Music School, Bogotá, Colombia. Schutmaat was an educator, theologian, and administrator, but first and foremost an artist. He spent his life using the arts in communicating the gospel.

ARGENTINA is an Argentine folk melody of unknown authorship harmonized by Schutmaat for his text.

433 There's a Spirit in the Air

Tune: LAUDS

The text was written by Brian Wren for the Pentecost worship at Hockley (1969). The intention is to celebrate the Holy Spirit's "Working in Our World." He revised the text in 1987.

Wren borrowed the repetition of two choruses from the Isaac Watts hymn "Give to Our God Immortal Praise" and applied it here: stanzas 1, 3, and 5—"Living, working in our world"; stanzas 2, 4, and 6—"Live tomorrow's life today." For comments on Wren, see hymn 71.

LAUDS was composed by John W. Wilson (b. 1905) as the setting for the text "Songs of Praise the Angels Sang" in *Hymns and*

Songs (1969). The present marriage of text and tune gives perfect expression to the Pentecost joy intended.

Wilson is treasurer of the Hymn Society of Great Britain and Ireland. After serving as music master at Tonbridge and Charterhouse, Wilson taught keyboard harmony at the Royal College of Music, London. With Leonard Blake, Wilson edited *Hymns for Church and School* (1964). Among Wilson's other works are *Short Companion to Hymns and Songs* (1970), *Hymns for Celebration* (1974), and *Sixteen Hymns of To-day for Use as Simple Anthems* (1977). In 1970, Wilson began the "Come and Sing" hymn-singing festivals at Westminster Abbey. These festivals are now an annual event.

434 Today We All Are Called to Be Disciples

Tune: KINGSFOLD

The text is by H. Kenn Carmichael, a retired Presbyterian pastor from Duarte, California. It was written in 1985 for the Support Agency (now the Stewardship and Communication Development Ministry Unit) of the Presbyterian Church (U.S.A.) as part of the 1986 Stewardship campaign entitled "Called to Be Disciples." It appeared on the back of denominational bulletins during the fall of 1986. For a biographical sketch of Carmichael, see hymn 62.

KINGSFOLD is from *English Country Songs* (1893). For comments on the tune and Ralph Vaughan Williams, see hymn 308.

435 We All Are One in Mission

Tune: ES FLOG EIN KLEINS WALDVÖGELEIN

This text by Rusty (Howard M. III) Edwards was written in 1985. It was inspired by a letter from Lutheran bishop Paul Erickson in which he said, "Our mission is to touch the lives of others, with Christ's love." The hymn was used in the 1986 mission appeal of the Evangelical Lutheran Church in America.

In the original poem, stanza 2, line 6, read "God's fantastic grace." It was changed to "God's surprising grace" by Edwards at the suggestion of the Presbyterian Hymnal Committee. The text was first published in *The Lutheran Journal* (1986), with AURELIA as the suggested tune. This is its first appearance in a denominational hymnal.

For comments on Edwards, see hymn 19.

ES FLOG EIN KLEINS WALDVÖGELEIN was harmonized by George Ratcliffe Woodward from a Memmingen manuscript. For comments on the tune, see hymn 184. For comments on Woodward, see hymn 68.

436 We Are Your People

Tune: WHITFIELD

Brian Wren wrote this text in August 1973 for *New Church Praise* (1975). It was indexed by him as a hymn for "Confirmation, Church Membership, Ordination and Induction, Church—Fellowship and Unity, and Church—Mission."

The first line was originally "We are your ministers" meaning all the people of God. Wren, fearing the hymn would be misunderstood and its use would be limited to ordination services, amended the line to "We are your people." For comments on the author, see hymn 71.

WHITFIELD was composed as the setting for this text by John W. Wilson. The hymn was sung for the first time at Westminster Abbey in 1977. Wilson named the tune WHITFIELD, his wife Mary's maiden name. Mary Whitfield Wilson died in 1974. For comments on the composer, see hymn 433.

437 Our Cities Cry to You, O God

Tune: SALVATION

This hymn about the modern city is by Margaret Clarkson (1981). Clarkson was born in 1915 in Saskatchewan, Canada. Her family moved to Toronto when she was four. Clarkson graduated from college in 1935 and began a thirty-eight-year elementary teaching career. Her first position was in a lumber village near Barwick, Ontario. After seven years Clarkson moved to a northern suburb of Toronto, where she still resides.

At age ten she secretly entered a children's poetry contest and won second place. Soon she was writing poems regularly and wrote her first Christian song at twelve. Her first hymn came to be written when Stacey Woods of Inter-Varsity Christian Fellowship asked for a hymn to link together the various groups that made up the student movement. That hymn, "We Come, O Christ, to Thee," was premiered in 1946.

Clarkson has written seventeen books on topics including music, bird and nature watching, education, and the meaning of suffering. Her collected hymns are published in *A Singing Heart* (1987). Clarkson has suffered from arthritis since age three. She writes, "God has so filled my heart and mind with himself, with a knowledge of his Word and with the glory of Christian praise, that it is sheer delight to serve my own generation in the will of God in the field of hymn writing" (*A Singing Heart,* p. 6; Carol Stream, Ill.: Hope Publishing Co., 1987).

SALVATION is an American folk melody from Ananias Davisson's *Kentucky Harmony* (Harrisonburg, Virginia, 1816). This was the first Southern shape-note tune book. The harmonization is from *Songs for Liturgy and More Hymns and Spiritual Songs* (1971).

438 Blest Be the Tie That Binds

Tune: DENNIS

The text whose original title was "Brotherly Love" was written by John Fawcett. As with most of his one hundred sixty-six hymns, this one was written to be used after a sermon. These texts were gathered and published in *Hymns Adapted to the Circumstances of Public Worship and Private Devotion* (Leeds, 1782).

John Fawcett (1740–1817) was born in Lidget Green, Yorkshire, and at sixteen was converted through the preaching of George Whitefield. He joined the Methodists but a few years later became a Baptist. At twenty-five he was ordained a Baptist pastor (1765) and served a congregation at Wainsgate for his entire ministry.

In 1772, after formally accepting it, he declined a call to follow Dr. John Gill as pastor of Carter Lane Baptist Church in London. He had preached his farewell sermon and the bags were packed and loaded on the wagon when the members' tears and his wife's sadness as well as his own led him to give the order to unpack. He later declined the presidency of the Baptist Academy at Bristol. In 1811, Fawcett was awarded an honorary doctorate from Brown University, Providence.

DENNIS was composed by Johann (Hans) Georg Nägeli. The present harmonization is by Lowell Mason from Mason and George Webb's *The Psaltry* (1845), where it was the setting for Philip Doddridge's "How Gentle God's Commands." In that volume Mason ascribed the tune to Nägeli but gave no source.

Johann Georg Nägeli (1773–1836) was born near Zurich, Switzerland. He served as president of the Association for the Cultivation of Music. As the founder of the Zürcherische Singinstitut he was known for his progressive steps in music education and greatly influenced Lowell Mason, who is generally understood to be the father of public school music in the United States.

As an editor and music publisher, Nägeli produced the first edition of *Beethoven's Sonatas, Opus 31* as well as vocal and instrumental works of his own.

For comments on Mason, see hymn 40.

439 In Christ There Is No East or West

Tune: ST. PETER

This text is by William Arthur Dunkerley, known in literary circles under the pseudonyms of John Oxenham and Julian Ross. It was originally part of *The Pageant of Darkness and Light*, a play written by Oxenham for the London Missionary Society exhibition on the Orient (1908). The hymn was first published in *Bees in Amber* (1913), a book he printed himself. It sold over 285,000 copies. In the United States the hymn was first published in H. Augustine Smith's *Hymns of the Living Age* (1925). It has been slightly altered for *The Presbyterian Hymnal* (1990).

John Oxenham (Dunkerley) (1852–1941) was born in Manchester, England, and educated in Manchester's Old Trafford School and Victoria University. He ran a successful wholesale grocery company while writing forty-two novels and twenty-five collections of poetry and hymns using different pseudonyms. Among his writings are *God's Prisoner* (1898) and *Hymns for Men at the Front*, World War I (which sold eight million copies).

ST. PETER was composed by Alexander R. Reinagle and named for St. Peter's-in-the-East Church, Oxford, where he was organist from 1822 to 1853. Originally the tune was the setting for Psalm 118 in *Psalm Tunes for the Voice and Piano Forte* (1836). The collection was for solo voice with piano accompaniment. Reinagle introduced the tune name in *A Collection of Psalm and Hymn Tunes, Chants, and other Music, as sung in the Parish Church of St. Peter's-in-the-East, Oxford* (1840). He later reharmonized the tune for *Hymns Ancient and Modern* (1861).

Alexander Robert Reinagle (1799–1877) was born at Kiddington, Oxford. He came from a musical family. His grandfather was trumpeter to the king of Austria, his father a cellist, and his uncle a well-known violinist, conductor, and composer, in England and the United States.

440 In Christ There Is No East or West

Tune: MC KEE

For comments on the text by John Oxenham, see hymn 439.

MC KEE is based on an African-American spiritual tune that served as the setting for "I Know the Angel's Done Changed My Name," in Theodore F. Seward and George L. White's collection *Jubilee Songs* (1884).

It was adapted by Harry T. Burleigh (1939) for the present text in *The Hymnal 1940*. Burleigh named the tune for Rev. Elmer M. McKee, rector of St. George's Protestant Episcopal Church, New York City (1936–1946).

Henry (Harry) Thacker Burleigh (1866–1949) was born in Erie, Pennsylvania, and studied at the National Conservatory of Music, New York, where he was a student of Anton Dvořák. Burleigh's singing of African-American spirituals stimulated Dvořák's interest in them and quite possibly influenced the major themes of the *New World Symphony*.

Burleigh was baritone soloist at St. George's Church (1894) for fifty-two years and was also soloist at Temple Emmanuel (1900–1925). He became music editor for G. Ricordi Music Publishers in 1911. His arrangements of spirituals for solo voice and piano, *Jubilee Songs of the USA* (1916), was a major contribution to the field of recital music. He composed more than two hundred pieces of music, including art songs, choral works, and solos but only two hymn arrangements. He was a charter member of the American Society of Composers, Authors, and Publishers. In 1917 he received from the National Association for the Advancement of Colored People the Spingarn Medal for the highest achievement by an African American in 1916. He was granted a Master of Arts degree from Atlanta University, and a Doctor of Music degree from Howard University. He died in Stamford, Connecticut.

441 I Love Thy Kingdom, Lord

Tune: ST. THOMAS

This is the oldest American hymn in common usage today. It was written by Timothy Dwight while he was president of Yale College and included in *The Psalms of David by Isaac Watts* (rev. 1800). The collection was the result of an invitation by the General Association of Connecticut (Presbyterian and Congregationalist) to revise Watts' *Psalms of David.* When completed, the revised edition included thirty-three of Dwight's own paraphrases. "I Love Thy Kingdom" is from Dwight's paraphrase of Psalm 137 entitled "Love to the Church."

A grandson of Jonathan Edwards, Timothy Dwight (1752–1817) was born in Northampton, Massachusetts, and entered Yale at the age of thirteen. He was a Congregational minister, chaplain during the Revolutionary War, and later president of Yale College (now Yale University). Throughout his life he suffered from poor eyesight as a result of eye strain due to studying by candlelight and the effects of smallpox.

ST. THOMAS was first published in Aaron Williams' *The New Universal Psalmodist* (1770) as the setting for Psalm 48, "Great Is the Lord Our God." An earlier extended form of the melody titled HOLBURN appeared in Williams' *The Universal Psalmodist*

(1763), where it was the setting for Charles Wesley's (see hymn 1) "Soldiers of Christ, Arise." Williams (1731–1776) was a composer, music engraver, publisher, and teacher in Smithfield, London. He was also music director and clerk of Scots Church, London Wall.

442 The Church's One Foundation

Tune: AURELIA

This text arose as a result of the Colenso affair (1866). This was a controversy in which John Colenso, bishop of Natal, South Africa, made critical statements about the Bible and questioned aspects of the Christian faith. The young curate of Windsor, Samuel John Stone, responded with this hymn of faith. The third stanza is a reference to the dispute.

Samuel John Stone (1839–1900) was born in Whitmore, Staffordshire, England, and was educated at Charterhouse, London, and Pembroke College, Oxford (A.B. 1862; A.M. 1872). He was curate of Windsor (1862–1870) and then St. Paul's (1870–1874). Stone was the author of several books and served on the committee of *Hymns Ancient and Modern.*

AURELIA was composed by Samuel Sebastian Wesley, apparently as the setting of John Keble's (see hymn 213) wedding hymn, "The Voice That Breathed O'er Eden" (1864). That same year it appeared in *A Selection of Psalms and Hymns Arranged for the Public Service of the Church of England, Edited by the Rev. Charles Kemble and S.S. Wesley* (1864) as the setting for three centos from Neale's (see hymn 4) translation of Bernard of Cluny's *Hora novissima*: "Jerusalem the Golden," "Brief Life Is Here Our Portion," and "For Thee, O Dear, Dear Country." It was the setting for "The Church's One Foundation" in the Appendix to *Hymns Ancient and Modern* (1868).

Samuel Sebastian Wesley (1810–1876) was the oldest of several children born to Samuel Wesley and his housekeeper, Sarah Suter. He was the grandson of Charles Wesley (see hymn 1). He is considered the greatest composer in the English cathedral tradition between Henry Purcell (see hymn 416) and Charles Villiers Stanford (see hymn 264). At ten he became a chorister at the Chapel Royal and by sixteen he was a church organist. He received a Doctor of Music degree from Oxford in 1839. Wesley was fond of fishing and it is said that he chose his church assignments in relation to the fishing possibilities in the area. On one occasion he had an assistant play a dedication service for him so he could fish. The assistant was instructed to tell the people attending the service that Wesley was unavoidably detained.

443 O Christ, the Great Foundation

Tune: AURELIA

The original text of this Chinese hymn was written by Timothy T'ingfang Lew in 1933. It appeared in T. C. Chao's collection *P'u T'ien Sung Tsan (Hymns of Universal Praise)* (1936). The English translation by Mildred A. Wiant (b. 1898) appeared in the 1977 revised edition of that collection sponsored by the Chinese Christian Literature Council of Hong Kong.

T'ingfang Lew (1891–1947) was a leading Chinese educator, author, and editor. He was educated in China and at Columbia University in New York City (M.A.; Ph.D.). His Bachelor of Divinity degree was from Yale and he studied at Union Theological Seminary, New York City, where he also taught Christian education. Lew lectured throughout America at schools and colleges from 1926 to 1928 and received an S.T.D. degree from Oberlin College.

In 1932, Lew began to chair the commission to prepare a Chinese Union hymnal. The resulting *Hymns of Universal Praise* was published in 1936. Its music editor was Bliss Wiant, a colleague of Lew's at Yenching University in Peking. Lew also edited the *Union Book of Common Prayer* which was used by four Protestant Chinese groups having approximately one-half million members. He represented China at the World Council of Churches meetings (1927–1939). He served as a member of the Chinese government's legislative body (1936–1941).

Lew is remembered for his work with Chinese Christian organizations in China and America where he resided from 1941 to 1947. He died while teaching at the University of New Mexico.

For comments on Mildred and Bliss Wiant, see hymn 65.

AURELIA was composed by Samuel Sebastian Wesley. For comments on the tune and the composer, see hymn 442.

444 We Gather Here to Bid Farewell

Tune: WINCHESTER NEW

This hymn is by Margaret Clarkson. It was written in February 1987 from notes made in 1970. In her collected hymns, *A Singing Heart*, this text bears the heading "For a Congregational Farewell." There are times in a church's life when people who have been vital to it leave. This hymn is for those occasions. For comments on the author, see hymn 437.

WINCHESTER NEW is from *Musikalisches Handbuch* (Hamburg, 1690). The original form of the tune appeared in *Foundery Tune-Book* (1742) under the title "Swift German tune" in long meter. In Moore's *The Psalm-Singer's Delightful Pocket Companion* (Glasgow, 1762) it was named WINCHESTER. The tune has appeared under the names FRANKFORT and CRASSELIUS in other collections.

The harmonization was composed by William Henry Monk during his time as choirmaster of King's College, London (1847). For comments on Monk, see hymn 543.

445 Great Day!

This African-American spiritual originated during the Civil War with the promised "Great Day" when all the slaves would be emancipated. Although their freedom was won through the fighting of humans, the slaves knew that ultimately their true freedom came from God. Characteristically this spiritual carries images from several passages of scripture, including Nehemiah 2–7 (restoration of the walls of Jerusalem), Revelation 21:15f. (eschatological [the end time] look at the walls of the New Jerusalem), Leviticus 25:8f. (year of Jubilee when all will be liberated).

The arrangement of the tune is by Joseph T. Jones (see hymn 153). Melva Wilson Costen adapted it for *The Presbyterian Hymnal* (1990). For comments on Costen, see hymn 29.

446 Glorious Things of Thee Are Spoken

Tune: AUSTRIAN HYMN

This text in praise of the church is by John Newton. It is based on Isaiah 33:20–21 and gives a general notion of the state of the redeemed in the kingdom of God. The hymn first appeared in the *Olney Hymns* (1779), the result of a collaborative effort between Newton and William Cowper (see hymn 270). For comments on John Newton, see hymn 280.

The Olney collection contains sixty-seven hymns by Cowper and two hundred eighty-one from Newton in three divisions. Book I, "On Select Texts of Scripture," presented hymns to be used to climax a sermon or illustrate prayer-meeting talks about Bible characters. "Glorious Things of Thee Are Spoken" is included in this section. Book II, "On Occasional Subjects," has poems relating to particular seasons or events. Book III, "On the Progress and Changes of the Spiritual Life," contains some autobiographical verses by Cowper, who as an adult struggled to maintain sanity.

AUSTRIAN HYMN was composed by Franz Joseph Haydn. For comments on the composer and the tune, see hymn 285. The descant is by Michael E. Young (1979).

447 Lead On, O King Eternal

Tune: LANCASHIRE

The hymn was written by Ernest Warburton Shurtleff for his graduation from Andover Theological Seminary (1887) at the request of fellow students. Shurtleff (1862–1917) was born in Boston and attended Harvard University, the New Church Theological Seminary, and Andover Theological Seminary. He was ordained to the Congregational ministry and served churches in California, Massachusetts, and Minnesota before moving to Frankfurt am Main, Germany, in 1905 to establish an American Church. In 1906 he began working with students in Paris, France, and remained there doing relief work until his death in 1917. Among his works are *Poems* (1883), *New Year's Peace* (1885), *Song of Hope* (1886), *Shadow of the Angel* (1886), *Hymns of Faith* (1887), and *Song on the Waters* (1913).

LANCASHIRE was composed by Henry Thomas Smart. For comments on the tune, see hymn 118. For comments on the composer, see hymns 22 and 417.

448 Lead On, O King Eternal

Tune: LLANGLOFFAN

The text was written by Ernest W. Shurtleff in 1887. For comments on the text and the author, see hymn 447.

LLANGLOFFAN is from Daniel Evans' *Hymnau a Thonau* (1865), the harmonization as in *The English Hymnal* (1906). For comments on this Welsh folk melody, see hymn 15.

449 My Lord! What a Morning

The words of this African-American spiritual refer to the " 'great getting up morning,' in which Christ would return to the earth. . . . It attests to 'an apocalyptic cosmic expectation which would accompany the ending of this present age just preceding the sound of the first trumpet' " (William B. McClain, *Come Sunday: The Liturgy of Zion*, p. 115).

When the words of the text began to appear in written form, the word "mourning" was mistakenly used for the word "morning" because of the similarity of sound. Today, both words are accepted. The scripture reference for this text is Matthew 24:29–30. Placed in the Church: Triumphant section of the hymnal, it is also an appropriate hymn for Advent.

This African-American spiritual is arranged by Melva Wilson Costen (1989). For comments on Costen, see hymn 29.

450 O Day of Peace

Tune: JERUSALEM

The text was written by Rev. Carl P. Daw, Jr. (b. 1944), and first published in *The Hymnal 1982*, where it is set to JERUSALEM. For comments on Daw, see hymn 314.

JERUSALEM was composed by C. Hubert H. Parry. For comments on the tune, see hymn 252. For a biographical sketch of Parry, see hymn 224.

The harmonization is by Richard Proulx (1986). For comments on Proulx, see hymn 573.

451 Ye Watchers and Ye Holy Ones

Tune: LASST UNS ERFREUEN

John A. L. Riley's text was written for the tune LASST UNS ERFREUEN to be included in *The English Hymnal* (1906). Riley was one of the compilers of that volume, contributing eight translations from Latin and Greek and three original poems.

John Athelstan Laurie Riley (1858–1945) was born in London, educated at Eton, and graduated from Pembroke College, Oxford (B.A. 1881; M.A. 1883). He wrote several pamphlets on the Eastern Christian Churches, published a revision of the Prayer Book, and wrote *The Religious Question in Public Education* (1911) and *Concerning Hymn Tunes and Sequences* (1915). Riley was a member of the House of Laymen of the Province of Canterbury. He died on the island of Jersey following World War II.

LASST UNS ERFREUEN is from *Geistliche Kirchengesäng* (1623) and harmonized by Ralph Vaughan Williams. For comments on the tune and the source, see hymn 229.

452 O Day of God, Draw Nigh

Tune: ST. MICHAEL

This hymn was written by Robert B. Y. Scott for the Fellowship for a Christian Social Order while he was its president. It was published in *Hymns for Worship* (1939), *The Hymnal 1940,* and the *Pilgrim Hymnal* (1958).

Robert Balgarnie Young Scott (1899–1987) was born in Toronto, Ontario, Canada, and educated at the University of Toronto and Knox College. He was ordained in the United Church of Canada (1926) and served as a pastor for two years before becoming professor of Old Testament studies, first in Vancouver and then Montreal. In 1955 he became professor of religion at Princeton University. He wrote books on the Psalms, wisdom literature, and was also interested in biblical archaeology.

ST. MICHAEL was either composed or adapted by Louis Bourgeois for Psalm 101 in the Genevan Psalter (1551). In 1561 the tune appeared as the setting of Psalm 134 in *Four Score and Seven Psalms*, printed in England. It fell out of usage until William

Crotch arranged it for *Psalm Tunes* (1836). Crotch gave it the name ST. MICHAEL.

William Crotch (1775–1847) was born in Norwich. He was a child prodigy, who at eighteen months began picking out tunes on the family's organ. At age two he taught himself to play "God Save the King." At three he was on tour and in 1779 played before the king and queen in Buckingham Palace. Already he was able to transpose a piece into any key and name the notes of any chord by ear.

Crotch studied at Cambridge from 1786 to 1788 and then at Magdalen College, Oxford. In 1790 he became organist and studied at Christ Church, Oxford (B.Mus. 1794; D.Mus. 1799). Crotch became known as a teacher, composer, and scholar. He was an associate of the London Philharmonic Society at its foundation and was appointed the first principal of the Royal Academy of Music in 1822. Crotch resigned that position in 1834. After 1836 until his death he devoted himself to sketching, composing, and writing. He composed works for choir, orchestra, and keyboard.

453 O Holy City, Seen of John

Tune: MORNING SONG

This text was written by Walter Russell Bowie during his first pastorate at Greenwood, Virginia. The inspiration for the hymn was John's vision on the isle of Patmos (Revelation 21–22). For comments on Bowie, see hymn 7.

MORNING SONG first appeared in John Wyeth's *Repository of Sacred Music, Part Second* (1813). For more on the tune, see hymn 600.

The harmonization is by C. Winfred Douglas for *The Hymnal 1940.* For comment on Douglas, see hymn 4.

454 Blessed Jesus, at Your Word

Tune: LIEBSTER JESU

This hymn is by Tobias Clausnitzer (1619–1684). He was chaplain of the Swedish regiment, Leipzig (1644), after having earned a Master of Arts degree at the University of Leipzig the previous year. Clausnitzer preached the Thanksgiving sermon at the accession of Queen Christina in St. Thomas Church, Leipzig, and to General Wrangel's army in Weiden at the end of the Thirty Years' War.

The text first appeared in the *Altdorffisches Gesang-Büchlein* (1663). The translation is by Catherine Winkworth and appears in her *Lyra Germanica* (2nd series, 1858). It was altered for *The Worshipbook—Services and Hymns* (1972). For comments on Winkworth, see hymn 3.

LIEBSTER JESU was composed by Johann Rudolph Ahle in 1664 for the text "Ja, er ist's, das Heil der Welt." For comments on Ahle, see hymn 493. The tune first appeared with the present text in 1687 after having been altered from the original. Thomas Hastings published the tune in a slightly altered form entitled NUREMBERG in *Musica Sacra* (U.S.A., 1834). Hastings' version appeared in the Presbyterian hymnals of 1895 and 1911.

The harmonization by Johann Sebastian Bach as found in *Choralgesänge* has been altered. Bach also wrote several organ pieces based on the tune. For more on Bach, see hymn 17.

455 All Creatures of Our God and King

Tune: LASST UNS ERFREUEN

The origin of this hymn text is "Altissimu, omnipotente, bon signore," known as "Canticle of the Sun" by Francis of Assisi. The poem was written in 1225 a year before his death. Blind and quite ill, he took refuge from the sun in a hut in the monastery gardens. The shelter was built by Clara, the first woman to take the vows of his order. Albert Edward Bailey, in *The Gospel in Hymns* (p. 266), reports:

> Then one day after a long conversation with Clara he took his place at the monastery table. The meal had hardly begun when suddenly he seemed to be rapt away in ecstasy, which lasted for some minutes. Then coming to himself, he cried, "Praise be to God!" He had just composed the Canticle of the Sun.

The English paraphrase was made by William Draper (c. 1910) for a children's Pentecost Festival in Leeds. It was first published in *Hymns of the Spirit* (1926).

William Draper (1855–1933) was born in Warwickshire, England. He was educated first at Cheltenham College, Oxford, and the Keble College, Oxford (B.A. 1877; M.A. 1880). He was ordained in the Church of England and served a variety of parishes throughout his ministry.

LASST UNS ERFREUEN is from *Geistliche Kirchengesäng* (1623) and harmonized by Ralph Vaughan Williams. For comments on the tune and the source, see hymn 229.

456 Awake, My Soul, and with the Sun

Tune: MORNING HYMN

King James II of England declared the author of this hymn, Thomas Ken, the most eloquent preacher among Protestants of his time.

Thomas Ken (1637–1711) was born at Little Berkhampstead, Hertfordshire, England, but went to live with his brother-in-law, Isaak Walton, after his parents died when Ken was nine years old. He was educated at Winchester and New College, Oxford (B.A. 1661; M.A. 1664). He was curate for Little Easton in Essex for three years after his ordination in 1662 and served for one year as a domestic chaplain to Bishop Morley. After his election as a fellow of Winchester College (1666), he was curate on the Isle of Wight (1667–1669), and for ten years, prebendary of Winchester Cathedral and College and chaplain to the bishop.

During this period Ken prepared his *A Manual of Prayers for the Use of the Scholars of Winchester College* (1674). In the second edition of this work (1695), Ken's hymns were included after having been separately published in 1692. He sang his hymns to the viol or spinet, but it is not known what tunes he used. The present text as well as "All Praise to Thee, My God, This Night" (hymn 542) became popular in English hymnals. His Doxology is the text used most often with OLD HUNDREDTH (see hymn 592).

Despite his adulation of Ken, King James II had him and six

other bishops imprisoned in the Tower of London for not subscribing to the King's Declaration of Indulgence. Later all seven were acquitted. Since Ken would not take the coronation oath to William of Orange (1691), he was deprived of his see. He retired to the home of his friend, Lord Weymouth, where he died.

MORNING HYMN was composed by François Barthélémon in 1785 at the request of Jacob Duché (1737–1798), a Philadelphia native who was then chaplain of the Female Orphan Asylum, Westminster Bridge Road, London. It appeared initially in the Supplement to *Hymns and Psalms Used at the Asylum for Female Orphans* (1789 or before).

François Barthélémon (1741–1808) was born at Bordeaux and was the oldest of sixteen children. His father was a French army officer and his mother an Irish lady from a wealthy family. He was widely educated in diverse fields and gave up a military career to pursue music. He was an expert violinist and became director of the Opera orchestra in London and later of the orchestra at Vauxhall Gardens (1770–1776). He wrote a variety of musical pieces. Barthélémon became a friend of Franz Joseph Haydn (see hymn 285) when Haydn visited London. Haydn later gave music lessons to Barthélémon's daughter.

The present tune is presented as it appeared in *The Church Hymnal for the Christian Year* (1917).

457 I Greet Thee, Who My Sure Redeemer Art

Tune: TOULON

This hymn first appeared in the French Psalter published in Strassburg (1545), published under the leadership of John Calvin. It has traditionally been ascribed to Calvin but that cannot be proved and many scholars deny Calvin's authorship.

The original in French, "Je te salue, mon certain Rédempteur," was translated by Elizabeth Lee Smith (1868) and first published in Philip Schaff's *Christ in Song* (1869).

John Calvin (1509–1564) was the leading theologian of the early Reformed theological tradition. His *Institutes of the Christian Religion* (various editions, 1536–1560) is one of the most important theological works ever written. Calvin was active in many dimensions of life in Geneva, where as a pastor, he preached, lectured, and wrote. His influence gave rise to Calvinism and the development of the Reformed faith throughout the world. Calvin was instrumental in the development of metrical psalmody. He encouraged the completion of the Genevan Psalters.

Elizabeth Lee Smith (1817–1898) was born in New Hampshire, where her father was president of Dartmouth University. She married Henry Boynton Smith in 1843 and moved to New York City in 1850, when her husband became a professor at Union Theological Seminary. Elizabeth Smith is remembered for this translation.

Philip Schaff (1819–1893) was born in Chur, Switzerland, and educated at Tübingen, Halle, and Berlin. In 1843 he emigrated to the United States, where he became a professor at the German Reformed Seminary, Mercersburg, Pennsylvania, and later professor of sacred literature, Union Theological Seminary, New York City (1870). He was a noted hymnologist and translator as well as one of the leading church historians of his day. In addition to many theological works, some of his others include *Deutsches Gesangbuch* (1860), *Hymns and Songs of Praise for Public and Social Worship* (1874), and with A. Gilman, *Library of Religious Poetry* (1881).

TOULON is adapted from Genevan 124 in the Genevan Psalter (1551). For comments on this tune, see hymn 375.

458 Earth and All Stars

Tune: DEXTER

This text was written by Herbert Frederick Brokering for the ninetieth anniversary of St. Olaf College, Northfield, Minnesota, in 1964.

Herbert Frederick Brokering was born in 1926 in Beatrice, Nebraska, and studied at Wartburg College, Waverly, Iowa; Wartburg Seminary, Dubuque, Iowa; and the Lutheran Theological Seminary, Columbus, Ohio. He graduated from the University of Iowa (M.A. in Child Psychology) and did additional work at the University of Pittsburgh and the universities of Kiel and Erlangen in Germany. After ten years in the pastorate in

Cedarhurst, New York, Pittsburgh, and San Antonio, he was in the education department of the American Lutheran Church from 1960 to 1970. Brokering is now a resource person and consultant. He has written more than thirty books.

DEXTER was composed for this text by David N. Johnson and first appeared in *Twelve Folksongs and Spirituals* (1968) and later in *Contemporary Worship—1* (1969).

David N. Johnson (1922–1987) was born in San Antonio and studied at Trinity University (B.Mus.) and Syracuse University (M.Mus.; Ph.D.). He was head of the music department of St. Olaf College, organist at Syracuse University, and organist and choir director of Trinity Episcopal Cathedral, Phoenix, before becoming professor of music at Arizona State University. He published approximately four hundred compositions for organ and choir and also served on the Lutheran Book of Worship Committee.

459 Father, We Praise Thee

Tune: CHRISTE SANCTORUM

This hymn text is attributed to Gregory the Great although speculation surrounding the authorship exists. Some say it was written by Alcuin (see hymn 340). The hymn is preserved in several eleventh-century manuscripts. The translation was prepared by Percy Dearmer for *The English Hymnal* (1906), which he edited with Ralph Vaughan Williams (see hymn 6).

Percy Dearmer (1867–1936) was born in London and educated at Westminster School and Christ Church, Oxford (B.A. 1890; M.A. 1896). He was ordained a deacon in 1891 and a priest in 1892. After serving several parishes, he was made vicar of St. Mary's, Primrose Hill, London (1901–1915), where his organist was Martin Shaw (see hymn 12). After serving as chaplain to the British Red Cross in Serbia during World War I, he was appointed professor of ecclesiastical art at King's College, London, where he remained until his death. He was granted a Doctor of Divinity degree by the University of Oxford and was made canon of Westminster in 1931.

Martin Shaw, Ralph Vaughan Williams, and Percy Dearmer

together edited *Songs of Praise* (1925), *The Oxford Book of Carols* (1928), and *Enlarged Songs of Praise* (1931).

CHRISTE SANCTORUM was first published in the Paris *Antiphoner* (1681). The present harmonization was by David Evans for the *Revised Church Hymnary* (1927). For more on the source, see hymn 147. For comments on Evans, see hymn 113.

460 Holy God, We Praise Your Name

Tune: GROSSER GOTT, WIR LOBEN DICH

The text is an English translation of the German versification of the Te Deum Laudamus by Clarence Augustus (later Alphonsus) Walworth. The hymn was first published in the *Catholic Psalmist* (Dublin, 1858). Later Hall and Lasar's *Evangelical Hymnal* (New York, 1880) dated the text to 1853.

The original German versification, attributed to Ignaz Franz (1719–1790) about 1774, was part of a collection commissioned by Maria Theresa, ruler of Austria.

Clarence Augustus Walworth (1820–1900) was born in Plattsburg, New York, and graduated in law from Union College (1838). He was admitted to the bar in 1841 and he attended General Theological Seminary in 1842. Born Presbyterian, Walworth studied for the Episcopal ministry but he was heavily influenced by the Oxford Movement and was subsequently ordained a Roman Catholic priest (1845), taking the name Clarence Alphonsus.

Walworth was one of the founders of the order of Paulists in the United States and from 1864/6 to 1900 was rector of St. Mary's Church, Albany, New York. He was blind for the last ten years of his life. He published *The Gentle Skeptic* (1863), *Andiatorocte, or the Eve of Lady Day and Other Poems* (1888), and *The Oxford Movement in America* (1895).

GROSSER GOTT, WIR LOBEN DICH is the tune long associated with this text. As was the German practice, it received its name from the first line of the poem. It was first published in *Allgemeines Katholisches Gesangbuch* (c. 1774). A number of variants of the tune were used in the nineteenth century. The present alteration appeared in Johann Gottfried Schicht's *Choral-Buch* (1819).

461 God Is Here!

Tune: ABBOT'S LEIGH

The text was written by Fred Pratt Green in 1979, at the request of Russell Schulz-Widmar, co-director of music at University United Methodist Church, Austin, Texas, who wrote:

> We are in need of a hymn. It would be sung for the first time at the closing service of an eight-month long festival centering round the themes of Worship, Music and the Arts. . . . We would prefer a meter of 8.7.8.7.D since we could then use your text to introduce the tune ABBOT'S LEIGH to our congregation. (Bernard Braley, *The Hymns and Ballads of Fred Pratt Green*, p. 93; Carol Stream, Ill.: Hope Publishing Co., 1982)

The hymn was revised in 1988 by Green for *The Presbyterian Hymnal* (1990).

ABBOT'S LEIGH was composed by Rev. Cyril Vincent Taylor on a Sunday morning during the spring of 1941. It was during World War II and Taylor was working in the wartime headquarters of the religious broadcasting department of the British Broadcasting Company located in the village of Abbot's Leigh. The village is across the Clifton suspension bridge from Bristol.

The tune was chosen for inclusion in the Revised Edition of *Hymns Ancient and Modern* (1950) as the setting for "Glorious Things of Thee Are Spoken." For comments on the composer, see hymn 74.

462 Christ, Whose Glory Fills the Skies

Tune: RATISBON

The text was written by Charles Wesley, the youngest son of the nineteen Wesley children. Together with his brother John, Charles Wesley led one of the greatest revivals in English history. He traveled hundreds of miles on horseback, preached to crowds of thousands in open fields and city streets. Charles Wesley remained loyal to the Anglican church all his life and disapproved of the separatists later called "Methodists" and John's informal ordinations. Charles is said to have written as many as 6,500 hymns. This hymn was published in 1740. For a biographical sketch of Charles Wesley, see hymn 1.

RATISBON was published in Johann A. Freylinghausen's *Geistreiches Gesangbuch* (1704), revised in Johann Gottlob Werner's *Choralbuch zu den neuen sächsischen Gesangbüchern vierstimmig für die Orgel* (1815). There it was the setting for "Jesu, meines Lebens Leben." Werner took Johann Crüger's tune JESUS, MEINE ZUVERSICHT as it had been adapted by several others, reworked it and placed it in his collection. The tune appears as in *Old Church Psalmody* (1847). It is named for the German city Ratisbon, now known as Regensburg. (For more on the tune's history, see Erik Routley, *The Music of Christian Hymns*, pp. 61f.)

Johann Gottlob Werner (1777–1822) was born in Hayn near Leipzig and was an organist. He was first at Frohburg (1798), then Hohenstein, Saxony (1808), and finally Merseburg (1819).

463 Christ, Whose Glory Fills the Skies

Tune: CHRIST WHOSE GLORY

For comments on Charles Wesley's text, see hymn 462.

CHRIST WHOSE GLORY was composed by Malcolm Williamson in 1961. It is one of sixteen tunes composed for texts of Isaac Watts and Charles Wesley. Williamson's practice has been not to name his tunes but to let them carry the name of the text for which they were composed. It appears here as in *The Hymnal 1982*.

Malcolm Williamson was born in 1931 in Australia and moved to England while young. He has become one of that country's finest contemporary composers. Growing up as a pre-Vatican Council II Roman Catholic, he was not exposed to congregational singing. Williamson has become "fascinated" with English hymnody and in particular with the works of Joseph Barnby. Among his compositions are *6 Carols for Children* (1963), *16 Hymns and Processions* (1975), and two chancel musicals: *Genesis* and *The Winter Star*.

464 Joyful, Joyful, We Adore Thee

Tune: HYMN TO JOY

The text was written by Henry van Dyke in 1907 while he was guest preacher at Williams College, in the Berkshires, Williamstown, Massachusetts. Tertius van Dyke told the story that his father "came down to breakfast one morning and placed the manuscript on the table before President James Garfield, saying: 'Here is a hymn for you. Your mountains were my inspiration. It must be sung to the music of Beethoven's "Hymn to Joy" ' " (William Chalmers Covert and Calvin Weiss Laufer, eds., *Handbook to The Hymnal*, pp. 7f.). It was first published in *Poems of Henry van Dyke* (1911) and was included in *The Hymnal* (1933).

The text was altered for *The Presbyterian Hymnal* (1990) in accord with Dr. van Dyke's ideal of hymn writing. He wrote:

> These verses are simple expressions of common Christian feelings and desires in this present time,—hymns of today that may be sung together by people who know the thought of the age, and are not afraid that any truth of science will destroy religion, or any revolution on earth overthrow the kingdom of heaven. Therefore these are hymns of trust and joy and hope. (Albert Edward Bailey, *The Gospel in Hymns*, p. 554)

For a biographical sketch of van Dyke, see hymn 305.

HYMN TO JOY was written by Ludwig van Beethoven (1770–1827) as the setting for Schiller's "An die Freude" in the final movement of Beethoven's Ninth Symphony, which premiered with Beethoven directing on May 7, 1824. It was published two years later. This was his last public concert. The story goes that after the final movement great applause erupted but Beethoven, by now totally deaf, continued conducting. The contralto soloist, Caroline Unger, walked over to him and gently turned him around toward the audience. Sir George Grove stated:

> His turning around and the sudden conviction thereby forced on everybody that he had not done so before because he could not hear what was going on acted like an electric shock on all present. A volcanic explosion of sympathy and admiration followed which was repeated again and again, and seemed as if it would never end. (Milton Cross and David Ewen, *Milton Cross' Encyclopedia of the Great Composers and Their Music*, rev. ed. 1:53; Garden City, New York: Doubleday & Co., 1962)

The adaptation of the tune for use as a hymn was by Edward Hodges (1796–1867) of Bristol, England. He emigrated to Canada (1838) and finally to New York City, where he was organist for more than twenty years first at St. John's Episcopal Church and finally at Trinity Church.

Beethoven's original rhythm for the twelfth and thirteenth measures has been restored for *The Presbyterian Hymnal* (1990).

465 Here, O Lord, Your Servants Gather

Tune: TŌKYŌ

This hymn was written by Tokuo Yamaguchi (b. 1900) in 1958 for the World Council of Christian Education Convention held in Tokyo, Japan. It was the poet's hope to lift up the theme of that convention: "Jesus Christ, the Way, the Truth, and the Life." Written at the dawning of the space age and the arms race, the hymn stresses that the answers to all human problems are ultimately found in Jesus the Savior and not in human-made weapons.

Everett M. Stowe (b. 1897) translated the text in 1958 for *Laudamus*, published by the Lutheran World Federation, Geneva. Stowe was a United Methodist missionary in Japan at the time.

TŌKYŌ was composed by Isao Koizumi (b. 1907) for this text. It was patterned after the ancient gagaku music of the imperial court of China dating back to the Tang dynasty.

466 O for a Thousand Tongues to Sing

Tune: AZMON

The text was written by Charles Wesley on the first anniversary of his spiritual conversion (1740). He was inspired to write the poem after a conversation with Moravian Peter Böhler during which Wesley asked him about praising Christ. Böhler replied, "Had I a thousand tongues, I would praise Him with them all."

The original hymn contained eighteen stanzas and was titled "For the anniversary day of one's conversion." The first stanza began, "Glory to God, and praise, and love."

The hymn has long been the first selection in Methodist collections. For a biographical sketch of Charles Wesley, see hymn 1.

AZMON was composed by Carl Gotthelf Gläser and arranged by Lowell Mason. For comments on the composer and the tune, see hymn 386. For comments on Mason, see hymn 40.

467 How Great Thou Art

Tune: O STORE GUD

The original text of this hymn is by Carl Gustav Boberg (1859–1940). It was written in 1885 as a result of his experience in a midday thunderstorm where moments of flashing violence were followed by a clear brilliant sun. After the storm he heard the song of birds in nearby trees. It is reported that Rev. Boberg fell on his knees in "humble adoration to God." Shortly after this experience he wrote the nine-stanza poem "O Store Gud." Several years later, he was visiting Varmland and was surprised to hear the congregation singing his poem to an old Swedish folk melody. He later published the poem in *Sanningsvittnet* (1891).

The hymn was translated into German by Manfred von Glehn and then into English by Rev. E. Gustav Johnson as "O Mighty God, When I Behold the Wonder" (1925). In 1927, I. S. Prohanoff translated the German version into Russian. Stuart Wesley Keene Hine (b. 1899), the author of the most popular English version, was a missionary to Russia. He and his wife often sang the Russian text as a duet as they worked among the Ukrainian people. The first three stanzas of his English version were written prior to 1939. With the outbreak of World War II, Hine returned to England, where he wrote the fourth stanza after the war.

The hymn in its present form was introduced to U.S. congregations by James Caldwell at Stony Brook Bible Conference Center, Long Island, New York, in 1951. But it was George Beverly Shea and Cliff Barrows of the Billy Graham Evangelistic Team who popularized it during a London Crusade in Harringay Arena.

In 1974 the hymn was picked as the most popular in America by the readers of *Christian Herald* magazine.

The hymn has become a favorite of the Korean Presbyterians, hence a phonetic rendering of the Korean, by Myung Ja Yue, is included in *The Presbyterian Hymnal* (1990).

O STORE GUD is an old Swedish melody long associated with both the original Swedish and the present English texts. The harmonization is by Stuart K. Hine (1949).

468 Let All the World in Every Corner Sing

Tune: AUGUSTINE

This hymn was written by George Herbert and published after his death in *The Temple: or Sacred Poems and Ejaculations* (1633), a collection of his English poetry. It was intended to be recited antiphonally.

George Herbert (1593–1632) was born in Montgomery Castle, Wales, and educated at Westminster School and Trinity College, Cambridge (B.A. 1611). In 1612 he published his Latin verses in a volume mourning the death of Prince Henry. Following the death of King James I, Herbert took holy orders and became rector of Bemerton (1630). He died of consumption shortly before his fortieth birthday.

AUGUSTINE was composed by Erik Routley for this text. For a biographical sketch of Routley, see hymn 218.

469 Morning Has Broken

Tune: BUNESSAN

The text of this hymn was written by Eleanor Farjeon (1881–1965) for the tune BUNESSAN. The text appeared first in *Enlarged Songs of Praise* (1931) and in its present form from *The Children's Bells* (1957). Farjeon wrote nursery rhythms and singing games for children. She was inspired to write this text at the suggestion of Percy Dearmer (hymn 459). A contemporary popular music recording by Cat Stevens helped make this text familiar to present-day culture. Farjeon was born in London and at seventeen became Roman Catholic. She considered her faith a progression toward which her spiritual life moved rather than a conversion experience.

BUNESSAN is a Gaelic melody first published in *Songs and Hymns of the Gael,* 1888. It later appeared with the Christmas text "Child in a Manger" (1917). The present arrangement was made for the *Psalter Hymnal* (1987) of the Christian Reformed Church by Dale Grotenhuis in 1985. Grotenhuis served on the revision committee for that hymnal.

470 O Day of Radiant Gladness

Tune: ES FLOG EIN KLEINS WALDVÖGELEIN

The text is a composite from several poets. The first two stanzas were written by Christopher Wordsworth and appeared as the opening hymn in *The Holy Year* (1862), where it had six stanzas. A few years later, in Tate and Brady's *Supplement to the New Version* (1874) it was reduced to four stanzas. For comments on Wordsworth, see hymn 318.

Stanza 3 was written by Charles P. Price at the request of the Standing Commission on Church Music of the Episcopal Church. Stanza 4 is the work of the Revision Committee for *The Hymnal 1982.* For a biographical sketch of Price, see hymn 13.

ES FLOG EIN KLEINS WALDVÖGELEIN was harmonized by George Ratcliffe Woodward from a Memmingen manuscript. For comments on the tune, see hymn 184. For comments on Woodward, see hymn 68.

471 O Praise the Gracious Power

Tune: CHRISTPRAISE RAY

This text was written by Thomas H. Troeger in 1984 for the ordination of Judith Ray as a teaching elder in the Presbyterian Church (U.S.A.). For a biographical sketch of Troeger, see hymn 73.

CHRISTPRAISE RAY was composed by Carol Doran in 1984 for this text. For a biographical sketch of Doran, see hymn 287.

472 Cantad al Señor O Sing to the Lord

This Brazilian folk hymn was translated into both Spanish and English by Gerhard Cartford. It appeared in *Songs of the People* published by the Division for Life and Mission in the Congregation of the American Lutheran Church and the Division for Parish Services of the Lutheran Church in America (1986).

Gerhard Cartford was born in 1923 at Fort Dauphin, Madagascar. He was in the U.S. Army (1943–1946) and graduated from St. Olaf College (B.Mus. 1948) and Union Theological Seminary, New York City (M.S.M.). He studied folk music and hymnody in Norway for a year under a Fulbright scholarship and continued his studies at Luther Seminary (1954–1955); St. John's University, Collegeville, Minnesota (1955); and the University of Minnesota (Ph.D. 1961). Cartford has served several Lutheran congregations as organist and choir director and taught at Luther College in Decorah, Iowa. He also taught in the music department of Texas Lutheran College, Seguin, Texas (1961–1974), where he was department chair for eleven years. At Luther-Northwestern Seminary, he was assistant professor of liturgy, church music, and the arts. Cartford worked on producing a Lutheran liturgy while living in South America. He contributed to the *Lutheran Book of Worship* and edited *Response*, a journal of the Lutheran Society for Worship, Music, and the Arts. Cartford has participated in a number of church music society organizations.

This Brazilian folk melody is contemporary with the text. The setting is from Editora Sinodal, São Leopoldo, Brazil.

473 For the Beauty of the Earth

Tune: DIX

The author of this text, Folliott Sandford Pierpoint (1835–1917), was born in Bath, England, and graduated from Queen's College, Cambridge (M.A. 1857). For a brief period he was headmaster and taught literature at Somersetshire College, but after receiving a small inheritance he spent the remainder of his life traveling and writing. He wrote numerous hymns and sacred poems for the church in seven volumes. Many dealt with love of nature. The present text, however, is the most well known.

This piece was originally written as a Communion hymn to infuse a note of joy into the otherwise solemn service. It now is used more generally and has been a particularly favored children's hymn. It was included in Orby Shipley's *Lyra Eucharistica* (2nd ed., 1864) and titled "The Sacrifice of Praise." There it consisted of eight six-line stanzas of which four are omitted in many hymnals. Originally the final two lines in the refrain read "Christ, our God, to Thee we raise this our sacrifice of praise." Hymnal editors later altered the final line to read "This our hymn of grateful praise" or "Lord of all, to Thee we raise this our hymn of grateful praise." It has been suggested the alterations were made to make the hymn more usable as a general hymn.

It is said Pierpoint wrote this hymn "one day in late spring near his native city of Bath, England, when violets and primroses were in full bloom and all the earth seemed to rejoice. He climbed up a hill and sat down to rest and meditate. The panorama before him inspired him to write these beautiful lines" (Armin Haeussler, *The Story of Our Hymns*, p. 66). The hymn is given completely to the praise of God and lists at least twenty-five causes for this praise. One original stanza gave thanks for God who is the source of all other joys and beauties:

> For Thyself, best Gift Divine! To our race so freely given;
> For that great, great love of Thine, peace on earth, and joy in heaven:
> Lord of all, to Thee we raise this our hymn of grateful praise.

DIX was composed by Conrad Kocher and abridged by William Henry Monk. The harmonization is from *The English Hymnal* (1906). For comments on the tune and the composer, see hymn 63.

474 O Splendor of God's Glory Bright

Tune: PUER NOBIS NASCITUR

Scholars have attributed the original Latin text "Splendor paternae gloriae" to Ambrose of Milan. This is based on the testimony of Fulgentius, bishop of Ruspe, North Africa (d. 533), the Venerable Bede (see hymn 141), and the Benedictine editors of his works. For comments on Ambrose see hymn 14.

This morning hymn addressing the Trinity was traditionally used at Lauds (sunrise) on Monday. The translation is a composite and appears as in *Rejoice in the Lord* (1985).

PUER NOBIS NASCITUR, from a Trier manuscript, was adapted by Michael Praetorius and harmonized by George Ratcliffe Woodward. For comments on the tune, see hymn 68.

475 O That I Had a Thousand Voices

Tune: O DASS ICH TAUSEND ZUNGEN HÄTTE

This text was written by the German hymn writer Johann Mentzer (1658–1734) in 1704. Mentzer was born in Silesia and studied theology at Wittenberg. He served pastorates throughout Germany until his death. Three other prominent hymn writers were among his good friends: Johann Christoph Schwedler, Henriette Catherine von Gersdorf, and Nikolaus Ludwig von Zinzendorf.

Not long after Mentzer arrived in the parish at Kemnitz, a nearby farmhouse was destroyed by lightning. Some believe Mentzer wrote this, his best hymn, to indicate the source of the Christian's thankfulness to God in all circumstances.

The hymn was first published in Johann A. Freylinghausen's *Geistreiches Gesangbuch* (Halle, 1704). The present translation is altered from *The Lutheran Hymnal* (1941), which was based on translations in Henry Mills' *Horae Germanicae* (1845) and Catherine Winkworth's *Lyra Germanica* (1st series, 1855).

O DASS ICH TAUSEND ZUNGEN HÄTTE is believed to have been composed by Johann Balthasar König. It appeared in his *Harmonischer Liederschatz* (Frankfurt, 1738) as the setting for "Ach sagt mir nichts von Gold und Schätzen" by Angelus Silesius.

König (1691–1758) was a German composer and appointed director of music at the Katharinenkirche, the second most important musical post in the city of Frankfurt. He later became Kapellmeister and was made a citizen of Frankfurt in recognition of his position. Under his leadership the quality of church and public music improved. He was concerned with congregational singing and his *Harmonischer Liederschatz*, a chorale book, was the most comprehensive work of its kind in the eighteenth century. It contained nearly two thousand melodies with continuo, and the tunes of the entire Genevan Psalter. Since two hundred ninety tunes are not known from other earlier sources, they are assumed to be from König.

476 O Worship the King, All Glorious Above!

Tune: LYONS

The text is a free paraphrase of Psalm 104. It was written by Robert Grant and was first published in Bickersteth's *Christian Psalmody* (1833). The text of stanza 2 was altered by the Presbyterian Hymnal Committee to reflect the language of the psalm more completely.

Robert Grant (1779–1838) was born in Bengal, India, educated in Oxford, admitted to the bar in 1807, and became a member of the British Parliament the next year. In 1833 he successfully introduced a bill into Parliament emancipating the Jews. He died in India at the age of fifty-nine. Grant's brother published twelve of his hymns in *Sacred Poems* (1839).

LYONS first appeared in William Gardiner's *Sacred Melodies* (London, 1815) where the source is stated as "Subject Haydn." It is not known whether Gardiner meant Franz Joseph or Johann Michael Haydn since a number of pieces by both contain the opening musical phrase. The first use of the tune in the United States was in Shaw's *Sacred Melodies* (1818).

Johann Michael Haydn (1737–1806) was a brother of Franz Joseph Haydn (see hymn 285). Like his brother before him, Michael was a boy soprano. It has been said he had a vocal range of three octaves. He was also an accomplished violinist, pianist, and later organist and choirmaster.

477 Ye Servants of God, Your Master Proclaim

Tune: HANOVER

The text was written by Charles Wesley as part of a hymn tract series issued for the Wesleys' class meetings. A caption to the hymn stated "To be sung in a tumult." The tract containing thirty-three hymns was titled *Hymns for Times of Trouble and Persecution* (1744). For a biographical sketch of Wesley, see hymn 1.

HANOVER was attributed to William Croft and published in Nahum Tate (see hymn 58) and Nicholas Brady's *A Supplement to the New Version of the Psalms* (6th ed., 1708). There a caption read "A New Tune to the 149th Psalm of the New Version, and the 104th Psalm of the Old." Later the tune appeared in Gawthorn's *Harmonia Perfecta* (1730) with the name HANOVER. During the eighteenth century the tune was known by several other names, including BROMSWICK, OLD 104TH, and TALLY'S among others. The name HANOVER was identified with the tune after George III ascended the throne. For a biographical sketch of Croft, see hymn 210.

478 Praise, My Soul, the King of Heaven

Tune: LAUDA ANIMA

This hymn text is one of two paraphrases of Psalm 103 by Henry Francis Lyte in *Spirit of the Psalms* (1834). The original hymn had five stanzas. The fourth has been omitted from Presbyterian hymnals since the turn of the century. It reads:

Frail as summer's flower we flourish;
Blows the wind and it is gone;
But, while mortals rise and perish,
God endures unchanging on:
Praise Him! praise Him!
Praise Him! praise Him!
Praise the high eternal One!

For comments on Lyte, see hymn 203.

LAUDA ANIMA was composed by John Goss in 1869 for this text. It was first published in Robert Brown-Borthwick's *The Supplemental Hymn and Tune Book* (3rd ed. with new appendix, 1869) in two forms, both of which appear in *The Presbyterian Hymnal* (1990). For comments on Goss, see hymn 51.

479 Praise, My Soul, the God of Heaven

The text is an altered form of Henry Francis Lyte's "Praise, My Soul, the King of Heaven" (see hymn 478). It was included in the inclusive-language hymn collection *Because We Are One People,* published by the Ecumenical Women's Center of Chicago Theological Seminary in 1974.

The Presbyterian Hymnal (1990) recommends using either arrangement of LAUDA ANIMA as a setting for this text.

480 Praise Our God Above

Tune: HSUAN P'ING

This text entitled "Harvest Song" in Frank W. Price's *Chinese Christian Hymns* (1953) is by Tzu-chen Chao (1931). The original Chinese was included in *Hymns of Universal Praise* (1936).

For comments on the author and the translator, see hymn 352.

HSUAN P'ING is a Confucian chant. It is a proclamation of peace and was harmonized for the revised *Hymns of Universal Praise* (1977) by W. H. Wong in 1973.

481 Praise the Lord, God's Glories Show

Tune: LLANFAIR

The text was Henry Francis Lyte's original version of Psalm 150. It appeared in *Spirit of the Psalms* (1834) and was altered by the author for the enlarged edition of 1836. The present collection is a slight variation of the 1834 text with the word "God's" replacing "His" in the first line. For comments on the author, see hymn 203.

LLANFAIR was composed by Robert Williams (1817) and harmonized by David Evans (1927). For comments on the tune and Williams and Evans, see hymn 113.

482 Praise Ye the Lord, the Almighty

Tune: LOBE DEN HERREN

This hymn text is based on Psalm 103:1–6 and Psalm 150. It was written by Joachim Neander and published in *A und Ω. Joachimi Neandri Glaub- und Liebesübung* (Bremen, 1680).

Joachim Neander (1650–1680) wrote some sixty hymns and has been called the "Paul Gerhardt of the Calvinists." As a youth in Bremen, he took the Calvinist faith seriously but also lived a rather unruly existence. His pastor, Theodore Under-Eyck of St. Martin's Church, affected him and led him to amend his ways. After a period as a tutor, Neander accompanied some of his students to the University of Heidelberg. Through them he came to know two important Pietists, Philipp Jacob Spener and Johann J. Schütz, the lyric poet. He was impressed by their faith and model of Christian living. In 1674, Neander became headmaster of the Düsseldorf grammar school and five years later he became an unordained assistant to Pastor Under-Eyck at St. Martin's. He died of tuberculosis. The valley of the Düssel near Mettmann, where he used to take long walks, was named Neanderthal in his honor. Here was where the skeleton of *Homo neanderthalensis* (Neanderthal man) was discovered in 1856.

Neander's hymns were sung by communities of faith and his *Bundeslieder* (covenant songs) celebrating God's covenant with humanity formed self-contained sections in the hymnals of many established churches in Germany. He wrote in the verse forms of the Genevan Psalter so his texts could be sung to the corresponding tunes. After his death, Neander's poetry was often given new melodies. Sixty-six of the outstanding ones were published by G. C. Strattner in 1691.

The text of this hymn in *The Presbyterian Hymnal* (1990) is an altered translation by Catherine Winkworth, included in her collection *The Chorale Book for England* (1863). For comments on Winkworth, see hymn 3.

LOBE DEN HERREN was first published with the text, "Hast du denn, Liebster, dein Angesicht gänzlich verborgen" in Part II of the Stralsund *Ernewerten Gesangbuch* (1665). It became associated with Neander's text in 1680 and may previously have been associated with secular texts before it was linked with religious ones. Johann Sebastian Bach used the melody in Cantatas 57 and 137 as well as in an unfinished cantata and an organ setting, "Kommst du nun, Jesu," in the *Schübler Chorales*.

The harmonization of this tune is from *Chorale Book for England* (1863). The descant is by Craig Sellar Lang (1953).

483 Sing Praise to God, Who Reigns Above

Tune: MIT FREUDEN ZART

The hymn was written by Johann Jacob Schütz and published in *Christliches Gedenckbüchlein* (1675). It was titled "Hymn of Thanksgiving." There was also a reference to Deuteronomy 32:3 attached. The hymn was later published in *Christliche Lebensregeln* (1677).

Johann Jacob Schütz (1640–1690) was born in Frankfurt am Main and educated at Tübingen, where he studied law after which he returned to Frankfurt and practiced law for the rest of his life. He sympathized with the pietistic (Evangelical) movement of the Lutheran Church. Later, under the influence of Philipp Jacob Spener and Johann Wilhelm Petersen, Schütz left the Lutheran Church and became a separatist.

The translation is that of Frances Elizabeth Cox (1812–1897). She was born in Oxford, England, and became one of the foremost translators of German hymns. This translation was published in *Lyra Eucharistica* (1864) and Cox's collection *Sacred Hymns from the German* (2nd ed., 1864). The hymn was introduced to America in the Lutheran *Church Book* (Philadelphia, 1868). Cox died at Headington.

MIT FREUDEN ZART was from the Bohemian Brethren's *Kirchengeseng* (1566). For comments on the tune and the source, see hymn 7.

484 Sing with Hearts

Tune: INTAKO

This text is a rendition of Psalm 100 written in 1983 by Jonathan Malicsi (b. 1932). Malicsi was a member of the President's Committee on Culture and the Arts in Manila, Philippines.

INTAKO is a Kalinga melody from northern Luzon, Philippines. The introduction is usually sung to bamboo buzzer accompaniment. These split bamboo tubes are hit on the palm of the hand on every beat. The tempo here is (quarter note = 92–100). The stanzas are more lyrical and sung at a slower tempo (quarter note = 66–72).

485 To God Be the Glory

Tune: TO GOD BE THE GLORY

This hymn was written by Fanny Crosby for children. She titled it "Praise for Redemption." It was published in William H. Doane and Robert Lowry's *Brightest and Best* (1875).

The hymn was all but forgotten until Cliff Barrows was gathering materials for the Billy Graham Greater London Crusade in 1954. Someone suggested this hymn. It became a favorite of the crusade and subsequently the hymn was reintroduced to the United States in the 1954 Nashville Crusade held at Vanderbilt University. The text differs from other Crosby gospel hymns in that it has an objective rather than subjective nature.

For a biographical sketch of Crosby, see hymn 341.

TO GOD BE THE GLORY was composed for this text by William Howard Doane for *Brightest and Best* (1875). For comments on Doane, see hymn 359.

486 When the Morning Stars Together

Tune: WEISSE FLAGGEN

This hymn text was written by Albert Frederick Bayly in 1969 and appeared in *Rejoice Always* (1971). It was included in *Rejoice in the Lord* (1985) with WEISSE FLAGGEN as the setting.

Some pronouns were changed from the third-person singular "him" and "his" to the second-person "you" and "yours" to provide more intimate language.

For a biographical sketch of Bayly, see hymn 297.

WEISSE FLAGGEN first appeared in *Tochter Sion* (Cologne, 1741). The melody is thought to have originated as a folk song. A variant of it appeared in the Cologne volume as the setting for "Lasst die weissen Flaggen wehen." There is also similarity to an anonymous melody in a Roman Catholic hymnal of 1732.

487 When Morning Gilds the Skies

Tune: LAUDES DOMINI

The text first appeared in *Katholisches Gesangbuch* (1828) and bore the title "A Christian Greeting." It had fourteen stanzas but no author's name. The text was translated by Edward Caswall. For comment on the translator, see hymn 51.

LAUDES DOMINI was composed by Joseph Barnby as the setting for Caswall's translation. For comments on the tune and the composer, see hymn 130.

488 The God of Abraham Praise

Tune: LEONI

The text in *The Presbyterian Hymnal* (1990) is quite close to the one found in *The Union Hymnal* edited by the Central Conference of American Rabbis. The 1885 translation is by Max Landsberg (1845–1928) and Newton Mann (1836–1926) and is based on the Jewish Creed set to meter, some say, by Daniel ben Judah, a fourteenth-century liturgical poet from Rome.

Moses Maimonides (1130–1205), the first to formulate the dogmas of Judaism, wrote the thirteen articles of the Jewish creed known as the *Yigdal.* This present translation is not to be confused with that of Thomas Olivers, although the first line is from his 1770 Christian version of the Yigdal.

LEONI, a Hebrew melody, was adapted by Thomas Olivers and Meyer Lyon (1770). For comments on the tune and on Olivers and Lyon, see hymn 274.

489 Open Now Thy Gates of Beauty

Tune: UNSER HERRSCHER

Benjamin Schmolck (1672–1737), the author of this text, was born in Silesia and was considered a splendid preacher, poet, and hymn writer. When he preached his first sermon in his father's pulpit, an influential member of the congregation was so impressed that he gave Schmolck a three-year allowance to study theology. At the University of Leipzig, he was influenced by Johannes Olearius and others from whom he received "a warm and living practical Christianity, but Churchly in tone and not Pietistic" (John Julian, ed., *A Dictionary of Hymnology*). He was ordained and served as assistant pastor with his father at Brauchitzchdorf.

After the Thirty Years' War and the Peace of Westphalia (1648), only one church and three clergy were permitted throughout an entire district of thirty-six villages. Schmolck ministered in this type of parish for the rest of his life. He was afflicted by strokes, partial paralysis, as well as cataracts.

Schmolck was the best-loved hymn writer of his day and wrote nine hundred hymns. He was crowned poet laureate in 1697. The present hymn was included in his *Kirchen-Gefährte* (1732).

The English translation is by Catherine Winkworth. For comments on Winkworth, see hymn 3. It was included in her collection *The Chorale Book for England* (1863).

UNSER HERRSCHER is also called NEANDER since Joachim Neander's hymn "Unser Herrscher, unser König" was published with this tune in *A und Ω. Joachimi Neandri Glaub- und Liebesübung* (Bremen, 1680). For a biographical sketch of Neander, see hymn 482. The tune was modified more toward its present form in Johann A. Freylinghausen's *Geistreiches Gesangbuch* (1704). The harmonization is altered from Catherine Winkworth's *The Chorale Book for England* (1863).

The descant is by John Dykes Bower (1905–1981), an English organist who spent his career in cathedral work. He taught at the Royal College of Music (1936–1969), received an honorary Doctor of Music degree from Oxford (1944), and was knighted in 1968.

490 With Glad, Exuberant Carolings

Tune: CAROL'S GIFT

This hymn, text and tune, is the result of collaboration between Thomas H. Troeger and Carol Doran (1984). The text is based on Ephesians 5:15–20 with particular emphasis on giving thanks to God at all times and for everything in the name of Jesus Christ. Although found in the Morning and Opening Hymns section of *The Presbyterian Hymnal* (1990), the hymn was written originally for use on the Thirteenth Sunday after Pentecost, Year B, according to the Common Lectionary. For a biographical sketch of Troeger, see hymn 73.

CAROL'S GIFT was composed for this text for *New Hymns for the Lectionary* (1985). For a biographical sketch of Doran, see hymn 287.

491 Stand Up and Bless the Lord

Tune: CARLISLE

This text which proclaims the good news was written by James Montgomery in 1824. Montgomery was England's most famous lay hymn writer. He is credited with having established English hymnological studies through his famous preface to *The Christian Psalmist* (1825). In the essay he critically reviewed the works of Watts, Wesley, and other Evangelical hymnists of the day. For further comment on the author, see hymn 22.

CARLISLE was composed by Charles Lockhart. It was originally titled INVOCATION but was later changed to CARLISLE after the former Carlisle Chapel, now Holy Trinity Church, London.

The descant is by Sydney Hugo Nicholson. For a biographical sketch of Nicholson, see hymn 371.

492 Baptized in Water

Tune: BUNESSAN

This hymn text by Michael A. Saward (1981) was published with this tune harmonized by Dom A. Gregory Murray (see hymn 193) in *Worship III* (1985). The present setting is from the *Psalter Hymnal* (1987) of the Christian Reformed Church.

BUNESSAN, a Gaelic melody, was arranged by Dale Grotenhuis. For comments on the tune's source and present setting, see hymn 469.

493 Dearest Jesus, We Are Here

Tune: LIEBSTER JESU

Benjamin Schmolck wrote the text in 1704. For a biographical sketch of the author, see hymn 489.

This English translation is by Catherine Winkworth. For comments on Winkworth, see hymn 3. Her original rendering of the opening phrase was "Blessed Jesus, here we stand" (*Lyra Germanica*, 2nd series, 1858). The present text has been considerably altered through the years.

LIEBSTER JESU was composed by Johann Rudolph Ahle in 1664. This tune was published in *Neue geistliche auf die Sonntage* (1664) as the setting for the Advent hymn by Franz Joachim Burmeister, "Ja, er ist's, das Heil der Welt." It became associated with the present hymn in *Das grosse Cantional: oder Kirchen-Gesangbuch* (Darmstadt, 1687).

Johann Rudolph Ahle (1625–1673) was born in Mühlhausen and was educated at the universities of Göttingen and Erfurt before becoming cantor of St. Andreas' Church and director of the Erfurt music school (1646–1654). He then became organist at St. Blasius' Church and was elected to his town council (1655) before becoming mayor (1661). He published many hymnals as well as a treatise on singing. He and others introduced a new style of music into churches which reflected the Italian opera. Ahle referred to his works as "sacred arias."

The harmonization by Johann Sebastian Bach has been altered. For comments on Bach, see hymn 17.

494 Out of Deep, Unordered Water

Tune: RUSTINGTON

This baptismal hymn by Fred Kaan was written for the Pilgrim Church, Plymouth, England, in 1965. It was sung at the 1984 Spring Synod of the West Midlands Province of the United Reformed Church during the debate on "Baptism, Eucharist and Ministry."

Biblical references in the hymn are Exodus 14:22 and 1 Corinthians 10:1–2.

RUSTINGTON was composed by C. Hubert H. Parry. For comments on the tune and the composer, see hymn 224.

495 We Know That Christ Is Raised

Tune: ENGELBERG

John Brownlow Geyer wrote this text, based on Romans 6, for this tune in 1969. It was first published in *Hymns and Songs, Supplement to the Book of Hymns* (1969) of the United Methodist Church. In personal correspondence Geyer wrote:

> "We know that Christ was raised" was written in 1967, when I was tutor at Cheshunt College, Cambridge. At that time a good deal of work was going on round the corner (involving a number of American research students) producing living cells. The hymn attempted to illustrate the Christian doctrine of baptism in relation to those experiments. Originally intended as a hymn for the Sacrament of Baptism, it has become popular as an Easter hymn.

(See also Stulken's *Hymnal Companion to the Lutheran Book of Worship*, p. 274.)

John Brownlow Geyer was born in 1932 in Wakefield, Yorkshire, England. He studied at Queen's College, Cambridge (1953–1956), where he was awarded the Kennett Hebrew Exhibition, and at Mansfield College (1956–1959). He was ordained in the Congregational Union of Scotland in 1959. He has served as chaplain at the University of St. Andrews; pastor of Drumchapel Congregational Church, Glasgow (1963); tutor at Cheshunt (1965) and Westminster (1967) colleges; and pastor of Little Baddow Congregational Church (1969). An interest in Old Testament studies has led him to write a commentary on *The Wisdom of Solomon* (1973) and several articles.

ENGELBERG was composed by Charles Villiers Stanford. For more on the tune and the composer, see hymn 264.

496 Lord Jesus Christ, Our Lord Most Dear

Tune: VOM HIMMEL HOCH

The text was written by Heinrich von Laufenberg (1429). John Julian notes he was "the most important and prolific hymn-writer of the 15th century." Catherine Winkworth, who translated the hymn into English (1869), said of his works, "He was a fertile composer and some of his hymns are very graceful and sweet, but many are prolix and fantastic; and though they seem to have been liked in the religious world of his own day they scarcely bear transplanting to ours."

Heinrich von Laufenberg (c. 1385–c. 1458) was born in Switerland and was first a priest at Freiburg and later a monk at the monastery of the Knights of St. John in Strassburg (1445). He translated many Latin hymns into German and transformed secular songs into religious pieces. He died in Strassburg.

For comments on Winkworth, see hymn 3.

VOM HIMMEL HOCH was first published in Schumann's *Geistliche Lieder* (1539). For comments on the tune, see hymn 54.

497 With Grateful Hearts Our Faith Professing

Tune: ST. CLEMENT

This text by Fred Kaan was written for *Pilgrim Praise* around 1963, where it was set to LES COMMANDEMENTS DE DIEU (see hymn 550). It is a baptismal hymn but Kaan believes it offers a wider challenge to those who bring up baptized children.

The last line was inspired by the regular contribution made by Kaan to the epilogue programs of Westward Television, Plymouth, England, entitled "Faith for Life."

This is the hymn's first appearance in a denominational hymnal in the United States.

ST. CLEMENT was composed by Clement Cotterill Scholefield. For comments on the tune and the composer, see hymn 546.

498 Child of Blessing, Child of Promise

Tune: KINGDOM

This hymn was written by Ronald S. Cole-Turner (1980) and first published in Ruth C. Duck (see hymn 219) and Michael G. Bausch's edited volume *Everflowing Streams* (1981).

Later the hymn was published in the children's baptismal

booklet *A Time to Remember.* There it appeared in both Spanish and English.

Ronald Stephen Cole-Turner was born in 1948 into a minister's family in Logansport, Indiana, and grew up in Ohio. He was educated at Wheaton College, Illinois (B.A. 1971), and Princeton Theological Seminary (M.Div. 1974; Ph.D. 1983). He was ordained a United Church of Christ minister (1974) and served several pastorates before becoming campus minister for Michigan Technological University, Houghton, Michigan. Presently, Cole-Turner is professor of systematic theology at Memphis Theological Seminary of the Cumberland Presbyterian Church. "Child of Blessing, Child of Promise" has enjoyed wide acceptance and has been published in hymn collections throughout the world.

KINGDOM was written by V. Earle Copes in 1959 and used at the National Convocation of Methodist Youth in 1960. It was written as a setting of "For the Bread, Which Thou Hast Broken" (see hymn 508) and appeared in anthem form before being published in *The Book of Hymns* (1964) of the Methodist Church. For a biographical sketch of Copes, see hymn 253.

499 Wonder of Wonders, Here Revealed

Tune: PENTECOST

This baptism hymn by Jane Parker Huber was written in 1980. She wished to emphasize two concerns: God loves each of us before we know how to love in return and baptism makes us part of a worldwide family unbound by time or space.

After writing the hymn, Huber became aware of the lack of hymns on the sacraments in Reformed hymnody. For a biographical sketch of Huber, see hymn 128.

PENTECOST was composed by William Boyd at the request of Sabine Baring-Gould for a meeting of Yorkshire colliers he had arranged for Whitsuntide. According to Boyd, "I walked, talked, slept, and ate with the words, and at last evolved the tune which I naturally named PENTECOST."

The tune appeared in *Thirty-two Hymn Tunes, Composed by Members of the University of Oxford* (1868). Sir Arthur Sullivan (see hymn 115) revised the tune, set it to the text "Fight the

Good Fight" (see hymn 307) and published it in *Church Hymns* (1874).

William Boyd (1847–1928) was born in Montego Bay, Jamaica, and educated at Hurstpierpoint and Worcester College, Oxford, where Baring-Gould was his tutor. He was ordained a deacon (1872) and later a priest (1882) in the Anglican Church. From 1893 until his retirement (1918) Boyd was vicar of All Saints, Norfolk Square, London.

500 Become to Us the Living Bread

Tune: O FILII ET FILIAE

This text was written by Miriam Drury for *The Worshipbook—Services and Hymns* (1972), where it was set to the present tune, without Alleluias.

Miriam Drury (1900–1985) was a native of California and lived there most of her life. Her husband was a faculty member at San Francisco Theological Seminary. After retirement, she lived in Monte Vista Presbyterian Retirement Home, Pasadena, California. Her hymn "Walk Tall, Christian" was also included in *The Worshipbook* (1972).

Drury composed many complete hymns (words and music), anthems, and poems for both children and adults. She was an award-winning composer for the Hymn Society of America and a number of her hymns were published by the society.

O FILII ET FILIAE, a fifteenth-century French melody, is found in *Airs sur les hymnes sacrez, odes et noëls* (1623). For comments on the tune, see hymn 116.

501 Bread of Heaven, on Thee We Feed

Tune: ARFON

The text was written by Josiah Conder. He published it in his collection *The Star in the East, and Other Poems* (1824). Conder titled it "For the Eucharist" and gave John 6:51–54 and John 15:1 as references.

Josiah Conder (1789–1855) was born and died in London. He worked as an author, editor, and publisher. He was owner and editor of the *Eclectic Review* and also editor of the *Patriot* newspaper.

The author of numerous poetry books and works of prose, Conder was also known as a hymnbook editor. His most important collections were *The Congregational Hymn Book: A Supplement to Dr. Watts's Psalms and Hymns* (1836; rev. 1844); and a revised edition of Dr. Watts' *Psalms and Hymns* (1851). He ranks close behind Watts and Doddridge as one of the most influential Congregational hymnists.

ARFON, a French and Welsh melody, was arranged by Hugh Davies. For comments on the tune and the composer, see hymn 99.

502 Bread of the World in Mercy Broken

Tune: RENDEZ À DIEU

This text by Bishop Reginald Heber was published after his death in the collection *Hymns Written and Adapted to the Weekly Church Service of the Year* (1827). There it was titled "Before the Sacrament." Originally it appeared as two stanzas of 9.8.9.8. In *The Presbyterian Hymnal* (1990) it appears in one stanza of 9.8.9.8. doubled. Commenting on this text in 1893, Charles Seymour Robinson stated, "It never had but these two stanzas in odd meter, but it has gone around the world." For a biographical sketch of Heber, see hymn 67.

RENDEZ A DIEU was composed or adapted by Louis Bourgeois in 1543. It was published in the Strassburg Psalter of 1545 and a revised version appeared in the Genevan Psalter (1551). For comments on the composer, see hymn 86.

503 Come, Risen Lord

Tune: SURSUM CORDA (SMITH)

This text was one of sixteen contributed to the volume *Songs of Praise* (1931), where the last line of stanza 1 was altered to read

"In this our sacrament of bread and wine." *The Presbyterian Hymnal* (1990) has restored the original text. The author, George Wallace Briggs, wrote:

> Dr. Percy Dearmer [see hymn 459], who edited *Songs of Praise,* had come to his own views about the institution of the Sacraments, and he was not prepared . . . to say that Christ ordered the *continuance* of the Sacrament. He therefore begged leave to alter the text. I reluctantly consented—and have ever since regretted it. As Professor F. C. Burkitt said, whether our Lord did or did not directly order the continuance of the Sacrament, it was undoubtedly His sacrament, or the Church would never have continued it.

George Wallace Briggs (1875–1958) was born in Kirby, England, and educated in classics at Emmanuel College, Cambridge. He was ordained in the Church of England and served as curate to a poor parish in Wakefield, Yorkshire, after which he served as a chaplain in the Royal Navy (1902–1909). He was vicar of St. Andrew's, Norwich (1909), rector of Loughborough (1918), and canon of Leicester Cathedral (1927–1934), then Worcester (1934–1956). Briggs was known as an educator and many of his hymns were written for the children of his weekly church school. His hymns and prayers have been published in *Prayers and Hymns for Use in Schools* (1927), *Little Bible* (1931), *Daily Service* (1936), and *Songs of Faith* (1945). Prime Minister Winston Churchill read one of Briggs' prayers when meeting with President Franklin Delano Roosevelt for the signing of the Atlantic Charter, August 10, 1941. With Ralph Vaughan Williams, Percy Dearmer, and Martin Shaw, he created the series of hymnbooks known as *Songs of Praise* (begun 1925).

SURSUM CORDA was composed by Alfred Morton Smith. For comments on the tune and the composer, see hymn 248.

504 Draw Us in the Spirit's Tether

Tune: UNION SEMINARY

This text was written by Percy Dearmer and included in *Enlarged Songs of Praise* (1931), which he edited with Ralph

Vaughan Williams (see hymn 6) and Martin Shaw (see hymn 12). Dearmer also compiled a handbook for the collection titled *Songs of Praise Discussed* (1933). For a biographical sketch of Dearmer, see hymn 459.

UNION SEMINARY was composed by Harold Friedell (1905–1958) just a year before his death.

505 Be Known to Us in Breaking Bread

Tune: ST. FLAVIAN

This hymn is one of four hundred written by James Montgomery. It was published in both *The Christian Psalmist* (1825) and *Original Hymns* (1853), where it was titled "The Family Table." The stanzas refer to the Emmaus road incident in Luke 24. For comments on the author, see hymn 22.

ST. FLAVIAN was first published in John Day's *Psalter* (1562) as the first half of the tune of Psalm 132. For comments on Day's *Psalter* and the tune, see hymn 81.

506 Deck Yourself, My Soul, with Gladness

Tune: SCHMÜCKE DICH

This hymn was written by Johann Franck. The first stanza appeared in Johann Crüger's *Geistliche Kirchen-Melodien* (1649), where it was set to SCHMÜCKE DICH. The hymn, with nine stanzas, later appeared in Crüger's *Praxis Pietatis Melica* (1656) under the title "Preparation for Holy Communion." For comments on Franck, see hymn 365.

Catherine Winkworth translated the hymn for her volume *Lyra Germanica* (1858) and rewrote it in metrical form for *The Chorale Book for England* (1863). For comments on Winkworth, see hymn 3.

The present form of the text is a composite of the Winkworth translation as well as one by John Casper Mattes (1913) as altered for *The Worshipbook—Services and Hymns* (1972).

SCHMÜCKE DICH was composed by Johann Crüger for this text for his 1649 collection. For a biographical sketch of the composer, see hymn 93.

507 I Come with Joy

Tune: DOVE OF PEACE

Brian Wren wrote this text as a summation of a series of sermons to his congregation at Hockley on the meaning of Communion (1968, rev. 1977). Important theological themes are explained using simple straightforward words. There is a general move from the individual ("I come") to the corporate ("together met, together bound"). Stanza 4 relates Christ's real presence and the communal nature of worship. For comments on the author, see hymn 71.

DOVE OF PEACE is an American folk melody first published in William Walker's (1809–1875) *Southern Harmony* (1854) (no. 89) as the setting for "O Tell Me Where the Dove Has Flown to Build Her Downy Nest." The present arrangement is by Austin C. Lovelace and is an adaptation of his 1973 anthem. The hymn setting was arranged for *Ecumenical Praise* (1977).

Austin Cole Lovelace was born in 1919 in Rutherfordton, North Carolina, and was educated at High Point College (A.B. 1939) and Union Theological Seminary School of Sacred Music, New York City (M.S.M. 1941; D.S.M. 1950). He has enjoyed a career as a music educator, teaching at the University of Nebraska; Queens College and Davidson College, North Carolina; Union Theological Seminary, New York City; Garrett Theological Seminary, Evanston, Illinois; Iliff School of Theology and Temple Buell College, Denver. Lovelace has served as minister of music in Methodist and Presbyterian churches nationally. He retired in 1986 after fifty-two years in church music. He was named minister of music emeritus of the Wellshire Presbyterian Church, Denver.

Lovelace is a prolific composer known for his contributions to choral, organ, and solo music and is the author of five books, including *Music and Worship in the Church* (1960; rev., 1976 with William C. Rice). Lovelace has served on five hymnal committees and is a fellow of the Hymn Society in the United States and Canada.

508 For the Bread Which You Have Broken

Tune: KINGDOM

The hymn written November 18, 1924, by Louis FitzGerald Benson was first published in his *Hymns, Original and Translated* (1925). The element of thanksgiving portrayed in the first stanza has gained universal acceptance, even though Christian communities differ in their understanding of what actually takes place during the sacrament of the Lord's Supper. Stanzas 2 and 4 move the singer to prayer. In stanza 3 worshipers are called to remember loved ones and other faithful saints who have died. For a biographical sketch of Benson, see hymn 308.

KINGDOM was composed by V. Earle Copes. For comments on the tune and a biographical sketch of the composer, see hymn 253.

509 For the Bread Which You Have Broken

Tune: CROSS OF JESUS

This hymn has written by Louis FitzGerald Benson in 1924. For comments on the text see hymn 508.

CROSS OF JESUS was written by John Stainer and published in his cantata *Crucifixion* (1887), where it was intended for congregational singing.

John Stainer (1840–1901) was born at Southwark, London, England. An accident at age five blinded his left eye. At seven, he began his musical career as a choirboy at St. Paul's Cathedral, London, and at fourteen became organist at St. Benedict and St. Peter's, Paul's Wharf. In 1856, Sir F. Gore Ouseley offered him the position of organist of the recently founded St. Michael's College. Stainer entered Christ Church, Oxford, in 1859 and graduated (B.Mus. 1860; B.A. 1864; D.Mus. 1865; M.A. 1866). He founded the Oxford Philharmonic Society (1866) and helped found the Musical Association (1874). In 1872 he succeeded Sir John Goss as organist of St. Paul's. He was knighted in 1888 and that same year left his position at St. Paul's because of failing eyesight. He taught at Oxford. He died suddenly while visiting Verona, Italy.

Today Stainer is better known as a musicologist than a composer, although his "Sevenfold Amen" and the cantata *Crucifixion* are still popular. His book *Early Bodleian Music* (1900) was the first attempt by an English scholar to explore music before Tallis (1505–1585) and Palestrina (1526–1594).

510 Jesus, Thou Joy of Loving Hearts

Tune: QUEBEC

This text is from the Latin poem "Jesu dulcis memoria" attributed to Bernard of Clairvaux (1091–1153). Whether Bernard wrote the hymn is much debated by scholars. Some believe the author to be an anonymous English person from the twelfth century.

The free translation into English by Ray Palmer is of stanzas 4, 3, 20, 28, and 10 of the forty-two-stanza poem. (The earliest manuscripts indicate forty-two stanzas, but by the end of the fourteenth century F. J. Mone's Frankfurt manuscript had fifty-one stanzas. An eighteenth-century manuscript found in the Benedictine edition of Bernard's *Opera* has forty-eight stanzas.) He used the Latin form of the poem as in Herman Daniel's *Thesaurus Hymnologicus* (1841–1855). The Palmer text was first published in *Sabbath Hymn Book* (1858). "Jesus, the Very Thought of Thee" (hymn 310) is another hymn using stanzas from the poem.

For comments on Bernard of Clairvaux, see hymn 98. For comments on Ray Palmer, see hymn 383.

QUEBEC was composed by Henry Baker (1835–1910). It appears in English hymnals as HESPERUS and WHITBURN. Baker is sometimes confused with Sir Henry W. Baker, secretary to the committee compiling *Hymns Ancient and Modern* (1861). The son of an Anglican priest, Baker was born in Nuneham, Oxfordshire, England, and educated at Winchester. He studied civil engineering and after graduation served many years with the railway in India. His interest in church music and the influence of John B. Dykes (see hymn 91) led him to pursue a musical degree at Exeter College, Oxford.

511 Jesus, Thou Joy of Loving Hearts

Tune: JESU DULCIS MEMORIA

This text is attributed to Bernard of Clairvaux and translated by Ray Palmer. For comments on the text, see hymn 510.

JESU DULCIS MEMORIA is based on plainsong, Mode II, and was arranged by James McGregor in 1984. McGregor (b. 1930) is choirmaster of Grace Episcopal Church, Newark, New Jersey.

512 Living Word of God Eternal

Tune: KOMM, O KOMM, DU GEIST DES LEBENS

The hymn text is by Jeffery Rowthorn (b. 1934). He wrote:

> It is based on the four characteristics of the first Christian community in Jerusalem, as described in Acts 2:42. Each of the first four stanzas addresses one of these characteristics: preaching, fellowship, the Lord's Supper, and the Prayers of the People. The fifth stanza revisits all four and is a summary of what has gone before.

For a biographical sketch of Rowthorn, see hymn 134.

KOMM, O KOMM, DU GEIST DES LEBENS is a German chorale tune dating to 1680, according to Conrad Kocher's *Zionsharfe* (1855). The earliest form of the tune is in *Neuvermehrtes und zu Übung Christliche Gottseligkeit eingerichtetes Meiningisches Gesangbuch* (1693), where it is the setting for "Ich begehr nicht mehr zu leben" by J. C. Werner. In 1698, the tune appeared in *Geistreiches Gesangbuch* with the text "Komm, o komm, du Geist des Lebens," from which it gets its name.

513 Let Us Break Bread Together

Tune: LET US BREAK BREAD

The original version of this African-American spiritual consisted of the now third stanza beginning with the words "Let us praise God." The spiritual was apparently used as a gathering song for secret religious meetings held before sunrise by slaves in Virginia. After 1676, the colony, afraid of group protests and attempted escapes, forbade the use of drums and horns by the slaves as a means for gathering. This spiritual and others took the place of those drums. Sometime after the Civil War the first two stanzas were added and it became a hymn for use during Holy Communion.

LET US BREAK BREAD is a Calhoun melody. Calhoun School (Alabama), Atlanta University, Tuskegee Institute, and other southern schools followed closely the work of Fisk University, which devoted itself to the careful collection and recording of the African-American spirituals. These other schools began their own studies and collections.

This tune was arranged for *The Presbyterian Hymnal* (1990) by Melva Wilson Costen (1988). For comments on Costen, see hymn 29.

514 Let Us Talents and Tongues Employ

Tune: LINSTEAD

This lively "Communion Calypso," as Fred Kaan titled the hymn, was written at the request of Jamaican composer Doreen Potter. Mrs. Potter, whose family lived on the same street in Geneva as the Kaans, brought the adaptation of a Jamaican folk melody to him and asked him to write a text. He decided on a hymn of celebration for the Lord's Supper.

The first international use of the hymn was at the World Council of Churches Nairobi Assembly (1975). It was used again by the WCC in Vancouver (1983). The hymn appeared in its present form in *Break Not the Circle* (1975) and the *Hymnal Supplement* (1984). For comments on Kaan, see hymn 109.

LINSTEAD is the Jamaican folk melody brought to Fred Kaan by Doreen Potter. For comments on Potter, see hymn 358.

515 Now to Your Table Spread

Tune: LOVE UNKNOWN

The text is by Shirley Erena Murray and is found in the booklet *In Every Corner Sing* (1987), where it bears the title "Hymn of

Approach to Communion." The booklet, made possible by a gift of the Church Worship Committee of the Presbyterian Church of New Zealand, contains twenty-eight of Murray's texts. For comments on the author, see hymn 105.

LOVE UNKNOWN was composed by John Ireland (1918). For comments on the tune and the composer, see hymn 76.

516 Lord, We Have Come at Your Own Invitation

Tune: O QUANTA QUALIA

This text was written by Fred Pratt Green at the request of Martin Ellis in 1977. Ellis wanted a hymn to be sung at the Taunton School Confirmation Service. The original form of the hymn was two stanzas of eight lines and set to Samuel Wesley's tune EPIPHANY. A four-stanza version was prepared for *Partners in Praise*. The present version of the text has dropped the last four lines of the poem:

> So, in the world, where each duty assigned us
> Gives us the chance to create or destroy,
> Help us to make those decisions that bind us,
> Lord, to yourself, in obedience and joy.

O QUANTA QUALIA from the Paris *Antiphoner* (1681) appears as in La Feillée's *Méthode du plain-chant* (1808). For comments on the tune, see hymn 147.

517 We Come as Guests Invited

Tune: WIE LIEBLICH IST DER MAIEN

This Holy Communion text is by Timothy Dudley-Smith. It was composed at Ruan Minor, Cornwall, in August 1975. According to Dudley-Smith the phrase "guests invited" is a reference to the recorded words of Jesus in Luke 22:19.

Stanza 2 incorporates the final words of the administration of the Lord's Supper from the *Book of Common Prayer*: "Feed on him in your hearts by faith with thanksgiving." The text moves from a recital of what is taking place to our participation and experience of Christ and then to the united family receiving the gifts of love (Timothy Dudley-Smith, *Lift Every Heart*, p. 268; Carol Stream, Ill.: Hope Publishing Co., 1984).

Timothy Dudley-Smith was born in 1926 and spent his youth in Derbyshire, where he developed a love for poetry. In his twenties he began writing and publishing poetry whose topics ranged from devotional to satirical subjects. Ordained in the Church of England (1950), he worked as curate in Erith and moved to East Anglia (1973) to be archdeacon of Norwich. In 1981 he was consecrated bishop of Tretford. Since 1969 the bishop and his family have spent summers in Ruan Minor, Cornwall, where he does most of his hymn writing.

WIE LIEBLICH IST DER MAIEN was composed by Johann Steurlein in 1575 as the setting for the secular song "Mit Lieb bin ich umfangen." The tune was first married to a sacred text in *Dauids Himmlische Harpffen* (Nuremberg, 1581).

Johann Steurlein (also Steuerlein) (1546–1613) was the son of Caspar Steurlein, the first Lutheran pastor in Schmalkalden. He studied law and was appointed town clerk of Wasungen. Later in Meiningen he became secretary in chancery (1589), notary public, and then mayor (1604). The Emperor Rudolph II crowned him a poet for his metrical version of Ecclesiasticus (Frankfurt, 1581). Steurlein was a musician and published works containing tunes and four-part settings all written by himself.

518 Una Espiga

Sheaves of Summer

Tune: UNA ESPIGA

The text and tune of this Communion hymn were composed as a unit by Cesáreo Gabaráin in 1973 for *Ediciones Paulinas* (1979). Although Spanish in origin, the hymn is a favorite in Latin America. The text has been translated into more than forty languages and the hymn is one of the top five in the Spanish hymn list.

The translation is by George Lockwood for *The United Meth-*

odist Hymnal (1989). For biographical sketches of Gabaráin and Lockwood, see hymn 296.

UNA ESPIGA: The harmonization of Gabaráin's tune is by Skinner Chávez-Melo and was published in *Albricias* (1987). For comments on Chávez-Melo, see hymn 377.

519 Thee We Adore, O Hidden Savior, Thee

Tune: ADORO TE DEVOTE

This poem of personal devotion was not intended to be a hymn. Initially it appeared in popular devotional collections of the Middle Ages. In the Roman *Missal* of 1570, Pope Pius V included the text as a poem among the Prayers of Preparation and Thanksgiving, where it has appeared ever since. The Latin text, ascribed to Thomas Aquinas, is believed to have been written when Thomas was preparing the Office Mass for the Festival of Corpus Christi, 1263.

Thomas Aquinas (c. 1225–1274) was the son of Count Landulph of Aquino, a nephew of Emperor Frederick I. When he was five, Thomas was sent to Monte Cassino to be educated at the Benedictine monastery. Later he studied at the University of Naples, where he decided to become a member of the Dominican Order. His mother, Theodora, a wealthy Neapolitan, greatly displeased by his decision, had Thomas apprehended and imprisoned for two years. Frederick, under the influence of the pope, ordered his release. In 1252 Thomas was appointed professor of the Dominican College at Paris and after receiving his doctorate in 1257, held a chair of theology in the Dominican College at Rome, among other appointments. He became lecturer at the University of Naples in 1272 and was to participate in the Second Council of Lyons but became ill while traveling and died at the Benedictine Abbey of Bossa Nuova. Thomas' *Summa Theologiae* became the standard theological work for the Roman Catholic Church.

The English translation is by James Russell Woodford (1850). It was first published in *Hymns arranged for the Sundays and Holy Days of the Church of England* (1852). Line 2 of stanza 1 has undergone many changes. The original read "Who in Thy Supper with us deign'st to be." The present first stanza seems to be a composite of Woodford's original and a variant found in Pott's *Hymns Fitted to the Order of Common Prayer* (1861), where the second line reads "Who in Thy feast art pleased with us to be."

James Russell Woodford (1820–1885) was born at Henley-on-Thames, England, and educated at Merchant Taylor's School, and Pembroke College, Cambridge (B.A. 1842). Woodford was ordained in 1843 and held numerous posts before becoming bishop of Ely (1873), a position he held until his death. He was honorary chaplain to Queen Victoria and author of several sermon and hymn collections. With H. W. Beadon and Greville Phillimore, Woodford edited *The Parish Hymn Book* (1863; enl., 1875).

ADORO TE DEVOTE is the tune long associated with this text. The earliest source is *Processionale* (1697), where it is the setting for the variant text "Adoro te supplex." Based on thirteenth-century Benedictine plainsong, Mode V, the tune is nonetheless an example of a seventeenth-century French church tune adapted from older plainsong melodies. The present arrangement is from *A Hymnal for Colleges and Schools* (1956).

520 Here, O Our Lord, We See You Face to Face

Tunes: ADORO TE DEVOTE or MORECAMBE

This text was written by Horatius Bonar (1855) at the request of his older brother, John James Bonar, pastor of St. Andrew's Free Church, Greenock, Scotland. John Bonar printed a leaflet after each Communion service with a hymn attached. The hymn was written in two days and published with the memorandum of October 1855. Later it appeared in Bonar's *Hymns of Faith and Hope* (1st series, 1857), where it was captioned "This do in remembrance of Me." For more on Bonar, see hymn 147.

The text may be sung to ADORO TE DEVOTE (hymn 519) or MORECAMBE (hymn 326).

521 You Satisfy the Hungry Heart

Tune: FINEST WHEAT

This hymn was the official hymn of the 41st Eucharistic Congress of the Roman Catholic Church held in Philadelphia (1976). Omer Westendorf wrote the text and sent it to his friend Robert E. Kreutz for a tune. They submitted their hymn to the international competition and won. For more on Westendorf, see hymn 259.

FINEST WHEAT was composed as the setting for this text by Robert E. Kreutz (b. 1922). Kreutz participates in the liturgical renewal movement within the Roman Catholic Church.

522 Lord, When I Came Into This Life

Tune: LAND OF REST

This text by Fred Kaan was written for the confirmation of his son Peter in 1976. "A hymn for confirmation," the title given to the poem by Dr. Kaan, was to represent him at the worship since he was in Canada at the time and unable to attend the service. Although the hymn was not sung on that occasion, it was sung at the confirmation of his two other children, Alison in 1977 and Martin in 1978.

When the Hymn Society of America asked him and two other hymn writers to submit an unpublished text, this was the one he chose. The hymn was part of the Hymn Society's 1980 Convocation held in Princeton, New Jersey.

The present form of the hymn uses the alternative stanza 1, written by Kaan, to be used when the person being confirmed was not baptized in infancy. The original first stanza was:

> You called me, Father, by my name
> when I had still no say;
> today you call me to confirm
> the vows my parents made.

LAND OF REST is an American folk melody arranged by Annabel Morris Buchanan (1938). For comments on the tune and the arranger, see hymn 603.

523 God the Spirit, Guide and Guardian

Tune: BETHANY (Smart)

This hymn text was written by Carl P. Daw, Jr., in 1988 for Jeffery Rowthorn (see hymn 134) as a hymn of consecration. For comments on Daw, see hymn 314.

BETHANY was composed by Henry Thomas Smart in 1867 and first published in the Presbyterian Church in England's *Psalms and Hymns for Divine Worship* (1867). For a biographical sketch of Smart, see hymn 22.

This tune is not to be confused with the tune BETHANY by Lowell Mason used for the hymn "Nearer, My God, to Thee."

524 Holy Spirit, Lord of Love

Tune: SALZBURG

This confirmation hymn was written by William Dalrymple MacLagen (also MacLagan). It was first published in Mrs. C. Brock's *Children's Hymnbook* (1884).

William Dalrymple MacLagen (1826–1910) was born in Edinburgh, entered the army at an early age and served in India. After retiring with the rank of lieutenant, he was educated at St. Peter's College, Cambridge (B.A. 1856; M.A. 1860). He was ordained in 1856 and served various pastorates before being consecrated bishop of Lichfield in 1878.

SALZBURG, attributed to Jacob Hintze, harmonized by J. S. Bach, appears as in *Hymns Ancient and Modern* (1861). For more on the tune, see hymn 159.

525 Here I Am, Lord

The text and tune of this hymn were written by Daniel L. Schutte in 1981 for a diaconate ordination at Oakland Cathedral in 1980.

Daniel L. Schutte (b. 1947) grew up in Milwaukee and studied at Jesuit seminaries in Minnesota, St. Louis, and Berkeley, California. He was ordained a priest and served in the Pine

Ridge Indian Reservation in southwest South Dakota. He is now a layperson. Schutte is a member of the Roman Catholic Liturgy Conference and presently serves as a musician and music director for Our Lady of Lourdes Parish in Milwaukee. He writes poetry and music.

The harmonization of Schutte's tune is by Michael Pope, Daniel L. Schutte, and John Weissrock (1983).

526 For All the Saints

Tune: SINE NOMINE

The text was written by William Walsham How for All Saints' Day, 1864. It is a commentary on the phrase "I believe in the communion of saints" from the Apostles' Creed. The text was first published in Earl Nelson's *Hymns for the Saints' Days* (1864), where it was titled "Saints Day Hymn—Cloud of Witnesses—Hebrew 12:1." The original hymn contained eleven stanzas, but most collections have edited them to six or fewer. For a biographical sketch of How, see hymn 327.

SINE NOMINE ("without a name") was composed by Ralph Vaughan Williams as the setting for this text in *The English Hymnal* (1906).

Erik Routley (see hymn 218) reported that the tune was at first rejected as being "jazz music," while Percy Dearmer (see hymn 459) stated that this tune is "one of the finest hymn tunes of the present century." Today most authorities agree with Dearmer. For a biographical sketch of Vaughan Williams, see hymn 6.

527 Near to the Heart of God

Tune: MC AFEE

The text and tune of this hymn were written by Cleland B. McAfee in 1901 while he was pastor of the First Presbyterian Church of Chicago. He wrote it when he received news that his two nieces had died from diphtheria. On the day of the double funeral, McAfee sang the hymn outside the quarantined house of his brother Howard. The choir of First Church sang it the following Sunday as a Communion hymn. McAfee's brother Lapsley carried the hymn back to his pastorate at the First Presbyterian Church of Berkeley, California.

Cleland Boyd McAfee (1866–1944) was born in Ashley, Missouri, and studied at Union Theological Seminary in New York City. He returned to his undergraduate college, Park College in Parkville, Missouri, to serve as a professor and pastor of the college church (1881–1901). He then went on to serve in Chicago and at the Lafayette Avenue Presbyterian Church in Brooklyn, New York. He was professor of systematic theology at McCormick Theological Seminary (1912–1930). Known as a fine theologian and outstanding speaker, McAfee became Moderator of the General Assembly of the Presbyterian Church U.S.A. He retired to Jaffrey, New Hampshire, where he continued to be active until his death. McAfee's granddaughter is Jane Parker Huber (see hymn 128), a popular contemporary hymn text writer.

MC AFEE was composed by Cleland Boyd McAfee in 1901. The hymn first appeared in the magazine *The Choir Leader* in 1903.

528 Give Thanks for Life

Tune: SARUM

This text was written by Shirley Erena Murray and published in the booklet *In Every Corner Sing* (1987), where it has four stanzas. There it is number 13 and is titled "Hymn for a Funeral." The final stanza, which was not included in *The Presbyterian Hymnal* (1990), reads:

> Give thanks for hope, that like the wheat, the grain
> lying in darkness does its life retain
> in resurrection to grow green again. Alleluia!

For comments on the author, see hymn 105.

SARUM was composed by Joseph Barnby in 1868 as the setting of the text "For All the Saints Who from Their Labors Rest." It appeared in *The Sarum Hymnal* (1869), a collection to be used by the diocese of Salisbury. The tune became known as NO. 229,

SARUM HYMNAL. Later the name was shortened to SARUM. For comments on Barnby, see hymn 130.

529 Lord of the Living

Tune: CHRISTE SANCTORUM

As a pastoral minister, Fred Kaan was frustrated by the absence of good funeral hymns in what were otherwise suitable hymnals. This text was added to the Pilgrim Church (Plymouth, England) hymnal supplement, *Pilgrim Praise* (1967).

Stanley L. Osborne, secretary of the Hymn Book Committee of the Anglican and United Churches of Canada, has said of this text that "its strength consists in its objective character and its emphasis upon Easter." While in the first edition of the supplement the text was set to DIVA SERVATRIX, in the edition of 1972 it is set to CHRISTE SANCTORUM.

CHRISTE SANCTORUM, from the Paris *Antiphoner* (1681), was harmonized by David Evans. For comments on the tune, see hymn 459.

530 O Lord of Life, Where'er They Be

Tune: GELOBT SEI GOTT

Frederick Lucian Hosmer (1840–1929) was born in Framingham, Massachusetts. Educated at Harvard College (1862) and Harvard Divinity School (1869), he was ordained in 1872 as a Unitarian minister. Hosmer is among the finest Unitarian hymn writers. His thorough knowledge of hymnody led Harvard to invite him to give a special lecture series on the subject in 1908.

Along with William Channing Gannett he wrote *The Thought of God in Hymns and Poems* (1885, 1894, 1918) and with Gannett and J. V. Blake *Unity Hymns and Chorals* (1880; enl. ed., 1911). He died in Berkeley, California.

GELOBT SEI GOTT was composed by Melchior Vulpius (1609) and appears as in *Pilgrim Hymnal* (1958). For comments on the tune and the composer, see hymn 111.

531 Not for Tongues of Heaven's Angels

Tune: BRIDEGROOM

This text based on 1 Corinthians 13 is by Timothy Dudley-Smith. He wrote it while at Ruan Minor, Cornwall, in August 1984. Robert Batastini had requested a text for the tune BRIDEGROOM. At the time Batastini was preparing *Worship III* for G.I.A. Publications, where he is vice-president and senior editor. It was first published in *New Songs of Praise 1* (1985). For comments on the author, see hymn 517.

BRIDEGROOM was composed by Peter Cutts. For a biographical sketch of Cutts, see hymn 135. For comments on the tune, see hymn 314.

532 O God, You Give Humanity Its Name

Tune: SURSUM CORDA (Smith)

Fred Kaan wrote this text to fill the void he felt concerning good hymns for Christian marriage. It was written while he served Pilgrim Church, Plymouth, England. This is its first appearance in a denominational hymnal in the United States.

The first line has been altered from "O God from whom mankind derives its name" to "O God, You give humanity its name" in order to be inclusive of all people. For comments on Kaan, see hymn 109.

SURSUM CORDA was composed by Alfred Morton Smith. For comments on the tune and the composer, see hymn 248.

533 O Perfect Love

Tune: PERFECT LOVE

This text was written by Dorothy F. B. Gurney (1858–1932) for her sister's wedding. Gurney said of the hymn:

> We were all singing hymns one Sunday evening and had just finished "Strength and Stay," a special favorite with my sister,

> when someone remarked what a pity it was that the words should be unsuitable for a wedding. My sister, turning suddenly to me, said: "What is the use of a sister who composes poetry if she cannot write me new words to this tune?" I picked up a hymn-book and said: "Well, if no one will disturb me I will go into the library and see what I can do." After about fifteen minutes I came back with the text, "O Perfect Love," and there and then we sang it.

Dorothy Frances Blomfield, the daughter and granddaughter of Anglican priests, was born in London. She married Gerald Gurney (1897), an actor who later was ordained in the Church of England. In 1919 the Gurneys left the Anglican Church and became Roman Catholic. Dorothy was a gifted writer, producing two volumes of poems and the devotional book *A Little Book of Quiet*. She is best known for this hymn and the often-quoted lines:

> The kiss of the sun for pardon,
> The song of the birds for mirth;
> One is nearer God's heart in a garden
> Than anywhere else on earth.

PERFECT LOVE was composed originally as an anthem setting for this text by Joseph Barnby, for the wedding of the Duke and Duchess of Fife in 1889. The anthem was adapted and arranged for congregational singing in *The Hymnal* (1892) of the Episcopal Church edited by Charles Hutchins. It is unaltered in *The Presbyterian Hymnal* (1990). For comments on Barnby, see hymn 130.

534 The Grace of Life Is Theirs

Tune: RHOSYMEDRE

Fred Pratt Green wrote this text in 1970 to fill the need for new hymns for the marriage service. It was published in the *Methodist Recorder* (1970), *26 Hymns* (1971), *Hymns of Faith and Life* (Free Wesleyan Church, U.S.A.), *The Marriage Service with Music* (Royal School of Church Music). It was also published in *Bride's* Magazine.

Green based the hymn on 1 Peter 3:7 and gave it the title "Christian Marriage."

RHOSYMEDRE, originally called LOVELY, was composed by John David Edwards (c. 1805–1885) and included in *Original Sacred Music Composed and Arranged by the Rev. John Edwards, B.A., Jesus College, Oxford* (c. 1840). Edwards was graduated from Oxford (B.A.) and ordained into the priesthood. For some time he served as vicar of Rhosymedre, Ruabon, Wales (c. 1843). He died at Llanddoget Rectory, Denbighshire. This is Edwards' most famous hymn tune.

535 Go with Us, Lord

Tune: TALLIS' CANON

Mary Jackson Cathey wrote this text in 1986 for the children's choir of National Presbyterian Church, Washington, D.C., where she was director of children's ministry. For comments on Cathey, see hymn 107.

TALLIS' CANON was composed by Thomas Tallis and adapted from Parker's *Whole Psalter* (c. 1561). For comments on the tune, see hymn 542. For a biographical sketch of Tallis, see hymn 186.

536 Lord, Make Us More Holy

This African-American spiritual is number 83 in John Work's *American Negro Songs and Spirituals* (1940). Its origins have been traced to coastal South Carolina, near Charleston, where it was used as a communal hymn of parting at religious gatherings. In Work's collection, the first line reads "Lord, make me more holy" and the four stanzas use the words "humble" and "righteous," in place of "loving" and "patient." These substitutions may be easily made.

537 Shalom, Chaverim!
Farewell, Good Friends

This Hebrew blessing is set to a traditional Israeli melody. The version in *The Presbyterian Hymnal* (1990) differs from others in its use of both the masculine *chaverim* and the feminine *chaverot*, plural Hebrew words for "good friends."

The Hebrew is pronounced: Shah-lohm, kah-vay-reem, shah-lohm, kah-vay-roht! Lah-heet-rah-oht.

538 Lord, Dismiss Us with Thy Blessing
Tune: SICILIAN MARINERS

This text is ascribed to John Fawcett in *A Selection of Psalms for Social Worship* (1786) and *A Collection of Psalms and Hymns* (1791). The text first appeared in *A Supplement to the Shawbury Hymn Book* (1773) with no name attached.

The sixth line of stanza 1 was altered from "In this dry and barren place" in Dr. Conyer's *A Collection of Psalms* (1774). Stanza 3 originally read:

> So whene'er the signal's given
> Us from earth to call away,
> Borne on angels' wings to heaven,
> Glad the summons to obey,
> May we ever
> Reign with Christ in endless day.

It was altered to the present form by Godfrey Thring (1823–1903). For comments on Fawcett, see hymn 438.

SICILIAN MARINERS is said to be of Sicilian origin but is not popular in Sicily today. It appeared in *The European Magazine and London Review*, November 1792, and William Tattersall's *Psalms selected from the version of the Rev. Jas Merrick* (c. 1790) as a setting for "O Sanctissima, O Purissima." Byron Underwood, in *The Hymn*, July 1976, writes: "*The European Magazine* states: the hymn was sung in unison by the whole crew of the Sicilian seamen on board their ships when the sun sets." Corri's *Select Collection of the Most Admired Songs, Duetts, Etc.* (c. 1794–1795) contains the tune with the caption "The Prayer of the Sicilian Mariner."

539 Savior, Again to Thy Dear Name We Raise

Tune: ELLERS

This hymn by John Ellerton was written for the festival of the Malpas, Middlewich, and the Nantwich Choral Festival in 1866. The original poem had six stanzas, but Ellerton reduced the number to four for the Appendix to *Hymns Ancient and Modern* (1868).

Louis Benson said of this hymn, "It seems the perfection of the blending of the corporate idea of worship with human individuality." James Davidson, in Julian's *Dictionary of Hymnology*, wrote that this hymn was "the most beautiful and tender" of Ellerton's works. For comments on Ellerton, see hymn 99.

ELLERS was composed by Edward John Hopkins for this text and appeared in Robert Brown-Borthwick's *The Supplemental Hymn and Tune Book* (3rd ed. with new appendix, 1869). The tune was originally set for unison singing, but in Samuel Smith's *The Appendix to the Bradford Tune Book* (1872) Hopkins harmonized it.

Edward John Hopkins (1818–1901) was born in Westminster, England, and educated in the Chapel Royal, St. James. In 1834 he became organist of Mitcham Church, Surrey, and in 1843 organist at Temple Church, London, where he remained for fifty years. Hopkins was one of the founders of the College of Organists and the Musical Association. He wrote much church music and many hymn tunes, but ELLERS is the only one well known today.

Hopkins served as music editor for various hymnals, but the contribution he made in his treatise *The Organ: Its History and Construction* (1855, rev., 1972) continues to be indispensable to researchers. He died in London.

540 God Be with You Till We Meet Again

Tune: RANDOLPH

This hymn text was written in 1880 by Jeremiah E. Rankin after a study of the derivation of the word "goodbye." When asked about the text he said:

> It was called forth by no person or occasion, but was deliberately composed as a Christian hymn on the etymology of

> good-by which is "God be with you." It was first sung on Sunday evening at First Congregational Church in Washington, of which I was then pastor.

Visitors to Rankin's church heard the hymn and carried it back to their congregations. In time, Dwight L. Moody and Ira D. Sankey heard the hymn and began using it in their services in both America and Europe. The hymn has become popular as a response to the benediction.

Jeremiah Eames Rankin (1828–1904) was born in Thornton, New Hampshire, and graduated from Middlebury College, Vermont, and Andover Theological Seminary. He held pastorates in New England and Washington, D.C., before becoming president of Howard University, Washington, D.C. (1889). Rankin was the editor of several collections, including *The Gospel Temperance Hymnal* (1878), *Gospel Bells* (1883), and *German-English Lyrics, Sacred and Secular* (1897).

RANDOLPH was composed by Ralph Vaughan Williams for this text when it was included in *The English Hymnal* (1906). For a biographical sketch of the composer, see hymn 6.

541 Now the Day Is Over

Tune: MERRIAL

This hymn text based on Proverbs 3:24 was written by Sabine Baring-Gould for the children of Horbury parish, where he was curate. The original hymn had eight stanzas and was published in *The Church Times* (1867). It then appeared in the Appendix to *Hymns Ancient and Modern* (1868). The present rendering of the hymn contains four of the original stanzas with a change in stanza 3. "Comfort those who suffer" has been substituted for "Comfort every sufferer." For comments on the author, see hymn 16.

MERRIAL was composed by Joseph Barnby for this text and was first published in his *Original Tunes to Popular Hymns* (1869). The hymn was introduced to the United States by Charles S. Robinson in his *Spiritual Songs for Social Worship* (1878). Since Barnby never named the tune, Robinson titled it EMMELAR after his daughter Mary whose initials were M.L.R. Later he changed the name to MERRIAL. For comments on Barnby, see hymn 130.

542 All Praise to Thee, My God, This Night

Tune: TALLIS' CANON

This text by Bishop Thomas Ken was one of three included in his *A Manual of Prayers for the Use of the Scholars of Winchester College* (1674). Designated "Evening Hymn," it contained twelve stanzas beginning with the phrase "All praise to Thee, my God, this night," and concluding with a doxology. In the 1695 edition the text began, "Glory to Thee, my God, this night." In 1709 the line was restored to the original. For a biographical sketch of Ken, see hymn 456.

TALLIS' CANON was composed by Thomas Tallis as one of nine tunes and several anthems for Archbishop Matthew Parker's *The Whole Psalter translated into English Metre, which contayneth an hundred and fifty Psalmes.* It was the setting for "God Grant Me Grace." The collection was written about 1555 and published several years later (c. 1561). For a biographical sketch of Tallis, see hymn 186.

543 Abide with Me

Tune: EVENTIDE

The text is by Henry Francis Lyte (1847). The hymn originally had eight stanzas but was introduced to America in Henry Ward Beecher's *Plymouth Collection* (1855) with only five.

It was not written as an evening hymn but rather is about death. The *Spectator*, October 3, 1925, presented evidence that Lyte wrote it (1820) after a visit with an old friend, W. A. Le Hunte, who continued to repeat the words "Abide with me" as he was dying. The original manuscript is in the Hunte family's private papers.

The British Weekly, April 3, 1947, reported, based on the gardener's recollections, that the hymn was written on Lyte's last Sunday in the pulpit, September 4, 1847. The gardener said:

> After tea on that last Sunday, Lyte walked in the valley garden in front of the home, then down to the rocks, where he sat and composed. It was a lovely sunny day and the sun was setting over distant Dartmoor in a blaze of glory. On the left lay Brixham harbor like a pool of molten gold, with its picturesque trawling vessels lying peacefully at anchor. After the sun had set Lyte returned to his study. His family thought he was resting, but he was putting the finishing touches to his immortal hymn. (Albert E. Bailey, *The Gospel in Hymns*, p. 171)

For comments on Lyte, see hymn 203.

EVENTIDE was written by William Henry Monk, music editor of *Hymns Ancient and Modern* (1861), for that collection. One story says he wrote it in ten minutes when, after a meeting of the committee, he realized there was no tune suitable for "Abide with Me." His concentration was such that a student sat two yards from him playing the piano without disturbing him. His widow, however, reported that EVENTIDE was written in her presence as the couple watched a glorious sunset in a time of personal sorrow.

William Henry Monk (1823–1889) was born and died in London. His musical education was early and thorough. He was appointed choirmaster (1847) and organist (1849) at King's College, London, and professor at the National Training School for Music (1876). Monk assisted in the development of the principles of plainchant for use in Anglican worship by contributing articles to the *Parish Choir* (1846–1951), the journal of the Tractarian Society for Promoting Church Music. He was awarded an honorary Doctor of Music degree at Durham in 1882.

544 Day Is Done

Tune: AR HYD Y NOS

This evening hymn was written by Roman Catholic James Quinn and published in *New Hymns for All Seasons* (1969). This collection was edited completely by Quinn. It contained one hundred hymns, some translations and some originals.

James Quinn (b. 1919) is a Lauriston Jesuit Father from Edinburgh, Scotland.

AR HYD Y NOS is a Welsh melody from the eighteenth century. It was first published in Edward Jones' *Musical Relicks of the Welsh Bards* (Dublin, 1784). *The Christian Lyre* (1830) stated the tune was set to "There's a Friend Above All Others," and noted, "This is a favorite piece among the Welsh and much used in their revivals. It was sent in manuscript from Bristol to a gentleman in New York, who kindly gave it to the Lyre."

Many know the tune as the setting for "All Through the Night."

545 Now, on Land and Sea Descending

Tune: VESPER HYMN

The text was one of two evening hymns written by Samuel Longfellow and included in his edited collection *Vespers* (1859). The other was "Again as Evening's Shadow Falls."

By the time Longfellow wrote this text he had abandoned all thoughts of the Trinity and considered the Holy Spirit to be the only form of God. In stanza 3 Longfellow's use of the word "his" referred to the Holy Spirit. In the present collection "his" has been changed to "God's" in accordance with Christian understandings that these characteristics are more appropriately ascribed to God "the Father" than to the Spirit. For a biographical sketch of Samuel Longfellow, see hymn 321.

VESPER HYMN has been attributed to Dimitri Stepanovitch Bortniansky. The tune also known as RUSSIAN AIR was first published in John Stevenson's *A Selection of Popular National Airs* (1818). For a biographical sketch of the composer, see hymn 209.

546 The Day Thou Gavest, Lord, Is Ended

Tune: ST. CLEMENT

This evening hymn by John Ellerton was written as a missionary hymn for *A Liturgy for Missionary Meetings* (1870) and revised for *Church Hymns* (1871). It was sung at the Diamond Jubilee Service of Queen Victoria in 1897. For comments on Ellerton, see hymn 99.

ST. CLEMENT was composed for this text by Clement C. Scholefield. It was first published in Arthur Sullivan's *Church Hymns with Tunes* (1874).

Clement Cotterill Scholefield (1839–1904) was born in Edgbaston, Birmingham, England, and educated at St. John's College, Cambridge (B.A. 1864; M.A. 1867). He was ordained pastor of Hove Church, Brighton (1867), served St. Peter's, South Kensington, London (1869), and St. Luke's, Chelsea (1879). He was chaplain of Eton College, Windsor (1880–1890), and then vicar of Holy Trinity, Knightsbridge, until his retirement in 1895. He was a self-taught musician and composer.

547 Awit Sa Dapit Hapon When Twilight Comes

This Filipino hymn was written by Moises Andrade. The English translation and paraphrase is by Father James Minchin of Holy Advent Church, Armidale, Victoria, Australia.

The musical setting is by Francisco F. Feliciano (b. 1941). The accompaniment, composed for two guitars, reflects contemporary practices in Filipino folk music. Feliciano is the director of the Asian Institute for Liturgy and Music at St. Andrew's Theological Seminary, Manila.

548 O Radiant Light, O Sun Divine

Tune: CONDITOR ALME SIDERUM

The Greek hymn Phos Hilaron (3rd century) is of unknown authorship. It is one of two extrabiblical hymn texts from the early Greek tradition still in use today. (The other is an expanded form of the Gloria in Excelsis Deo; see hymns 566 and 575.) St. Basil (c. 365) quotes it as a familiar hymn of unknown authorship and date.

It has been suggested that the hymn "certainly goes back to the days when Christians worshiped 'underground' (literally so when they were in the catacombs), and when light had a special significance for people whose only safe place was in the dark" (Erik Routley, *A Panorama of Christian Hymnody*, p. 78). The hymn was sung in the ancient church at the lighting of the evening lamps and was commonly called the "candlelighting or lamplighting hymn." Today it is used at Evensong.

The earliest printed form is in Archbishop Usher's *De Symbolis* (1647), where the text is adapted from twelfth- and fourteenth-century manuscripts. The present translation is that of William G. Storey, a contemporary Episcopalian born in 1923.

CONDITOR ALME SIDERUM is a Sarum plainsong melody from the early Middle Ages (ninth century). The harmonization is by C. Winfred Douglas, as it appeared in *The Hymnal 1940.* The handbell intonations are by Kenneth E. Williams, contemporary Presbyterian church musician and member of the Psalter Task Force of the Presbyterian Church (U.S.A.). For more on the tune and a biographical sketch of Douglas, see hymn 4.

549 O Gladsome Light

Tune: LE CANTIQUE DE SIMÉON

This translation of the Phos Hilaron (3rd century) is by Robert Seymour Bridges. The second stanza of Bridges' original translation read:

> As fades the day's last light,
> We see the lamps of light.

The term "light" in the phrase "lamps of light" was changed to "lamps of night" for *The Presbyterian Hymnal* (1990). For comments on the Phos Hilaron see hymn 548. For comments on Bridges, see hymn 93.

LE CANTIQUE DE SIMÉON is from the Genevan Psalter (1551). For comments on the Genevan Psalter see hymns 86 and 194. The harmonization is by Claude Goudimel (1565). For comments on Goudimel, see hymn 194. (See also hymn 605.)

550 O Light Whose Splendor Thrills

Tune: LES COMMANDEMENTS DE DIEU

This paraphrase of the third-century Phos Hilaron was written by Carl P. Daw, Jr., in 1989. For comments on Daw, see hymn 314.

LES COMMANDEMENTS DE DIEU, also known by its German chorale name "Wenn wir in höchsten Nöten sein," was written by Louis Bourgeois as the tune for the Ten Commandments in the Genevan Psalter (1543). For comments on Bourgeois, see hymn 86.

The harmonization is altered from Claude Goudimel (1564). For comments on Goudimel, see hymn 194.

551 Come, Ye Thankful People, Come

Tune: ST. GEORGE'S WINDSOR

This text by Dean Henry Alford is considered one of the finest harvest hymns in all hymnody. It was first published in *Psalms and Hymns* (1844). For comments on Henry Alford, see hymn 399.

ST. GEORGE'S WINDSOR was composed by Sir George Job Elvey as the setting of James Montgomery's "Hark! the Song of Jubilee." It was named for St. George's Chapel, Windsor, where Elvey spent much of his musical career.

The tune first appeared with this text in *Hymns Ancient and Modern* (1861). For comments on Elvey, see hymn 151.

552 Give Thanks, O Christian People

Tune: ES FLOG EIN KLEINS WALDVÖGELEIN

This thanksgiving hymn was written by Mary Jackson Cathey to celebrate the ministry of a fellow Christian educator who was leaving the Washington, D.C., area. Cathey said the hymn was a tribute to her friend and all others who serve Christ through work in the church. It was first published in *Fresh Winds of the Spirit* (1986). For comments on the author and the source, see hymn 107.

ES FLOG EIN KLEINS WALDVÖGELEIN was harmonized by George Ratcliffe Woodward from a Memmingen manuscript. For comments on the tune, see hymn 184. For comments on Woodward, see hymn 68.

553 For the Fruit of All Creation

Tune: EAST ACKLAM

At a conference of the Methodist Music Society of Great Britain, Fred Pratt Green heard the tune EAST ACKLAM. At the suggestion of John Wilson, he wrote "Harvest Hymn" to go with the music.

The text appeared in the *Methodist Recorder* in August 1970, with a footnote stating permission granted on application to Fred Pratt Green. Within a few weeks he received one hundred twenty-five requests from all over the British Isles. It has truly become a hymn of the world. By 1982 there were already fourteen hymnals that included the text. Austin Lovelace used the text for an anthem.

EAST ACKLAM was written by Francis Jackson (b. 1917) in 1957 for the text "God That Madest Earth and Heaven" as an alternative for AR HYD Y NOS (hymn 544). The change never caught on and the tune might have been lost were it not for Green's text.

554 Let All Things Now Living

Tune: ASH GROVE

Katherine Kennicott Davis wrote this text for this tune in the 1920s. It was published in 1939 under the pseudonym John Cowley in a four-part anthem with descant. "His law he enforces" has become "By law God enforces" in stanza 2 of *The Presbyterian Hymnal* (1990).

Katherine Kennicott Davis (1892–1980) was born in St. Joseph, Missouri, and received a B.A. degree from Wellesley College (1914). She did postgraduate study from 1916 to 1918 and from 1921 to 1929 taught in private schools in Concord, Massachusetts, and Philadelphia. After 1929 she did free-lance work and published nearly eight hundred separate items, primarily choral pieces and arrangements. She frequently used the pseudonyms John Cowley or C.R.W. Robertson, and it was under a pseudonym that her "The Little Drummer Boy" was published. Stetson University honored Davis with a doctorate. She was active as a composer until 1977, when failing eyesight forced her to stop. Davis is buried in Sleepy Hollow Cemetery in Concord.

ASH GROVE is a Welsh folk melody. Davis cited the *Book of National Songs*, a small pamphlet published by Novello and Company, as her source for this tune. The present harmonization is by Gerald H. Knight (1908–1979), who was born in Cornwall and was an English church musician. From 1937 to 1952 he served as organist of Canterbury Cathedral and then became director of the Royal School of Church Music (1952–1972). His work there helped raise standards for Anglican Church choirs and also to extend instruction and make better music available.

555 Now Thank We All Our God

Tune: NUN DANKET ALLE GOTT

This hymn was written about 1636 by Martin Rinkart. It was translated into English by Catherine Winkworth for her *Lyrica Germanica* (2nd series, 1858).

The hymn, known as the German Te Deum, was written near the close of the Thirty Years' War and is still sung in German churches on New Year's Eve. Rinkart composed the first two stanzas as a grace to be sung before meals at his family table. The hymn was sung at both the dedication of the Cologne Cathedral (1882) and the Diamond Jubilee Service of Queen Victoria (1897).

Martin Rinkart (1586–1649) was born in Eilenburg, Saxony, and studied at St. Thomas School, Leipzig. After completing an M.A. (1616), he served in several capacities before returning to Eilenburg to minister to the village. He was there for thirty-two years. In 1637 disease ravished the community and Rinkart buried four thousand of the eight thousand who died.

He wrote dramas and hymns. This hymn is thought to have been included in *Jesu Hertz-Büchlein* (1636), but the earliest copy available today is the 1663 edition of this volume.

For comments on Winkworth, see hymn 3.

NUN DANKET ALLE GOTT was composed by Johann Crüger in 1648 and appeared with Rinkart's text in *Praxis Pietatis Melica* (2nd ed., 1647). The harmonization is adapted from Felix Mendelssohn's *Lobgesang* (1840).

For a biographical sketch of Crüger, see hymn 93. For comments on Mendelssohn, see hymn 31.

556 The World Abounds with God's Free Grace

Tune: HALIFAX

This Thanksgiving hymn was written by David G. Mehrtens in 1980 and submitted as a new text for consideration by the Presbyterian Hymnal Committee. Mehrtens, who lives in Waynesboro, Virginia, titled the hymn "Give Thanks." His hymn "Dear Lord, You are Power" was selected for inclusion in *The Hymn*, journal of the Hymn Society in the United States and Canada (January 1991, p. 43).

HALIFAX was composed by George Frederick Handel (1748) and harmonized by C. Winfred Douglas. For comments on the tune, see hymn 167. For comments on Handel, see hymn 59. A biographical sketch of Douglas may be found at hymn 4.

557 ¿Con Qué Pagaremos? O What Shall I Render?

Tune: GRATITUD

The author of the Spanish original of this Latin American hymn is unknown. It is a hymn of thanksgiving for all God has done in Jesus Christ.

The translation is by George P. Simmonds for the *Spanish/ English Hymnal* (1968). For comments on Simmonds, see hymn 157.

GRATITUD is a Latin American folk melody by an unknown composer. It was arranged and harmonized by Ethel Lee Winn (b. 1914) for *El Himnario* (1964).

558 Come, Sing a Song of Harvest

Tune: CHRISTUS, DER IST MEIN LEBEN

The text was written by Fred Pratt Green for *Together for Festivals* (1976). It was one of two submitted to the Anglican Board of Education when the editor wrote to Green and others seeking material for the publication.

In *The Hymns and Ballads of Fred Pratt Green* the hymn is selection 62 and bears the title "The Festival of the First-Fruits." It is based on Deuteronomy 26:1–15 and was first sung at the Harvest Thanksgiving Festival of St. Mary's Church, Diss, Norfolk, England, on September 26, 1976. Green described the day as "a memorable Sunday!"

The hymnal has dropped one stanza and altered the present stanza 2, line 3, from "with science in our pockets" to "view science as our savior."

CHRISTUS, DER IST MEIN LEBEN was composed by Melchior Vulpius (1609). For comments on the tune, see hymn 179. For comments on the composer, see hymn 111.

559 We Gather Together

Tune: KREMSER

This folk hymn dating from the seventeenth century was first written during Holland's struggles for independence from Spain. The political environment played a role in the writing of the text. Frederick Henry, prince of Orange, had just assumed leadership of the Dutch provinces following the assassination of his father, William the Silent (1625). A capable politician and military leader, Frederick led the way for Dutch independence. He ruled for more than a quarter of a century. Peace came to the Netherlands in 1648. The hymn was published in Adrian Valerius' *Nederlandtsch Gedenckclanck* (1626) and attributed to no author.

The English translation is by Theodore Baker (1851–1934). Baker was born in New York City and was literary editor for G. Schirmer Music Publishers (1892–1926). His *Biographical Dictionary of Musicians* (first published in 1900) became a standard reference work for musicologists. After his retirement he moved to Dresden, Germany, where he had been a student, remaining there until his death.

KREMSER, thought to be a folk tune from the Netherlands, was the original setting of the text. Eduard Kremser (1838–1914), a Viennese composer and choir director, rediscovered the hymn after two centuries of neglect. He arranged the tune for male voices and published it in 1877. In subsequent collections the tune has been named for him. Kremser was born and died in Vienna, Austria. He was also known for his instrumental works.

560 We Plow the Fields and Scatter

Tune: NYLAND

The original German text of this hymn "Wir pflügen und wir streuen" was written by Matthias Claudius (1782). It was the "Peasants' Song" from the poem *Paul Erdmann's Festival* (Feast). The poem tells of a harvest festival in north Germany in which the village people sing this song on the way to Paul's house for a thanksgiving celebration. The original song had seventeen stanzas each sung by a different soloist, with all joining in the refrain.

Matthias Claudius (1740–1815) was born at Reinfeld, Germany, and educated in Jena. He entered the university to study theology but turned to law and languages. In 1771 he became a literary editor in Hamburg and in 1776 was appointed the commissioner of agriculture and manufactures of Hesse-Darmstadt. There he befriended Goethe. He temporarily abandoned his faith, but a severe illness in 1777 persuaded him of his spiritual emptiness. Claudius returned to the Lutheran faith of his youth and to the newspaper, where he wrote poetry of such religious depth that three of his poems have become hymns in Germany.

The English translation is by Jane Montgomery Campbell (1861). It was first published in *The Garland of Songs; or an English Liederkranz* (1862). The collection was the collaborative effort of Campbell and Charles S. Bere. They also produced *The Children's Chorale Book* (1869). In addition Campbell wrote *A Handbook for Singers.*

Jane Montgomery Campbell (1817–1878), the daughter of an Anglican priest, was a gifted poet and musician. Her life revolved around her father's parish at Paddington, where she trained children's choirs. She died of injuries incurred in a carriage accident.

NYLAND is a tune from the Finnish Province of Nyland, adapted and harmonized by David Evans. For comments on the tune, see hymn 389. For comments on Evans, see hymn 113.

561 My Country, 'Tis of Thee

Tune: AMERICA

The hymn was written by Samuel Francis Smith (1808–1895), a Bostonian linguist and prominent Baptist minister. At the time of his death he was fluent in fifteen languages and was seeking a Russian text in order to learn that language. When he wrote this "national song" he was twenty-four years old and a student at Andover Theological Seminary. In 1843, along with Baron Stow, Smith edited *The Psalmist: A New Collection of Hymns,* the most important Baptist hymnal of that era.

Smith was inspired to write the text after reading a German patriotic hymn given to him by musician and educator Lowell Mason. "I instantly felt the impulse to write a patriotic hymn of my own, adapted to the tune. Picking up a scrap of waste paper which lay near me, I wrote at once, probably within half an hour, the hymn 'America' as it is known everywhere."

The original text contained five stanzas, including one that dropped out of use because of its strong anti-British bias.

AMERICA: Of the tune Smith writes:

> I found the tune in a German music-book brought to this country by the late William C. Woodbridge and put into my

> hands by Lowell Mason, because (so he said) I could read German and he could not. Lowell Mason arranged it as it is known in the United States and gave it the name AMERICA.

The hymn was first sung at Park Street Church, Boston, July 4, 1831, by Mason's children's choir and was included in Mason's *The Choir, or Union Collection of Church Music* (1832).

Much has been written on the origin of the tune. In England it was first published in honor of George II and given the title "National Anthem" or "God Save the King." It has been ascribed to various people, including Henry Purcell (1696), John Bull (1619), and Thomas Ravenscroft. Parts of it have been found in Gregorian chant and a Scottish carol (1609). However, French critics claim that Jean Baptiste Lully composed the original music, which was sung by three hundred young women to King Louis XIV, at St. Cyr, where Handel found it in 1721. Further, there are several German hymns which use this tune as a setting and until 1833 the Russian national anthem was set to this tune. The melody as we have it comes from *Thesaurus Musicus* (London, 1740).

562 Eternal Father, Strong to Save

Tune: MELITA

The text was written by William Whiting for a student who was about to set sail for America (1860). It was published in an altered form in *Hymns Ancient and Modern* (1861). In America the hymn is known as the Navy Hymn because it is used at the Naval Academy at Annapolis. It is also sung on English ships. The text has been translated into French.

This was the favorite hymn of President Franklin Delano Roosevelt and was sung at his funeral in Hyde Park (1945). It also was played by the Navy band in 1963 as John F. Kennedy's body was carried up the steps of the Capitol building to lie in state.

William Whiting (1825–1878) was born in Kensington and educated at Chapham and Winchester. Because of his musical ability he became master of Winchester College Choristers' School. While he is best known for this text, he also published two poetry collections: *Rural Thoughts* (1851) and *Edgar Thorpe, or the Warfare of Life* (1867). He died at Winchester.

MELITA was composed by John Bacchus Dykes (1861) for this text and has always been associated with it. Melita is the ancient name of the island of Malta, where Paul was shipwrecked (Acts 28:1–2). Benjamin Britten used the hymn in *Noye's Fludde.* For a biographical sketch of Dykes, see hymn 91.

563 Lift Every Voice and Sing

Tune: LIFT EVERY VOICE

This hymn, which has become the official song of the National Association for the Advancement of Colored People (NAACP), was a collaborative effort of two brothers, James Weldon Johnson (1871–1938) and J. (John) Rosamond Johnson (1873–1954). It was first published as sheet music in 1921.

James Weldon Johnson was born in Jacksonville, Florida, and educated at Atlanta University (B.A. and M.A.). He was self-taught in law and was admitted to the Florida bar. Johnson became U.S. consul in Puerto Cabello, Venezuela, and later in Corinto, Nicaragua. He was visiting professor of creative literature at Fisk University and for fourteen years served as national secretary of the NAACP.

Among Johnson's writings are *The Book of American Negro Poetry* (1922), *God's Trombones* (1927), *Negro Americans, What Now?* (1934). *The Book of American Negro Spirituals* (1925) and *The Second Book of Negro Spirituals* (1926) were written with his brother Rosamond. James Weldon Johnson died at Wiscasset, Maine.

LIFT EVERY VOICE was composed by J. Rosamond Johnson (1921) for his brother's text. Rosamond Johnson was educated at the New England Conservatory of Music (Boston) and was awarded an honorary master's degree from Atlanta University. For a time he was music supervisor for the Jacksonville public schools.

After a career that included touring in vaudeville, serving as music director of the Hammerstein Opera House, London, and the Music School in New York City, Rosamond Johnson composed the scores for many Broadway musicals, including *The Red Moon.* He appeared in *Porgy and Bess* and *Cabin in the Sky.*

In 1901 the Johnsons and Robert Cole became the first black songwriters to sign a contract with the Tin Pan Alley publisher Joseph W. Stern and Company.

564 O Beautiful for Spacious Skies

Tune: MATERNA

Katharine Lee Bates (1859–1929), born in Falmouth, Massachusetts, attended Wellesley College and stayed on as professor of English literature until her death. She was not affiliated with any church, but the college was maintained as a distinctly Christian nondenominational institution.

Two events in her life in the summer of 1893 precipitated the writing of this hymn. First, she visited the World's Columbian Exposition at Chicago, of which she wrote:

> The White City made such strong appeal to patriotic feeling that it was in no small degree responsible for at least the last stanza of "America the Beautiful." . . . We went on, my New England eyes delighting in the wind-waved gold of the vast wheat fields.

Second, she ascended Pikes Peak, Colorado, and her soul was stirred by the expansive earth below and the spacious skies above. She wrote, "It was there as I was looking out over the amber skies, that the opening lines of this text formed themselves in my mind." She immediately set to writing the hymn in Colorado Springs.

MATERNA was written by Samuel Augustus Ward (1847–1903), who was born and died in Newark, New Jersey. He spent his life selling musical supplies, pianos, and organs, and directed the Orpheus Club for fourteen years.

The tune first appeared in the Episcopal *Hymnal* (1892) as the setting of the text "O Mother Dear, Jerusalem." *The Hymnal* (1895) of the Presbyterian Church and *The Hymnal* revised (1911) preserved that setting. However, during World War I the tune became associated with Bates' hymn text and in 1912 Ward's widow gave official permission for the tune to be used with this text. In a postcard to Louis Benson dated January 17, 1895, Ward stated that he wrote the tune in 1882.

SERVICE MUSIC

565 Lord, Have Mercy

The text of this Kyrie is from *Prayers We Have in Common* (1970, 1971, 1975), prepared by the International Consultation on English Texts. John Weaver prepared the musical setting in 1984 for the congregation of Madison Avenue Presbyterian Church, New York City. It was first published in *Reformed Liturgy & Music,* vol. 19, no. 1 (Winter 1985).

The son of a Presbyterian minister, John Weaver was born in 1937 in Jim Thorpe (then Mauch Chunk), Pennsylvania. He grew up in Baltimore and was educated at Juilliard School of Music and Union Theological Seminary's School of Sacred Music, New York City. During his military service he was organist at West Point, after which he became organist at Holy Trinity Lutheran Church, New York City.

Since 1970 Weaver has been music director at Madison Avenue Presbyterian Church. Currently, he is organist-in-residence at Juilliard School of Music, New York City, and Curtis Institute of Music, Philadelphia. Weaver served on the Presbyterian Hymnal Committee, and several of his arrangements as well as original compositions are included in *The Presbyterian Hymnal* (1990).

566 Glory to God in the Highest

The text is from the English Language Liturgical Consultation revision of 1987. This Gloria in Excelsis is appropriately sung as an act of praise following the Declaration of Pardon. The setting by John Weaver is part of the Service for the Lord's Day music (565–571) he contributed to *The Presbyterian Hymnal* (1990). For comments on Weaver, see hymn 565.

567 Glory to the Father

The text of this Gloria Patri is from *Prayers We Have in Common* (1970, 1971, 1975), prepared by the International Consultation on English Texts. The setting, which may be sung as a canon, is by John Weaver, who composed it in 1978 for the congregation of Madison Avenue Presbyterian Church, New York City. For comments on Weaver, see hymn 565.

568 Holy, Holy, Holy Lord

The text for this Sanctus is from *Prayers We Have in Common* (1970, 1971, 1975), written by the International Consultation on English Texts. It is to be sung as part of the Great Prayer of Thanksgiving and is reminiscent of the song of the heavenly host (Isa. 6:1–5; Rev. 4:8). The setting is by John Weaver and was published in *Reformed Liturgy & Music*, vol. 19, no. 1 (Winter 1985). For comments on Weaver, see hymn 565.

569 Christ Has Died

The text of the Memorial Acclamation is from the English translation of *The Roman Missal* (1973) by the International Committee on English in the Liturgy. It is meant to be sung as part of the Great Prayer of Thanksgiving during the celebration of the sacrament of Holy Communion. The setting by John Weaver was composed for the 1987 Montreat Conferences on Worship and Music. It was published in *Reformed Liturgy & Music*, vol. 22, no. 4 (Fall 1988). For comments on Weaver, see hymn 565.

570 Amen

This Amen was written by John Weaver in 1978 for the Service of Holy Communion, to be sung after the Great Prayer of Thanksgiving. It was first used at Madison Avenue Presbyterian

Church, New York City. For comments on Weaver, see hymn 565.

571 Our Father in Heaven

John Weaver composed this setting of the Lord's Prayer for *Reformed Liturgy & Music*, vol. 22, no. 4 (Fall 1988). The text is a product of the English Language Liturgical Consultation (1987). For comments on Weaver, see hymn 565.

572 Lord, Have Mercy Upon Us

The text of the Kyrie Eleison is from *Prayers We Have in Common* (1970, 1971, 1975), prepared by the International Consultation on English Texts.

The setting by John Merbecke (also Marbeck) (c. 1510–1585) was composed when he was organist at St. George's Chapel, Windsor, England. Merbecke was the first person to compose a complete setting of the Anglican service which he titled *The Booke of Common Praier Noted* (1550).

His life was full of controversy. At one point he was condemned for heresy but was saved through the intervention of the Bishop of Winchester. In his later years, Merbecke became more associated with theology and published several tracts on the subject.

The present arrangement is by Healey Willan (1930). For comments on Willan, see hymn 56.

573 Lord, Have Mercy

This setting of the Kyrie was made for *Worship III* by Richard Proulx (1984). Proulx (b. 1937) is an active composer and musician. He served as consultant to the Standing Committee on Church Music of the Episcopal Church. Currently he is director of music at the Cathedral of the Sacred Heart in Chicago. Proulx is coauthor of *Songs of Thanks and Praise.*

574 Lord, Have Mercy Upon Us

This setting of the Kyrie was composed by David N. Johnson for *The Worshipbook—Services and Hymns* (1972). For a biographical sketch of Johnson, see hymn 458.

575 Glory to God in the Highest

This early hymn of the Greek Church, the Gloria in Excelsis, known as the Greater Doxology, appeared no later than the fourth century and quite possibly dates from the second century. It is an elaboration on Luke 2:14. The present form of the text is by the English Language Liturgical Consultation (1987).

The "Old Scottish chant," not otherwise identified, is one of the best-known settings for the Gloria in Excelsis. In the United States the chant was first published in William Smith's *Churchman's Choral Companion* (1809). In order to accommodate the present text some alterations in notation and harmonization were made by John Weaver (see hymn 565). For an abbreviated form of the chant, see hymn 578.

576 Gloria, Gloria

The Latin text of Luke 2:14 was set to music by Jacques Berthier for the Taizé community in 1979. The canon is sung by the congregation with different voices entering at each double bar line indicated by the letters A, B, etc. Instruments may be added at the beginning of each instrumental sequence designated by the numbers 1, 2, etc. A secondary canon for cantors or choir is available in *Music from Taizé* (1978, 1980, 1981; vocal ed., p. 97).

Jacques Berthier (b. 1923) is composer and organist at St. Ignatius Church, Paris. Since 1975 he and Brother Robert of the Taizé community have developed liturgical repertoire for the brothers.

In 1940, Brother Roger started the Taizé community "on account of Christ and the Gospel." During World War II, his house served as a refuge for those fleeing the Nazis. By 1949, there were seven men who joined together committing themselves to celibacy and communal living. Although Roger was Protestant, the present community is ecumenical in nature. The brothers work toward the goal of reconciliation among all Christians. (For more on Taizé, see J. L. Gonzalez Balado, *The Story of Taizé*; Oxford: A. R. Mowbray & Co., 1980; and Rex Brico, *Taizé: Brother Roger and His Community;* London: William Collins & Co., 1978.)

577 Glory Be to the Father

The Gloria Patri, known as the Lesser Doxology, has its roots in the second century. The Trinitarian language comes from Matthew 28:19, the Great Commission. For many years the Gloria was sung after the reading of the Psalm. Today it is often sung in response to the Declaration of Pardon.

The arrangement of the text and composition of the music are by Richard K. Avery and Donald S. Marsh. It was first published in *Hymns Hot and Carols Cool* (1967).

Richard K. Avery was born in 1934 in Visalia, California, and educated at the University of Redlands, California, and Union Theological Seminary, New York City. His entire ministry has been as pastor of First Presbyterian Church, Port Jervis, New York, where he stresses music and the dramatic arts as components of worship.

Donald S. Marsh was born in 1923 in Akron, Ohio, and studied at the University of Houston (B.S. and M.S.). He specialized in art, music, and theater. He worked in New York City in theater, nightclubs, and television production before settling in Port Jervis, where he is choirmaster and director of the Presby Players. With Avery, he wrote *Hymns Hot and Carols Cool* (1967), *More, More, More* (1970), *Songs for the Search* (1970), *Alive and Singing* (1971), and *Songs for the Easter People* (1972).

578 Glory Be to the Father

This hymn, the Gloria Patri, dates to the beginning of the Christian church. Known as the Lesser Doxology, it derives its Trinitarian language from Matthew 28:19. Within Presbyterian/Reformed liturgies the Gloria Patri is sung as a response after the Declaration of Pardon or after the Psalm.

The "Old Scottish chant" (see hymn 575) is used here in an abbreviated form.

579 Glory Be to the Father

For comments on the text, see hymn 578.

The tune was composed by Henry Wellington Greatorex and published as "Gloria Patri No. 1 in his *Collection of Psalm and Hymn Tunes, Chants, Anthems and Sentences for the use of the Protestant Episcopal Church in America* (1851). The collection contained thirty-seven original tunes and several adaptations of melodies by Greatorex as well as his father and grandfather's compositions.

Henry Wellington Greatorex (1813–1858) was born at Burton-on-Trent, Derbyshire, England, and received much of his musical training from his father. He came to the United States in 1836 and was organist of Center Church and later St. John's, Hartford. He moved to New York City, where he served St. Paul's (1846) and then Calvary Protestant Episcopal Church (1851). In 1853 he moved to Charleston, South Carolina, where he died of yellow fever.

580 Holy, Holy, Holy

This setting of the Sanctus is from John Merbecke's *Booke of Common Praier Noted* (1550). For comments on Merbecke, see hymn 572.

The harmonization is by Healey Willan. For comments on Willan, see hymn 56.

581 Holy, Holy, Holy Lord

This setting of the Sanctus is by Joseph Roff. It was published by G.I.A. Publications in 1980. Roff's "eucharistic acclamations" were brought to the attention of Presbyterians through *Reformed Liturgy & Music*, vol. 22, no. 4 (Fall 1988), p. 220.

Roff was born in Brooklyn, New York, in 1935 and is pastor emeritus of St. Patrick's Roman Catholic Church in Brooklyn, where he still resides.

582 Dying, You Destroyed Our Death

The setting of this Memorial Acclamation is by Joseph Roff (1980). This and other settings by Roff were introduced to Presbyterians through *Reformed Liturgy & Music*, vol. 22, no. 4 (Fall 1988). For comments on Roff, see hymn 581.

583 Amen

This Amen was composed by Marty Haugen (1984) and appeared in *Worship III* (1985).

584 Amen

This Amen was probably composed by Johann Gottlieb Naumann (1741–1801) for the royal chapel at Dresden. It was published in the Zittau choir book.

The so-called Dresden Amen was used by Felix Mendelssohn (see hymn 31) in Symphony No. 5, *Reformation* (1832), and later immortalized by Richard Wagner in the opera *Parsifal* (1882).

585 Amen

This musical setting of Amen is by McNeil Robinson II (b. 1943). It is part of his musical setting of the Lord's Supper composed for *The Hymnal 1982* of the Episcopal Church.

586 Amen

This Threefold Amen is from anonymous Danish sources.

587 Amen

This Amen is based on the African-American spiritual "Amen, Amen." For more information, see hymn 299.

588 Amen

The musical setting of Amen is by Joseph Roff for G.I.A. Publications. For comments on Roff, see hymn 581.

589 Our Father, Which Art in Heaven

This musical setting of the Lord's Prayer (Matt. 6:9–13) is from the West Indies. The melody was transcribed by Olive Pattison for the *Edric Connor Collection of West Indian Spirituals and Folk Tunes* (1945).

John Weaver of the Presbyterian Hymnal Committee harmonized the tune for *The Presbyterian Hymnal* (1990). For comments on Weaver, see hymn 565.

This hymn is set in a traditional leader-response style.

590 Our Father, Lord of Heaven and Earth

Tune: VATER UNSER

This contemporary versification of the Lord's Prayer is by Henry J. de Jong (b. 1956). It was first published in the *Psalter Hymnal* (1987) of the Christian Reformed Church.

VATER UNSER was adapted by Martin Luther for his versification of the Lord's Prayer in Valentin Schumann's *Geistliche Lieder auffs new gebessert und gemehrt* (1539). Earlier forms of the tune are found in a manuscript given to Luther by Johann Walther (1530) and Michael Weisse's *Ein New Gesengbuchlen* (1531). Since 1560 the tune has appeared in English-language hymnals as a setting for the Lord's Prayer and Psalm 112. The harmonization is from the *St. John Passion* (1723) by Johann Sebastian Bach. He used the tune in his Cantatas 90, 101, and 102, and prepared several organ settings found in *Orgelbüchlein* and the *Clavier Übung*. The tune, which was a favorite of John Wesley (see hymn 253), is also known as OLD 112TH. For comments on Bach, see hymn 17.

591 Praise God, from Whom All Blessings Flow

Tune: OLD HUNDREDTH

This form of the Doxology was written by Neil Weatherhogg in 1988. It is an inclusive-language versification originally used by the congregation of Harvey Browne Memorial Presbyterian Church, Louisville, Kentucky, where he is pastor and head of staff. This is the first published form of the text.

OLD HUNDREDTH, from the Genevan Psalter (1551), appears here with an English version of the last musical phrase. For more on the tune, see hymn 220.

592 Praise God, from Whom All Blessings Flow

Tune: OLD HUNDREDTH

This text of the Doxology by Thomas Ken was included as the final stanza of both his morning hymn "Awake, My Soul, and with the Sun" (see hymn 456) and his evening hymn "All Praise to Thee, My God, This Night" (see hymn 542) in *A Manual of Prayers for Use of the Scholars of Winchester College. And all other Devout Christians. To which is added three Hymns for Morning, Evening, and Midnight; not in former Editions: By the Same Author. Newly Revised. London, Printed for Charles Brome at the Gvn, at the West end of St. Paul's Church* (2nd ed., 1695). The original phrase "angelick host" was modified to "ye heavenly host" in the 1709 edition. It has become known as the

Protestant Te Deum. For a biographical sketch of Ken, see hymn 456.

OLD HUNDREDTH is from the Genevan Psalter (1551). For comments on the tune, see hymn 220.

593 Praise God, from Whom All Blessings Flow

For comments on this text of the Doxology, see hymn 592. For a biographical sketch of Thomas Ken, see hymn 456.

The tune was composed by Richard K. Avery and Donald S. Marsh for use by their congregation in Port Jervis, New York. It was published in *Hymns Hot and Carols Cool* (1967). For biographical sketches of Avery and Marsh, see hymn 577.

594 This Is the Feast of Victory

Tune: FESTIVAL CANTICLE

The text of this tune is adapted by John W. Arthur (1978). For a biographical sketch of Arthur, see hymn 124.

FESTIVAL CANTICLE was composed by Richard W. Hillert in 1978. Since 1959, Hillert has served as a professor of music at Concordia College in River Forest, Illinois. He was born in 1923 in Wisconsin and educated at Concordia Teachers College, River Forest (B.S. in Education 1951), and holds degrees in composition from Northwestern University, Evanston, Illinois (M.Mus. 1955; D.Mus. 1968). Hillert has also served as director of music for various Lutheran churches in Missouri, Wisconsin, and Illinois. He has written a variety of compositions, including choral works, gospel motets, hymn tunes, carols, and chamber music as well as pieces for piano and organ.

Hillert was a member of the Liturgical Music Committee for the Lutheran Church from its inception in 1966, and his work is represented in a number of places in the *Lutheran Book of Worship*. Previously he was music editor for *Worship Supplement* (1969) and a contributor to *The Lutheran Hymnal*. His work is featured in "Composers for the Church: Richard Hillert," *Church Music* 72:1.

595 Heleluyan Alleluia

Tune: HELELUYAN

This alleluia is from the Muscogee Native American community. The Muscogee-Creek people often regard it as their "tribal anthem." Its first appearance in print was in *The United Methodist Hymnal* (1989), being transcribed in musical notation there by Charles Webb, a hymnal committee member, for its inclusion in that volume.

Historically, this hymn has been most often led by a male who begins a new stanza while others complete the previous one. It has been used in a variety of settings and is best sung without any accompaniment. It has often been taught by rote. Frequently now the hymn is used as a response in World Communion Sunday services, at Easter, Pentecost, or on Sundays giving particular attention to Native American awareness.

The hymn may be sung as a canon.

596 May the Lord, Mighty God

Tune: WEN-TI

This blessing is an adaptation of several verses of scripture, including Psalm 29:11 and Numbers 6:24–26.

WEN-TI, a Chinese folk tune, was composed by Pao-chen Li (1907–1979) and was adapted for this text. It appeared in *Hymnal Supplement* (1984).

597 Bless the Lord, O My Soul

This paraphrase of Psalm 103:1–2 is from the third musical setting of the Service for the Lord's Day, Musical Responses—Setting Three (Folk Style), in *The Worshipbook—Services and Hymns* (1972).

The musical setting is an arrangement of an Appalachian folk melody by Richard D. Wetzel. Wetzel composed some of the tunes and arranged all the music for Setting Three in *The Worshipbook—Services and Hymns* (1972). For more on Wetzel, see hymn 30.

598 This Is the Good News

This affirmation is a paraphrase of 1 Corinthians 15. It was first published in *The Worshipbook—Services* (1970). It appears in *The Worshipbook—Services and Hymns* (1972) as part of Musical Responses—Setting Three (Folk Style) in the Service for the Lord's Day. The phrase "and that He appeared to the women" was added to the affirmation by the Presbyterian Hymnal Committee to reflect more closely the biblical narrative.

The tune was adapted from a Native American (Dakota) melody by Richard D. Wetzel. For more on Wetzel, see hymn 30.

599 Jesus, Remember Me

These words of the thief on the cross beside Jesus (Luke 23:42) have been set to music by Jacques Berthier for the Taizé community. The first English publication was in *Music from Taizé* (1981). The present arrangement is from *Worship III* (1985). "Jesus, Remember Me" is an ostinato and is intended to be sung in a meditative, calm mood as it is continuously repeated by the congregation. The instrumental countermelodies are to be treated as solo voices that may be added at the beginning of each sequence designated by the numbers 1, 2, etc. For comments on Berthier, see hymn 576.

600 Song of Mary

Tune: MORNING SONG

This form of the Magnificat is by Sister Miriam Therese Winter. It was originally written for use by the Medical Mission

Sisters in 1978. Winter revised the hymn in 1987 to make the language more inclusive. The revision first appeared in *The United Methodist Hymnal* (1989). For comments on the author, see hymn 386.

MORNING SONG is an Aeolian melody first published in John Wyeth's *Repository of Sacred Music, Part Second* (1813), where it is named CONSOLATION. There it was the setting for Isaac Watts's text, "Once More My Soul, the Rising Day." For comments on the source of the tune, see hymn 355.

The harmonization is by C. Winfred Douglas for *The Hymnal 1940* of the Protestant Episcopal Church. For comments on Douglas, see hymn 4.

601 Song of Zechariah

Tune: KINGSFOLD

This paraphrase of the Benedictus Luke 1:68–79 is by Father James Quinn (b. 1919). It was written in 1969 and altered by the Psalter Task Force of the Presbyterian Church (U.S.A.) in 1985. The present setting is from *A Psalm Sampler* (1986). Traditionally the Song of Zechariah was sung during the Service of Morning Prayer. For comments on Quinn, see hymn 544.

KINGSFOLD is from *English Country Songs* (1893). It is arranged and harmonized by Ralph Vaughan Williams (1906). For comments on the tune and the source, see hymn 308. For a biographical sketch of Vaughan Williams, see hymn 6.

602 Song of Zechariah

Tune: MERLE'S TUNE

This paraphrase of the Benedictus Luke 1:68–79 was written by Michael A. Perry in 1973 and published with Hal H. Hopson's tune in *The Upper Room Worshipbook* (1985) and again in *Daily Prayer* (1987).

Michael A. Perry (b. 1942) is rector of Eversley and chaplain/lecturer at the National Police Staff College in Bramshill, England. He was editor of *Carols for Today* and *Carol Praise.*

MERLE'S TUNE was composed for this text by Hal H. Hopson in 1983. It was first published in *The Upper Room Worshipbook* (1985). The tune is named for Hopson's oldest sister, Merle, who was his first piano teacher. For a biographical sketch of Hopson, see hymn 182.

603 Song of Simeon

Tune: LAND OF REST

The text is a paraphrase of the Nunc Dimittis Luke 2:29–32 by Father James Quinn (b. 1919). It first appeared in the collection *New Hymns for All Seasons* (1969), published by the Geoffrey Chapman division of Cassell Publishers Ltd., London. For comments on Quinn, see hymn 544.

LAND OF REST is an anonymous American folk melody arranged by Annabel Morris Buchanan (1888–1983) in *Folk Hymns of America* (1938). She headed the tune with the following: "Heard as a child from my grandmother, Mrs. S. J. (Sarah Ann Love) Foster." Buchanan believed the tune to be a variant of some old folk tune of Scottish or Northern English origin. Her grandmother's version was brought to Texas from South Carolina via Tennessee. Born Annabel Morris in Groesbeck, Texas, she graduated from Landon Conservatory, Dallas, in 1907 and the Guilmant Organ School, New York City, in 1923. She was a student of Dr. H. A. Clarke and John Powell. Until her death in 1983, she taught piano, organ, theory, and composition.

Buchanan is noted for her extensive work in American folk music. She is the author of several books, including *Folk Hymns of America* (1938) and *American Folk Music* (1939), and served as editor for two series: *White Top Folk Song Series* and *Early American Psalmody.* Her library was donated to the University of North Carolina, Chapel Hill, in 1978.

604 Song of Simeon

Tune: SONG 1

This paraphrase of the Nunc Dimittis Luke 2:29–32 by Rae E. Whitney first appeared in the collection *Hymns for Church and*

School (1964). The present form of text and tune is from *The Hymnal 1982* of the Protestant Episcopal Church.

SONG 1 was composed by Orlando Gibbons (1623) and arranged by Ralph Vaughan Williams (1906). For comments on the tune and the composer, see hymn 385.

605 Song of Simeon

Tune: LE CANTIQUE DE SIMÉON

This paraphrase of the Nunc Dimittis Luke 2:29–32 by Dewey Westra (1899–1979) was for the *Psalter Hymnal* (1934). In stanza 2 the original phrase "That peoples might adore Thee" was altered to read "Fulfilling prophets' story," and the phrase "To nations gone astray" now reads "To Gentiles gone astray." The present version of the text is from the *Psalter Hymnal* (1987) of the Christian Reformed Church.

LE CANTIQUE DE SIMÉON was composed by Louis Bourgeois for Jean Crespin's 1551 edition of the Genevan Psalter. Although the edition has been lost, there is documentary evidence in the Swiss archives of his involvement in the creation of the Genevan Psalters from 1547 to 1561. For comments on Bourgeois, see hymn 86 (compare 549).

The harmonization is by Claude Goudimel (1564). For comments on Goudimel, see hymn 194.

SELECTED BIBLIOGRAPHY

Bailey, Albert Edward. *The Gospel in Hymns: Backgrounds and Interpretations.* New York: Charles Scribner's Sons, 1950.

Benson, Louis F. *Studies of Familiar Hymns,* 1st series. New edition (orig. ed., 1903). Philadelphia: The Westminster Press, 1917.

———. *Studies of Familiar Hymns,* 2nd series. Philadelphia: The Westminster Press, 1923.

Brown, Theron, and Hezekiah Butterworth. *The Story of the Hymns and Tunes.* New York: American Tract Society, 1906.

Colquhoun, Frank. *A Hymn Companion: Insight Into 300 Christian Hymns.* Wilton, Conn.: Morehouse-Barlow Co., 1985.

Covert, William Chalmers, and Calvin Weiss Laufer, eds. *Handbook to The Hymnal.* Philadelphia: Presbyterian Board of Christian Education, 1935.

Eskew, Harry, and Hugh T. McElrath. *Sing with Understanding: An Introduction to Christian Hymnology.* Nashville: Broadman Press, 1980.

Farlander, Arthur, and Leonard Ellinwood. *The Hymnal 1940 Companion.* New York: Church Pension Fund, 1949.

Frost, Maurice, ed. *Historical Companion to Hymns Ancient & Modern.* London: William Clowes & Sons, 1962.

Haeussler, Armin. *The Story of Our Hymns.* St. Louis: Eden Publishing House, 1952.

Hughes, Charles W. *American Hymns Old and New: Notes on the Hymns and Biographies of the Authors and Composers.* 2 vols. New York: Columbia University Press, 1980.

Hustad, Donald P. *Jubilate! Church Music in the Evangelical Tradition.* Carol Stream, Ill.: Hope Publishing Co., 1981.

Johnson, James Weldon, and J. Rosamond Johnson. *The Books of American Negro Spirituals.* New York: Viking Press, 1925–1926; reprint Da Capo Press, 1977.

Julian, John, ed. *A Dictionary of Hymnology.* Reprint of the 1907 edition. 2 vols. New York: Dover Publications, 1957.

Kennedy, Michael. *The Oxford Dictionary of Music.* New York: Oxford University Press, 1985.

Leaver, Robin A., and James H. Litton, eds. *Duty and Delight: Routley Remembered.* Carol Stream, Ill.: Hope Publishing Co., 1985.

Lovelace, Austin C. *Hymn Notes for Church Bulletins.* Chicago: G.I.A. Publications, 1987.

McClain, William B. *Come Sunday: The Liturgy of Zion.* Nashville: Abingdon Press, 1990.

McCutchan, Robert Guy. *Hymn Tune Names: Their Sources and Significance.* Nashville: Abingdon Press, 1957.

Morehead, Philip D. *The New American Dictionary of Music.* New York: E. P. Dutton, 1991.

Oliver, Paul, Max Harrison, and William Bolcom. *The New Grove Gospel, Blues and Jazz with Spirituals and Ragtime.* New York: W. W. Norton & Co., 1986.

Osbeck, Kenneth W. *Amazing Grace: 366 Inspiring Hymn Stories for Daily Devotions.* Grand Rapids: Kregel Publications, 1990.

———. *101 Hymn Stories.* Grand Rapids: Kregel Publications, 1982.

———. *101 More Hymn Stories.* Grand Rapids: Kregel Publications, 1985.

Patrick, Millar. *Four Centuries of Scottish Psalmody.* London: Oxford University Press, 1949.

Reynolds, William Jensen. *A Survey of Christian Hymnody.* New York: Holt, Rinehart & Winston, 1963.

———. *Songs of Glory: Stories of 300 Great Hymns and Gospel Songs.* Grand Rapids: Zondervan Publishing House, 1990.

Robinson, Charles Seymour. *Annotations Upon Popular Hymns.* New York: Hunt & Eaton, 1893.

Ronander, Albert C., and Ethel K. Porter. *Guide to the Pilgrim Hymnal.* Philadelphia: United Church Press, 1966.

Routley, Erik. *Christian Hymns Observed: When in Our Music God Is Glorified.* Princeton, N.J.: Prestige Publications, 1982.

———. *Hymns and the Faith.* Greenwich, Conn.: Seabury Press, 1956.

———. *The Music of Christian Hymns.* Chicago: G.I.A. Publications, 1981.

———. *A Panorama of Christian Hymnody.* Chicago: G.I.A. Publications, 1979.

Sadie, Stanley, ed. *The New Grove Dictionary of Music and Musicians.* Reprint of the 1980 edition. 20 vols. London: Macmillan Publishers, 1987.

Sanchez, Diana, ed. *The Hymns of The United Methodist Hymnal: Introduction to the Hymns, Canticles, and Acts of Worship.* Nashville: Abingdon Press, 1989.

Schweitzer, Albert. *J. S. Bach*, trans. Ernest Newman. 2 vols. reprint. New York: Dover Publications, 1966.

Simmons, Morgan F. "Hymnody: Its Place in Twentieth-Century Presbyterianism," in *The Confessional Mosaic: Presbyterians and Twentieth-Century Theology*, ed. Milton J Coalter, John M. Mulder, Louis B. Weeks. Pp. 162–186. Louisville, Ky.: Westminster/John Knox Press, 1990.

Stulken, Marilyn Kay, *Hymnal Companion to the Lutheran Book of Worship*. Philadelphia: Fortress Press, 1981.

Sydnor, James Rawlings. "Sing a New Song to the Lord: An Historical Survey of American Presbyterian Hymnals," *American Presbyterians*, vol. 68, no. 1 (Spring 1990), pp. 1–13.

Temperley, Nicholas. *The Music of the English Parish Church*. Cambridge Studies in Music. 2 vols. Cambridge: Cambridge University Press, 1979.

Terry, Lindsay. *Stories Behind Popular Songs and Hymns*. Grand Rapids: Baker Book House, 1990.

JOURNALS

The Hymn: A Journal of Congregational Singing. The Hymn Society in the United States and Canada (formerly The Hymn Society of America).

Reformed Liturgy & Music. Presbyterian Association of Musicians.

Reformed Worship: Resources in Music and Liturgy. Christian Reformed Church Publications.

INDEXES

The following indexes refer to *The Presbyterian Hymnal.*

INDEX OF AUTHORS, TRANSLATORS, AND SOURCES

INDEX OF COMPOSERS, ARRANGERS, AND SOURCES

INDEX OF TUNE NAMES

INDEX OF FIRST LINES AND COMMON TITLES